THE
ASIAN AMERICAN
ENCYCLOPEDIA

THE
ASIAN AMERICAN
ENCYCLOPEDIA

Volume 3

Ho, Chinn – Korean martial arts

Editor
FRANKLIN NG

Managing Editor
JOHN D. WILSON

Marshall Cavendish
New York • London • Toronto

Published By
Marshall Cavendish Corporation
2415 Jerusalem Avenue
P.O. Box 587
North Bellmore, New York 11710
United States of America

∞ The paper in these volumes conforms to the American National Standard for Permanence of Paper for Printed Library Materials, Z39.48-1984.

Library of Congress Cataloging-in-Publication Data

The Asian American encyclopedia / editor, Franklin Ng.
    p. cm.
   Includes bibliographical references and index.
   Contents: v. 3. Ho, Chinn—Korean martial arts.
   1. Asian Americans—Encyclopedias. I. Ng, Franklin, 1947-   .
E184.O6A827 1995
973′ .0495′003—dc20   94-33003
ISBN 1-85435-677-1 (set).   CIP
ISBN 1-85435-680-1 (vol. 3).

First Printing

Contents

THE
ASIAN AMERICAN
ENCYCLOPEDIA

Ho, Chinn (Feb. 26, 1904, Honolulu, Territory of Hawaii—May 12, 1987, Honolulu, Hawaii): Developer and investment banker. Ho was the grandson of an immigrant who arrived in Hawaii in 1875. His Honolulu-born father operated a small grocery store and also worked as a clerk and as a bartender. Ho was a sickly child and entered Kaahumanu School when he was eight. He enrolled at McKinley High School, where he joined the school marching band. He was so poor that he played the least expensive instrument he could buy, an eleven-dollar piccolo; but he displayed an early flair for business by organizing his first *hui*, Commercial Associates, to raise funds for the school. Graduating from McKinley in 1924, Ho took University of Hawaii extension courses and worked as clerk at Honolulu's Bishop Bank before becoming clerk in a brokerage house.

Ho organized Capital Investment of Hawaii in 1944, and in 1947 the company purchased nine thousand acres of Waianae Sugar Company, the largest land purchase by any Asian in Hawaii up to that time. In 1961 Ho took over and built the Ilikai hotel-apartment complex and pioneered the concept of condominium ownership in Hawaii. He was the first Asian to serve as director of one of the islands' "Big Five" companies, Theo. H. Davies. He also was director of Host International, World Airways, Hawaiian Airlines, Pacific Insurance Co., Pioneer Mill Company, Honolulu Stadium, and the *Honolulu Advertiser*. In 1962 he organized an investor group that bought the *Honolulu Star-Bulletin* and supported a joint production arrangement that saved the *Advertiser* from failure and made both papers profitable. When the *Star-Bulletin* merged with the Gannett Company, Ho became board chairman of Gannett Pacific Corporation. Ho was director of Victoria Ward, which managed the Ward Estate, where his grandfather once worked. He was also managing trustee of the Mark A. Robinson Trust.

In his later years Ho had many investments outside Hawaii. He built Guam's largest office building, helped acquire and renovate Hong Kong's Empress Hotel, and was chairman of the American group owning 40 percent of the Great Wall Hotel in Beijing. In California he invested in the Peacock Gap development in Marin County. Ho founded the Chinn Ho Foundation; some beneficiaries of the foundation were Harvard University's East Asian Studies Program and Beijing's Capital Hospital.

Ho, David (b. 1950's): Physician and researcher. Ho has emerged as one of the world's foremost authorities

Physician David Ho is an authority on the HIV virus, which causes AIDS. (David D. Ho)

on the human immunodeficiency virus (HIV), which causes acquired immune deficiency syndrome (AIDS). When he was twelve, he and his family left Taiwan to immigrate to the United States, settling in California. The son of an engineer, Ho graduated from the California Institute of Technology (Cal Tech) and Harvard Medical School. He decided to become a full-time HIV researcher when, as a medical resident at a Los Angeles hospital in 1981, he observed two of the city's first five cases involving the deadly disease.

Ho has headed New York's pioneering Aaron Diamond AIDS Research Center since its inception in 1990. The $7 million center is one of the largest research laboratories in the world focusing exclusively on the pathology of AIDS. Ho and his research team were the first to demonstrate that the HIV is seldom present in human saliva and therefore seldom transmitted casually. He was also the first to isolate the virus in otherwise healthy carriers and to identify the bodily cells that the virus targets for attack. Ho made headlines again by becoming the personal physician of former National Basketball Association (NBA) star Earvin "Magic" Johnson, following the announcement in late 1991 that Johnson was HIV-positive.

Ho, Fred (Fred Wei-Han Houn; b. 1957, Palo Alto, Calif.): Musician and composer. Drawing on a rich array of sources, both Asian and Western (and especially African American), Ho has created avant-garde jazz inspired by a Marxist commitment to revolutionary social change.

After receiving a bachelor's degree in sociology from Harvard University, Ho worked at various jobs while pursuing a career as a musician, playing baritone saxophone and composing. He also began to publish articles on Asian American musicians, Asian American history, and other topics. He formed two multiracial jazz groups: the Afro-Asian Music Ensemble and the Asian American Art Ensemble.

Among Ho's many albums are *Blues for the Freedom Fighters* (1985), *Tomorrow Is Now! Suite* (1985), *Bamboo That Snaps Back* (1986), *A Song for Manong* (1988), and *We Refuse to Be Used and Abused* (1988). His jazz opera *Chinaman's Chance*, which premiered in San Francisco in 1987 without a staged production, received a full production in 1989. He has also composed in a variety of other forms, including ballet and multimedia.

Ho has been the recipient of numerous commissions and awards, including the Duke Ellington Distinguished Artist Lifetime Achievement Award. He lives in New York City. A fuller account of his life and work can be found in Wei-hua Zhang's "Fred Ho and Jon Jang: Profiles of Two Chinese American Jazz Musicians," *Chinese America: History and Perspectives* (1994): 175-199.

Ho Ah-kow v. Nunan: Case decision made in the Ninth Circuit Court in California in 1879. A law known as the Queue Ordinance was passed in San Francisco that required all male prisoners in city and county jails to have their hair shaved to within one inch of their scalp. Although it was ostensibly passed in order to prevent the spread of head lice, the ordinance was part of a series of discriminatory laws

Jazz musician Fred Ho, founder of the multiracial Afro-Asian Music Ensemble. (Asian Week)

used to harass Chinese workers, who kept their hair braided in long ponytails known as queues. One Chinese prisoner, Ho Ah-kow, sued Sheriff Matthew Nunan for damages because of the haircut Nunan gave him. In ruling the ordinance unconstitutional because it unfairly discriminated against the rights of a particular group, the circuit court also ordered that compensation be awarded to Ho Ah-kow in the amount of $10,000.

Ho Chi Minh City: Largest city in Vietnam; formerly known as Saigon. It lies on the Saigon River just north of the Mekong Delta. The city was renamed in 1975 for the deceased Ho Chi Minh, president of North Vietnam from 1945 to 1969.

Saigon became a Vietnamese settlement shortly before the end of the seventeenth century, when it was captured from a declining Cambodian kingdom. Relations with Westerners soured during the reigns of Emperor Gia Long's successors, and in 1858 Vietnam was attacked by the French. Though it took France nearly twenty-five years to conquer the whole of present-day Vietnam, Saigon was ceded to France in 1862 by the Vietnamese emperor Tu Duc, at which time the city was named the capital of French Cochinchina (southern part of Vietnam). With the signing of the Geneva accords in 1954, Saigon became the capital of South Vietnam and remained as such until the Communist takeover in 1975.

Structurally, Ho Chi Minh City suffered relatively little damage from the long years of fighting. French colonialization and the decades of American presence have left some indelible marks on the city. Although many of the bars and military facilities have disappeared, it is still Vietnam's most cosmopolitan city and boasts French colonial architecture, tree-lined streets, and Western-style hotels. Following 1975, the south, particularly Ho Chi Minh City, was slow to embrace the socialist policies of the north. As early as 1976, there was a thriving black market in Ho Chi Minh City, supplied to a major extent by goods sent into the country by Vietnamese living abroad. When the government tried to accelerate reforms, many more thousands Vietnamese fled their country for, it is suspected, better economic conditions elsewhere in the world.

As a result of the decreased isolation, the Vietnamese economy began improving, as evidenced by the profusion of imported goods in Cholon, the Chinatown of Ho Chi Minh City. Also, foreign companies began showing an interest in Vietnam, and what was once a country heavily dependent on the Soviet Union turned to courting capitalist economies. One important exception, however, is the United States, which has yet to normalize relations with Hanoi. The city's population in 1992 was estimated at 6,075,700.

Hokkaido: Northernmost of the four main islands of Japan. It is bordered on the north by the Sea of Okhotsk, to the east and south by the Pacific Ocean, and to the west by the Sea of Japan. It occupies an area of about 30,314 square miles, which includes some adjacent islands, and forms about 21 percent of Japan's territory. Its main cities are Sapporo (the industrial and commercial center and the capital of Hokkaido Prefecture), Hakodate, and Utashinai. It produces white potatoes, oats, barley, and rice. Its chief industries are agriculture, mining, and fishing. Hokkaido's population is 5,649,000 (1991 estimate).

Hokkien: One of two dialects of Chinese spoken in Fujian Province, the coastal province adjacent to Taiwan across the Taiwan Strait. It is spoken in the northern part of the province; Hoklo or Minnan is spoken in the southern part and is the basis for the language spoken by the Fujian Taiwanese in Taiwan. Hokkien is also called Minpei or the Foochow dialect of Chinese.

Hokkien is also one of several groups of Chinese dialects that are considered to have preserved the ancient pronunciation of Chinese better than other Chinese dialects.

Hokoku Seinen-dan (Young Men's Organization to Serve Our Mother Country): Japanese patriotic organization that existed during World War II at the TULE LAKE relocation center. The group was founded originally as the Sokoku Kenkyu Seinen-dan (Young Men's Association for the Study of the Mother Country) in 1944 at Tule Lake. The latter was the segregation internment camp for Japanese earmarked for repatriation or who had refused to serve in the U.S. military and their families. The organizations' purpose was to prepare its members to become useful Japanese citizens following deportation. Much time was therefore spent studying Japanese language, culture, and history.

Some Hokoku members threatened, harassed, and assaulted internees who were not willing to pledge their loyalty to Japan. Many young internees at Tule Lake joined the group as a result of intimidation. In addition, a large number of Tule Lake internees were coerced into renouncing their American citizenship. (See DENATIONALIZATION ACT OF 1944.)

Hokoyama, J. D.: Educator, administrator, and community leader. Hokoyama is president and executive director of LEADERSHIP EDUCATION FOR ASIAN PACIFICS (LEAP), a nonprofit Asian American community organization which teaches leadership skills to Asian Pacific Americans. In 1992 he presided over the formation of LEAP's Asian Pacific American Public Policy Institute. In 1993, in conjunction with the Asian American Studies Center of the University of California, Los Angeles (UCLA), the institute issued *The State of Asian Pacific America: Policy Issues to the Year 2020.*

Educated at Loyola University of Los Angeles, where he received a B.A. in English literature and an M.Ed. in educational administration, Hokoyama volunteered to serve in the Peace Corps in Ethiopia. In addition to his work with LEAP, he is active in many other Asian American community programs.

Hokubei Mainichi: Japanese American newspaper based in San Francisco, California. Kiyoshi "Jimmy" Hirasaki, known as the "Garlic King," used profits from his agricultural enterprises to help finance the publication of *Hokubei Mainichi* and served as the first president of the paper's board of directors beginning in 1948. Howard Imazeki, a noted Japanese American journalist, took over as editor of the paper's English section in 1954 and continued in this post through the 1970's. Imazeki was credited with introducing a number of innovative features in *Hokubei Mainichi*, including annual community forum sections known as *zadankai* addressing public issues of interest to the paper's Japanese American readers. Nisei novelist and short story writer Toshio Mori published many of his stories in the pages of *Hokubei Mainichi*. As one of the few major Japanese American papers that continues to publish a Japanese-language section, the paper has continued to appeal as a source of information to the increasing number of post-1965 immigrants from Japan, including visiting tourists and businesspeople working for subsidiaries of Japanese companies in the United States.

Hole hole bushi: Work songs characteristic of early Japanese immigrant laborers who came to Hawaii to work the sugar plantations. These immigrants arrived in the islands armed with a tradition of work songs. For example, in Japan, as the women threshed rice, they sang together. In Hawaii immigrants adapted familiar work song melodies to their new working conditions. Today these songs are an invaluable source of information on the early immigrants' plantation experiences.

Hole hole is the repetition of the Hawaiian word that means to "peel or strip," and *bushi* (*fushi*) is Japanese for "melody" or "tune." The creators of *hole hole bushi* were the laborers who stripped dried leaves from the sugarcane stalks to allow the plant to become larger and juicier. Among the different plantation jobs, *hole hole* was considered one of the easiest and was therefore assigned mostly to women.

Hole hole bushi often plaintively express the feelings and frustrations of the immigrants. A discernible theme is a shift from the desire to go back to Japan to the realization that Hawaii is to be their home. One song laments: "Go on to America? / Return to Japan? / This is the problem / Here in Hawaii." Another declares: "When I left Yokohama / I cried as I sailed out, / But now I have children / And even grandchildren, too."

Many songs deal with hardships and disappointments, as in the following song: "Hawaii, Hawaii / Like a dream / So I came / But my tears / Are flowing now / In the canefields." The next song is even more explicit: "Wonderful Hawaii, or so I heard / One look and it seems like Hell / The manager's the Devil and / His lunas [field supervisors] are demons."

Some songs deal with topics that reflect the earthier concerns of the immigrants: sex, drinking, and gambling. In fact these activities were fairly widespread before the "picture brides" came, which resulted in a family life that brought stability to the Japanese community. Often non-Japanese words, such as Hawaiian words, were used to express what the singers were probably embarrassed to say in Japanese. An example of such a song questions: "Why settle for 35 cents / Doing *hole hole* all day / When I can make a dollar / Sleeping with that pake [Chinese]?"

Holt International Children's Services: Adoption agency founded by Harry and Bertha Holt and incorporated as the Orphan Foundation Fund on October 12, 1956. In 1955, the Holts were greeted by the U.S. mass media when they returned to the United States with eight Korean children, whom they adopted in February, 1956. With the help of David H. Kim, who became its executive director, the agency established an office in the Salvation Army Academy building in Seoul on March 5, 1956. With seven U.S. regional offices and branches in ten nations, the agency has arranged more than thirty thousand adoptions for American families.

The Hawaiian landscape has been converted by developers from farmland to housing developments and golf courses; members of the Home Rule movement are concerned with maintaining the balance among the urban, rural, agricultural, and conservatory uses of land. (Dennis Rose)

Home Rule movement (1973): Not to be confused with the former Home Rule Party of Hawaii, which ceased to exist in 1912, the Hawaiian Home Rule movement was still very much alive in the waning years of the twentieth century. The central issue of home rule, in both Hawaii and the rest of the United States, is land use.

Protecting the Land. Hawaii's controversy over land use grew from the desire to preserve limited agricultural lands and the environment, while simultaneously providing a healthy economic climate and adequate housing for all. Although a high point in Hawaiian home rule activism was reached in 1973, the movement actually began in 1961, with passage of the Hawaiian Land Use Law. That law was based on the concept that all land within the state, including privately owned land, is a public resource, rather than purely a commodity to be bought and sold. Virtually identical in principle to the laws governing land use throughout Great Britain, Hawaii's Land Use Law was the first among the fifty U.S. states to recognize that private lands (which constitute approximately 75 percent of all land in the forty-eight contiguous states) may require the same sort of legal protection against unregulated commercial exploitation that public lands are explicitly granted.

In Hawaii, the land-use issue first arose on the island of Oahu, where the city of Honolulu, expanding rapidly during and after the 1950's, began to lose some of the best agricultural land in the state to commercial development. In response to this commercial growth boom, the Hawaiian Land Use Law was used to establish a Land Use Commission, which was ultimately tasked with zoning all Hawaiian land into four types: conservation, agricultural, rural, and urban. Under this zoning system, only urban lands were to be developed

Development has transformed Honolulu into a busy resort. The move from rural to urban land use has threatened the islands' environment but has also brought income and jobs. (John Penisten, Pacific Pictures)

extensively. Unfortunately, these attempts to control development saw limited success: Economic pressures often led to rezoning of protected areas, thus opening them to commercial development.

Adding to the environmental strain of increasing urbanization is the accompanying transformation of the Hawaiian landscape. Many Hawaiians, initially jubilant over the increased popularity and prosperity brought by statehood, began to have second thoughts about how to use their natural resources. That dawning awareness resulted, in 1973, in Hawaii's landmark decision to refuse developers the freedom to convert twenty-three hundred acres of choice Oahu farmland into a housing project. Yet voters may sometimes be persuaded to place housing and jobs ahead of the environment: On Kauai, to circumvent the Hawaii Supreme Court ruling against a large development project at Nukolii Beach, developers simply paid for a special 1984 election, the result of which was the lifting of the original zoning restrictions.

Federal, State and Local Government Conflicts.

Hawaii's land-use proposals have been examined by legal scholars throughout the United States, where increasing urbanization has brought land-use issues and environmental activism into the forefront of debate during the last quarter of the twentieth century. Increasingly determined to exercise their home-rule rights, many state and local governments have tried to curb and shape the development of land and resources by enacting more restrictive zoning laws regarding building codes, siting of waste and industrial facilities, road and airport expansions, and various other uses of both public and private lands.

By contrast, in some situations where local governments have given free rein to or even encouraged economic forces, the federal government has intervened, with bitterly divisive conflicts arising. The most visible conflicts have centered around the locally controversial but nationally acclaimed Environmental Policy Act (in effect since 1970) and land set-aside programs involving eminent domain.

Steps to protect the environment, while broadly recognized by the public as essential, are often opposed locally by those who stand to lose economically when the costs of compliance directly affect them. Even when money is not a direct issue, as in the case of state or federal acquisition of land—including land offered by willing sellers—local opposition has occasionally been heated by emotions. The fear of local communities is that land taken over by government is unlikely ever to be returned to local or private ownership. Yet the argument for central government control of some lands, especially those marginally profitable under private ownership or those prone to environmental degradation, is that such lands (including their native flora and fauna) should be preserved in their natural state for the enjoyment and benefit of all rather than be lost to unwise private management practices; furthermore, those public lands, if managed properly, may produce income from renewable resources or from public recreational use.

Weighing the Benefits. The question of land use is often reduced to one of who will take better care of it: the private owner or the government. That question is misleading, however, because the answer may have changed as the late twentieth century trend toward increasing corporate/absentee ownership of larger and larger tracts of land has evolved. Undoubtedly, the answer in each case depends on a complex array of variables, including (but not limited to) the amount of land involved, the user's/owner's attitudes, and the temptation to abandon the long-term benefits of sound agricultural practices for the short-term profits of urban development.

Hawaii, because of its small size and rapidly growing population, is simply one of the first places in the United States where the strain of finite resources and limited growth options has erupted into serious land-use conflicts. For example, if the major producers of Hawaii's principal exports, sugar and pineapple, no longer find those products profitable, should they be allowed to idle the rich Hawaiian soil permanently by converting it to immediately profitable urban uses? Or should they (and other rural and agricultural landowners) be forced to accept smaller profits, even losses, at risk of bankruptcy?

Unfortunately, the choices are not always so clearly defined; even when they are, the answers are seldom easy. Yet with the prospect of an ever-increasing population and the never-increasing availability of land, the choice to act conservatively, to protect all arable lands and other nonrenewable resources as much as possible, seems the only prudent alternative.—*William Matta*

SUGGESTED READINGS: • Callies, David L. *Regulating Paradise: Land Use Controls in Hawaii.* Honolulu: University of Hawaii Press, 1984. • Chaplin, George, and Glenn D. Paige, eds. *Hawaii 2000.* Honolulu: University of Hawaii Press, 1973. • Horwitz, Robert H., and Norman Meller. *Land and Politics in Hawaii.* 3d ed. Honolulu: University of Hawaii Press, 1966. • Miller, James Nathan. "Hawaii's 'Quiet Revolution' Hits the Mainland." *National Civic Review* 62 (September, 1973): 412-420. • Rayson, Ann. *Modern Hawaiian History.* Honolulu: Bess Press, 1984. • Wright, Theon. *The Disenchanted Isles: The Story of the Second Revolution in Hawaii.* New York: Dial Press, 1972.

Home Rule Party: Native Hawaiian political party that started a movement in 1895 to overthrow the Caucasian-dominated Republic of Hawaii and restore Queen LILIUOKALANI to the throne. Using "Nana I Ka Ili!" (look to the skin) as its motto, the party gained a majority in both houses of the territorial legislature in 1900. Its influence declined after 1904, because former Prince Jonah Kuhio divided the native Hawaiian vote by supporting the BIG FIVE sugar companies and the Republican Party.

Honda, Harry K. (b. Aug. 12, 1919, Los Angeles, Calif.): Editor and journalist. After graduating from Belmont High School in Los Angeles, California, in 1946, Harry K. Honda went to work as a sports writer for the Japanese-language paper *Rafu Shimpo.* In 1938, he became the editor of the English-language section of the *Sangyo Nippo* (*Japanese Industrial Daily*). Honda joined the U.S. Army on October 20, 1941, before the Japanese attack on Pearl Harbor, and he served in the Quartermaster Corps until December 24, 1945. After being honorably discharged from the Army, Honda attended Loyola University in Los Angeles and received a bachelor's degree in political science in 1950. From 1950 to 1952, Honda was assistant English-language editor of *Shin Nichibei Shimbun* (*New Japanese American News*). In 1952, he went to work for the weekly paper *Pacific Citizen,* serving first as editor, then as general manager/operations, next as senior editor, and finally as editor emeritus, a position that he still holds. Honda is also active in the JAPANESE AMERICAN CITIZENS LEAGUE (JACL), the organization that adopted *Pacific Citizen* as its official publication on July 27, 1932. He has been the recipient of many awards for his work as an editor and for his service to the community.

Honen: Japanese term designating a year with a bountiful rice crop.

Hong Kong: Crown colony of Great Britain, scheduled to revert to China on July 1, 1997. The island of Hong Kong lies at the mouth of the Pearl River, about ninety miles from Canton. In addition to the island, Hong Kong consists of Lantau Island and many smaller islands, the Kowloon Peninsula, and the New Territories on mainland China. The population of Hong Kong in 1993 was approximately 5.8 million. Provided with an excellent natural harbor, Hong Kong is one of the world's busiest ports; it is also one of the world's leading financial centers.

The treaty of Nanjing, which China was forced to sign in 1842 after being defeated in the First Opium War, gave Hong Kong Island to Britain "in perpetuity." The British annexed the Kowloon Peninsula in 1860. In 1898, Britain leased the New Territories from China for ninety-nine years, giving Hong Kong its present dimensions.

Negotiations between Britain and the People's Republic of China (PRC) over the future of Hong Kong

HONG KONG

began in the 1980's. In 1984 they reached an agreement whereby Hong Kong will revert to Chinese sovereignty upon expiration of the lease on the New Territories in 1997. The agreement requires the PRC to maintain Hong Kong as a "special administrative region" for fifty years after that date, maintaining its capitalist economy and its current freedoms.

As the 1997 deadline approaches, conflict has intensified between Britain and the PRC over the political transition from British to Chinese rule. Particularly at issue in 1993 and 1994 was the makeup and status of Hong Kong's legislative body. This debate, however, was only the latest development in the profound economic, political, and cultural transformation which Hong Kong has experienced in the post-World War II period.

Economic Development. From a Chinese fishing village in the nineteenth century, Hong Kong has become one of the most vigorous industrial states of the world. With a territory about one-third the size of Rhode Island, the smallest state in the United States, Hong Kong exports more commodities than the entire nation of India. What explains this extraordinary economic success?

First, in the early 1950's, as a result of the victory of the Communists in China's civil war and the establishment of the PRC in 1949, the sudden and massive influx of refugee capitalists and refugee laborers from the mainland sparked an industrial revolution in Hong Kong. These refugees brought capital, management skills, international connections, and cheap and docile labor to Hong Kong. It was as if the best of mainland China's assets in terms of capital and labor had been transplanted to Hong Kong to reap the benefits of the postwar economic boom.

Second, there is dynamism among the small firms of Hong Kong. More than 90% of Hong Kong's industrial firms employ fewer than fifty workers. Being small, these firms are obstructed less by bureaucratic red tape, are more adaptable to new markets and more readily able to try new methods of production, and need a relatively small amount of capital to get started.

Third, the colonial government of Hong Kong provided an excellent urban infrastructure for industrialization. Its large-scale, low-rent public housing projects served to lower labor costs, provided secure shelter for the urban population, promoted familism, and dampened working-class radicalism. Moreover, during the 1970's, the colonial government increased expenditures for education, health care, and social work and established regulations on industrial safety, severance pay, and child labor.

Downtown Hong Kong. Anticipating the reversion of control of this British colony to the Chinese in 1997, many Hong Kong residents have moved to the United States and Canada. (AP/Wide World Photos)

A Hong Kong businessman, one of many immigrants to Canada. (Florent Flipper, Unicorn Stock Photos)

Finally, since mainland China adopted an open-door policy in 1978, there has been a massive northward shift of Hong Kong's labor-intensive industries to South China. It is estimated that more than three million South China workers are currently employed in Hong Kong-owned enterprises. This northward shift not only has released pressure on labor and land resources, but also has allowed Hong Kong to concentrate its energy on economic diversification and structural transformation. As a result, Hong Kong has upgraded itself to be the financier, investor, promoter, exporter, and technical consultant of mainland China's economy.

Political Transformation. Under British rule, Hong Kong has been headed by a governor, appointed by the crown, and a nonelective legislative council. After the 1984 agreement with the PRC, the colonial government of Hong Kong sought to initiate political reforms that would produce a democratically elected legislature in 1988. Some observers viewed this as a face-saving gesture, conceived to allow Britain to claim that sovereignty had been returned to the people of Hong

Kong rather than to the Communist regime of the PRC. The British colonial government maintained that the reforms were needed to safeguard Hong Kong's freedoms after reversion to Chinese sovereignty.

In response to the colonial government's proposals for reform, Hong Kong's middle class of educated professionals suddenly became politicized. There was a proliferation of new political organizations calling for democratic reforms. In the view of many middle-class professionals, democratization was the only way to protect themselves and the people of Hong Kong from excessive interference by the PRC after 1997. For example, college professors and journalists were worried about the record of censorship of the mainland regime, and they defended their interests in the name of freedom, liberty, the rule of law, human rights, and democratization.

The PRC strongly opposed these developments, fearing that democratization would disrupt Hong Kong's political stability and might even turn Hong Kong into a base of counterrevolution against the mainland. A PRC-appointed committee comprising representatives from Hong Kong and the mainland was formed to draft a constitution (the Basic Law) clarifying Hong Kong's post-1997 status. The PRC announced that there could be no major political reform in Hong Kong before the promulgation of the Basic Law in 1990. At the same time, in order to gain support in Hong Kong, the PRC established cordial relations with Hong Kong businesspersons, warning them that democratization would lead to higher taxes and more regulations on the corporate sector. As a result of this alliance between mainland Communists and Hong Kong businessmen, the proposal for direct election of the legislature in 1988 was shelved.

In 1992, however, under Governor Chris Patten, proposals for democratic reform were revived and pressed forward. In February, 1994, the legislative council approved Patten's proposal for single-member voting districts and a fully democratic parliamentary body for the elections of 1994-1995. In response, the PRC announced that it would not recognize any such legislative body when it resumes sovereignty in 1997.

Changing Cultural Values and Ethnic Identity. It is obvious that the 1997 issue has greatly transformed the political culture of Hong Kong. There was a distrust of the Chinese government, a strong sense of political helplessness, a carefree attitude toward public affairs, and a shift to such values as "it is of utmost importance to make as much money as possible" and "enjoy life and forget about the future." In part as a result of this political alienation, 60,000 emigrated from Hong Kong in 1990.

Furthermore, a new political identity emerged among Hong Kong residents. A survey by Ming-Kwan Lee shows that only 29 percent regarded themselves as "Chinese," with the majority identifying themselves as "Hong Kong persons." Proud of their material wealth and urban sophistication, many Hong Kong people tend to look down on the relatively less developed mainland Chinese.

While the 1997 issue has been a motive for immigration, it would be misleading to see immigration from Hong Kong exclusively in that context. Substantial immigration from Hong Kong to the United States and Canada, especially since the immigration reforms of the 1960's, and Hong Kong investment abroad are paralleled by developments in Taiwan, for example, and must be seen in the larger context of the Chinese diaspora.—*Alvin Y. So*

SUGGESTED READINGS: • Leung, Benjamin K. P.

Immigration from Hong Kong to the U.S., 1951-1990

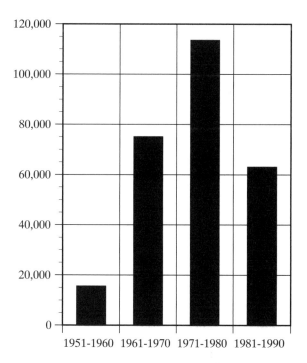

Sources: Min Zhou, *Chinatown: The Socioeconomic Potential of an Urban Enclave.* Philadelphia, Pa.: Temple University Press, 1992. Susan B. Gall and Timothy L. Gall, eds., *Statistical Record of Asian Americans.* Detroit: Gale Research, Inc., 1993.

Social Issues in Hong Kong. Hong Kong: Oxford University Press, 1990. • McGurn, William. *Perfidious Albion: The Abandonment of Hong Kong, 1997.* Washington, D.C.: Ethics and Public Policy Center, 1992. • Scott, Ian. *Political Change and the Crisis of Legitimacy in Hong Kong.* Honolulu: University of Hawaii Press, 1989. • Wong, Richard Y. C., and Joseph Y. S. Cheng, eds. *The Other Hong Kong Report, 1990.* Hong Kong: Chinese University Press, 1990.

Hong Xiuquan (Jan. 1, 1814, Fuyuanshui, Guangdong Province, China—June 1, 1864, Nanjing, Jiangsu Province, China): Leader of the TAIPING REBELLION (1850-1864). Excoriated by the ruling Manchus and the Chinese who accepted their dynasty as legitimate Confucian rule, Hong was first welcomed by foreign powers as a modern and Christian alternative to the Manchus, was finally rejected by these powers as mad and disruptive, and was venerated by later Chinese, especially SUN YAT-SEN, as prophet of a Chinese nationalism based on race and populist ideology. Some call Hong's movement not a "rebellion" but a "revolution."

Born into a Hakka family, Hong first tried to revive family fortunes by studying the Confucian classics and taking the imperial examinations. He failed four times. In the early 1840's, he suffered a spiritual crisis, reporting that he had gone into a forty-day trance and had been welcomed to Paradise by the white-bearded Heavenly Father of the Old Testament. After studying Christianity with Chinese and foreign teachers, he convinced relatives and Hakka villages in mountainous and chaotic neighboring Guangxi Province to join his God Worshippers Society and eventually to raise the flag of rebellion in January, 1851.

Hong's anti-Confucian, anti-Manchu ideology was drawn from biblical and ancient Chinese ideals: universal brotherly love; a prohibition on opium, prostitution, and mixing of the sexes; equal status for women (including the right to own property, join the army, and unbind their feet); abolition of landlordism in favor of equal holdings and communal farming; openness to new technology; and equality for all nations. He was evidently an astute judge of talent, for he recruited imaginative military leaders whose campaigns are classic. Yet he was defeated both by a rejuvenated Confucianism and by an inability to create institutions that would embody his charismatic ideas. After his movement took Nanjing in 1853, he increasingly withdrew; he could not quell bloody dissension or carry out the programs that he espoused. Just before vengeful

Qing armies retook Nanjing in June, 1864, he poisoned himself; his corpse was found in a sewer, wrapped in imperial yellow satin.

Hongo, Florence M. (b. Nov. 21, 1928, Cressey, Calif.): Educator and administrator. She became a faculty member at the College of San Mateo (California) in 1983 and has served as the general manager and board president of the Japanese American Curriculum Project (JACP), a nonprofit educational corporation dedicated to developing Japanese American curriculum materials. She also served as an adviser to the San Mateo City Elementary School District (1969-1971) and edited *Japanese American Journey* (1985), a book containing history, biographies, and short stories.

Hongo, Garrett Kaoru (b. May 30, 1951, Volcano, Hawaii): Poet. An accomplished, prize-winning talent, Hongo became director of the Creative Writing Program at the University of Oregon. His book of poems *The River of Heaven* (1988) was a finalist for the Pulitzer Prize in poetry and won the Lamont Prize. Hongo's sharply imaged and powerfully cadenced verse has been compared to the poetry of Walt Whitman. His poems display a multitude of emotions ranging from meditative recollection to humorous scorn, from angry denunciation to lyrical praise.

A Yonsei (fourth-generation) Japanese American, Hongo had a grandfather who was unjustly arrested during World War II on suspicion of being a saboteur. The arrest has lingered in Hongo's consciousness and has compelled him to honor the Japanese American past, which, he believes, has been maligned by American history. Much of his poetry thus explores and celebrates his Japanese American and Hawaiian roots, and he often returns to Volcano to compose his poetry and prose.

By 1957 Hongo and his family had moved from Hawaii to Southern California, and he attended a racially mixed high school in a working-class section of South Los Angeles. Hongo attended elite Pomona College on a state-funded scholarship, graduating cum laude in English. After traveling in Japan on a fellowship, he pursued Japanese studies at the University of Michigan, where he won a Hopwood Prize for Poetry. He earned an M.F.A. degree from the University of California, Irvine, where he also began working toward a doctorate in critical theory. Hongo has since taught at the Universities of Washington, Southern California, Missouri, and Oregon. He married Cynthia Anne Thiessen in 1982, and they have two children.

Hongo's initial book of poems was *The Buddha Bandits Down Highway 99* (1978), published in collaboration with Japanese American Lawson Inada and Chinese American Alan Chong Lau. From 1976 to 1978 Hongo directed a theatrical company in Seattle that he had founded; it staged during those years several important Asian American plays, including Frank Chin's *The Year of the Dragon* (orig. pr. 1974), Wakako Yamauchi's *And the Soul Shall Dance* (pr. 1977), and his own *Nisei Bar and Grill*. *Yellow Light* (1982) was Hongo's first individual book of poems. It was followed by *The River of Heaven*. *The Open Boat*, an anthology of Asian American poetry edited by Hongo, was published in 1993.

Honouliuli: Detention camp administered by the U.S. War Department on Oahu, Hawaii. The compound contained mostly Issei prisoners and a few German and German American prisoners of war. It closed in September, 1945.

Honshu: The largest of the four primary islands that constitute the major portion of the territory of Japan, Honshu is considered to be the Japanese mainland. Almost all of Japan's major population centers are located on the island of Honshu.

Hood River: Farming community in Oregon where Japanese immigrants settled at the end of the nineteenth century and the beginning of the twentieth century. Located on the Columbia River at the foot of Mount Hood, the Hood River Valley had been heavily logged. With great labor the Issei pioneers cleared the land and developed it into apple orchards (Hood River apples were world-famous) and productive farmland. In 1910, Japanese made up about 6 percent of Hood River's population of 8,016.

In Oregon as in California, the Issei soon had to contend with ALIEN LAND LAWS and other discriminatory laws and practices. They persevered nonetheless, establishing a thriving Japanese American community. Many participated actively in the affairs of the larger community. That harmony was shattered in 1942, when the Japanese Americans in Hood River, along with approximately 120,000 other Japanese Americans on the West Coast, were forcibly evacuated and sent first to temporary assembly centers, then to relocation centers administered by the WAR RELOCATION AUTHORITY (WRA).

In October, 1943, the Hood River American Legion unveiled a plaque listing the names of county residents

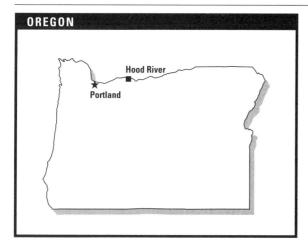

OREGON

Hood River

Portland

who had served or were serving their country in the military during World War II. Nisei from Hood River were among the thousands who served in the U.S. armed forces. In November, 1944, however, the names of sixteen Nisei servicemen were removed from the plaque, which was located at the county courthouse in Hood River. Shortly thereafter, when the first Japanese American internees from Hood River began to return to their homes, they encountered hostility on the part of some local residents, who sought to keep the Japanese from returning.

The treatment of the Japanese in Hood River drew national publicity, most of it strongly critical. In April, 1945, the Hood River American Legion voted to restore the names of the Japanese American servicemen to the plaque, and in May, a group called the Hood River League for Liberty and Justice was formed to support the right of Japanese residents to return to their homes. Slowly, the Japanese American community in Hood River was rebuilt.

Hop pun: System of cooperative farming adopted by Chinese rice farmers in Hawaii. A phrase meaning "partnership" in Chinese, *hop pun* generally referred to an arrangement made by a small group of farmers by which they distributed responsibilities for and profits from cultivating rice crops on land they leased jointly. Under this system, a representative from the group was usually selected to undertake the negotiations to lease the property from a wealthy landowner. Such arrangements were common in the area of southern China, where many of these farmers had been originally recruited as contract laborers.

Hosokawa, William K. (b. Jan. 30, 1915, Seattle, Wash.): Journalist. Hosokawa is best known to Japa-

nese Americans as the popular historian of the Japanese American Citizens League (JACL). His two books on the organization, *Nisei: The Quiet Americans* (1969) and *JACL in Quest of Justice* (1982), chronicle the history of the JACL from its birth through the early 1980's. He is also the author of several other noteworthy books, including *Thirty-Five Years in the Frying Pan* (1978), a collection from his column that has appeared in the JACL newspaper *Pacific Citizen* since 1942, and *They Call Me Moses Masaoka* (1987), an autobiography of the controversial JACL leader.

Hosokawa was born to immigrant parents. He was graduated from the University of Washington in 1937 with a B.A. degree. In 1938 he started his career in journalism by accepting a position with a newspaper in Singapore and later Shanghai. By 1941 Hosokawa had realized that war with the United States was near and quickly departed for his homeland. Soon after he and the rest of his family were interned at the Puyallup assembly center and then at the Heart Mountain concentration camp in Wyoming. His experience of escaping the war in the Pacific to live in the "frying pan" of a concentration camp led him to title his newly formed *Pacific Citizen* column, "From the Frying Pan." While at Heart Mountain he became editor of the camp newspaper, the *Heart Mountain Sentinel*. Hosokawa left Heart Mountain with his family in 1943 to accept a position with the *Des Moines Register* in Des Moines, Iowa. In 1946 he moved to Denver, Colorado, to work for the *Denver Post*, where he eventually became an editor for the paper.

Hosokawa has won numerous awards, including Nisei of the Biennium (1958), the Colorado Society of Professional Journalists' Outstanding Journalist award (1976), the Denver Press Club's Outstanding Colorado Communicator award (1985), and the Decorated Japanese Order of the Rising Run (1987). He and his wife continue to reside in Denver.

House Select Committee to Investigate Un-American Activities (also, Dies Committee): U.S. Congressional body established in 1938 and chaired by Martin Dies, a Texas representative. It activities were inspired by jingoism and fanatic anticommunism. After the bombing of Pearl Harbor, Dies claimed that the West Coast would be invaded unless the government took care of the Japanese American "problem." Even after Japanese Americans were in concentration camps, the committee criticized the U.S. War Relocation Authority (WRA) for making the camps too comfortable and hospitable.

House Un-American Activities Committee. *See* **House Select Committee to Investigate Un-American Activities**

Houston, Jeanne [Toyo] Wakatsuki (b. Sept. 26, 1934, Inglewood, Calif.): Writer. In 1973, with her novelist husband, James D. Houston, Houston wrote *Farewell to Manzanar: A True Story of Japanese American Experience During and After the World War II Internment. The book helped to draw national attention to the wartime injustice suffered by Japanese Americans.*

Born to Ko Wakatsuki, an Issei fisherman, and Riku Sugai Wakatsuki, Jeanne spent her childhood in Long Beach, California. When she was seven years old her happy childhood suddenly ended. The Wakatsukis were forced to leave their fishing business and were interned in the Manzanar relocation center, which was located in the high-mountain desert of California, east of the Sierras. Manzanar was the first of ten concentration camps where 120,000 people of Japanese ancestry were interned under EXECUTIVE ORDER 9066 (1942). With 10,000 other internees the Wakatsukis spent nearly four years surrounded by barbed wire and guard towers. Although Jeanne did not understand the political implication of their internment experience, she kept her traumatic childhood memory to herself.

After returning to normal life Jeanne Wakatsuki studied sociology and journalism at San Jose State College, where she met her future husband. They married in Hawaii in 1957. Following a tour of duty with the U.S. Air Force in Europe, they stayed for an extra year and studied at the Sorbonne, University of Paris. They have three children.

At age thirty-seven, after twenty-six years of painful silence, Jeanne Wakatsuki Houston tried to reconstruct her lost internment experience from the perspective of an informed adult. In Farewell to Manzanar, through her calm, restrained style, she recaptured the fear, anxiety, agony, and confusion experienced by a sensitive child in Manzanar.

Houston's *Farewell to Manzanar* vividly depicts

Jeanne Houston's book Farewell to Manzanar *depicts the hardships endured by Japanese Americans interned in that camp during World War II; here, pilgrims to the site pay their respects in 1983.* (Michael Yamashita)

hardships which Japanese Americans endured, along with the dignity and personal integrity sustained by them even in a humiliating environment. Houston also authored the teleplay *Farewell to Manzanar*, broadcast in 1976 and based on her book. For this screenplay she received the Humanitas Prize and the Christopher Award, as well as an award from the National Women's Political Caucus.

Houston, Velina Hasu (b. May 5, 1957, Junction City, Kan.): Playwright and poet. The daughter of an African American man and a Japanese woman, Velina Hasu Houston grew up near Fort Riley, Kansas, in a community whose members consisted of American military men, their Japanese wives, and their Amerasian children. Inspired by her mother's love of her Japanese heritage, Houston began writing haiku when she was six. When Houston was twelve, one of her teachers encouraged her to write a play. At that point, Houston has said, "I fell in love with dramatic literature." She later attended Kansas State University, where she studied theater, philosophy, journalism, and mass communications, and the University of California, Los Angeles, where she earned a master's degree in theater and playwriting. After her graduation, Houston became an assistant professor at the University of Southern California School of Theater, where she teaches modern drama and playwriting. She is also the president and cofounder of the Amerasian League, "a nonprofit organization dedicated to educational awareness of Amerasian culture."

Racism, culture clashes, and ethical responsibility are frequent themes in Houston's plays. She is a prolific playwright; among her most acclaimed works is a trilogy that includes *Asa Ga Kimashita* (pr. 1981), *American Dreams* (pr. 1984), and *Tea* (pr. 1987). Some of Houston's other dramatic works are *Necessities* (1991), *Thirst* (pr. 1986), *The Legend of Bobbi Chicago* (as *Tips on How to Store Breast Milk*, 1985), and *Father I Must Have Rice* (pr. 1987). She edited *The Politics of Life: Four Plays by Asian American Women* (1993).

Houston is not only a busy playwright but also an active poet who gives readings in both the United States and Japan. She also lectures on such subjects as theater, Amerasian culture, and African American-Asian American relations. Houston has been the recipient of numerous awards and honors, including the Lorraine Hansberry Playwriting Award (1982) and various *DramaLogue* Outstanding Achievement in Theater Awards.

Howe, James Wong (Wong Tung Jim; Aug. 28, 1899, Yong'an Village, Taishan, Guangdong Province, China—July 12, 1976, Los Angeles, Calif.): Cinematographer. Howe came to America with his father, who opened a general store in Pasco, Washington, in 1904. In 1914 his father died. Howe did not get along with his stepmother and left home. For a short time he was a professional boxer in Portland. In 1916 he drifted to Los Angeles. He worked as janitor of the camera room for Lasky Studios, where he familiarized himself with photographic equipment in the studio during his spare moments. A break came in 1919, when his work as fourth assistant cameraman on the Cecil B. DeMille silent film *Male and Female* impressed the producer.

Howe became first cameraman and established a reputation after actress Mary Miles Minter picked him to be her cameraman in 1922. In 1929 he went to China and stayed for a year. After his return he found that cinematography had changed to accommodate sound and that his experience was now obsolete. He made a Japanese American film that was a failure. He reestablished his reputation in cinematography, however, with his work in the film *Transatlantic* (1931), and by the 1930's he was well known internationally. In 1938 Howe received the first of ten nominations for an Academy Award for his work in *Algiers*.

In 1948 Howe went to China intending to produce Lau Shaw's "Rickshaw Boy," but the unstable political situation in the country prevented completion of the project. It remained one of Howe's greatest disappointments that he was never able to make such a film in the land of his birth expressing his own emotions and ideas.

When Howe returned to the United States, the anti-Communist witchhunt was already on. Although he was not blacklisted as a communist, the House Un-American Activities Committee placed him on a so-called grey list, and for awhile he could find work only in low budget pictures. In 1953 he formed Living Art Production and produced his only documentary, *The World of Dong Kingman*. A slow resurgence of Howe's career began and resulted in an Academy Award for his work in *The Rose Tattoo* (1955), followed by another award for *Hud* (1963). Howe passed away at his home in Los Angeles.

Hsi Lai Temple: Buddhist temple founded in 1981 in Hacienda Heights, California, an unincorporated suburb of Los Angeles. As the largest Buddhist edifice in the Western Hemisphere, the temple serves as a spiritual home to some 20,000 worshippers from Southern California's growing Taiwanese immigrant community. In addition to housing approximately fifty Buddhist monks and nuns, the temple has made an effort to reach beyond its Chinese membership by supporting charitable efforts in the local area and inviting local residents to participate in its annual celebration of Chinese New Year as well as other festive events. Although the establishment of the temple initially generated great concern among some non-Asian residents of the community regarding changes that its presence would bring, most have come to accept the temple, and its outreach activities have served as a springboard for greater understanding and interaction among the town's ethnic groups.

Hsu, Francis Lang Kwang (b. Oct. 28, 1909, Zhuanghe, Manchuria, China): Scholar. Hsu earned a B.A. degree at Shanghai University in 1933 and a Ph.D. degree at the University of London in 1940. From 1947 until 1978 he taught anthropology at Northwestern University, eventually becoming full professor there and serving as anthropology department chair from 1957 until 1975. His many books include *Americans and Chinese: Two Ways of Life* (1953; 3d ed. 1981), *Americans and Chinese: Purpose and Fulfillment in Great Civilizations* (1970), *The Challenge of the American Dream: The Chinese in the United States* (1971), and *Iemoto: The Heart of Japan* (1975). He was a Rockefeller Foundation Fellow (1955-1957) and a Carnegie Corporation grantee (1964-1965).

Hsu, Kai-yu (July 5, 1922, China—Jan. 4, 1982): Scholar, journalist, and administrator. Hsu coedited *Asian-American Authors* (1972), one of the first anthologies of Asian American writing. He was educated at National Tsinghua University (B.A., 1944) and Stanford University (Ph.D., 1959). From 1943 to 1947 he served in various military capacities with the Chinese and U.S. governments. Between 1948 and 1952 he was with *The Chinese World Daily* (San Francisco), beginning as a reporter and rising to editor. Hsu left journalism to pursue a career as a university professor and administrator. In addition he directed educational projects involving studies in Chinese language and culture. He published widely in professional journals and in reference sources such as the *Encyclopaedia Britannica. Asian-American Authors*, the pioneering anthology he edited with Helen Palubinskas, included poetry and prose by Chinese American, Japanese American, and Filipino American writers. Hsu also

was the editor and translator of *Twentieth Century Chinese Poetry: An Anthology* (1963) and the author of *Chou En-lai: China's Gray Eminence* (1968), the first biography of Chou in English.

Hua Long: San Francisco-based artists and writers collective. The group takes its name from a Chinese saying, *hua long dian jing* ("adding the eyes to a painted dragon"; that is, adding the finishing touch). The group has collaborated on books and other projects to promote knowledge and appreciation of Asian and Asian American culture.

HUAC. *See* **House Select Committee to Investigate Un-American Activities**

Huang Zunxian (1848, Chia-ying [now Meixian], Guangdong Province, China—Mar. 28, 1905, Chia-ying, China): Poet and government official. In these dual capacities, Huang instituted both literary and social reforms.

As a diplomat serving the Chinese government, Huang visited Japan, the United States, and England. His travels expanded his view of the world and provided him with fresh material for his poetry and prose. Yet it was his new style of poetry, gleaned from listening to the speech patterns of commoners in his hometown, that lifted his work to a new level of mass popularity. Proclaiming "I write as I speak," Huang incorporated vernacular Chinese into his verse. He also tapped the styles and rhythms of local folk songs and added them as well. By adopting new forms, Huang started a new trend in Chinese verse.

Huang was assigned to the Chinese legation in Tokyo, Japan, in 1876. During this time, he noted the Japanese government's attempts to reform Korea and came to believe that Japan might someday lay claim to the Korean peninsula. He wrote a policy treatise urging the Koreans to improve foreign relations with both Japan and the United States. Huang also published a history of Japan.

While stationed in San Francisco, Huang observed the prejudice shown by Americans against the Chinese and recorded his observations in numerous poems. Opponents of Chinese exclusion quoted his verse to bolster their arguments.

After 1889 the Chinese emperor, an admirer of Huang's reformist principles, called him back to China. There Huang advised many reform-minded Chinese officials and helped found a school where revolutionary leaders discussed their ideas.

Huaqiao. *See* **Chinese diaspora**

Hu-DeHart, Evelyn (b. Mar. 12, 1947, Chongqing, China): Scholar. In 1988 she became a professor of history and the director of the Center for Studies of Ethnicity and Race in America at the University of Colorado, Boulder. The recipient of numerous awards, including two Fulbrights, she has lectured in the United Kingdom, Mexico, Peru, Cuba, the People's Republic of China, and Taiwan and has written two books on the Yaqui Indians of northern Mexico and Arizona.

Huiguan: Mutual-aid networks, or "companies," that evolved into large social and political organizations of benefit to Chinese immigrants and that played a major part in the Chinese American community's growth and development. *Huiguan* were traditional and lawful societies both in China and in the overseas Chinese communities. Whenever large numbers of Chinese from one place or with identical surnames were thrown together in another place, they immediately formed a *huiguan* for their own protection and general welfare.

As a consequence, in major Chinese cities all kinds of *huiguan* were organized by merchants and sojourners. In a cosmopolitan city such as Shanghai or Hong Kong, there were the Ningbo Huiguan, the Fujian Huiguan, the Shanxi Huiguan, and so forth. Thus it was natural that the Chinese organized such associations as soon as they arrived in the New World. In North America, the various *huiguan* became known as companies.

A second basis of social organization in China, and a much tighter one, rested on a coincidence between blood and region. In an agrarian society, the people of any one clan, those claiming a common ancestor, usually inhabited a village or cluster of adjacent villages; consequently the Wang Village, the Liang Village, the Wu Village, and so forth became commonplace in rural China. Agnatic descendants maintained these lineage alignments by keeping a common estate and by forming a clan association for the contact and common interests of their kin. Another basis of organization, again agnatically defined, was the blood-ties *huiguan*. Chinese who had the same surname, though they might come from different parts of China, could

Convention of the Benevolent Association, a San Francisco huiguan. (International Daily News)

Edifice of the Bing Kung Association, one of many huiguan *in the United States.* (Wing Luke Museum)

organize a *huiguan* on the grounds that they had a common ancestor in the distant past. In the modern city of Manila, the Chinese have formed many such associations: the Chen Clan Huiguan, the Li Clan Huigan, the Huang Clan Huiguan. The same situation existed when the Chinese emigrated to America: Among the biggest such associations was the Wong Clan Huiguan, with its headquarters in San Francisco.

When a Chinese laborer arrived in the United States, the first thing he or she did was to seek people who spoke the same dialect; if such could be found, a bond of solidarity soon was forged. The linguistic bond accounted to a great degree for the rise of so many *huiguan* in Chinese communities. It is believed that in 1852 an influential Chinese, Yu Laoji, from the Si-yi district, founded the first *huiguan*, the Kong Chow Company (or Ganzhou Huiguan) in San Francisco. Membership was open to all Chinese except people from the San-yi district and the Hakkas. Within a year the San-yi people organized their own Sam Yup Company (or Sanyi Huiguan) with branches in San Francisco and Stockton. Soon the Hakkas and other dialect/regional groups also formed their own *huiguan*. There followed a period of spin-offs and mergers until finally all the various *huiguan* joined the all-inclusive umbrella organization, the Zhonghua Huiguan, or CHINESE CONSOLIDATED BENEVOLENT ASSOCIATIONS (CCBA), more popularly known to the American public as the "Chinese Six Companies."

Judging from its functioning and history, a *huiguan* played a big role in easing the new arrivals' entry into a foreign setting. As soon as an immigrant ship arrived from China, the *huiguan* sent an interpreter to the wharf to welcome the arrivals. In the *huiguan* headquarters the new immigrants were furnished with water, fuel for cooking, and a room in which to spread their mats. Chinese laborers from inland towns and mining camps, embarking for return to China, often stayed in the *huiguan* lodges. In most of the *huiguan* buildings there were special sections devoted to religious purposes. In some *huiguan* buildings an apartment was used for the worship of the spirits of deceased members. In it was an altar before which a candle light was constantly kept burning. Bones of the deceased were usually exhumed as soon as possible and sent back to China for permanent burial. The Six Companies kept a register of names and addresses of all the Chinese in the United States; in 1876, for example, it listed a total of 150,130 members. Virtually everyone belonged to the Six Companies. A few years later the Sam Yup Company listed twelve thousand members, the Yeong Wo Company thirteen thousand, the Kong Chow Company sixteen thousand, the Yan Hop Company a few thousand, the Hop Wo Company forty thousand, and the Ning Yeung Company seventy thousand.

The leaders of the *huiguan* were mostly successful businessmen who were wealthier and better educated than most of their fellow immigrants; many occupied positions of honor and power. The merchant *huiguan* leaders generally promoted learning, stressing the importance of traditional education. By the 1890's the *huiguan* made great efforts to bring respected scholars from China to serve as their presiding officials. In 1906, for example, there were four Juren (holders of the second civil-service examination degree, equivalent to an M.A.) among the *huiguan* presidents, and they were paid handsomely for coming to the United States. Of the fourteen presidents of the Sam Yup Company from 1881 to 1927, three had Jinshi degrees (Ph.D.), nine had Juren degrees, and one had a Gongsheng degree (B.A.).

The Six Companies and its member *huiguan* were often viewed as secretive, extralegal organizations because they arbitrated cases of misunderstanding or quarrels among the Chinese. They also decided strategies for contesting or seeking relief from unconstitutional or burdensome laws, devised ways and means to curb the importation of prostitutes and opium, and arranged for public dinners and other celebrations. Yet the fact that thousands of Chinese immigrants acquiesced in the *huiguan* decisions led many white Americans to believe that the Chinese in America feared jurisdiction under their *huiguan* more than they did the U.S. laws or courts. Such beliefs failed to take into account the strong Confucian traditions that called for respect and obedience of the older, better-educated superiors who held positions of authority and honor. Frequently the *huiguan* officials led the fight against legal impositions and social indignities imposed upon the Chinese immigrants. *Huiguan* had indeed become the most important and generally effective voice of the Chinese community speaking to the outside world, functioning as representatives for the whole Chinese American population. Even after the Chinese government had established legations and consulates in the United States, the *huiguan* continued to dominate the internal affairs of Chinatowns.—*Shih-shan H. Tsai*

SUGGESTED READINGS: • Daily, Carl Livingston. "The Chinese as Sojourners: A Study in the Sociology of Migration." Ph.D. dissertation, New York: City University of New York, 1978. • Lai, Him Mark, and

Philip P. Choy, eds. *LuMei sanyi zong huiguan jianshi* (A Brief History of the Whole San-yi Association in the United States). San Francisco: Chinese American Studies Planning Group, 1976. • Lee, Rose Hum. *The Chinese in the United States of America*. Hong Kong: Hong Kong University Press, 1960. • Lyman, Stanford M. "Conflict and the Web of Group Affiliation in San Francisco's Chinatown, 1850-1910." In *The Asian American: The Historical Experience*, edited by Norris Hundley, Jr. Santa Barbara, Calif.: ABC-Clio, 1976. • Sung, Betty L. *Mountain of Gold*. New York: Macmillan, 1967.

Hula: Popular, entertaining dance among Hawaiian people. The hula is danced with chants that give meaning to the body movements. The hula existed in prehistoric or pre-1778 Hawaii, but it is impossible to document any rituals associated with the hula at that time. What remains today of any older rituals is based on late-nineteenth century training practices. These are the chants and dances that survived the attempt by early nineteenth century missionaries to extinguish hula entirely.

Calvinist missionaries from America arrived in Hawaii in 1820. After converting several tribal chiefs, they began to attack the hula as being "heathen" and "lascivious" and made every effort to drive it out of the culture. For example, the queen regent Kaahumanu, who had been accepted into the church in December of 1825, issued an edict forbidding public performance of the hula in 1830. In 1851 an act was passed to require licensing and heavy fees for each public hula performance.

Away from the mission stations and the pious chiefs, however, the hula continued to be taught and practiced. Secret dance schools operated throughout the islands in the 1860's. Some rulers and chiefs of the kingdom openly reverted to the old custom of having hula people, *poe* hula, available to provide entertainment. These individuals kept the art alive, and from them came the traditional nineteenth century hula, which is called "ancient hula" today.

Full reacceptance of the hula as public entertainment happened in the reign (1874-1891) of King David KALAKAUA. Elaborate dances were performed at both his coronation ceremonies in 1883 and his

Ray Fonseca's hula school during a performance of modern hula, or hula auana. (Lyman House Memorial Museum)

fiftieth birthday celebration in 1886. Many of the hula danced today are revivals or revisions of those composed and performed in the Kalakaua years. After the end of the Hawaiian monarchy, public performances of the hula again declined. Yet by the mid-twentieth century, the popularity of the hula as entertainment had begun to flourish again and became linked to the tourist industry in Hawaii.

Originally the hula was performed to chants. Gesticulation was appreciated for its grace but was not used to illustrate the meaning of the chant until more modern times. The modern hula was quite different from that performed as Hawaiian entertainment for Hawaiians. Many innovations were made in both song and dance forms to appeal to audiences who did not understand the Hawaiian language. Hula had undergone a radical change, from a dance form subordinate to the poetry of the chant to which it was danced, to a style of dancing in which gesture became the important feature.

The most detailed work on the rituals and practices of the hula of the late nineteenth and early twentieth century is N. B. Emerson's *The Unwritten Literature of Hawaii: The Sacred Songs of the Hula* (1909). This book has become the classic authority for studying hula.

Hulbert, Homer B. (Jan. 26, 1863, New Haven, Vt.— Aug. 5, 1949, Seoul, Republic of Korea): Diplomat. After serving in Korea from 1886 to 1905, he became adviser to Korea's penultimate king, Kojong. Hulbert led a secret mission to the Second Hague Peace Conference in 1907, at which delegates denied the king's petition asserting the illegality of the 1905 Japanese Protectorate treaty. Hulbert appealed to U.S. president Theodore Roosevelt for assistance in accordance with the 1882 Korean-American Treaty but was refused. Hulbert was one of the earliest and most widely accepted authors of western works on Korea, including *The History of Korea* (1905) and *The Passing of Korea* (1906).

Hulugan: Economic association formed among Filipinos in Hawaii. Members of a *hulugan* pooled their savings in order to provide the necessary capital in making loans for various projects and investments. Started in the 1920's, these *hulugans* resembled similar savings associations established in the Chinese community and provided a rotating system by which members could bid for the privilege of receiving a loan.

Hundred Days of Reform (1898): Period noted for the series of progressive edicts issued by the Chinese emperor in an effort to revolutionize the country. These reforms, also known collectively as the "Reform Movement of 1898," are often seen as a political morality tale: "Progress," represented by the reforms of Emperor Guangxu and his advisers KANG YOUWEI and LIANG QICHAO, was stifled in a reactionary coup by the EMPRESS DOWAGER Cixi and Yuan Shikai. Recently historians have disputed this view. They point out that the movement originated from the self-serving writings of Kang's followers, who exaggerated their own roles and nature of the reforms and maligned the Empress Dowager, and that the sickly emperor himself, recognizing failure and fearing imperialist depredations, ceded control. Whether the reforms were bungled and feckless or simply premature, the Hundred Days of Reform stand as intriguing political drama.

China's defeat by Japan in 1895 had ruined the previous generation's limited program of "Self-Strengthening." Kang Youwei, an unconventional young Cantonese scholar, represented a new generation; he wanted to use foreign ways to save the dynasty, to emulate the sweeping institutional reforms of Peter the Great of Russia and the Meiji emperor of Japan. This passionate program caught the Chinese emperor's eye. He appointed Kang, his pupil Liang, and reform students to office and for (roughly) one hundred days, from June to September, 1898, issued decree after decree. With no political preparation the reforms found scant support in the bureaucracy, while an emerging public remained helpless. The emperor simply proclaimed the establishment of new schools and universities to replace the examination system, commanded reformation of the armed forces, and abolished many bureaucratic positions and procedures. He seemed to replace Confucianism with Western natural and political science and to favor Chinese over Manchus. In September some reformers apparently tried to enlist Yuan, a reform-minded general, in plans to assassinate the Empress Dowager and others; instead Yuan triggered a countercoup. Kang and Liang fled to Japan, while other reformers were summarily executed. After the BOXER REBELLION (1900) and imperialist retribution, the Empress Dowager effectively implemented many of the proposals. The frustrated reformers were thus impelled toward overseas Chinese for support; with the notable exception of Kang they evolved toward revolutionary Republicanism and anti-Manchu nationalism.

Hune, Shirley (b. Toronto, Canada): Scholar. She is a professor of urban studies specializing in U.S. immigration policy, Asian American studies, and global policies and their relationship to Third World states and migrant workers. She has published widely in these areas. In 1993 she was appointed acting associate dean for Graduate Programs at the University of California, Los Angeles (UCLA); previously she was associate provost at Hunter College, City University of New York. A past president of the Association for Asian American Studies, she holds a Ph.D. degree in American civilization from George Washington University.

Shirley Hune, scholar and university administrator. (Asian Week)

Hungsa-dan (Corps for the Advancement of Individuals): Korean nationalist cultural organization founded in San Francisco by Ahn Chang-ho on May 13, 1913. Based on Ahn's belief that political action on behalf of Korean independence would not be effective unless accompanied by national regeneration, the organization influenced Korean students, intellectuals, and professionals in Korea under Japanese colonial rule. When Korea was divided after World War II, Hungsa-dan became an educational organization in South Korea.

Hurh, Won Moo (b. Sept. 24, 1932, Chungju, Choong-Nam, Korea): Scholar. A professor of sociology at Western Illinois University, he immigrated to the United States in 1965. His fields of interest include race and ethnic relations, social psychology, and sociological theory. He has coconducted three major research projects on Korean immigrants. His publications include *Comparative Study of Korean Immigrants in the United States: A Typological Approach* (1977), *Korean Immigrants in America: A Structural Analysis of Ethnic Confinement and Adhesive Adaptation* (1984), coauthored with Kwang Chung Kim, and *Assimilation Patterns of Immigrants in the United States* (1978), with Hei Chu Kim and Kwang Chung Kim.

Hwang, David Henry (b. Aug. 11, 1957, Los Angeles, Calif.): Playwright, screenwriter, and drama critic. Hwang's parents emigrated from China to the United States. Hwang grew up in California. He is divorced from Ophelia Chong, an artist.

Hwang's is one of the leading Asian American voices in American theater. As the son of first-generation Chinese American immigrants, he is aware of the cultural conflict between the East and the West. His plays, besides presenting a more pluralistic interpretation of the culturally diversified American experience, also reveal the playwright's determination to destroy cultural stereotypes.

Hwang indicated his interest in playwriting while he was an undergraduate student at Stanford University. *F.O.B.* (pr. 1978) was first staged at Stanford when Hwang was a senior there. Later the play was developed at the O'Neill National Playwrights Conference in the summer of 1979 and presented at the New York Shakespeare Festival in 1980. The play won the Obie Award for the best new play of the 1980-1981 season.

After graduating from Stanford, Hwang attended Yale School of Drama. The success of *F.O.B.* was followed by *The Dance and the Railroad* (pr. 1981). The play ran for 181 performances at both the New Federal Theater and the New York Shakespeare Festival. *Family Devotions* (pr. 1981) and *Sound and Beauty* (pr. 1983) were staged at the Public Theater at the New York Shakespeare Festival. *Rich Relations* (pr. 1986) was produced at Second Stage in New York City.

Hwang's Broadway debut was as successful as his appearance in the Off-Broadway productions. *M. But-*

Playwright David Henry Hwang is well known for both his stage plays and his screenwriting. (AP/Wide World Photos)

terfly (pr. 1988) first opened at the National Theater in Washington, D.C., where *West Side Story* (pr. 1957) and *Amadeus* (pr. 1979) had premiered. It was later moved to the Eugene O'Neill Theater and won the Tony Award for Best Play of 1988. In 1993 *M. Butterfly* was released as a feature film, for which Hwang wrote the screenplay. Hwang also wrote the screenplay for the 1994 film *Golden Gate*.

Hwang also collaborated with composer Philip Glass and designer Jerome Sirlin on *One Thousand Airplanes on the Roof* (pr. 1988), which debuted in Vi-

enna. His plays are included in *Broken Promises: Four Plays by David Henry Hwang* (1983) and in the anthology *New Plays USA* (1982). He has received Guggenheim, Rockefeller, National Endowment, and New York State fellowships. He was also appointed to the board of directors of Theatre Communications Group.

Hwangsong Sinmun: Daily Korean- and Chinese-language newspaper, also known as *Capital Gazette*, founded by Ok Namgung in 1898 and published until 1910 in Korea. An organ of the Independence Club, it focused on Confucianist reform elements. Along with other Korean newspapers, its publication was terminated by Terauchi Masatake, the Japanese resident general, in May, 1910.

Hyun, Peter (Aug. 15, 1906, Lihue, Hawaii—Aug. 25, 1993, Oxnard, Calif.): Theater director and writer. He participated in Korea's March First movement in 1919 and escaped a year later with his family to Shanghai, where his father, Reverend Soon Hyun, and other patriots founded the independent Korean provisional government in exile. Graduating from DePauw University in Greencastle, Indiana, he became active in theater in New York and Massachusetts. In 1936, he was named director of the Children's Theater of the New York Federal Theater, a Works Progress Administration project. During World War II he served in Army intelligence; he was stationed in Korea after the war ended, as a liaison officer in the American military government. In the postwar years, in addition to directing plays and teaching, he established a Chinese restaurant, the House of Hyun, in Laguna Beach, California. His autobiographical book, *Man Sei! The Making of a Korean American* (1986), gives insight into Korean immigrant life in Hawaii, California, and other parts of the United States.

I

I Wor Kuen (IWK): Revolutionary collective of Asian Americans founded in New York's Chinatown in 1969. The group took its name (meaning "Righteous and Harmonious Fists") in tribute to the militant peasant movement that sought to expel foreigners from China in the BOXER REBELLION (1900). IWK's founding members included American-born and immigrant college students, workers, and high school youth who wanted to do community work. In June of 1971 IWK merged with the Red Guards, based in San Francisco's Chinatown, and became a national organization.

IWK was one of a number of Asian American revolutionary organizations strongly influenced both by the Marxist-Leninist philosophy of Mao Zedong and by the militant African American organization, the Black Panther Party. Members of IWK saw their role as organizing Asian Americans for fundamental change and bringing an end to the capitalist system of economic exploitation, racial oppression, and social injustice. IWK saw itself as an integral part of the multinational revolutionary movement in the United States and believed in the formation of a communist party that would lead the working-class struggle for equality and justice.

Between 1969 and 1978 IWK had chapters in Boston, New York, San Francisco, Los Angeles, Honolulu, Atlanta, Chicago, Sacramento, and Seattle. Including more than two hundred active members at its peak, IWK was the largest national Asian American revolutionary organization.

IWK tackled issues of concern to Asian American working people. Such issues included land use, workers' rights, support for Third World countries fighting U.S. imperialism, relevant education, and equal access to health and human services.

Some of IWK's campaigns included support for the People's Republic of China (PRC) and for the normalization of diplomatic relations between the United States and the PRC. IWK conducted door-to-door tuberculosis tests in Chinatown tenements and offered free health clinics. It also held free outdoor breakfasts for children and the elderly, organized bilingual child care programs for garment workers, and conducted draft and youth/gang counseling. IWK fought land developers to preserve low-income housing and advocated the physical preservation of the historic Chinatowns and Nihonmachis.

After 1978, IWK merged with the August Twenty-ninth Movement (ATM) to form the League of Revolutionary Struggle (LRS), which lasted until 1990.

Ichihashi, Yamato (1878, Aichi Prefecture, Japan—1965, Stanford, Calif.): Scholar. Son of a former samurai family, Ichihashi was educated at public school in Nagoya before traveling to San Francisco in 1894 in order to complete his education. After graduating from Lowell High School in 1902, he enrolled at Stanford University. Choosing to major in economics, Ichihashi received his bachelor's degree in 1907 and taught classes in the economics department while working on his master's degree, which he received in 1908. In addition to his graduate work, Ichihashi worked on a project for the U.S. Immigration Commission to study Japanese immigration to the United States. He left Stanford to enter a doctoral program at Harvard University, where he received his Ph.D. in 1913 after completing a dissertation on immigration and the Japanese immigrant community in the United States.

Ichihashi returned to California in 1913 to accept a one-year appointment at Stanford to teach Japanese history and politics—an appointment that was secretly funded through the efforts of the Japanese Foreign Ministry in order to counteract anti-Japanese propaganda in the state. After Ichihashi's temporary appointment was renewed for a three-year period in 1914 and again in 1917, the foreign ministry helped channel funds for an endowment to establish a permanent faculty position. During this period, Ichihashi published several pamphlets and books on the subject of Japanese immigration and compiled impressive statistics that challenged the assumptions of the anti-Japanese movement.

After being granted tenure at Stanford in 1928, Ichihashi published his landmark study *Japanese in the United States* (1932). During World War II, Ichihashi and his family were interned at MANZANAR, TULE LAKE, and GRANADA. After the war ended, Ichihashi returned to Stanford, where he lived until his death in 1965.

Ichioka, Yuji (b. June 23, 1936, San Francisco, Calif.): One of the first scholars to research Asian Americans as agents of history, he received his M.A. degree in history from the University of California, Berkeley, in

1968. While there, he cofounded the Asian American Political Alliance. He coined the term "Asian American" to replace the ethnocentric term "Oriental," and in 1969 he became associate director of the Asian American Studies Center at the University of California, Los Angeles, where he has been instrumental in developing and cataloging Japanese American archives. His book *The Issei: The World of the First Generation Japanese Immigrants, 1885-1924* (1988) won an award from the Association for Asian American Studies. His research has provided the foundation for subsequent research by other scholars investigating the Japanese immigrant experience.

Idul-Adha: Muslim festival. Also known as Id-al-Qurban (feast of sacrifice), it is celebrated in the last lunar month of the Islamic religious calendar. Idul-Adha is the highest holy day in the Islamic calendar; it commemorates the sacrifice of Abraham and the end of the *hajj*. This festival, as well as other Islamic religious events, is increasingly celebrated among Muslims (including Asian Muslims) in North America, where mosques and Islamic centers play an important role in facilitating Muslims' practice of the teachings of Islam.

There are two Islamic festivals that are celebrated all over the Islamic world: the *hajj* (pilgrimage), which culminates in Idul-Adha in the last lunar month, and Ramadan, the month of fasting, which ends with the celebration of Idul-Fitr (feast of the breaking of the fast).

Hajj, or the pilgrimage to Mecca, is the fifth and final pillar of Islam. Unlike the other four requirements, however, *Hajj* is not obligatory. Its performance is contingent on the believer's financial situation and family circumstances. Like the month of Ramadan, the time appointed for the pilgrimage, which is ten weeks after the festival of the breaking of the fast, is fixed according to the lunar calendar and rotates throughout the year.

The various activities during the pilgrimage culminate, on the tenth day, in Idul-Adha, during which pilgrims sacrifice animals as a reenactment of Abraham's willingness to sacrifice his son, who was saved when the archangel Gabriel brought a ram that was used as a sacrifice instead.

The Grand Mosque would be a destination in Muslims' pilgrimage to Mecca. (AP/Wide World Photos)

New York City Muslims pray in celebration of the end of Ramadan, the month of fasting. (Frances M. Roberts)

The sacrifice of animals during Idul-Adha is not only the high point of the pilgrimage to Mecca but also the time when the whole Muslim community is called upon to repeat the sacrifice at home. The performance of the sacrifice is done by pointing the animal's head toward Mecca, saying, "God is great" and "In the name of God," and then slitting the animal's throat. The animal's blood is then thoroughly drained and the meat butchered, in a way similar to the Jewish practice of koshering meat. The meat is then divided into three portions: one for the poor, one for the neighbors, and one for the family.

Besides the animal sacrifice, Idul-Adha is also celebrated by wearing new clothes, visiting friends and family, and sharing special food prepared for the occasion.

Idul-Fitr: Muslim festival. It is observed at the end of the month of Ramadan (the month of fasting) and celebrates the breaking of the fast. Because of the growing Muslim community in North America, including that of Asian Muslims, the celebration of Idul-Fitr is becoming common in the United States. Muslims in larger metropolitan areas, such as Chicago and New York, gather in mosques and Islamic centers to pray, greet other Muslims, and share festival meals.

Fasting during the month of Ramadan requires abstention from food, drink, and other worldly pleasures, from dawn until dusk. The fasting is meant to purify the soul, inculcate a sense of discipline, create compassion for the have-nots in society, and develop appreciation of the blessings of God. The Quran (Islamic scriptures) was also first revealed in the month of Ramadan.

Muslims observe a twelve-month lunar calendar in which each month begins and ends with the appearance of the new moon; therefore, a month may have thirty or twenty-nine days. If the moon is not sighted on the twenty-ninth day, the Idul-Fitr celebrations are postponed for the next day. Several days before the end of Ramadan, Muslims start the preparations for the festival. New clothes, shoes, and jewelry are purchased, and people stock up on fruits, meats, and various other foods to prepare special meals for the festival.

There are two canonical obligations on the day of Idul-Fitr: The first is alms giving to the poor, mostly in the form of cash; the second is gathering for a special prayer meeting, which usually takes place in the largest public grounds available or in the biggest mosque. After the service, members of the congregation greet one another and return home, where they spend the rest of the day receiving guests, exchanging gifts, taking children to amusement parks, and consuming food prepared especially for Idul-Fitr.

Iemoto: *Iemoto-sei* is a Japanese social organizational form that literally means "origin of the household system." It is most clearly found in the traditional arts such as flower arrangement and tea ceremony. The head of a particular school of art is called the *iemoto*. Numerous vertical links tie him to those lower in the inverted V-shaped social network that makes up the school.

If one is a member of a particular school, the *iemoto* system does not allow one to mix with members of other schools or change masters within the same school. The system requires that the individual retain the single vertical master-disciple relationship. This has significant social implications in that an individual cannot utilize elements from different *iemotos*. To do so would make one's loyalty suspect. Moreover one does not necessarily ascend the social hierarchy of the *iemoto* based upon competence, as considerable emphasis is placed on the personal relationship between superior and subordinate.

This pattern of organization is found, to a certain degree, in other spheres of Japanese life such as professional organizations. The spirit, albeit not the form, is said to prevail in universities, businesses, and other modern Japanese organizations. Thus there is little horizontal mobility in, for example, Japanese universities or corporations. Further it has been argued that the *iemoto* social template prevents the Japanese from easily forming voluntary organizations that are common in societies, such as that of the United States, which require the formation of horizontal linkages among individuals.

The nature of the social relationships among individuals in the *iemoto* has been characterized as quasi-kin in that these relationships have a kinlike quality. There are elements of not only authority and subordination but also mutual dependence, allegiance, and responsibility. An important quality of the *iemoto* system is that it can be applied to a wide range of social groupings and thus may be used to facilitate the organization and mobilization of a group in its efforts to reach some goal. Some have argued that it was a key factor in the rapid industrialization of Japan beginning in the late nineteenth century.

Iglesia ni Kristo: Philippine Church of Christ. Despite the Philippines' large Roman Catholic majority, native Christian groups make up a small percentage of the Filipino nation. Many stem from the turmoil against the friars, or Catholic religious orders, and had performed an important part in the struggle for independence from Spanish rule. One cult, the Iglesia ni Kristo, won converts rapidly after World War II, and by the latter 1960's the organization's adherents numbered possibly half a million.

The strongly anti-Catholic Iglesia ni Kristo was formally established by Felix Manalo Ysagun in 1914. The magnetic Manalo, who dropped the name Ysagun once he founded his cult, hailed from Laguna de Bay and an indigent background. Without much schooling and influenced by his mother's Catholicism, he dallied with Mount Banahaw's religious sects and associated with recently disembarked American Protestant missionaries sent by the Methodists, Presbyterians, Disciples, and Seventh-day Adventists.

Manalo withdrew from the Adventists and, carrying off a number of defecting members, decided to create his own church. His instability, alleged sexual immorality, and disagreements with Adventist leaders all prompted the break. Most significantly, however, Manalo wanted to begin a new church unbeholden to foreigners and under Filipino control.

The Iglesia ni Kristo is perceived by its adherents as the sole lawful Christian denomination in the world, after an interval of close to twenty centuries when no legitimate religious body prevailed. Manalo, who died in 1963, believed himself to be the fifth heavenly host of the revelation. The cult rejects Christ as a divine being but sees Him as the only mediating agent between the Almighty and humans. Manalo presumed that Christ freed and saved from sin's consequences only those joining the church.

Members of Iglesia ni Kristo are expected to submit to a strict regimen including mandatory presence at two weekly church services and exemplary private conduct. Prohibited behaviors encompass wagers, intemperance, faith renunciation, unsanctioned wedlock, and trade union enrollment. Social services provided by Iglesia ni Kristo include literacy programs, employment searches, and investment opportunities. The church seeks new adherents by way of mass meetings, and members form a powerful voting combination during electoral campaigns.

A 1990 census found that 2.3 percent of Philippine households identify themselves with Iglesia ni Kristo, although some observers believe that actual membership is higher. The church has congregations in the United States.

Ilocanos: A cultural and linguistic group of people in the Ilocos region of northwestern Luzon in the Philippines. Ilocos Norte, Ilocos Sur, and La Union are the major Ilocos provinces from which agents from Hawaii recruited laborers, many of whom sought to leave depressed economic conditions at home. Ilocano is one of the Philippines' major spoken dialects.

Ilse: Korean term for Koreans who emigrate and reside outside Korea.

Ilustrados: Filipino educated class. The *ilustrados*, or enlightened ones, arose during the late nineteenth century. This upper-class group, consisting principally of Chinese mestizos, developed a Philippine national consciousness.

Educated at Filipino universities, *ilustrados* studied European political thought and emerged as the native intelligentsia. Generally, their members hoped to become government officials in Spain's colonial administration. Many also wanted entry into the priesthood; the Spanish clergy, however, blocked their ambition, and the issue of indigenous priest investment encouraged their nationalism.

The *ilustrados* disapproved of revolution. Their upper-class origins and wealthy landholding followers turned them against radicalism. For example, José Protasio Rizal, a founder of the Filipino national spirit, rejected sweeping change and favored reform of the Spanish imperial system.

Following the Cavite mutiny in the Philippines and the execution of native priests in 1872, Spanish authorities persecuted the *ilustrados*, many of whom fled abroad. While in exile, they created the Propaganda movement, which favored political and clerical equality as well as a program to advance Filipino language and culture. The organization criticized Spain's friars through the newspaper writing of Marcelo H. del Pilar in *La Solidaridad* and the fiction of Rizal's *Noli me tangere* (1886; *The Social Cancer*, 1912).

While Rizal was coming back to the Philippines in 1892 to face arrest and banishment to Mindanao, the Filipino patriot Andres Bonifacio established the Katipunan, or "Highest and Most Honorable Society of Sons of the Country." This revolutionary association, despite its wish to enlist *ilustrados*, actually alarmed many, such as Antonio Luna, the revolutionary Apolinario Mabini, and the deported Rizal. As Bonifacio's uprising against the Spanish carried across Manila, most *ilustrados* remained unsupportive.

Spanish repression and Rizal's execution in 1896 by

the Spanish colonial government for treason, however, drew *ilustrados* to the Katipunan. When the Spanish-American War started in 1898, Spain hoped to win over the educated elite with the offer of a consultative assembly. Instead, most *ilustrados* supported the leadership of Emilio Aguinaldo, the revolutionary who had wrested control of the Katipunan, yet they pressured the Katipunan to moderate its program and urged conservative reform along with a strong legislature in an independent republic.

Once the Philippine-American War broke out in 1899 and the U.S. Army gained the upper hand, Filipino resistance weakened, and ties between the elite and Aguinaldo loosened. Although some *ilustrados* remained loyal, many defected to the Americans and accepted American diplomat Jacob Schurman's pledge that Washington would encourage *ilustrado* participation in an American-sponsored Filipino government. Eventually, three top *ilustrados* were placed on a seven-panel governing commission. Yet by 1907, *ilustrado* influence began to decline as parties advocating independence won a majority in National Assembly elections.

Imam: Arabic term meaning "leader" or "pattern." The word has multiple uses. Among its most general references is to the prayer leader of a mosque, but one who is without divine ordination or special spiritual powers beyond the ability to carry out this task. Some also use it to mean any scholar of Islamic law. Many among the sect of Sunni Muslims use the term to mean the leader of the Islamic community—the *caliph*, or earthly successor to Muhammad. Among Shiite Muslims, for whom the *imam* is revered as a figure of unquestioned spiritual authority, the term becomes more complicated. Generally, however, among Shiites the *imam* is that particular descendant of the House of Ali recognized as God's designated successor to the absolute spiritual authority and insight inherent in that appointed lineage.

Imamura, Yemyo (1867, Fukui, Japan—1932): Bishop. Landing in Hawaii in 1899, he began his work among followers of the Jodo Shinshu Buddhist sect, the largest in the islands. As bishop of the Honpa Hongwanji, he attempted to bridge the gap separating Christianity and Buddhism. He also helped establish a Young Men's Buddhist Association (YMBA), modeled after the Young Men's Christian Association (YMCA), to assist Hawaii's Japanese immigrants in their struggle to learn English and adapt to a foreign way of life.

Imazeki, Howard (b. 1907, Japan): Newspaper editor. Imazeki served for many years as the English-section editor of the *Hokubei Mainichi*. In 1918 he came to the United States with his family. After attending Sacramento Junior College, he went to work for the *Nichibei Shimbun*, a San Francisco Issei newspaper. A little later he returned to school, this time at the University of Missouri, from which he was graduated with a journalism degree in 1934. Back in San Francisco, he got a job with the *Shin Sekai-Asahi Shimbun* as its English-section editor.

Toward 1940, with a family to support, Imazeki left journalism so that he and his father could enter the poultry business. A few years later he and his family were removed to the *Tule Lake* relocation center in northern California. There he edited the *Tulean Dispatch*, the camp newspaper. Following his release in 1943 he taught Japanese language for the U.S. Navy and broadcast propaganda overseas for the Office of War Information.

After World War II ended, Imazeki moved to Japan, where he worked as an interpreter and translator. He returned to the United States in 1954 as a naturalized American citizen and joined the staff of the *Hokubei Mainichi*.

Imin: Japanese term for Japanese people who emigrate to another country. The word is used in a derogatory way, referring as it does to a lower-class person.

Imingaisha: Or "emigration companies," private Japanese firms that recruited, sponsored, processed, and shipped Japanese emigrants during 1894-1908, principally to Hawaii. Sugar plantations in the islands required a steady supply of cheap labor. Before 1885, the Japanese government had forbidden emigration. In that year, however, Japanese officials dropped objections and entered into an agreement with the government of the Hawaiian Republic in the belief that emigration would relieve agrarian distress at home, while remittances from overseas would bring in much-needed capital. Japanese farmers were attracted by the higher wage rates abroad and believed that they could work for three or four years and save enough to return to buy land or pay off family debts.

From 1885 to 1894, the two governments exercised close control over the emigrants, almost all of whom were under three-year contracts with specified terms as to wages, deductions, and living and working conditions. After 1894, the Japanese government elected to place the emigration business in the hands of private companies, the *imingaisha*, for a variety of reasons. First, the government had already had considerable success with creating other pilot enterprises that had been placed with private management. Second, the Sino-Japanese War (1894-1895) diverted government shipping. Finally, there turned out to be more would-be emigrants than anticipated, and a number of countries besides Hawaii began requesting Japanese workers.

Between 1894 and 1908, fifty-one firms, both large and small, shipped 125,000 emigrants to Hawaii and about thirty thousand to Canada, the United States, Australia, the Philippines, various Pacific islands, and Latin America. Paid a flat reimbursement from the planters for each contracted worker, the *imingaisha* recruited emigrants, booked passage, provided interim boardinghouse accommodations, screened emigrants, did the emigration paperwork, and made loans for surety money requirements. There was much abuse in these services.

After 1900, labor contracts were made illegal in the United States and Hawaii. Without the assurances of the contracts, the *imingaisha* competed fiercely for independent emigrant business, and profits fell. The GENTLEMEN'S AGREEMENT (1907-1908) between the United States and Japan obliged the latter to cease issuing passports to laborers who wished to emigrate to the United States. Most of the *imingaisha* ended operations. About forty-eight thousand relatives of previous emigrants crossed over between 1908 and 1924, when all Japanese emigration to the United States was legally ended.

Immigration Act of 1882: Legislation that marked the increasing determination of the federal government to exercise centralized control over immigration into the United States. Among its provisions, the act imposed a head tax on every incoming immigrant and barred entrance to "any convict, lunatic, idiot, or any person unable to take care of himself or herself without becoming a public charge."

The 1882 act has been interpreted by some scholars as a significant step toward limiting immigration. Several months earlier, it is true, Congress had passed the CHINESE EXCLUSION ACT OF 1882, the first in a series of acts restricting Chinese immigration, and then Asian immigration in general, culminating in the IMMIGRATION ACT OF 1924. However, during the period between 1882 and the 1920's, despite the increasingly restrictive limits on Asian immigration, immigration overall reached record levels. Thus, although already by 1882 nativist sentiments were being vocally ex-

pressed, it is farfetched indeed to see the 1882 act as significantly restrictive.

What the 1882 act signified, rather, was the growing demand for the federal government to assert control over a process that had largely been left to state and local authorities. Regulation, not restriction per se, was the goal. This was not the first such step; it was one of a series of acts over a period of decades during which immigration came under gradually tighter control.

In the absence of federal laws regulating the flow of foreigners into the country, the states asked the government to establish a national policy. One particular concern among some state legislatures was securing protection for their citizens against foreign convicts who had been allowed to enter the country. Another significant concern was the financial burden of processing immigrants (prior to the passage of the 1882 act, New York had threatened to close its immigrant depot at Castle Garden, near Manhattan).

The 1882 act spoke to these concerns. The head tax of fifty cents on every alien arriving by vessel—a figure that was raised periodically, reaching eight dollars by 1917—was earmarked for the processing of immigrants and the expense of enforcing regulation. This permitted the opening of New York's Ellis Island immigration depot in 1892; in 1910, the ANGEL ISLAND IMMIGRATION STATION was opened in San Francisco Bay.

Immigration Act of 1907: Legislation that consolidated and extended controls on immigration established by the acts of 1882, 1891, and 1903. (See IMMIGRATION ACT OF 1882.) One section of the 1907 law was designed primarily to limit Japanese immigration; Korean immigrants were also affected.

Addressing the 59th Congress, Theodore Roosevelt had urged lawmakers to impose tighter limits on immigration. In response, numerous regulatory or restrictive immigration bills were drafted, introduced, and debated on the floors of both the House and the Senate. Finally, after much discussion and refining of the various bills, during the second legislative session a draft was agreed upon and was signed into law on February 20, 1907.

Like many immigration laws, the 1907 act included widely diverse provisions. To the groups excluded by earlier immigration acts, such as paupers, convicts, polygamists, epileptics, anarchists, and persons suffering from "loathsome and contagious diseases," the 1907 act added would-be immigrants with tuberculosis and persons who had been convicted of a crime involving moral turpitude.

Another class of exclusions involved the mentally ill—a significant concern to immigration inspectors, since many of the immigrants who became public charges were mentally ill. The act of 1882 had barred "any . . . lunatic, idiot, or any person unable to take care of himself or herself without becoming a public charge." The act of 1903 barred the "insane." To these the 1907 act added persons who were imbeciles, feeble-minded, or mentally defective. The overlapping terms attested the lack of precision in diagnosis of mental handicaps and disorders. In practice, inspections were generally perfunctory; very few prospective immigrants were excluded under these provisions.

On a different front, the law's first section included a provision intended to limit Japanese immigration. In response to the agitation of the anti-Japanese movement, Roosevelt was seeking to control the flow of Japanese laborers to the United States. On the basis of the so-called GENTLEMEN'S AGREEMENT (1907-1908), Japan agreed to stop issuing passports to laborers destined for the continental United States. Meanwhile, section 1 of the act of 1907 was designed to stop the secondary migration of Japanese (and Korean) laborers from Hawaii, Canada, or Mexico to the United States. Without referring specifically to the Japanese, the law authorized the president to deny entry to any alien suspected to have obtained a passport to a U.S. territory or another country for the purpose of entering the United States. Given that authority, the president issued an executive order on March 14, 1907, which made the specific application envisioned when the law was framed, that "Japanese or Korean laborers, skilled or unskilled, who have received passports to go to Mexico, Canada, or Hawaii and come therefrom, be refused permission to enter the continental territory of the United States."

Immigration Act of 1917. *See* **Barred Zone Act of 1917**

Immigration Act of 1924: U.S. law that codified existing legislation and established the national-origins quota system that would essentially remain in force until the IMMIGRATION AND NATIONALITY ACT OF 1965. The 1924 law included discriminatory provisions that gave preference to immigrants from Northern and Western Europe and that virtually excluded Asian immigrants.

The Immigration Act of 1924, sometimes referred to as the National Origins Act or the Johnson-Reed Act of

The Immigration Law of 1924 was signed into law by President Calvin Coolidge. (White House Historical Association)

1924, was signed into law by President Calvin Coolidge on May 26, after passage by the 68th Congress of the United States. Its purpose was "to limit the immigration of aliens into the United States, and for other purposes." The legislation arose from bills introduced by Congressman Albert Johnson, a Republican from Washington, and Senator David Aiken Reed, a Republican from Pennsylvania. Building on the immigration laws of 1907, 1917 and 1921, it enforced new quotas which limited severely the immigration of persons from specific national groups, and totally barred Japanese. This act abrogated the 1907-1908 GENTLEMEN'S AGREEMENT with Japan. Nonquota status was given only to immigrants from North, Central and South America. The law took effect on July 1, 1924.

Previous Legislation. Immigration legislation leading up to the Immigration Act of 1924 demonstrated growing concern in the United States about the makeup of the population, and a special concern about the numbers of Asian immigrants. The CHINESE EXCLUSION ACT OF 1882 and a series of subsequent acts severely curtailed Chinese immigration. As Japanese immigration began to increase, calls were sounded for Japanese exclusion as well.

By means of the secret GENTLEMEN'S AGREEMENT,

Japan agreed to regulate Japanese emigration to the United States, generally barring laborers unless they previously had been in the United States and allowing for the immigration of children, spouses and parents of laborers currently in the United States. Japan's annexation of Korea in 1910 had the effect of significantly curtailing Korean emigration to the United States, as Koreans were treated as Japanese nationals. The BARRED ZONE ACT OF 1917 prohibited immigration from parts of China, all of India, Burma (now Myanmar), Siam (now Thailand), Malaysia, Asian Russia, parts of Arabia and Afghanistan, the Polynesian Islands, and the East India Islands. Japan, still governed by the Gentlemen's Agreement, and the Philippines, an American protectorate, were not included.

Anti-Japanese groups, especially in California, argued that the Japanese were violating the Gentlemen's Agreement by allowing the practice of picture brides. Unmarried men were having their families in Japan arrange marriages for them through an exchange of photographs. The marriages, without the husbands present, took place in Japan, creating new brides eligible for entry into the United States. The Japanese government eventually acted on the rising protests and in March of 1920 ceased issuing passports to these picture brides.

The Immigration Act of 1921 introduced a quota system to regulate and limit immigration. The quotas were based on the census of 1910. Each nation was allotted an annual quota for immigration equivalent to 3 percent of the total number of persons of that nationality residing in the United States in 1910. Japan's status did not change. This measure was to be in effect for just one year, but in 1922 it was extended for two more years while Congress pursued discussion of immigration.

The 68th Congress. Agitation continued for further restrictions on immigration during the 68th Congress,

Representative Albert Johnson was part of the 68th Congress that established the national-origins quota system that existed until 1965. (AP/Wide World Photos)

Asian Immigration to the U.S. Before and After the Immigration Act of 1924

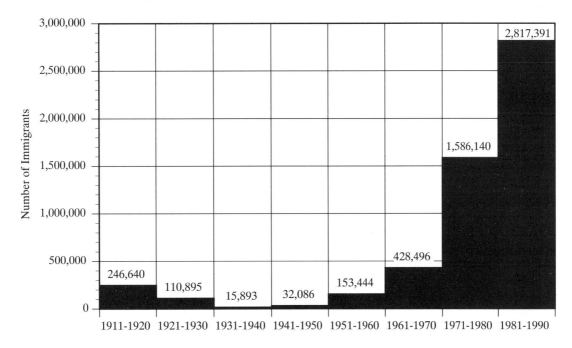

Source: Susan B. Gall and Timothy L. Gall, eds., *Statistical Record of Asian Americans.* Detroit: Gale Research, Inc., 1993.
Note: According to the Immigration and Naturalization Service definition, Asia includes the Middle East.

which convened in December of 1923. A California Joint Immigration Committee pressed for total Japanese exclusion. Knowing that the Senate needed more convincing than the House, delegates of the group, including V. S. McCLATCHY, a retired newspaper publisher, former California senator James Duval Phelan, and California Attorney General Ulysses S. Webb, presented their case to the Senate Committee on Immigration in March of 1924.

Albert Johnson presented a bill to the House calling for a 2 percent quota (rather than the 3 percent of the 1921 law) based on the 1890 census (rather than the 1910 census). Rolling back the base census figures greatly favored immigrants from Northern and Western Europe, since people from these areas constituted a significantly higher percentage of the U.S. population in 1890 than they did in 1910, following two decades of massive immigration.

Johnson's bill also contained a clause restricting entry of immigrants who were not eligible to become American citizens. U.S. naturalization laws allowed citizenship only to whites and African-born persons or persons of African descent. A November, 1922 Supreme Court decision in the case of *Ozawa v. United States* upheld this racial criterion, smoothing the way for the inclusion of the clause in the final legislation. The Senate bill, managed by David A. Reed, called for the same quota system without the citizenship clause, thus including the Japanese, and had the base year of 1910 for calculating the number of immigrants eligible, which would have increased significantly the numbers of Japanese eligible.

Secretary of State Charles Evans Hughes argued for Reed's bill but with the GENTLEMEN'S AGREEMENT left intact, in an effort to support the administration's reluctance to offend the Japanese. Because some members of Congress complained about the secret nature of the Gentlemen's Agreement, Hughes suggested to Japanese Ambassador Hanihara Masanao that he write a letter summarizing the Gentleman's Agreement. Hanihara did so, and ended the letter by speaking of "grave consequences" if the exclusion clause in the Johnson Bill was retained. When Hughes sent the entire letter for publication in the Congressional Record of April 11, its contents provoked strong reactions in Congress. On April 14, Senator Henry Cabot LODGE, a Republican from Pennsylvania, singled out the "grave consequences" phrase and declared it a "veiled threat" against the United States. Despite Hanihara's protest over Lodge's interpretation, this proved to be the turning point in the congressional debate as votes in the Senate shifted toward total exclusion of the Japanese. The Senate amended the bill to make 1890 the base year for determining the quota.

The Senate voted in April to reject an amendment which would have recognized the Gentleman's Agreement, and accepted a new amendment, which called for the exclusion of any "alien ineligible to citizenship." The Senate voted on April 18 (62-6, with 28 not voting) in favor of the bill, which included the citizenship clause and the base year of 1890. The House vote passed the bill on May 15 (308-62-63). House-Senate conference reports cleared up any disagreements still existing between the House bill and the Senate bill, with the final document (43 Stat. 153) sent to the president for his signature on May 26, 1924.

Consequences. The Immigration Act of 1924 reinforced previous legislation barring the immigration of most Asian peoples. Without naming the Japanese, it singled them out in section 13 (c). The legislation created bad feelings between the United States and Japan, especially since the GENTLEMEN'S AGREEMENT was abrogated without negotiation; the 1924 act was seen as an insult to the Japanese. This legislation virtually ended Asian immigration until after World War II.—*Ann M. Harrington*

SUGGESTED READINGS: • Chan, Sucheng. *Asian Americans: An Interpretive History.* Boston: Twayne Publishers, 1991. • Chuman, Frank F. *The Bamboo People: The Law and Japanese-Americans.* Del Mar, California: Publisher's Inc., 1976. • Daniels, Roger. *The Politics of Prejudice: The Anti-Japanese Movement in California and the Struggle for Japanese Exclusion.* Berkeley: University of California Press, 1962. • Divine, Robert A. *American Immigration Policy, 1924-1952.* New Haven, Conn.: Yale University Press, 1957. • Hutchinson, E. P. *Legislative History of American Immigration Policy, 1798-1965.* Philadelphia: University of Pennsylvania Press, 1981.

Immigration Act of 1943: Legislation sponsored by Senator Warren G. Magnuson of Washington State and passed by the U.S. Congress in December 1943 allowing Chinese to become naturalized citizens in the United States. It gave Chinese a quota—of 105—to immigrate legally to the United States.

The 1943 act, also known as the Magnuson Act, represented a significant philosophical change in U.S. immigration policy because it repealed the Chinese

Exclusion Acts, which had barred Chinese immigration. The Chinese Exclusion Acts were the first immigration laws that blocked entrants of a specific race or national group. (See CHINESE EXCLUSION ACT OF 1882.) And while the quota was so low as to hardly be meaningful (and half of it was stipulated for people with skills needed in the United States), the 1943 act affected thousands of Chinese aliens in the United States in following years, largely through nonquota immigration.

The act reflected the fact that China was a U.S. ally during World War II; America's exclusionist immigration policy had long been a source of displeasure to China.

Immigration Act of 1990: U.S. legislation that retained the family reunification categories that dominated the IMMIGRATION AND NATIONALITY ACT OF 1965 and added provisions for additional employment-related immigrants. In addition it gave special consideration to countries that had experienced little recent immigration and that were perceived to have been unfairly treated by the 1965 legislation. The new act took effect in October, 1991.

The major provisions include an overall limit of 700,000 immigrants (to be reduced to 675,000 beginning in fiscal year 1995); this limit does not include refugees and can be "pierced" if the number of immediate relatives rises beyond 239,000.

Family-based immigrants (immediate relative and family-sponsored immigrants) are limited to 480,000 annually (465,000 beginning in fiscal year 1995). Immediate relatives (spouses, unmarried children, and parents of U.S. citizens) are exempt from numerical limitations. Other family members are restricted as follows: unmarried adult sons and daughters of citizens, 23,400; spouses and minor children and unmarried adult sons and daughters of permanent resident aliens, 114,200; married sons and daughters of U.S. citizens, 23,400; and brothers and sisters of adult U.S. citizens, 65,000.

Employment-based immigrants (limited to 140,000) are distributed as follows: priority workers (persons of extraordinary ability, such as outstanding professors and researchers), 40,000; other professionals and workers of exceptional ability, 40,000; skilled and unskilled workers, 40,000; certain special immigrants, 10,000; and employment-creating immigrants (agreeing to invest $1,000,000 in capital), 10,000.

Diversity immigrants are limited to 55,000 per year. They are to be mostly from low-admission states in low-admission regions, although some may be from low-admission states in high-admission regions.

Individual countries are limited to slightly more than 25,000 immigrants each year, up somewhat from the 20,000 maximum previously in effect.

The new law will undoubtedly have some effect on Asian immigration. Increased country limits will probably result in higher immigration for those countries (China, India, and the Philippines) that were already at the 20,000 ceiling under the old law. Countries that were not at the limit may show increases because immigration is now more possible for so-called "new-seed" immigrants who do not already have relatives living in the United States. Overall it is likely that immigration from Asia will increase.

Immigration and Nationality Act of 1952. *See* **McCarran-Walter Act of 1952**

Immigration and Nationality Act of 1965: The Immigration and Nationality Act, also known as the Hart-Celler Act, was passed by the U.S. Congress in October, 1965. While technically an amendment to the McCarran-Walter Act of 1952, this law constituted a major departure from U.S. immigration legislation up to that time. In fact, it may be seen as a repudiation or a cancellation of McCarran-Walter. This is certainly true of its main feature: provisions that abolished the national-origins quota system that had governed U.S. immigration policy since the Immigration Act of 1924 and that gave preferences to relatives of U.S. citizens, people with special or needed skills, and refugees fleeing persecution. It also had the effect of permitting an enormous increase in Asian immigration.

Background. Although the act was passed during the Johnson Administration and supported strongly by President Johnson, it is, however, not accurate to say that Lyndon Johnson was the originator of the legislation. What he pushed through Congress had been proposed for the most part by two earlier presidents—Eisenhower and Kennedy—particularly the latter. In fact, when Kennedy was elected, new legislation changing or repealing the McCarran-Walter Act was anticipated. And in 1963, just before he was assassinated, Kennedy had sent a special message to Congress asking for the abolishment of immigration quotas.

The Preference System. In the Immigration and Nationality Act there are listed seven preferences for granting visas to immigrants and/or the right of immigrants to become naturalized American citizens. First

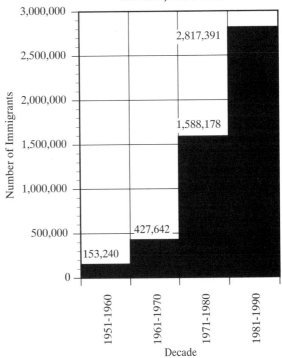

Emigration from Asia to the U.S., 1951-1990

Number of Immigrants (y-axis) — *Decade* (x-axis)

Decade	Number of Immigrants
1951-1960	153,240
1961-1970	427,642
1971-1980	1,588,178
1981-1990	2,817,391

Sources: Alison Landes, Betsie B. Caldwell, and Mark A. Siegel, eds., *Immigration and Illegal Aliens: Burden or Blessing?* Wylie, Tex.: Information Plus, 1991. Susan B. Gall and Timothy L. Gall, eds., *Statistical Record of Asian Americans.* Detroit: Gale Research, Inc., 1993.

Note: According to the Immigration and Naturalization Service definition, Asia includes the Middle East.

priority is given to unmarried grown sons and daughters of U.S. citizens (spouses, minor children, and parents were allowed free entry). The second category is for relatives of citizens and resident aliens. The third preference is granted to members of professions and persons with special abilities in the sciences or arts. The fourth and fifth also are for relatives of citizens and resident aliens. The sixth group consists of "skilled labor in great demand." The seventh preference goes to refugees. According to the law when one category was not filled, slots filtered down to the next categories.

Originally, category one was to get about 10 percent of the visas; groups two, four, and five were to get 74 percent; preference three was to have 10 percent; and preference seven was to have 6 percent. However, "skill groups" took more than the share originally allo-

President Lyndon B. Johnson speaks at the signing ceremony for the Immigration and Nationality Act of 1965, which permitted an enormous increase in Asian immigration. (AP/Wide World Photos)

cated. The seventh, or refugee category, has varied considerably in terms of its size.

The Western Hemisphere was given an initial advantage since a lid of 170,000 was placed on nonhemisphere immigrants. However, a cap of 120,000 was put on hemisphere entrants, as of July, 1968. In addition, no more than 20,000 quota immigrants could be admitted from a single country each year; when nonquota immigrants were added, totals frequently exceeded the 20,000 limit.

Intentions and Consequences. Some interpreted the act as reflecting political liberalism in the United States at the time, and even more specifically the Civil Rights movement. The act was debated and passed by Congress at almost the same time as the Voting Rights Act. President Johnson signed the bill in a highly publicized ceremony at the foot of the Statue of Liberty, and clearly those who formulated the legislation thought of it as ending the discriminatory quota system. On the other hand, many supporters of the act felt that provisions mortgaging quotas and defining nationality were at minimum untidy and were in fact discriminatory. Furthermore, there had been already numerous debates in Congress concerning needed changes in the country's immigration laws, particularly concerning refugees, and it was obvious something had to be done.

The act was considered to have provided a solution to the refugee issue and the contention between Congress and the Executive branch about refugees that had long been a problem. As it turned out, it offered only a partial solution. The act, however, produced major changes in immigration patterns. After its passage the percentage of immigrants from Europe, Canada and Central America dropped. The number of immigrants from Asia rose dramatically. Also the act resulted in a noticeable change in the makeup of the immigrant population: higher level of skills and a higher percentage of educated people.

Because of the large number of immigrants with high skill and educational levels after 1965, the act is said to have created a "brain drain" from other countries to the advantage of the United States and the disadvantage of some other nations or areas of the world. This was said particularly of Asian countries. Notwithstanding this problem, the act was generally welcomed by Asian people and countries.—*John F. Copper*

SUGGESTED READINGS: • Hutchinson, Edward P. *Legislative History of American Immigration Policy, 1798-1965.* Philadelphia, 1981. • *Immigration and Nationality Act.* Washington, D.C.: Government Printing Office, 1980. • Reimers, David M. *Still the Golden Door: The Third World Comes to America.* New York: Columbia University Press, 1985.

Immigration Convention of 1886: Compact concluded between Hawaii and Japan under which the former agreed to provide better treatment of Japanese immigrant laborers in the islands. The agreement was negotiated after the Japanese government dispatched a representative to Hawaii to investigate complaints that Japanese there were being mistreated. Under the terms of the convention, Japan was to monitor the migrant-selection process more carefully and to pay the laborers' transportation costs to Hawaii. Hawaii consented to supply the laborers with doctors and interpreters, and American diplomat Robert Walker IRWIN was placed in charge of regulating immigration matters in the islands. Voting and naturalization rights for the immigrants were also stipulated. About a year later, however, an internal conflict in the Hawaiian government forced a revision of the convention unfavorable to the laborers.

Immigration policy: Until the late nineteenth century, the Congress pursued a policy of free immigration, based on the view that the United States was an asylum for anyone seeking to escape political persecution or economic deprivation. This policy also reflected the needs of employers for low-paid unskilled and semi-skilled labor. In 1882, Congress abandoned the policy of open borders by excluding Chinese immigrants, a policy extended to all other Asians in 1917. In 1921, Congress also reversed its policy of free immigration for Europeans by adopting a literacy test and by placing severe numerical restrictions on immigrants— policies designed to exclude entrants from southern and eastern Europe. These actions were taken in the name of preserving racial, ethnic, and religious homogeneity. The change also reflected the growing influence of organized labor. Asians were the primary beneficiaries of abandonment in 1965 of the preference for northwestern Europeans contained in the 1924 and 1952 comprehensive immigration acts. The current policy is one of a worldwide annual quota for immigrants, with preference given to accommodation of refugees, family reunification, and access to needed skills. Between 1882 and 1986, the focus of immigration policy was on the Eastern Hemisphere. Since 1986, the primary concern has been immigration from Latin America, especially Mexico.

The U.S. policy of open borders was first altered in 1882 to exclude Chinese immigrants. This cartoon reflects the xenophobic fears of the times. (Library of Congress)

Early Policy. During the Colonial period, agents of the various North American colonies recruited immigrants from the north and west of Europe. The preference for free immigration led to conflict with the British government. One of the grievances cited to justify the dissolution of the relationship with the mother country cited in the Declaration of Independence is the charge that King George III "has endeavored to prevent the population of these states; for that purpose obstructing the laws for naturalization of foreigners; refusing to pass others to encourage their migration hither." Following independence, the United States actively recruited European immigrants and encouraged them to become permanent settlers. The first federal immigration law, "An Act to Encourage Immigration," was passed in 1864. The law was in response to complaints from employers that the Civil War had reduced the flow of European immigrants on which the country's economic growth was dependent.

The nation's political leaders expected the newcomers to be primarily British and Protestant. An influx of Germans in the eighteenth century led to the first cries for limits on immigration. Large immigration of Irish Catholics in the mid-nineteenth century led to formation of the Know-Nothing Party and organized efforts to prohibit their entry. The influx of millions from southern and eastern Europe in the decades following the Civil War led to further demands to restrict immigration. The eighteenth and nineteenth century open-borders policy was based on the principle of asylum—the United States was a place offering protection or safety to all those seeking religious or political security or economic opportunity. The sanctuary concept coincided with the demand of business for increasing numbers of unskilled and semiskilled laborers.

Chinese Exclusion Act. The first regulation of immigration by Congress came in 1875, when it enacted a statute barring entry of convicts and prostitutes. In 1882 the categories of disqualification were expanded to include persons likely to become public charges, idiots, and lunatics. The current immigration law contains thirty-three grounds for exclusion of an individ-

ual. Congress, however, soon departed radically from the approach of judging the fitness of entrants merely by their individual characteristics. Because of pressure from California, in 1882 the Congress passed the first Chinese Exclusion Act, not repealed until 1943. It had already declared Asians ineligible for naturalization as citizens. Although under the fourteenth Amendment, ratified in 1868, anyone born in the United States was a citizen, naturalization of the foreign-born was a privilege granted only to Caucasians and, after 1870, persons of African nativity or African descent. The primary purpose of the Chinese exclusion was to protect U.S. labor from competition with low-wage workers. The initial exclusion act was a temporary measure

Immigrants Admitted to the U.S., 1871-1990

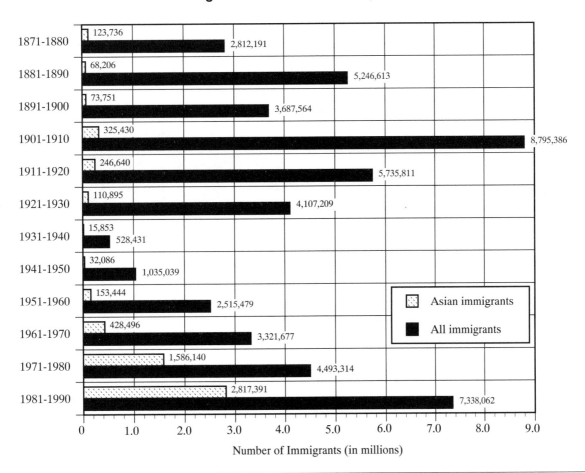

Period	Asian immigrants	All immigrants
1871-1880	123,736	2,812,191
1881-1890	68,206	5,246,613
1891-1900	73,751	3,687,564
1901-1910	325,430	8,795,386
1911-1920	246,640	5,735,811
1921-1930	110,895	4,107,209
1931-1940	15,853	528,431
1941-1950	32,086	1,035,039
1951-1960	153,444	2,515,479
1961-1970	428,496	3,321,677
1971-1980	1,586,140	4,493,314
1981-1990	2,817,391	7,338,062

Number of Immigrants (in millions)

Sources: Ong Bill Sing, *Making and Remaking Asian America Through Immigration Policy, 1850-1990.* Stanford, Calif.: Stanford University Press, 1993. Alison Landes, Betsie B. Caldwell, and Mark A. Siegel, eds., *Immigration and Illegal Aliens: Burden or Blessing?* Wylie, Tex.: Information Plus, 1991. Susan B. Gall and Timothy L. Gall, eds., *Statistical Record of Asian Americans.* Detroit: Gale Research, Inc., 1993.

Note: According to the Immigration and Naturalization Service definition, Asia includes the Middle East.

but was extended after each ten-year expiry and made permanent in 1904. China complained that the exclusions violated treaty obligations of the United States, but the U.S. Supreme Court disagreed. In 1885 Congress, also in response to labor union urging, forbade the importation of contract laborers.

The contradiction in the government's policy became apparent when employers simply replaced Chinese with Japanese aliens, for Congress was attempting simultaneously to further labor and business interests. Organized labor triumphed again upon completion of the so-called GENTLEMEN'S AGREEMENT (1907-1908) between the U.S. government and the government of Japan, which effectively excluded Japanese workers. These policies reflected the judgments both that the low wages earned by Asians in the United States lowered the overall wage level and that Chinese and Japanese could not easily be American-

ized. The Gentlemen's Agreement was abrogated by Congress in 1924 through passage of legislation including a Japanese exclusion clause. The Japanese considered the exclusion to be an insult, and the Tokyo newspapers declared July 1, 1924, a day of mourning.

By 1882, a policy of restriction had replaced free immigration. Three elements constituted the policy: disqualification of undesirable individuals, discrimination against certain races, and protection for domestic workers. The policy remained in effect until 1965. A law of 1903 reaffirmed the principle of individual selection, adding epileptics, beggars, anarchists, and all those who advocated the forceful overthrow of government to the excluded list.

The Barred Zone Act of 1917. Economic depression in the 1870's and 1880's led to popular disaffection with the country's liberal immigration policy. Also influencing the change in public opinion was the in-

Immigrant workers such as these railroad laborers helped to develop the American West. (Asian American Studies Library, University of California at Berkeley)

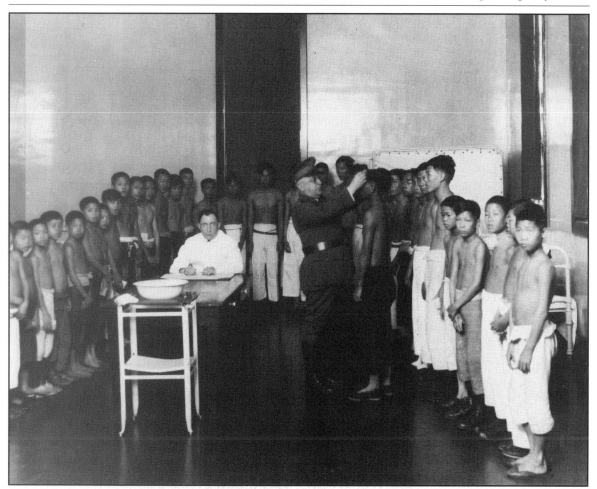

Angel Island immigration center in California reflected changes in U.S. immigration law as U.S. employers replaced excluded Chinese with Japanese laborers, who were then excluded as well. (National Archives)

flux of immigrants from southern and eastern Europe, anti-Catholic feeling, the closing of the frontier, an association of immigrants with socialism and anarchism—ideologies blamed for World War I and the Russian Revolution of 1917—and a belief in the superiority of the Anglo-Saxon race, fueled by a new "science" of race. The most influential writer on the link between eugenics and immigration policy was Madison Grant, a wealthy New York lawyer. In 1916 he published *The Passing of the Great Race*, in which he argued that racial mixing was destroying the superior races and the cultures that they had created.

The era 1881 to 1924 was the period of greatest immigration in the nation's history. In the 1880's, 5.2 million foreigners migrated to the United States, followed by 8.8 million in the first decade of the twentieth century, 5.7 million between 1911 and 1920, and 4.1 million in the 1920's. In each of the years 1905, 1906, 1907, 1910, 1913, and 1914, more than 1 million immigrants entered the country. The ethnic and religious makeup of the immigrant pool changed dramatically during this period. Between 1881 and 1890 more than 80 percent had come from northern and western Europe, the majority of whom were Protestant. Between 1911 and 1920, by contrast, 77 percent of the immigrants came from southern and eastern Europe, mostly Catholics and Jews. In that decade, more than 2 million entered from Italy, 2 million from Austria-Hungary, and 1.5 million from Russia.

Congress, responding to domestic pressures, sought to preempt permissive state policies and to restrict this new immigration, while the president, influenced by foreign-policy considerations, fought to maintain an open-door policy with respect to Europeans. Presidents Grover Cleveland, William Howard Taft, and Woodrow Wilson vetoed bills prohibiting entry of aliens above age sixteen who could not read, in 1897, 1913, and 1915. In his 1915 veto message, Wilson

Between 1881 and 1890 between 77 and 80 percent of immigrants to the U.S. came from Europe. (Library of Congress)

accused Congress of attempting to depart from the traditional American belief that the United States was a sanctuary for the world's poor and oppressed. He said it was contradictory to depict America as a land of opportunity and then limit right of entry to those who had already had the opportunity of an education.

In 1917 Congress, overriding Wilson's veto, finally imposed a literacy test, the first substantial limitation on European immigrants, thus dramatically abandoning its liberal policy. Although on the surface the literacy test seemed consistent with the principle of individual selection, its proponents admitted that it was aimed at immigrants from southeastern Europe, many of whom could not read and write. The bill's sponsors expected the test to produce a 25 percent reduction in the flow of entrants. At the same time, the act established the Asiatic Barred Zone, which blocked further immigration from Asia.

The 1917 enactment represented a victory of the principle of group selection. Influencing Congress were such considerations as patriotic fervor whipped up by the war effort, a feeling that the United States should not get involved again in European conflicts, the increased competition with foreign labor that rapid urbanization was bringing, and the large numbers seeking to immigrate from southeastern Europe. The formation of the Third International by the Communists in 1919 further increased Americans' fear of foreigners. Race riots and industrial strikes made racial and ethnic heterogeneity seem increasingly frightening. Republican Warren G. Harding's victory in the presidential election of 1920 signaled the triumph of isolationist sentiment.

The Immigration Act of 1924. In 1921, however, some 800,000 immigrants entered the United States, a return to prewar levels, sparking the outcry of organized labor, fearful of losing jobs to low-paid foreign workers, and business leaders, frightened of radical influence from the new immigrants. Congress responded by passing a temporary quota act in 1921, the first numerical limitations ever placed on immigration. Quantitative restrictions had now replaced qualitative ones as the primary bar to entry. Immigration was confined to three percent of the number of foreign-born of each European nationality living in the United States in 1910. A ceiling of 355,000 a year was applied to European immigration, 55 percent from northwestern Europe and 45 percent from southeastern Europe. In 1924 Congress made the quota permanent, sharply limiting the number of immigrants, to 164,000 yearly. This landmark legislation remained in effect until 1952. In 1927 the quota was set at 150,000 annually, with the wives and children of U.S. citizens also permitted to come. The law continued in effect the racially based national-origins quota, aimed at discouraging growth in immigration from eastern and southern Europe. The law established visa quotas for each country proportionate to the percentage of the U.S. population sharing that particular national origin as of 1920. It included a minimum quota of 100 for each nationality but barred all non-whites. Most Asian

countries remained in the barred zone. Thus, more than 70 percent of the quota was allocated to Great Britain, Ireland, and Germany, a quota that was rarely filled.

The ceiling applied only to immigration from the Eastern Hemisphere. Immigration from the Western Hemisphere remained numerically unrestricted until 1968. By 1924 U.S. immigration policy embodied a hemispheric dual standard. Domestic considerations led to severe restraints upon immigration from Europe and Asia, while foreign-policy concerns produced a completely free policy with regard to immigration from Canada and Latin America. With regard to the latter sources of immigrants, the maintenance of good neighborly relations overrode all caveats with respect to labor competition and assimilation. The quota would have severely limited immigration from the Western Hemisphere. Relatively few Canadians, Mexicans, and South Americans were U.S. citizens or permanent residents in 1920. Moreover, it was unfeasi-

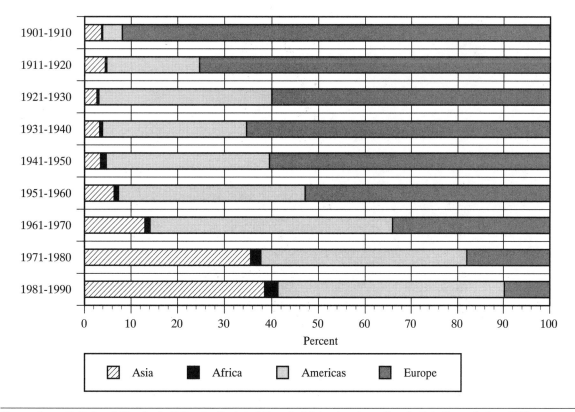

Sources of Immigration to the U.S. by Region, 1901-1990

Legend: Asia, Africa, Americas, Europe

Source: Susan B. Gall and Timothy L. Gall, eds., *Statistical Record of Asian Americans.* Detroit: Gale Research, Inc., 1993.
Note: According to the Immigration and Naturalization Service definition, Europe includes the former Soviet Union, Asia includes the Middle East, and the Americas include Canada, Mexico, the Caribbean, Central America, and South America.

ble to patrol effectively the country's extensive northern and southern borders.

The replacement of qualitative by quantitative restraints was motivated by the consequences of World War I and by the growing influence of science on policy making. Congress was told by witnesses during legislative hearings in the 1920's that as many as three million Polish Jews and eight million Germans wanted to migrate to the United States. Harry N. Laughlin, who served as a eugenics consultant to the Immigration and Naturalization subcommittee of the Judiciary Committee of the House of Representatives, characterized the national-origins quota as the triumph of the biological idea over the asylum concept. The national-origins quota system remained in effect until 1965.

World War II. The 1940's saw the overshadowing of domestic considerations by foreign-policy considerations. The prohibition on Asian immigration that marked early twentieth century U.S. immigration policy was one of the sources of friction with Japan that contributed to the outbreak of the Pacific war in 1941. American participation in World War II led to a fundamental rethinking of U.S. immigration policy. The Chinese Exclusion Acts were repealed by the Immigration Act of 1943, and small quotas were established for Chinese in recognition of the wartime alliance with China. The 1943 act also made Chinese immigrants eligible for naturalization. Congress admitted 150,000 foreign brides of U.S. servicemen, regardless of the woman's race. The Displaced Persons Act of 1948 resulted in the admission of 600,000 refugees and displaced persons from eastern and southern Europe and Asia, all of whom were permitted to settle permanently in the United States.

The Cold War. The Cold War with the Soviet Union produced a new disqualification and a different category of refugee. The Internal Security Act of 1950 declared Communists ineligible for entry. This was

China's alignment with the Allies in WWII caused immigration restrictions for Chinese to be relaxed significantly. (Library of Congress)

Net Asian Immigration to the U.S., 1908-1957						
	Total	Chinese	Japanese	Asian Indians	Koreans	Filipinos
Number admitted	268,560	76,683	167,238	8,117	3,534	12,988
Number departed	173,282	88,545	60,579	8,004	1,872	14,282
Net immigration	95,278	-11,862	106,659	113	1,662	-1,294

Source: Herbert Barringer, Robert W. Gardner, and Michael J. Levin, *Asians and Pacific Islanders in the United States.* New York: Russell Sage Foundation, 1993.

Note: No data are available for 1932-1938. Data for Filipinos begin in 1939.

followed by the MCCARRAN-WALTER ACT OF 1952, the first major piece of immigration legislation since 1924. It made no fundamental changes in the national-origins system basically codifying the 1917 and 1924 statutes. The annual quota for Eastern Hemisphere immigration was set at 154,657. President Harry S Truman, influenced as Wilson had been in 1917 by foreign-policy concerns, vetoed the bill but was overridden by Congress. The failure to repeal the national-origins quota reflected not only the outbreak of the Cold War and the fear of Communist aggression but the isolationist sentiment gripping the country following the second U.S. involvement in a European conflagration in the twentieth century. Somewhat discredited by the experience with Nazism, the biological theory of the superiority of the Anglo-Saxon race, which had heavily influenced the 1924 legislation, was recast as a sociological theory, which argued the inability of persons from alien cultures to assimilate in the United States.

The 1952 statute did, however—in conjunction with the IMMIGRATION ACT OF 1943 and the LUCE-CELLER BILL OF 1946—mark a significant change in policy toward Asian immigration and the eligibility of Asian immigrants for naturalization. The McCarran-Walter Act removed the virtual ban on immigration from Japan and other Asian countries not included in previous reforms; moreover, the act removed all racial barriers to naturalization.

In the 1950's 40,000 Hungarians entered the United States as refugees following the Communist suppression of an uprising in their home country. Following a Communist takeover, in the 1960's 700,000 Cubans came to the United States as refugees. The Kennedy Administration attempted to hold them to the 120,000 Western Hemisphere quota in effect at that time, but a U.S. district judge held that refugees are nonquota entrants. Another 100,000 came during the Cuban boat lift of 1980.

The Immigration and Nationality Act of 1965. By

the 1960's the national-origins approach had become unworkable because of its inability to accommodate refugees and other nonquota entrants and its racially discriminatory effect. Fewer than half of the immigrants who entered the United States during the 1950's did so under the quota. Most entered as refugees under special temporary laws, as family members outside the quota, or from the Western Hemisphere.

In July, 1963, President John F. Kennedy recommended to Congress abolition of the national-origins quota system. Congress took no action on the bill before his assassination in November, 1963. In 1964, Kennedy's vice president, Lyndon B. Johnson, was elected in a landslide, which also produced lopsided Democratic majorities in both houses of Congress. With the support of the 89th Congress, Johnson brought forth a program of legislation he termed the "Great Society," which included a war on poverty, the economic development of Appalachia, an effort to rebuild the inner cities, medical care for the poor and elderly, federal funding for education, and a comprehensive civil-rights initiative. Included in this initiative was a first-come, first-served racially neutral immigration policy. The abandonment of the national-origins approach was a product not only of the 1964 Democratic landslide but also of changes in public attitudes toward race precipitated by the campaign led by the Supreme Court since 1954 to desegregate public facilities. The Immigration and Nationality Act Amendments of 1965 were accompanied by a Voting Rights Act in the same session and preceded by a 1964 Civil Rights Act.

The amendments replaced the national-origins system with an equal limit of 20,000 immigrants annually for every country, with a ceiling of 170,000 for the Eastern Hemisphere and 120,000 for the Western Hemisphere. The imposition of a ceiling on immigration from Canada and Latin America marked a sharp break from the past and reflected fear of the pressures being generated on U.S. borders by the population

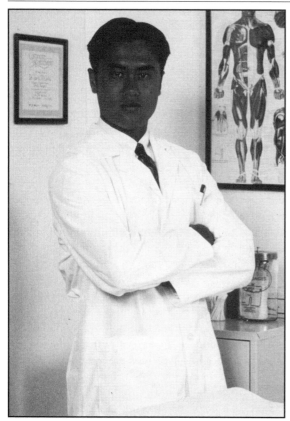

The Immigration and Nationality Act of 1965 gave preference to family members and persons with special skills, such as medical professionals. (Tom McCarthy, Unicorn Stock Photos)

explosion in Latin America. The 20,000-per-country limit represented a particularly major change in policy toward Mexico. (The limit of 20,000, however, applied to quota immigrants only; actual immigration often greatly exceeded this limit.) Preference was given to applicants with close relatives in the United States, those possessing special skills, and refugees. In 1978 Congress reduced the worldwide limit to 270,000 immigrants per year, excluding minor children and spouses. The effect of the policy change was to favor the most recent immigrants, particularly Asians, many of whose family members were still residing outside the United States. Relatively few of the total immigrant population have entered under the labor certification provisions of the act.

In 1968 Congress, in response to complaints from the Mexican government and from employers, abolished the 10,000-per-country limit with regard to immigration from the Western Hemisphere but maintained the 120,000 annual ceiling. In 1976, however, Congress reimposed the 10,000-per-country limit on Mexico and other countries in the Western Hemisphere. The decision to end preferential treatment for Canada and Mexico was based on foreign-policy considerations, a desire by Congress to treat all countries the same. Also in the name of uniform treatment, in 1978 legislation was enacted combining the two hemispheric quotas into a single worldwide quota of 290,000. By 1978 in U.S. immigration policy the principle of equal treatment for all nationalities finally had supplanted completely the discriminatory principle of national origin.

Refugee Policy. The REFUGEE ACT OF 1980 authorized a substantially higher number than the 1965 law. It allowed routine admission of 50,000 refugees a year, a number that could be raised by the president following consultation with Congress. The act established uniform procedures for processing refugees from South Vietnam, Laos, and Cambodia, which had fallen to the Communists in 1975. In keeping with United Nations' practice, it broadened the definition of a refugee to include anyone fleeing persecution because of race, religion, nationality, political opinion, or membership in a social group. Earlier law had limited refugee status to those fearing political persecution. The act was also a recognition that exiles would regularly be coming to the doors of the United States and that a permanent refugee law was necessary.

Presidents use their authority under the act to set annual ceilings for refugees. It is the president's practice to allocate this quota by region, favoring those areas where U.S. national interests are most implicated. Since the act's passage the quota has been allocated to Southeast Asia (69 percent), Eastern Europe (14 percent), the Middle East (9 percent), Africa (4 percent), and Latin America (4 percent). The number of refugees admitted has dropped considerably since Republican president Ronald Reagan took office in 1981, when 159,252 were admitted, a number that fell to 61,681 in 1983. Most of the refugees have come from Southeast Asia, approximately 755,000 between 1975 and 1984. Illegal aliens apprehended in the United States have the option of applying for asylum if they fear persecution on return to their home country, but only about 3 percent of such applications are successful.

Mexican Immigration Policy. Those who employed Asian and Mexican laborers did not expect them to settle permanently in the United States and become citizens. Both groups were expected to return to their countries of origin. During World War I Congress first formalized the temporary-worker arrangement governing the employment of Mexican labor. The enactment in 1917 of the temporary-alien-worker program was the product of pressure from employers affected by the departure of agricultural workers to participate in the war effort or to work in higher-paying war-production jobs and by the 1917 Immigration Act, which for the first time imposed restrictions on immigration from Mexico, including a literacy test, a ban on contract labor, and a head tax. The program remained in effect until 1921, when the soldiers returned and reentered the agricultural workforce.

Employers suffered similar labor shortages in World War II. Congress responded with enactment of the bracero program in 1942, under which nearly 5 million temporary agricultural workers from Mexico found employment before its expiration in 1964. The 1952 codification of the immigration law had no effect on the bracero program because Congress did not view the Mexican workers as permanent residents of the United States or as infiltrated by Communist agitators. The farm bloc in the House of Representatives and Senate, moreover, would have blocked any attempt to dismantle the program in the 1950's, prior to the extensive mechanization of the agricultural sector of the economy that occurred in the 1960's. Mechanization, in addition to opposition from organized labor and efforts by public interest advocates to improve the plight of migrant workers, led to the cessation of the bracero program in 1964, over the protests of the Mexican government. It was later revived as the so-called H-2 program, which, like its predecessor, allowed Mexican and other foreign workers into the United States temporarily to work in agricultural jobs. Under the program, 20,000 aliens enter the country each year.

The Immigration Reform and Control Act of 1986. In response to the flood of illegal immigrants from Mexico, estimated to be between 500,000 and 1 million a year, Congress, after a five-year struggle, enacted a comprehensive statute in 1986 designed to stem the tide of illegal migration across the Rio Grande River and to stop the exploitation of undocumented workers. Also known as the Simpson-Rodino Act, the Immigration Reform and Control Act (IRCA) was the first comprehensive reform of the nation's immigration law since 1952. The act contained a num-

A Mexican boy returns to Mexico across the bridge from El Paso after being prevented by border guards from crossing illegally into the U.S. (R. Del Percio, UNHCR)

ber of new policy instruments, including employer sanctions, amnesty, and federal assistance to compensate state and local governments for serving legalized immigrants. The act made it an offense for employers knowingly to hire illegal immigrants and granted amnesty to many Mexican laborers who had come to the United States illegally. Employers for the first time faced fines and jail terms. Illegals were eligible for amnesty if they could prove that they had resided in the United States continuously since 1982. Special provision was made for up to 350,000 Mexican farmworkers, who only needed to prove that they had resided in the United States for at least three years in order to qualify for legal-resident status. Some of the economic goals of the reform were to encourage investment in the United States by immigrants, many of whom remitted much of their earnings to Mexico, and to guarantee to employers access to low-wage agricultural labor. The law was passed despite the opposition of Hispanic and civil-rights groups, which were concerned that employers would discriminate against Hispanic-looking job applicants.

The law requires employers for the first time to verify the legal status of each newly hired person and

employees to attest in writing that they are legally permitted to work in the United States. Those qualifying for amnesty could become permanent residents eligible for citizenship after eighteen months if they can show understanding of English and knowledge of the history and government of their new country. Mexicans traditionally have the lowest rate of naturalization among all immigrant groups. The bill appropriated large sums of money to reimburse the states for the costs associated with legalizing aliens, who, as undocumented workers, had not qualified for any form of public assistance. The bill also raised the legal immigration ceiling for HONG KONG, from 600 to 5,000, in response to the plight of those wishing to flee the British crown colony before it became part of the People's Republic of China in 1997.

Asians benefited most from the abolition of the national-origins approach and the designation of family reunification as the cornerstone of U.S. immigration policy. Asian immigration increased almost four times between the period 1956 to 1965 and 1967 to 1976, rising from 224,000 to more than 1 million. The largest percentage increases (more than 2,000 percent) occurred in immigration from Thailand, Vietnam, and

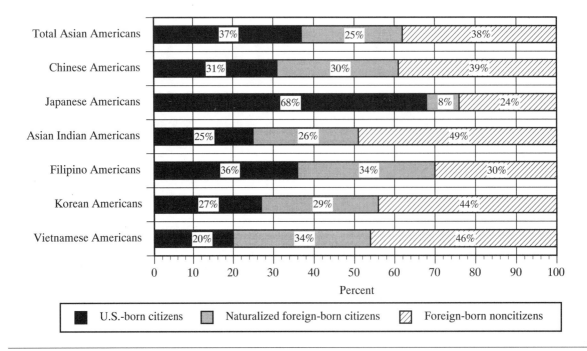

Citizenship Status of Asian Americans, 1990

Source: U.S. Bureau of the Census, *1990 Census of Population: Asians and Pacific Islanders in the United States,* 1993.

India, and the greatest absolute increases (more than 120,000 individuals) were in immigration from the Philippines, Korea, and China. Through the early 1990's, approximately 600,000 immigrants enter the United States legally each year. Approximately half are Asian and a quarter are Hispanic. Another 200,000 enter illegally, mostly from Latin America.

Pressures for Immigration Policy Change. Congress in the 1990's and beyond will face several policy issues concerning immigration that were not addressed by the 1986 reform:

☐ Should an overall annual ceiling be set for the total number of immigrants, including nonquota immigrants, refugees, asylum grantees, and illegals?

☐ How many new immigrants can the U.S. economy actually absorb without depressing the wages of the most recent entrants?

☐ Should a stronger effort be made to control the influx of illegal immigrants? The IRCA has not proven effective in stemming the tide of undocumented workers across the Rio Grande. One suggestion is the issuance of a national work card, which could be verified and not easily counterfeited.

☐ Should amnesty be granted to those who did not qualify under the IRCA? Although 2 million undocumented workers received amnesty under the legislation, another 2 million new illegals were working in the United States as of 1993.

The answers to these questions will be shaped by the changed realities of the 1990's, including a population explosion in Asia and Latin America, growing disparities in wealth between the Northern and Southern hemispheres, declining demand for unskilled labor, the high cost of social-welfare entitlement programs, and a rising federal budget deficit. The prospect, then, is for a more restrictive immigration policy in the twenty-first century.—*Kenneth Holland*

SUGGESTED READINGS:

• Baker, Susan Gonzalez. *The Cautious Welcome: The Legalization Programs of the Immigration Reform and Control Act*. Santa Monica, Calif.: RAND, 1990. This study chronicles the design, implementation, and effects of the provisions of the IRCA legalizing certain illegal aliens and farmworkers. The author contends that immigration policy has been too oriented toward punitive sanctions and has not taken full advantage of positive incentives to achieve its goals. A useful source of the details of the IRCA's legalization sections.

• Bean, Frank D., Georges Vernez, and Charles B. Keely. *Opening and Closing the Doors: Evaluating Immigration Reform and Control*. Santa Monica,

Calif.: RAND, 1989. The authors survey the history of U.S. immigration policy and describe current policy, with an emphasis on implementation and consequences of the IRCA. They seek to provide an objective, nonpartisan assessment of the IRCA and suggest some policy changes. A helpful source of the pressures that led to the IRCA.

• Calavita, Kitty. *Inside the State: The Bracero Program, Immigration, and the I.N.S.* New York: Routledge, 1992. This book is a history of the bracero program, the largest foreign-worker program in U.S. history. The author focuses on how the principal government agency in the program's administration, the Immigration and Naturalization Service of the Department of Justice, used its power to make policy. A good source for understanding the role of the executive branch in formulating immigration policy.

• Cose, Ellis. *A Nation of Strangers: Prejudice, Politics, and the Populating of America*. New York: William Morrow, 1992. The author provides a valuable reference work, which chronicles the story of American immigration policy since 1790, with an emphasis on the conflict between the openness dictated by the principles of the Declaration of Independence and the impulse to exclude that has gripped native-born Americans periodically. There is extensive treatment of the efforts to restrict immigration and naturalization of Chinese and Japanese. The fashioning of policies with regard to Southeast Asian refugees is also discussed.

• Divine, Robert A. *American Immigration Policy, 1924-1952*. New Haven, Conn.: Yale University Press, 1957. The author summarizes the history of U.S. immigration policy since the Colonial period, with emphasis on the course of the restrictive immigration policy adopted in 1924. He neither praises nor condemns restriction but uncovers the forces that brought about the policy and summarizes the arguments on both sides of the issue. A good source for the details of the 1924 and 1952 immigration acts.

• Glazer, Nathan, ed. *Clamor at the Gates: The New American Immigration*. San Francisco: ICS Press, 1985. This edited volume contains fourteen separate papers dealing with the history, impact, and prospects of immigration policy. It provides information and analysis that influenced the drafting of the IRCA in 1986. There is a chapter on the Koreans in Los Angeles ("immigrant entrepreneurs") and one particularly useful chapter describing the history of immigration policy toward Asians.

• Higham, John. *Strangers in the Land: Patterns of*

American Nativism, 1860-1925. New Brunswick, N.J.: Rutgers University Press, 1955. In this classic work, the author traces the history of U.S. immigration policy, from the period of open borders to the passage of the percentage law restricting European integration in 1924. He analyzes the phenomenon of nativism, which played a critical role in bringing about the discussion of the Chinese and Japanese exclusion.

• Reimers, David M. *Still the Golden Door: The Third World Comes to America*. New York: Columbia University Press, 1985. This book focuses on the consequences of the 1965 immigration act, which the author contends were neither intended nor foreseen. The author analyzes the pressures that built up between 1943 and 1965 to abandon the racially discriminatory immigration policy. Individual chapters are devoted to the opportunities that the 1965 reform presented for Asians, Latin Americans, and Third World refugees wishing to migrate to the United States. Useful for understanding the dynamics of the "new" Asian immigration.

• Riggs, Frederick Warren. *Pressures on Congress: A Study of the Repeal of Chinese Exclusion*. New York: King's Crown Press, 1950. The author analyzes the forces that made possible the repeal of the Chinese Exclusion Act in 1943 and the liberalization of policy on immigration from India and the Philippines in 1946. The author shows how legislation restricting immigration and naturalization of Asians became a serious irritant in relations between the United States and the countries of Asia.

• Rolph, Elizabeth S. *Immigration Policies: Legacy from the 1980s and Issues for the 1990s*. Santa Monica, Calif.: RAND, 1992. This report focuses on the continuing questions of integration of immigrants in the life of the country and the demands immigrants are placing on public education and other local government services. After proving that the main effect of the IRCA was to open the gates to Third World immigration, the author concludes with a call for greater restrictions. A useful source of the pressures likely to determine immigration policy in the next century.

Imperial conferences (1920's and 1930's): Series of conferences at which the new relationship between Great Britain and territories within its Empire was discussed. During World War I (1914-1918), the relationship between Great Britain and its dominions—Australia, New Zealand, Canada, and South Africa—and colonies, especially India, changed dramatically as the Empire made major contributions to the war

effort and wanted greater respect, equality, and freedom as a result. Several conferences followed to work out this new relationship between Great Britain and its foreign possessions.

The imperial conference of 1921 came to the conclusion that a new formal relationship was not necessary but that future conferences would work out any differences between them. The 1926 imperial conference was an important development in the constitutional relationship between Great Britain and the dominions when the dominions were promised virtual independence. The imperial conference of 1930 finally removed any legal limitations on the freedom of the dominions, and these changes were enacted as the Statute of Westminster of 1931.

The British had promised India independence in 1917 but issued new regulations in 1919 that restricted Indian freedom. Thus the British were making liberal constitutional changes, as in the Government of India Act of 1919, which extended the franchise and allowed more Indians to sit in regional and national legislatures, and at the same time were introducing repressive measures to keep opposition to a minimum. As a result, Mahatma GANDHI, the leader of the Indian National Congress, started a civil disobedience movement against the British in August, 1920, and during the 1920's, people of all classes became politically active. Partly as a result of this pressure, from 1930 to 1932 the British held a series of three Round Table Conferences in London with representatives from India. The outcome was the Government of India Act of 1935, which gave India greater freedom and was the basis for the act leading to independence in 1947. The independence of other nations in the British Empire quickly followed. These conferences leading to the freedom of India gave Indian Americans as well as other Asian Americans a greater sense of pride in that Asian nations were no longer subject to an imperial relationship.

In re Ah Chong (1880): Ruling issued by the U.S. Ninth Circuit Court of Appeals, striking down a California statute that barred aliens from catching and selling fish. The petitioner, Ah Chong, had been arrested for taking fish from San Pablo Bay, north of San Francisco, and for selling them in violation of a law passed by the California state legislature. This law prohibited "aliens ineligible to vote" from fishing or procuring any type of fish for the purpose of selling them. After he had been sentenced to a thirty-day jail sentence, Ah Chong filed for a writ of *habeas corpus* before the federal circuit court. The court ruled that the state law unfairly singled out Chinese for exclusion, since other aliens were eligible to become citizens and to attain voting privileges. Furthermore, the court ruled that the law violated the property rights of alien residents in California. The exclusionary nature of the California law was deemed unconstitutional because it directly violated the Fourteenth Amendment as well as provisions guaranteed in the 1868 BURLINGAME TREATY between China and the United States. Subsequent anti-Asian legislation, however, overrode this decision.

In re Ah Fong: Case decision made in the Ninth Circuit Court in California in 1874. The case was brought before the federal circuit court on a writ of *habeas corpus* by Ah Fong, a woman who represented a group of twenty other Chinese immigrant women who had been detained at Angel Island after arriving in California on August 24, 1873, on the steamship *Japan*. The state commissioner of immigration had refused the group's request for permission to land because he considered them to fall within a class of individuals, including criminals, paupers, and people with physical or mental disabilities, who were deemed eligible for exclusion. The American steamship company filed a petition for the writ of *habeas corpus* on behalf of its passengers, but a California district court and the state supreme court both upheld the 1870 state law under which the commissioner derived his authority to exclude immigrants. A third petition was filed before the federal circuit court, which overturned the previous rulings. The court ruled that the state law was in direct violation of the Fourteenth Amendment, the Civil Rights Act of 1870, and the terms of the BURLINGAME TREATY signed by China and the United States in 1868. As a result of the circuit court decision, twenty of the women were released; one woman, Chy Lung, remained in custody pending the outcome of her appeal to the U.S. Supreme Court on a writ of error. (See *CHY LUNG V. FREEMAN.*)

In re Look Tin Sing (1884): Federal court case in California that allowed an American-born Chinese to be readmitted to the United States after a trip to China, notwithstanding the Chinese Exclusion Acts of 1882 and 1884. The Exclusion Acts barred many Chinese American residents who had gone to China and had been out of the country when the laws were passed. When these people attempted to reenter, they were blocked.

Look Tin Sing was born in California in 1870 of Chinese parents who had come to the United States in approximately 1864. In 1879 his father sent him back to China for a period of five years but intended for him to return to the United States. When Look Tin Sing went to China in 1879, birth certificates were not required for reentry into the United States; however, Congress passed the Chinese Exclusion Acts, which required such documents. When Look Tin Sing attempted to reenter in September, 1884, he was blocked on grounds that he was a potential laborer and/or that he had renounced his U.S. citizenship by going to China.

Look Tin Sing's father insisted that his son should be included in the same employment category as himself (merchant) and that he was too young to renounce his citizenship. The unanimous three-judge panel agreed. The court also determined that Look Tin Sing's parents were not diplomats, which might have been a ground for denying their American-born son his U.S. citizenship. They further pointed out that Look Tin Sing had not been convicted, or even accused, of being a criminal, which would have been the only other ground for revoking his citizenship under the Fourteenth amendment.

In re Tiburcio Parrott (1880): Federal court case from California that declared unconstitutional a provision in the second California constitution prohibiting corporations from employing any "Chinese or Mongolian." This case involved an American corporation that had been fined for employing a Chinese person contrary to state laws.

The second California constitution was drafted by an anti-Chinese convention and forbade any corporation from employing any "Chinese or Mongolian"; it directed the legislature to set criminal penalties against any corporate official who violated the law. The convention delegates targeted corporations, recognizing that the U.S. Supreme Court would void any act that impacted the hiring practices of an individual proprietor since he or she would be a "person" protected by the Fourteent Amendment. They thought, however, that they might get away with prohibiting corporate hiring since states normally are allowed to set special conditions for granting charters to corporations. This subterfuge was strongly denounced by the federal court as still in violation of the Fourteenth Amendment. The unanimous decision was accompanied by a lengthy, strongly worded statement by the court chastising the California legislative bodies for knowingly violating federal law and pointing out that numerous previous statutes had been stricken as unconstitutional on comparable grounds. In fact, in the late 1880's twenty-three out of twenty-five California laws dealing with Chinese American relationships were stricken as unconstitutional. The court also found the state to be in violation of the federal BURLINGAME TREATY, which had been ratified by the U.S. government in 1868; California was therefore infringing on the U.S. Constitution's supremacy clause as well.

The court went to great lengths to defend its decision, saying that the Burlingame Treaty and other U.S. laws had to be enforced as the "supreme Law of the Land." The court did, however, express concern over the unrestricted Chinese immigration into the United States and suggested that it might be advisable to amend the treaty to restrict Chinese entry. Eventually, in 1893, the Supreme Court upheld congressional exclusion of Chinese.

Inada, Lawson Fusao (b. 1938, Fresno, Calif.): Poet. A third-generation Japanese American, Inada was born in the central California community of Fresno. During World War II, he and his family were interned in camps in Arkansas and Colorado.

Inada's first volume of poetry, *Before the War: Poems As They Happened* (1971), reflected his interest in jazz as well as the experience of the incarceration. Together with Frank CHIN, Jeffery Paul CHAN, and Shawn WONG—fellow members of the San Francisco-based Combined Asian-American Resources Project—Inada edited the pathbreaking collection *Aiiieeeee! An Anthology of Asian American Writers* (1974) and its sequel *The Big Aiiieeeee! An Anthology of Chinese American and Japanese American Literature* (1991). In 1992, Inada published his second collection of poems, *Legends from Camp*. A professor of English at Southern Oregon State College, he has received two fellowships from the National Endowment for the Arts.

India, Republic of: Republic located in southern Asia on the Indian subcontinent. It is bounded on the northwest by Pakistan; on the north by China, Nepal, Sikkim, and Bhutan; on the east by Burma, Bangladesh,

India's Taj Mahal is believed to be one of the most beautiful structures in the world. (Government of India Tourist Office)

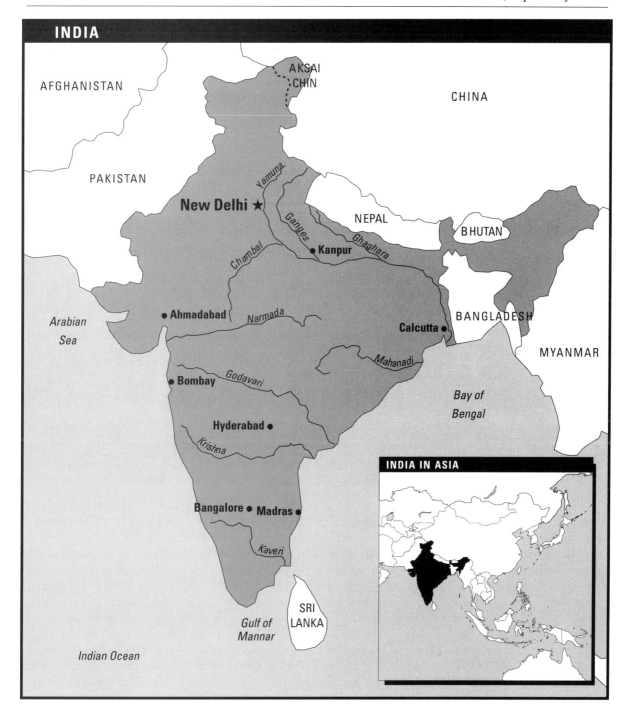

INDIA

AFGHANISTAN

PAKISTAN

AKSAI CHIN

CHINA

New Delhi ★

Yamuna

Ganges

Chambal

● Kanpur

Ghaghara

NEPAL

BHUTAN

● Ahmadabad

Narmada

Calcutta ●

BANGLADESH

MYANMAR

Arabian Sea

Mahanadi

● Bombay

Godavari

Hyderabad ●

Bay of Bengal

Krishna

Bangalore ● Madras ●

Kaveri

SRI LANKA

Gulf of Mannar

Indian Ocean

INDIA IN ASIA

and the Bay of Bengal; on the south by the Indian Ocean; and on the west by the Arabian Sea and Pakistan. India is the world's second most populous nation and the seventh largest country in the world. During the medieval period, Muslim rulers called it "*Hind*" or "Hindustan." The name "India," which is derived from the name of the *Indus* River, was used by the ancient Greeks and Persians and was later popularized by British colonial rulers beginning in the sixteenth century. After independence, "India" and "Bharat" were both chosen to be the official names of the republic.

People and Population. India is home to a population of about 889,700,000 (1992 estimate) in a densely

The bustling city of Bombay, India. (Government of India Tourist Office)

populated area of about 1,222,396 square miles. The ratio of urban to rural population is 26 percent to 74 percent, respectively, with an adult literacy rate of 36 percent. India presents striking extremes of wealth and poverty. It is second only to the United States as an exporter of software, yet bullock carts remain the main method of transportation in most villages. A traditional caste-based social hierarchy and strains of fanatic religiosity are coupled with a political system based on the Western democratic model.

India has eighteen officially recognized languages and several thousand dialects. Hindi remains the official language along with English, which has become the language of the elite. Indians are predominantly Hindu (82.7 percent), but other major religions represented in India are ISLAM (11.4 percent), Christianity (2.6 percent), SIKHISM (2 percent), BUDDHISM (.5 percent), and JAINISM (.4 percent).

Ancient India. Indian culture is of great antiquity. The earliest known Indian civilization developed in the Indus Valley from 4000 B.C.E. to 2500 B.C.E. Archeological discoveries in *Mohenjo-Daro* and *Harrapa* (in present-day Pakistan) have revealed that the Indus Valley civilization was sophisticated, literate, and urban, but its script has not yet been deciphered. The exact causes of this civilization's disappearance are not known, though the region's climate, floods, and forest fires may have contributed to it.

Aryan invaders began to enter India from the northwest around 1500 B.C.E. The conquerors subjugated the native population yet intermingled with the people and even adopted some of the Harrapan cultural traits. The successor culture was definitely inferior to its predecessor. The Aryans were not literate and did not develop writing for at least another thousand years, but they had a strong oral tradition and an extraordinary capacity for metaphysical speculation. The Vedas, which are the four scriptures, or pillars, of Hindu thought, were composed by the early Aryan sages and passed on as an oral tradition for a millennia before their codification. No concrete evidence of the Aryans' way of life is available in the absence of archeological remains or artifacts, and their practice of burning the bodies of their dead has added to this gap. The Aryan culture is known to the modern world through the epics of the *Mahabharata* and the *Ramayana*, which were composed toward the end of the first century B.C.E.

The foundations of Indian society, including HINDUISM and the caste system, were laid by the Aryans. The Indian tradition is unique in that it has developed continuously since that time. BUDDHISM and JAINISM also developed in ancient India. After a glorious zenith of the Hindu civilization under the *Maurya* (c. 321 B.C.E.-c. 181 B.C.E.) and *Gupta* dynasties (early fourth to the mid-sixth century C.E.), the Hindu Empire declined into chaos and feuding small kingdoms.

India Under Foreign Influences. India was subjected to strong Islamic influences following the Islamic invasions beginning in the eleventh century. Between the thirteenth and sixteenth centuries, India remained under Muslim rule, and Hindus were treated as second-class citizens. Culturally, however, India developed through the syncretization of the Islamic and Hindu cultures in the areas of language, literature, poetry, dance, music, cuisine, art, medicine, science, and architecture. Thus emerged the Indian cultural tradition, which is not the same as the Hindu tradition.

Beginning in the sixteenth century, Western colonial powers began to make incursions into India. The British triumphed, gradually establishing control. In 1750, India was formally transferred to the British crown.

India attained independence from British rule in 1947 as a result of its national independence movement, but because of deep-seated conflict between the Muslim minority, represented by the Muslim League, and the Indian National Congress Party, mainly dominated by Hindus, independent India was partitioned

Cattle are vitally important animals in India, revered for their religious significance and prized as beasts of burden. Here a veterinarian advocates a bullock's inoculation against disease. (Library of Congress)

into the sovereign states of India and Pakistan.

Modern India. Independent India became a secular democracy modeled on the British parliamentary system. It also borrowed from American, French, and Swiss constitutional practices in having an elected head of the republic, a federation of states with unitary tendencies, and a multiparty system. The liberal goals of the constitutional system, based on Western political thought and the principles of individualism, equality, and gender equality, were superimposed on traditional Indian society, which continued to practice casteism, communalism, untouchability, and gender discrimination.

Independent India became a leader of the newly liberated Third World nations through its championship of a policy of nonalignment with Western nations and the Communist Bloc during the Cold War. Despite its professed commitment to peace and mediation in international conflicts, however, India entered into a border war with China in 1962 (resulting in a stalemate) and three armed conflicts with neighboring Pakistan in 1948, 1965, and 1971.

India has progressed considerably in the political and economic areas since its independence. It has remained a stable and functional democracy, and it is among the few democracies to have elected a female head of the government. In the absence of a social revolution, however, conservatism, backwardness, and lack of commitment to democratic values are widespread. India became the only democracy in the world to have a single family rule for almost four decades. Moreover, economic and educational opportunities have not been evenly distributed among the population.

India in the 1990's, then, is a nation marked by great tensions but also by great promise. While civil strife is a real threat to stability, India is enjoying unprecedented economic growth. The steady development of the middle class—now constituting about 150 million people—also bodes well for the future—*Indu Vohra*

SUGGESTED READINGS: • Brass, Paul. *The Politics of India Since Independence.* New York: Cambridge University Press, 1990. • Nyrop, Richard F., ed. *India: A Country Study.* Washington, D.C.: U.S. Government Printing Office, 1986. • Roach, James R., ed. *India 2000: The Next Fifteen Years.* Riverdale, Md.: Riverdale, 1986. • Smith, Vincent A. *The Oxford History of India.* Edited by Percival Spear. 3d ed. Oxford, England: Clarendon Press, 1967. • Wolpert, Stanley. *A New History of India.* New York: Oxford University Press, 1989.

India Abroad: New York-based weekly newspaper, founded in 1970, that reports events of interest to the Asian Indian diaspora.

India Currents: Monthly magazine founded in 1987 and based in San Jose, California. It reports events of interest to the Asian Indian community in California, with a special focus on the San Francisco Bay Area. Originally committed to documenting only cultural events, the publication began to offer short features on Asian Indian American political activity.

India League of America: Organization formed by concerned Asian Indians in New York City in the mid-1930's. The league published a monthly bulletin, *India Today*. As the drive for Indian independence from the British intensified internationally, the league became a catalyst for the movement in America. The group also supported the naturalization rights of Asian Indians in America.

India League of America, Madison, Wisconsin: Organization formed through the merging of eleven Asian Indian associations in Madison in 1964. With numerous local chapters throughout the United States, the league attempts to unite immigrants from India, instill pride in Indian heritage, and assist the acculturation process.

India Studies Chair, University of California, Berkeley: Professor Robert Goldman, of the South Asian Studies Department at the University of California, Berkeley, initiated the India Studies Chair project in August, 1990. He did this in an attempt to get the Indian American community more involved in campus activities. The genesis of this project could not have come at a worse time for the university, as it was facing one of the most devastating financial crises in its history. State budget cuts were imminent, and the situation would become far worse before it got better. Furthermore, help from the university could not be expected since it had already made cutbacks in many departments. Thus it became evident that the South Asian community would have to raise the $400,000 needed to fund the Indo-American Community Chair, as it is officially titled.

A very active Indian counsulate general in San Francisco, with an interest in education, became one of the primary forces behind the establishment of the chair. He went to certain wealthy members of the community, as well as the South Asian community at large, and solicited donations. The result of the fund-raising drive was more than one thousand contributions from all across the country, and from people from all class backgrounds. In under six months, the effort had raised $450,000—a remarkable tribute to the mobilizing powers of the community despite tough economic times.

The chair has sponsored guests from India, England, and the United States. A selection committee, composed primarily of South Asians and those whose work centers on South Asia, determines whom to invite. The committee welcomes recommendations, and students have been especially encouraged to submit recommendations. Among those who have spoken are John Kenneth Galbraith from Harvard, S. Chandrasekhar—a Nobel Prize winner—from the University of Chicago, Andre Beteille from Delhi University, Upendra Baxi from Delhi University, and Mrinal Dattachaudhuri from the Delhi School of Economics.

India-West: California-based weekly newspaper, founded in 1975, devoted to South Asian Indian current events in North America and abroad. The publication attempts to link events in South Asia to the immigrant community in the United States and is distributed primarily throughout the Pacific Coast.

Indian dance. *See* **Indian music and dance**

Indian independence: India attained independence from British colonial rule and became a sovereign nation-state on August 15, 1947. Indian independence was the result of indigenous nationalism rooted in anti-British sentiment since about the mid-nineteenth century. On the eve of its independence, India was partitioned into two separate states, INDIA and PAKISTAN. The Indian National Congress, under the leadership of Mahatma GANDHI (Mohandas Karamchand Gandhi), was the main political organization responsible for India's independence.

Origins. The beginning of Indian nationalism is generally traced to the war of independence of 1857, and event termed by British historians as the Indian "Sepoy Mutiny." One of the three armies of the BRITISH EAST INDIA COMPANY revolted over the widespread rumor that the new Enfield rifles were greased with the fat of beef and pork, which was against the Hindu and Muslim religious beliefs. The affected native princes and influential landlords also played an important role in stirring up the anti-British sentiments. The "mutiny" was suppressed with great sever-

ity by the British, which left a legacy of bitterness in the Indian psyche. The Government of India Act of 1858 transferred the rule of British India, which, with the exception of more than five hundred small princely kingdoms, encompassed virtually the entire Indian subcontinent, to the British crown.

Indian Nationalism. The emergence of Indian national consciousness was a slow and diverse process underlined by variations in religion, class, caste, and region. It was also the sum total of both negative and positive responses to the British consolidation of power in India. At one level, the movement was perceived as a socio-religious challenge to the predominantly Hindu society, which necessitated socio-religious reform and revival of the ancient Hindu tradition. A number of societies and movements such as the Brahmo Samaj, the Arya Samaj, the Prarthna Samaj, and many others were formed by the middle-to-upper-class intelligentsia. At another level, admiration of Western achievements in technology, science, statecraft, and worldwide political power led many to advocate the assimilation of Western values and attitudes as the only way to modernize India. The perspectives afforded by both levels were nationalistic and had

Mahatma Gandhi showed great courage in the fight for Indian independence with his adherence to non-violent civil disobedience. (AP/Wide World Photos)

supporters among all religions and classes.

Indian nationalist sentiments took a distinctly anti-British turn on a large scale toward the late nineteenth century. The economic ruin and drain imposed on the Indian agricultural and feudal economy; indifference toward the plight of artisans and farmers suffering from unemployment; poverty and famines; and British racist practices that refused to appoint Indians to high-level positions and because of which Britishers refused to socialize with Indians or accept them as equals all contributed to the emergence of nativist consciousness.

Many upperclass Indians, who had benefited from the British system of education and had become well versed in Western liberal philosophy as well as the recent history of Western nationalism, soon became restless about the "white man's" double standards vis-à-vis the "colored people." The British efforts to unify and modernize India for their own political and economic interests (the introduction of mass-level education, the English language, the press, railways, and new British manufacturing technology) also helped to create and intensify the national consciousness in India.

Indian National Movement. Indian nationalism began to surface in the wake of the founding of the Indian National Congress in 1885 as a forum for the expression of public opinion in India through the indigenous elite. This phase of Indian nationalism (1885-1905) is called the "moderate" era, as petitions and appeals were made by the early Indian leaders to the British conscience for better treatment of Indians and a greater equality of opportunity. While the moderate aspect of the nationalist movement remained predominant until the early 1920's, a number of terrorist organizations and secret societies began to emerge in many regions of India, and some had their agents or chapters in the Western world, including the United States. Around the outbreak of World War I, "extremist" elements having strong fundamentalist and Hindu chauvinistic tendencies began to gain popularity over the moderate leadership within the Indian National Congress.

In the post-World War I period, the diversified and fragmented Indian nationalism was largely brought under a single umbrella under the leadership of Gandhi by the year 1920. Thereafter, the Indian national movement became a mass movement encompassing the rank and file in India. The goal of the Indian National Congress now was nothing less than complete *swaraj*, or self-rule, for India. Indian nationalism had received a boost from World War I, where Indian soldiers had fought and died defending the principles of democracy and self-determination of nations. The blueprint for the future of India along democratic lines and parliamentary principles, however, began to cause a wedge between the Hindu and Muslim populations, as the Muslims began to speculate about their future in a predominantly Hindu India. From the 1920's until India's independence in 1947, while the singular goal of complete independence of India was unanimously upheld, the prospects of two separate states in the aftermath of the British withdrawal remained potent. The Muslim League began to demand a separate state for the Muslims.

During the decades between World Wars I and II, the British became accommodative under the mounting pressure of mass-scale Indian nationalist mobilization under Gandhi, which was characterized by methods of non-cooperation, civil disobedience, boycott of foreign goods, strikes, fasts unto death, and nonviolence. Toward the late 1920's, the British began to propose dominion status for India, instead of complete independence. To take advantage of the rift between

Jawaharlal Nehru served as first prime minister of the Republic of India. (AP/Wide World Photos)

Indian women receive instruction prior to entering the voting booth in Delhi, India, 1951, to participate in what was at the time the largest free election in history. (National Archives)

Muslims and Hindus, the British introduced elections in India based on a "separate electorate" for different religious communities and the "untouchables." While the charismatic Gandhi could persuade the Christians, Sikhs, untouchables, and other groups to remain united in the demand for one free India, the Muslim League remained adamant. Meanwhile, the riots between the Hindus and the Muslims became too frequent.

The Government of India Act of 1935, which became effective in 1937, provided provincial autonomy in India based on a federal model, in order to give the Indians a sense of responsibility before granting them the transfer of power. This period, however, was also the beginning of the intensification of Muslim distrust of the Indian National Congress and of separatism.

With the ensuing World War II, the Indian National Congress increased its pressure on the British to declare their postwar aims and policy for India. In August, 1942, the congress launched the "Quit India" movement to force the British to relinquish power on penalty of mass civil disobedience. Because of the prospect of India's noncooperation in the British war effort, and the dire need for Indian resources and first-rate trained Indian soldiers, the British conceded in

1940 that after the war, the framing of a new constitution would be primarily the responsibility of the Indians themselves, but that the British would not tolerate the coercion of minorities. A series of deadlocked conferences took place between 1942 and 1946 to resolve the differences between the Indian National Congress and the Muslim League. The diplomatic mission of Sir Stafford Cripps in 1942, the Simla conference with Viceroy Lord Wavell in 1945, and the Labour Cabinet mission in 1946 are noteworthy. Meanwhile the British administrators in India, whose days of actual rule were over, were becoming demoralized. Britain was exhausted from the war, and the overseas empire was beginning to feel burdensome.

On February 20, 1947, British prime minister Clement Attlee announced that by June, 1948, power would be transferred to a responsible government, whether or not an agreement between the various parties had been reached. The British government reserved the right to choose to whom the power would be transferred. In March, 1947, Lord Louis Mountbatten arrived in India to expedite the process, and in June a final agreement was reached.

The British Parliament passed the India Independence Act, which came into force on August 15, 1947, conferring complete independence on India as a self-governing dominion within the British Commonwealth of Nations with the right to secede from this organization. Britain also terminated its suzerainty over the Indian princely states. The independent state of Pakistan was given a similar status. The partition of India led to the accession of East Bengal and West Punjab to Pakistan and the migration of at least twelve million people between the two countries. Hindu-Muslim hatred and animosity led to some of the worst kind of killing that the world had ever seen. Subsequently, in 1950 India emerged as a "Sovereign Democratic Republic" and "Union of States" under its own constitution.—*Indu Vohra*

SUGGESTED READINGS: • Edwardes, Michael. *A History of India from the Earliest Times to the Present Day.* New York: Farrar, Straus and Cudahy, 1961. • Mason, Philip. *The Guardians.* Vol. 2 in *The Men Who Ruled India.* London: Jonathan Cape, 1963. • Sitaramayya, B. Pattabhi. *History of the Indian National Congress.* 2 vols. Bombay: Padma, 1946-1947. • Smith, Vincent A. *The Oxford History of India.* Edited by Percival Spear. 3d ed. Oxford: Clarendon Press, 1967. • Wolpert, Stanley. *A New History of India.* 4th ed. New York: Oxford University Press, 1993.

Indian music and dance: India is a diverse nation with literally thousands of different genres and styles of traditional performing arts. At the same time, there are areas of consistency among many of them, especially the classical forms. Some of these traditions are flourishing in the United States.

Early History. One of the most important unifying concepts in the arts of India is the idea of *sangeet* (*sangit*), which encompasses vocal music, dance, and instrumental music, originally composed and performed for religious purposes. Indian philosophers and theologians have also asserted a relationship between musical phenomena (such as resonance) and meditation. In both *Bhakti* yoga and Sufi mysticism, music is regarded as a means of attaining spiritual union. Hindu tradition associates both music and literature with the goddess Saraswati, and musical rhythm is said to reflect cosmic motion and vast cycles of time (the dance of Shiva). From the very beginning, the arts were an important part of Indian life. A pre-Vedic sculpture, for example, dating back to c. 2500 B.C.E. and found in the Indus valley region, portrays a young dancer.

One of the oldest layers of Indian music is Vedic chant, a practice probably as old as the Vedas them-

selves, at least three thousand years. The earliest known theoretical document relating to music and dance is the *Natya-sastra* (theory of dramaturgy), attributed to the sage Bharata and written sometime between 100 B.C.E. and 500 C.E. Included in this document is a scientific system, now used throughout the world, of classifying musical instruments according to their elements of vibration. Sculpture and painting from this period show a great number of musical instruments, including many kinds of string, wind, and percussion instruments. Temples were important centers for music, and women associated with the temples were proficient in both music and dance. By classifying melodies and rhythms according to structure, early theorists founded the modern Hindustani and Karnatic systems of raga (melodic form) and tala (rhythmic cycle). In both systems, a drone instrument (usually the tamboura) supplies a tonal reference for complex melodic structures.

Hindustani Music and Dance. After the Mughal conquests in the sixteenth and seventeenth centuries, most of North India and parts of central India were culturally influenced by nations to the west, most notably Persia. The area under Mughal control eventually encompassed present-day Pakistan and Bangladesh as well as North India and was known as "Hindustan." A new musical system gradually emerged in the courts of this area, in which Hindu musical forms and instruments were influenced by Muslim ones, resulting in new vocal styles such as khyal and new instruments such as the sitar (a plucked lute) and the tabla drums. Music and dance techniques were closely guarded at this time and were passed down through families known as *gharanas.* New dance genres such as *kathak* were created, and Hindu narrative themes were maintained, even in the context of entertainment for Muslim rulers. There was much variance in the social status of these performers, some of whom were courtesans. After the dissolution of the Mughal Empire, Hindustani *sangit* survived in the courts of patrons who worked within the British colonial system. Political, technological, and economic changes in the nineteenth and twentieth centuries eventually made these artistic traditions accessible to increasingly larger groups of people.

Karnatic Music and Dance. Many areas of southern India resisted Islamic political and cultural influences, and the performing arts developed in different ways, forming the basis of the Karnatic system. Musical genres that were created at this time include the *kriti,* based on classical devotional songs with texts in South

Indian languages. South Indian dance genres such as *bharata-natya* are taught all over India and abroad. The principal percussion instrument of Karnatic music is the *mridanga*, a double-headed drum, and many kinds of melodic instruments are used, including the vina, flute, and violin. The Karnatic theoretical system of *raga* and *tala* classification is somewhat more standardized than its Hindustani counterpart.

Music and Dance for the Cinema. Since the advent of motion pictures with sound, film has become the primary vehicle for the development of popular music and dance throughout South Asia. These new genres, fusing elements of Indian folk and classical music and dance with international popular styles, are so popular that films are often created as mere vehicles for recording stars and their song-and-dance pieces. Classical musicians such as Ravi SHANKAR have also provided sound tracks for film authors with a more independent, less commercial approach to this new art form.

Developments in the United States. South Asian performing artists have established teaching studios serving Indian and other South Asian communities abroad. In the United States, non-Indian students have often enrolled as well, inspired by increasingly available recordings, or by concerts featuring visiting artists. Some are privately operated, while others are affiliated with Indian cultural associations. One of the oldest Indian music schools in the United States is the Ali Akbar Khan College of Music in San Rafael, California. Some teachers, including Veena Chandra in New York, Hamid Hossain in Maryland, and Sushil Mukherjee in Massachusetts, have combined private teaching with an academic affiliation. While Indian music and dance have found audiences worldwide in the twentieth century, their emphasis on systematic improvisation and a clearly articulated music theory has captured the imagination of many American jazz, popular, and classical musicians, who, like their Indian counterparts, have experimented with blended styles.

Academic interest in Indian music and dance has been especially strong in the United States. Many universities and colleges with programs in ethnomusicology have offered classes taught by Indian musicians and scholars, most notably at the University of California, Los Angeles (Nazir Ali Jairazbhoy) and Wesleyan University (T. Viswanathan and T. Ranganathan).

Two young girls receive instruction in Hindustani dance forms at the Hindu Temple Society in Queens, New York. (Hazel Hankin)

American scholars such as David Reck, Charles Capwell, Bonnie C. Wade, and Jon Higgins, to name but a few, have also contributed to the process of sharing these venerable traditions with new audiences in the United States.—*John Myers*

SUGGESTED READINGS: • Manuel, Peter. *Popular Musics of the Non-Western World*. New York: Oxford University Press, 1988. • Sambamoorthy, P. *South Indian Music*. (6 vols.) Madras: Indian Music Publishing House, 1958-1969. • Sarabhai, Mrinalini. *Understanding Bharata Natyam*. 3d ed. Ahmedabad, India: Darpana Academy of Performing Arts, 1981. • Shankar, Ravi. *My Music, My Life*. New York: Simon & Schuster, 1968. • Wade, Bonnie C. *Music in India: The Classical Traditions*. Englewood Cliffs, N.J.: Prentice-Hall, 1979.

Indian religions: India has been the place of origin of several of the major religions of Asia and Asian Americans, including HINDUISM, BUDDHISM, JAINISM, and SIKHISM. These religions share the view that human beings live many lifetimes, being reborn repeatedly according to their actions (Karma), with good actions leading to a good rebirth, bad actions to a bad rebirth. This is the eternal cycle of rebirth, the ending of which is regarded as the goal of religious practice for all these religions. Statistics for 1991 give the following estimates for members of these Indian religions living in North America: 1,269,000 Hindus, 558,000 Buddhists, and 254,000 Sikhs.

Indian American women leave a Hindu temple in Queens, New York. (Hazel Hankin)

Hinduism. The vast majority of people living in India are Hindus. This highly diverse religious tradition has very ancient roots. Hinduism can be traced back to the Indus Valley civilization (about 2500 B.C.E.) and the Aryan people, who migrated into India about 1500 B.C.E. The blending of these two groups and their cultures gave rise to classical Indian culture and its religious traditions. Hindus regard as sacred the ancient religious poems of the Vedas, composed in the period c. 1500 B.C.E. to 1200 B.C.E.

Hindus have developed three "paths," or ways of being religious. The oldest of these paths is the way of sacrifice. Although in recent centuries this way of being religious has not been popular, in ancient times it was the primary way for the Aryan people. Animals, particularly cattle, were killed and burned in fire in an elaborate ritual that included the recitation of the Vedas by priests. This sacrifice was regarded as pleasing to the gods, who were asked to provide long and happy lives to the humans who made these sacrifices. The second way of being religious is the path of knowledge gained through meditation. Knowledge of the self (*atman*) and knowledge that the self was identical with Brahman, the sacred power that lies behind all reality, is sought through various practices, including *yoga*, a spiritual discipline of meditation. The path of knowledge was developed around the sixth century B.C.E. The third way of being religious is the path of devotion, which became popular around the first century B.C.E. This path is based on developing a loving attitude toward God. Hindus conceive God in various ways, including as Vishnu or Shiva, who are male, or as Durga or Kali, who are female, and many Hindus are polytheistic, believing that multiple gods exist. Hindus display devotion through small offerings such as food, incense, and flowers, often made before a statue or image of God. Hindu society is organized into four hereditary groups, ranked according to their status; this ranking, known as the "caste system," is regarded as having divine origin. Thus, Hindus have a wide array of ways in which to express their religious sentiments.

Buddhism and Jainism. These two religious traditions began in the sixth century B.C.E. in North India. While BUDDHISM has spread throughout Asia, and in recent times to Europe and North America, JAINISM remains a small religious tradition found only in India. Buddhism began with the experience of one man, Siddhartha Gautama, who came to be known as the "Buddha" (Awakened One) as a result of attaining enlightenment (*Nirvana*). Buddhism is based on the idea of avoiding extremes of self-denial or luxury, developing compassion, and terminating anxiety and rebirth through the attainment of *Nirvana*. Buddhism's major ideas are found in the Four Noble Truths, which state that life is characterized by suffering and a sense of unsatisfactoriness; that this suffering is a result of one's tendency to desire and crave things that are impermanent, leading to feelings of unsatisfaction, to a desire for more life, and to rebirth; that this cycle of rebirth and suffering can be broken if one stops desiring these impermanent things; and that the method to stop desiring is the Eightfold Path of Buddhist religious practice, which leads to *Nirvana*.

Jainism, founded by a man known as the "Jina" (conqueror), is similar in its emphasis on the need to control one's emotions and desires so that one can break out of the rebirth cycle. Both religious traditions emphasize the importance of nonviolence and vegetar-

ian diets, Jainism to an even greater degree than Buddhism. Both religions also criticized the Hindu tradition of animal sacrifice, insisting that such actions were bad *Karma*. Finally, both religions founded orders of monks and nuns that continue to function. Buddhists and Jains together total slightly less than 1 percent of India's large population, though there are hundreds of millions of Buddhists outside India.

Sikhs are shown in their temple in Sacramento, California, 1994. (Ben Klaffke)

Statue of Buddha preaching, Sarnath, India. (Library of Congress)

Sikhism. The Sikh religion began in the sixteenth century, much later than the other religions of India. Founded by Guru Nanak, the tradition of the Sikhs (disciples) emphasizes the equality of all humanity before God. Though the Sikh worldview does not differ significantly from that of Hindus, accepting rebirth according to one's *Karma*, Sikhs reject other aspects of Hinduism, including the caste system and the use of images of God during worship, and they are monotheistic, believing that there is only one God. In this regard, Sikhs are similar to Muslims. Despite this similarity, the Mughal emperors of the sixteenth through eighteenth centuries, who were Muslims, persecuted Sikhs in an effort to eliminate the Sikh religion. Sikhs defended their faith effectively, and the teachings of the pacifist Nanak were preserved through armed force. Their sacred book is a collection of the teachings of Nanak and nine later gurus (teachers), and their temples are known as *gurdwara*s. Although Sikhs are a small minority within modern India, constituting about 2 percent of the population, they are literate, often successful in business, and influential.

In the nineteenth and twentieth centuries, Hindu, Buddhist, and Sikh immigrants have come to North America by the thousands. In addition, some North Americans have converted to these Indian religions. Particularly in larger cities, one finds yoga classes, Buddhist temples, meditation centers, and Sikh *gurdwara*s.—*Bruce M. Sullivan*

SUGGESTED READINGS: • Basham, A. L. *The Wonder That Was India: A Survey of the Culture of the Indian Subcontinent Before the Coming of the Muslims.* London: Sidgwick and Jackson, 1954. • Embree, Ainslie T., and Stephen Hay, eds. *Sources of Indian Tradition*, 2d ed. 2 vols. New York: Columbia University Press, 1988. • Jaini, Padmanabh. *The Jaina Path of Purification.* Berkeley: University of California Press, 1979. • Kinsley, David R. *Hinduism: A Cultural Perspective.* Englewood Cliffs, N.J.: Prentice-Hall, 1982. • McLeod, W. H. *The Evolution of the Sikh Community.* Oxford, England: Clarendon Press, 1976. • Robinson, Richard H., and Willard L. Johnson. *The Buddhist Religion: A Historical Introduction.* 3d ed. Belmont, Calif.: Wadsworth, 1982.

Indian religious movements in the United States: American Transcendentalists such as Ralph Waldo Emerson and Henry David Thoreau evinced a keen interest in Indian religious thought. Subsequently, Edwin Arnold's *The Light of Asia* (1879) (a poetic biography of the Buddha) and *The Song Celestial* (1885; translation of the Bhagavadgita, c. first or second century C.E.) made an impact on many Americans. The Theosophical Society, founded by Madame Helena Blavatsky and Colonel Henry Olcott in New York City in 1875 and grounded in the Neoplatonic occult and mystical tradition, as well as the Christian Science movement of Mary Baker Eddy in Boston and its offshoot, the New Thought movement started by Phineas Quimby in the 1860's, had been greatly influenced by Vedantic philosophy. Thus when Indian religious reformers and preachers began to arrive in the country during the 1880's and 1890's, they found at least a minority of interested and knowledgeable Americans supportive of their cause.

Beginnings of Hindu Evangelicalism. The first Indian religious teacher to lecture in the United States was Protap Chunder Mozoomdar in 1883, whose Brahmo Samaj (originally started by Ram Mohan ROY) had already developed a cordial relation with the Unitarian Church of America. He was followed by Swami VIVEKANANDA, a disciple of the Hindu mystic Ramakrishna Paramahamsa, who addressed the World Parliament of Religions in Chicago on September 11, 1893.

Vivekananda's Vedantic message was that anyone could realize God and that the plurality of faiths and sects were nothing but so many paths to the Divine. His extensive tours and lectures in the country culminated in the founding of the Vedanta Society in New York City in 1896. This was the beginning of the Vedanta movement, leading to the construction of monasteries and missions mainly in California, Connecticut, and New York in the course of the next quarter century. With 12 independent centers and their subcenters, convents, and monasteries and with approximately 22,000 members, the Vedanta Society is the most influential Hindu organization established before the twentieth century.

Throughout the late 1890's right up to World War I, the activities of a number of Hindu evangelists were complemented by the literary and missionary works of men such as William Walker Atkinson, who wrote on Hindu teachings under the pen name of Swami Ramacharaka, and Philip Bernard who, calling himself Omnipotent, founded the Tantric Order of America.

Indian religious movements confronted a crisis after the war as a result of growing anti-Asian sentiment resulting in the Exclusion Act of 1917. A few years later the U.S. Supreme Court ruled Indians ineligible for American citizenship. Anti-Indian stereotypes were promoted by works such as Katherine Mayo's 1927 bestseller *Mother India*. In spite of these difficulties, the Vedantist mystic Paramahamsa Yogananda (Mukundalal Ghosh), founded the Yogoda Satsang, later called SELF-REALIZATION FELLOWSHIP, on Mount Washington in Los Angeles in 1935.

Explosive Growth. Indian religious movements in the United States began to experience explosive growth in the 1960's, in conjunction with the dramatic flourishing of the counterculture. Rejecting mainstream traditions, many Americans—especially young people—were drawn to various Indian movements.

One of the most influential of these movements, the INTERNATIONAL SOCIETY FOR KRISHNA CONSCIOUSNESS (popularly known as Hare Krishna), was founded by A. C. Bhaktivedanta Swami Prabhupada in the mid-1960's in New York City, later moving to the West Coast and finally to a grand spiritual sanctuary called

Maharishi Mahesh Yogi, founder of transcendental meditation. (AP/Wide World Photos)

New Vrindavan near Moundsville, West Virginia, in the 1980's.

Also, in 1966 was launched the Student's International Meditation Society—an extension of the transcendental meditation (TM) begun by Maharishi MA-HESH YOGI in 1959 in California—an organization based on monistic mysticism and yet secular enough, requiring no religious commitment, it being a group practicing techniques for achieving concentration and tranquility of the mind. The TM movement was brought under the World Plan Executing Council in 1972 with a view to ushering in an Age of Enlightenment.

Of the three noteworthy movements of the 1970's, the first is the SAI Foundation of California founded by Satya Sai Baba. The thrust of the movement is veneration of Sai Baba and teaching of mainline Hinduism. The second movement is the Siddha Yoga Dham of American (SYDA) Foundation, established by Swami Muktananda in Oakland in 1974. It was later relocated to South Fallsburg, New York. The third movement is that of the Ananda Marga, which made rapid progress betweeen 1969 and 1973 with more than 100 centers and about 3,000 members. Its founder, Sri Sri Anandamurti (Prabhat Ranjan Sarkar), taught not only a yogic philosophy toward the path of bliss (*ananda marga*) but also a sociopolitical activism known as the Progressive Utilization Theory (Prout) under a sister organization called Proutist Universal.

The Rajneesh Foundation International was started by Bhagwan Shree Rajneesh in Antelope, Oregon, sometime after 1981. Beginning as a large community practicing a variety of techniques connected with left-hand tantra as well as Zen Buddhism in search of enlightenment and personal freedom, the movement suffered a major setback in 1985 following several allegations against the Bhagwan and his principal associates, his subsequent departure from America, and the eventual disintegration of the Antelope commune.

The Meher Baba Movement. The Meher Baba movement is difficult to categorize because its founder Merwan Sheriar Irani, who became known as Meher Baba (compassionate father), was born in a Zoroastrian household, trained in a Christian school, followed the mystical Sufi religion, and claimed to be the last in the series of *avatars* (incarnations) of God such as Zoroaster, Rama, Krishna, Buddha, Jesus, and Muhammad. He preached Karma, reincarnation, nirvana, and above all, the absolute importance of showing compassion to everybody. The Baba Lovers movement has two organizations: The Society for Avatar Meher Baba in New York City and Sufism Reoriented near San Francisco. The largest center is in Myrtle Beach, South Carolina.

The Sikh and Jain Movements. Yogi Bhajan (Sahib Harbhajan Singh) founded the Sikh Dharma movement in 1969 in New York and California. The movement's educational wing, Healthy, Happy, Holy Organization (3HO), has about 125 branches in the United States.

The two Jain organizations, International Mahavir Jain Mission, founded by Guruji Muni Suhil Kumar in Staten Island and in upstate New York in the late 1970's, and the New Life Now, founded by Gurudev Sri Chitrabhanu in 1974 (later renamed Jain Meditation International Center in New York City), with branches in Boston, South Norwalk in Connecticut (headquarters of Jain Peace Fellowship), Pittsburgh, Philadelphia, West Orange in New Jersey, and Toronto, are quite active among Jain immigrants as well as non-Indian Americans. There are, in all, sixty-three Hindu, ten Sikh, and two Jain organizations in the United States.—*Narasingha Sil*

Suggested Readings: • Judah, J. Stillson. *The History and Philosophy of the Metaphysical Movements in America*. Philadelphia: The Westminster Press, 1967. • Leviton, Richard. "How the Swamis Came to America." Yoga Journal (March/April, 1990). • Melton, J. Gordon. The Encyclopedia of American Religions. 2d ed. Detroit: Gale Research, 1987. • Miller, Timothy, ed. When Prophets Die: The Postcharismatic Fate of New Religious Movements. Albany: State University of New York Press, 1991. • Miller, Timothy, ed. *America's Alternative Religions*. Albany: State University of New York Press, 1993. • Shulman, Albert M. *The Religious Heritage of America*. San Diego: A. S. Barnes & Company, 1981. • Zaretsky, Irving I. and Mark P. Leone, eds. *Religious Movements in Contemporary America*. Princeton, N.J.: Princeton University Press, 1974.

Indian restaurants and cuisine: Indian restaurants in the United States have seen tremendous changes in the 1970's and 1980's. From the old and dark curry houses that were popular in the 1960's and that were usually found in the poor sections of such cities as San Francisco and New York, Indian restaurants have been transformed into refined and spacious dining rooms that attempt to offer a wide range of India's gastronomic regionalism.

Because of the large size of India, its various ethnic groups and religions, and the influence of Persian and Chinese cuisines, Indian foods vary from one region to another. In the United States, most Indian restaurants, such as Akbar and The Bombay Palace, provide combinations of these various cuisines, such as the vegetarian and nonvegetarian dishes of South and North India, respectively, the famous tandoor cooking of the Punjab and northwestern Pakistan, the seafood specialties of Bengal, and the sweet and sour dishes of West India.

Curry. When one thinks of Indian cuisine, the first word that often comes to mind is "curry." Curry, however, is neither the name of a dish nor the name of a single spice. Curry is actually a flavorful combination of several ground spices, including turmeric, cardamom, cumin, cassia, pepper, ginger, fennel, coriander, and nutmeg, that are used to flavor various stewlike dishes.

Certainly, curries are the unique and unifying features of Indian cooking, and they have gained such prominence that international versions have emerged. A curry for example is extremely popular in Japan, and various types of curry powder are sold in grocery stores all over the world. To the Indians, curry represents a wide variety of dishes made with fish, chicken, vegetables, lentils, and even fruits. Curry powder, however, is not considered to be a standard Indian spice; as a spice it is primarily meant for foreign consumption. Instead of curry powder, some basic spices such as turmeric, chilies, and cumin are used in Indian cooking, and the combination of these spices is usually a highly guarded family secret. Another stereotypical notion of Indian food is that it is extremely hot and spicy. Although spices are important in Indian dishes, they are not necessary. In many families and groups, spicy food is totally discouraged on physical and spiritual grounds and is often referred as *tamsik*, that is, food having evil or dark qualities.

Vegetarian Dishes. Indian cuisine has evolved over the past four thousands years and offers a dazzling array of vegetarian dishes. Usually, the Indian definition of "vegetarian" is much narrower than perceived in the West, and in the narrowest definitions, even onions and garlic are excluded. Spices and vegetarianism are two unifying features of Indian cuisine. Instead of turning to meats, Indians often rely on lentils and milk products. Nonvegetarian food, however, is also an integral part of present-day Indian dishes, which are not free from foreign influences.

Indian cuisine has its own regional, religious, and seasonal forms. South Indian food is usually vegetarian, the two most popular dishes being *dosa* and *idlies*. Both are made with a mixture of fermented rice and lentils. *Dosas* are griddle-fried, delicate paper-thin pancakes stuffed with vegetables, whereas *idlies are steamed-rice dumplings. They are served with sambhar—a combination of arhar* lentil with tamarind, spices, and vegetables—and coconut chutney. Soup dishes include *rasam* (lentil-based soup), which is served with rice and two or three vegetables, cooked coconut, and yogurt. Many restaurant chains, such as Madras, Woodlands, and others, specialize in South Indian cooking. South Indian dishes are popular throughout India, Sri Lanka, and Nepal. In India, South Indian food is no longer seen as a regional cuisine.

Nonvegetarian Cooking. North Indian cuisine is usually known for its nonvegetarian food. That is not to say that vegetarianism is not common in the North. North Indian food is influenced by Muslim and Central Asian preparations and features minced or ground-meat dishes such as *kabobs* and *keema*. Numerous indigenous varieties of *kabob* (such as *sheek kabob, boti kabob,* and *shammi kabob*), which use skewered, marinated meat grilled or broiled on charcoal embers, have developed over the last fifteen hundred years. Well known among curry dishes are *rogan josh, korma,* and *koftas* (meat balls). These dishes consist of meat cooked with cream and clarified butter (*ghee*), thickened with almonds, cashews, and other nuts, and flavored with spices, onions, and garlic. They are usually served either with plain rice called *basmati* (fragrant rice,) or with *pulaos* or *biryani* (rice with saffron and marinated lamb). Chicken curries are also popular in North Indian cuisine.

New York City residents visit Taj Mahal Restaurant booth at Indian Street Fair. (Richard B. Levine)

Indian Americans prepare "paan" at Indian Street Festival in New York City. (Richard B. Levine)

Indian Americans enjoy traditional foods on Sikh Independence Day in New York City. (Richard B. Levine)

Tandoori Baking. The tandoor (clay oven) is particularly famous in the Punjab and the Northwestern part of Pakistan for its mouthwatering dishes. Famous tandoori preparations include *tandoori chicken*, a small chicken marinated with yogurt and spices and served with a tortilla-type wheat bread called *rotis* (cooked in tandoors or baked). An important variant of a tandoori *roti* is *naan*, a long, triangular bread sprinkled with poppy seeds. These dishes may be accompanied with *daal makhani* (a special lentil preparation) and *raita*, or with chutney and pickles.

Seafood Specialties. Fish dishes, famous in Bengal, are cooked in a number of ways: *macher jhol* (fish stew), *macher jhal* (fish with mustard seed), *bekti* (fried or grilled fish), and *Hilsa,* (smoked fish). A typical dish of Bengal is *chingri malai* (prawns cooked with coconut and spices). This region is particularly known for its sweet dishes, such as *Sandesh* and *rassogullas*, which are made with cottage cheese, and *misti doi* which is made with yogurt.

Sweet-and-Sour Cooking. Sweet-and-sour vegetarian dishes are preferred in western India. Maharash-trian and Gujarati cooking involves sprouted lentils and subtle spicing, and *Dhokla* and *paav bhaaji* are the most popular dishes in this region. *Dhokla* is a steamed savory cake made of yogurt and lentils. Ethnic Parsi food in Bombay and Portuguese-influenced food in Goa are two other unique features of western Indian food.

Among Indian fried food, the favorites are *puris* (fried round bread), *pakoras* (fried vegetables with a coat of chick-pea flour, similar to Japanese Tempura), and its South Indian cousin *bondas*. Usually *ghee* and various types of oils (mustard, peanut, coconut, sesame) are used for frying purposes. Among the snacks, the most popular are *samosas*, triangular egg rolls stuffed with potatoes and peas and mixed with spices, which are served in most Indian restaurants.

Customs and Table Manners. Religion, seasons, and other factors play important roles in dictating menus in homes and in restaurants. Hindus usually do not eat beef, whereas Muslims do not eat pork. During the winter season, the greatest delicacies one can enjoy in Punjab and its countryside restaurants are *sarson kaa saag* (mustard greens cooked with a special regional touch) and *makkai/baajre ki roti* (baked Indian corn bread).

Food in India is not only meant for worldly pleasures but also has a strong affinity with some spiritual values, which have affected the presentation of food and the style of eating. Eating with the hands is preferred over the use of forks and knives; if, however, it is impossible to eat some food items with the hands, then the spoon is used. The use of the hands in the traditional Indian setting is considered sacred. The use of forks and knives is associated with Western values, and, in some circles, it is still considered inauspicious to bring unnecessary intervention between human beings and food. It should be added that eating with the hands involves complex rules; the use of the right hand is almost a requirement, and the eloquent use of fingers is still considered a skill, which distinguishes a cultured person from a rustic individual. In the traditional setting, the connoisseur sits on the floor with legs crossed. In urban areas, however, and Western-style restaurants, it is perfectly acceptable to eat Indian food with forks and knives while seated on a chair at a table.

Indian restaurants attempt to offer a wide range of food that reflects the diversity of Indian cuisine. Indian restaurants usually specialize in either vegetarian or nonvegetarian cooking. National and international chains such as Siddhartha, Madras, and Woodlands specialize in South Indian vegetarian food. Notable among the nonvegetarian chains are The Bombay Palace, Gaylord, and Akbar. Tandoor and seafood cooking are offered by Indian restaurants specializing in non-vegetarian cuisine.—*Shobha K. Bhatia*

SUGGESTED READINGS: • Dalal, Tarla. *Low Calorie Healthy Cooking*. Bombay, India: Sanjay, 1989. • Devi, Yamuna. *The Best of Lord Krishna's Cuisine: Favorite Recipes from the Art of Indian Vegetarian Cooking*. California: Bala Books, 1991. • Jaffrey, Madhur. *Madhur Jaffrey's World-of-the-East Vegetarian Cooking*. New York: Alfred A. Knopf, 1981. • Kirchner, Bharati. *The Healthy Cuisine of India: Recipes from the Bengal Region*. Los Angeles: Lowell House, 1992. • Ray, Sumana. *Indian Regional Cooking*. New Jersey: Chartwell Books, 1986.

Indochina: Term used in the nineteenth century by Europeans to designate that region (mainland Southeast Asia) lying between India and China. When the French gradually began controlling the area consisting of CAMBODIA, VIETNAM, and LAOS in the second half of the nineteenth century, they called the area "French Indochina." Indochina is located on the eastern side of mainland Southeast Asia. It consists of mountains, the Red and Mekong river valleys, the Great Lake of Cambodia, and an extensive coastline. The region has a great complexity of peoples, cultures, and languages. Major political struggles in the twentieth century have led to great population shifts within it and abroad. Since 1975, hundreds of thousands of its people have come to the United States.

Geography. Indochina is bounded to the north by the People's Republic of China, to the east by the South China Sea, to the south by the Gulf of Thailand, and to the west by Thailand (plus a small part of Myanmar). Its core is a mountain range (the Long Mountains, Truong Son) stretching south from China. The Red River Delta of northern Vietnam (Tonkin) and the narrow plains of central Vietnam (Annam) lie to its east. To the west is the Mekong River valley, also coming out of China. The upper Mekong region has Laos mainly on the east bank and northeast Thailand on the west. Farther south the Mekong flows through Cambodia to its delta in southern Vietnam (Cochinchina). The Tonle Sap connects the Great Lake of central Cambodia with the Mekong. The long Vietnamese coast stretches from China to Cambodia. Indochina's major cities are HANOI, Hue, and HO CHI MINH CITY (in northern, central, and southern Vietnam, respectively); PHNOM PENH (in Cambodia); and Vientiane (in Laos).

Peoples and Cultures. A great variety of peoples and languages exist in Indochina, one of the most diverse regions on earth. Speakers of the Sino-Tibetan, Austroasiatic, Tai-Kadai, and Austronesian language families live here, as do adherents of the major world belief systems: Mahayana and Theravada BUDDHISM, HINDUISM, ISLAM, CONFUCIANISM, and Catholic and Protestant Christianity.

On the lowlands and along the coasts live the major ethnic groups: Vietnamese, KHMER, and Lao, predominantly raising wet rice and fishing. The homeland of the Mahayana Buddhist and Confucian Vietnamese civilization is in the Red River Delta of northern Vietnam around Hanoi. In the past four centuries, Vietnamese moved south down the coast into what is now central and southern Vietnam. In the center, they encountered and scattered the CHAM, an Austronesian, Hindu-Buddhist civilization, whose remnants either settled along the coast or adopted Islam and moved west into Cambodia. In the south, the Vietnamese permeated among the resident Khmer and gradually gained political control. With French contacts and then colonial control, about 10 percent of the Vietnamese population became Roman Catholic.

The Khmer civilization of CAMBODIA is centered inland around the Great Lake. North up the Mekong lie the Lao principalities, related by language and culture to the Thai state on the other side of the river. The two peoples, the older Khmer and the more recent Lao, both Theravada Buddhists, live between two major powers, Vietnam and Thailand, and through the nineteenth century suffered from the competition between them.

The Chinese commercial population thrived in the cities, particularly under the French. From southeast China, those in Vietnam are predominantly Cantonese, while those in Cambodia (and elsewhere in Southeast Asia) are Teochiu from Fujian Province. Another major lowland minority are the Muslim Cham in Cambodia and southwest Vietnam. The other significant minorities are the MONTAGNARDS, highlanders living mainly on dry rice and hunting and gathering. The north of Laos and Vietnam has Tai-speaking peoples such as the TAI DAM (or Black Tai) and the Nung, related linguistically to the Thai and the Lao. At higher elevations are the HMONG and the MIEN. The south (the central highlands of Vietnam, the Bolovens plateau of southern Laos, and the highlands of Cambodia) has a great variety of Mon-Khmer tribal groups. The central highlands of Vietnam, close to the old Cham empire, also has Austronesian speakers, such as the Rhade and the Jarai. Many highlanders accepted Protestantism from American missionaries.

Politics. Twentieth century politics has caused shifts in these ethnic groups. During the colonial period, the French encouraged fragmentation among the three parts of Vietnam, consolidation in Cambodia and Laos, and separation of lowlanders and highlanders. The French also favored Chinese urban dwellers and the growth of the Catholic church. Nationalist movements against the colonial power, mainly Vietnamese, were disruptive before World War II (1939-1945) and afterward began to succeed. The Indochinese Communist Party, under Ho Chi Minh, led the August Revolution of 1945 and fought the French in the First Indochina

Rice harvest, Bac Thai Province, Vietnam. (Eric Crystal)

War (1946-1954), which ended at Dien Bien Phu and Geneva. Vietnam was split at the seventeenth parallel, and pro-French Vietnamese, mainly Catholics, together with anti-Communist nationalists and the Nung, almost a million people, moved south. There, these northerners joined a variety of southerners, including Vietnamese Buddhist sects such as the Cao Dai and the Hoa Hao, to set up a republic, supported by the United States.

The government in Saigon tried to control the countryside and the mountains of the south. The Second Indochina War (1954-1975) saw heavy fighting and bombing drive many into government-controlled areas, especially the cities. Highland populations were greatly affected by both sides. Gradually, the warfare pushed into Laos and Cambodia, especially as the Ho Chi Minh Trail from north Vietnam to the south was developed down the eastern edges of these two countries. The fall of the Cambodian leader Norodom Sihanouk led to savage fighting between the army and the KHMER ROUGE, while the Pathet Lao kept pressure on Vientiane. American forces encouraged highlanders, particularly the Hmong of Laos, against the Communists.

The fall of both Saigon and Phnom Penh and the Pathet Lao takeover of Vientiane in 1975 led to large population movements. Anti-Communist Vietnamese fled their country, mainly to the United States. Hmong and Lao moved to northeast Thailand. The Khmer Rouge horrors (1975-1978) were perpetrated upon Khmer, Cham, and Chinese. Many fled Cambodia during the Vietnamese invasion of late 1978. Internal economic policies and external troubles with China led thousands of Chinese to flee Vietnam after 1978. Hundreds of thousands of Vietnamese followed them. The result of American involvement in Indochina has been the resettlement of more than a million refugees from Vietnam, Laos, and Cambodia in the United States.—*John K. Whitmore*

SUGGESTED READINGS: • Adams, Nina S., and Alfred W. McCoy, eds. *Laos: War and Revolution*. New York: Harper & Row, 1970. • Chandler, David P. *The Tragedy of Cambodian History: Politics, War, and Revolution Since 1945*. New Haven, Conn.: Yale University Press, 1991. • Karnow, Stanley. *Vietnam: A History*. New York: Viking Press, 1983. • Keyes, Charles F. *The Golden Peninsula: Culture and Adaptation in Mainland Southeast Asia*. New York: Macmillan, 1977. • Kunstadter, Peter, ed. *Southeast Asian Tribes, Minorities, and Nations*. 2 vols. Princeton, N.J.: Princeton University Press, 1967. • Whitmore,

John K., ed. *An Introduction to Indochinese History, Culture, Language, and Life*. Ann Arbor: Center for South and Southeast Asian Studies, University of Michigan, 1979.

Indochina Migration and Refugee Assistance Act of 1975: U.S. legislation enacted by Congress to broaden the definition of "refugee." Under the earlier Migration and Refugee Assistance Act of 1962, the term encompassed only those people fleeing from countries in the Western Hemisphere. Under the new amendment, the term included people emigrating from Vietnam, Laos, and Cambodia.

The 1975 law appropriated $455 million toward the costs of assisting the settlement of Indochinese refugees. All funds, however, were to be discontinued after September, 1977. Meanwhile, the president was empowered to continue to assist refugees from the countries listed above and to direct both funding and manpower into areas of the world where this purpose would be served.

Indonesia, Republic of: Country in Southeast Asia. A young nation in the midst of major social and economic development, Indonesia enjoys growing regional and worldwide prominence. Located between the Indian and Pacific Oceans, this archipelagic country is composed of nearly 13,700 islands that span a distance of more than three thousand miles. Altogether, the country is more than 741,000 square miles in size. With about 185 million citizens inhabiting its twenty-seven provinces (as of 1992), Indonesia is one of the most populated countries on earth. Jakarta is its capital city.

At various points in their history, the Indonesian islands were home to ancient maritime kingdoms, were crisscrossed by trade routes stretching to China, India, the Middle East, and Europe, and were subject to colonization by various foreign powers, in particular the Dutch. Throughout the centuries, foreign visitors have introduced new religions, ideologies, and customs to the region, which were then refashioned and adopted by local peoples. This process has contributed to Indonesia's uniqueness and has enhanced its cultural variety.

Indonesia's national motto, Unity of Diversity, was aptly chosen. Since declaring its independence from Dutch colonial rule on August 17, 1945, Indonesia has endeavored to foster harmony between the members of its diverse citizenry through five Principles of State (Pancasila), which emphasize cooperation and mutual

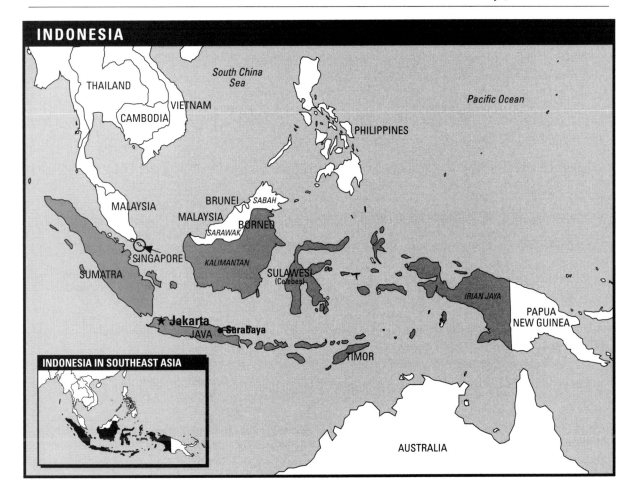

INDONESIA

THAILAND
South China Sea
VIETNAM
CAMBODIA
Pacific Ocean
PHILIPPINES
MALAYSIA
BRUNEI SABAH
MALAYSIA
BORNEO
SARAWAK
SINGAPORE
KALIMANTAN
SUMATRA
SULAWESI
(Celebes)
IRIAN JAYA
PAPUA NEW GUINEA
★ Jakarta Surabaya
JAVA
TIMOR
AUSTRALIA

INDONESIA IN SOUTHEAST ASIA

self-help. Members of more than three hundred ethnic groups coexist in Indonesia. Each has its own traditions and often its own language. To bridge the communication gap between its citizens, the state has adopted a national language, Indonesian, which is taught at school and used in everyday conversation outside the home. Almost all Indonesians are fluent in at least two languages, the language of their particular ethnic group and the national language.

Indonesia is also characterized by religious pluralism. Approximately 85 percent of Indonesians are adherents of Islam, but the government also recognizes Protestant and Catholic Christianity, Hinduism, and Buddhism as official religions. In addition, many Indonesians practice animism, which involves a belief in nature spirits and usually ancestor worship.

The government of Indonesia is popularly referred to as a Pancasila democracy. Much of its power is concentrated in the hands of top officials. The national parliament (Dewan Perwakilan Rakyat, or DPR) is composed of delegates elected by province. An even higher administrative body is the People's Consultative Assembly (Majelis Perwakilan Rakyat, or MPR), which is composed of DPR delegates as well as other elected and appointed members. The members of the MPR are responsible for electing the president, who serves a five-year, renewable term of office.

Indonesia remains a largely agricultural nation. While its primary crop is rice, it also encourages the planting of estate crops, including tea, coffee, rubber, and spices. At the same time, Indonesia ranks among the world's largest producers of petroleum products and liquefied natural gas. Indonesia also continues its efforts to industrialize. A growing number of multinational corporations operate factories in Indonesia, and participation in the world market has helped Indonesia to become better known throughout the world.

Inouye, Daniel Ken (b. Sept. 7, 1924, Honolulu, Territory of Hawaii): Politician. Daniel Inouye is the product of two very different cultures: those of Japan and the United States. He spoke Japanese before he learned to speak English, and he attended a Japanese school for two hours every day after his English-language public school let out.

Inouye was a high school senior when Japanese military forces attacked Pearl Harbor on December 7, 1941, and the shame he felt about what the Japanese had done reinforced his loyalty to the United States. After he graduated from high school in 1942, Inouye enlisted as a private in the 442ND REGIMENTAL COMBAT TEAM, the famous Japanese American unit that fought for the United States during World War II. He was promoted to second lieutenant in 1944 and served in Italy, where he lost his right arm fighting the Germans in 1945.

The loss of his arm meant that Inouye could not pursue the surgical career that had originally been his goal, so he decided to study law instead. In 1950, he graduated from the University of Hawaii, where he studied government and economics, and then he studied law at George Washington University Law School in Washington, D.C. He chose to study in Washington because he wanted to learn firsthand about government and politics. In 1952, Inouye graduated from law school, and in 1954, he began to practice law in Honolulu.

A dedicated Democrat, Inouye was elected to the Territorial House of Representatives (Hawaii was not yet a state) in 1954, where he served as majority leader for four years, and later he was elected to the Senate. After Hawaii gained its statehood in March of 1959, Inouye was elected as the Hawaiian member of the U.S. House of Representatives. He served two terms in the House and then was elected to the Senate.

Inouye was a strong supporter of the John F. Kennedy and Lyndon Johnson administrations, and he was a champion of civil rights legislation. Among other things, he introduced legislation intended to repeal the INTERNAL SECURITY ACT OF 1950, which had provided the legal basis for the establishment of internment camps for Japanese Americans during World War II. The act was repealed in 1971. In 1968, Inouye was honored by being chosen to deliver the keynote address at the Democratic National Convention. He served on the Senate Watergate Committee and was one of the first members of Congress to request that Richard M. Nixon resign the presidency.

In 1976, on the strength of his impressive performance on the Senate Watergate Committee, Inouye was appointed chairman of the Senate Select Committee on Intelligence. Eight years later, he became the chairman of the Select Committee on Secret Military

Portrait of Daniel Inouye against the backdrop of the flag of the 442nd Regimental Combat Team with which he fought during WWII. (Library of Congress)

Assistance to Iran and the Nicaraguan Opposition, which investigated the Iran-Contra episode. Later, Inouye took over the leadership of the Select Committee on Indian Affairs, the Appropriations Subcommittee on Defense, the Commerce Subcommittee on Communications, and the Senate Democratic Steering Committee.

Insular Cases (1901-1904): Group of U.S. Supreme Court rulings that defined the constitutional status of the country's island territories. The *Insular Cases* originated from the American victory against Spain in 1898 as well as the United States' appearance as a colonial power with foreign dependencies. Beginning in 1901 the Court decided how such possessions would be administered within the meaning of the Constitution.

Assuming an imperialist viewpoint, the Court perceived the new territories as subordinate lands that were owned by the United States but physically apart from it. Until these dependencies became incorporated or were supposed to be preparing for statehood status in the Union, their peoples were considered unincorporated and denied all the rights and privileges enjoyed by American citizens. While Hawaii and Alaska were designated as incorporated areas, the Philippines, Samoa, and Puerto Rico were classified as unincorporated.

Yet neither were unincorporated territories described as foreign nor were their export commodities regulated by U.S. tariff laws except for special congressional legislation. In fact lawmakers could levy such taxes as they wished. For example the Court ruled by a five-to-four margin that the Philippine Islands could not be considered alien lands in a constitutional sense and that Congress would have to act in order to prohibit tariff-free imports from such a possession.

The Court also clarified the meaning of fundamental rights as opposed to procedural rights. The former were made available to peoples who resided under the control of the United States, and the latter were granted to inhabitants of unincorporated provinces solely when the legislative branch so stated explicitly. In *Dorr v. United States* (1904), the Court decided by an eight-to-one vote that an editor of the *Manila Freedom* was not denied his constitutional right when placed on trial for libel without a jury in a federal court in the Philippine Islands. The Constitution was inapplicable, ruled the justices, since the Philippines was excluded from the United States, and therefore the idea of trial by jury was alien to the customs of its inhabitants, unless Congress so chose to require it.

Internal Security Act of 1950: U.S. legislation intended to impose the strictest control over the Communist Party and other subversive organizations in the United States. Also known as the McCarran Act, it was enacted in September, 1950, following China's fall to the Communists in 1949 and the outbreak of the Korean War in June, 1950. Several years before, all Eastern European countries had already fallen to the Communists. The act strengthened existing laws controlling espionage, sedition, and sabotage.

Under this act, both the Communist Party and its members were required to register with the attorney general of the United States. Failing to do so constituted a crime. Once registered, however, both party and members were subject to government harassment and prosecution. Members of the party were not permitted to hold any nonelective federal offices, nor were they allowed to hold any office in a labor union. They were also prohibited from applying for or using a United States passport. Furthermore, a Communist

alien (non-American national) who violated any provision of this act was subject to deportation. For the purpose of enforcing this act, Congress created the Subversive Activities Control Board. The board, the Un-American Activities Committees of Congress, and Senator Joseph R. McCarthy contributed to much of the witch hunting. A prominent rocket expert of Chinese descent, Qian Xuesen, left for China in the wake of McCarthyism.

The Internal Security Act raised serious constitutional questions, particularly regarding the First (freedom of speech and assembly) and Fifth (protection against self-incrimination) amendments. The Supreme Court declared the passport provision unconstitutional in 1964 as a violation of citizens' right to travel. In 1967, the Court struck down the registration requirement for the individuals on the ground of self-incrimination. The Subversive Activities Control Board was abolished in 1973. First with the relaxation of tension between the United States and the Soviet Union in the late 1980's, and then with the collapse of Communism in Soviet Union and Eastern Europe beginning in 1989, the Cold War finally came to an end.

International District: Nihonmachi or Japantown section of Seattle, Washington, originally established in 1891. Seattle was a primary port of entry for Japanese immigrants to the Pacific Northwest, and many newly arrived Issei settled in the waterfront district of the city. The Nihonmachi prospered as a result of income from Japanese-owned businesses, and, by the 1920's, the district boasted a Buddhist temple, a Japanese-language school, and several Japanese-owned theaters. As the district's Nisei population increased, James Sakamoto established the *Japanese American Courier*, one of the first English-language newspapers for Japanese Americans in the United States. The Seattle Progressive Citizen's League, founded in 1921, provided a support base that resulted in the organization of the national JAPANESE AMERICAN CITIZENS LEAGUE (JACL), which held its first national convention in Seattle in 1930. Evacuation orders handed down in April of 1942 forced the evacuation of most residents of the Nihonmachi, many of whom were held in the Puyallup Assembly Center before being relocated to the MINIDOKA relocation center in Idaho. After World War II, many Japanese Americans returned to Seattle, but the Japanese American population of the original district decreased from 7,000 in 1940 to some 5,800 in 1950 as the neighborhood experienced an influx of African American resi-

Headquarters of Hip Wah Hing, a Chinese association in the International District of Seattle, Washington. (Wing Luke Museum)

dents. The district began to attract attention during the 1960's and 1970's when a coalition of Asian Americans—including residents of Japanese, Chinese, and Filipino descent—protested full-scale redevelopment of the area and began to lobby for preservation of the houses, theaters, and other cultural landmarks in the Nihonmachi and neighboring Chinatown areas. These neighborhoods were renamed the International District to reflect the diverse nature of its Asian cultural heritage.

International Examiner (Seattle, Wash.): Semimonthly catering to the Asian American community. It is the oldest regularly published pan-Asian American newspaper in the United States. It aims to give voice to topics of concern to the Asian American community and to promote the unity of all Asian and Pacific Islander groups. Its accomplishments include the education of its readers about their history, culture, social issues, and civil rights.

The newspaper, which published its first issue in June, 1974, was started by two Seattle businessmen from the INTERNATIONAL DISTRICT who wanted to

upgrade the area's image and promote its small businesses. The first issues, four-pages long and monthly, contained extensive coverage of local businesses. In 1975, the Alaska Cannery Workers Association (ACWA) purchased the paper. The April, 1975, issue reflected the priorities of the new ownership, featuring greater coverage of social and political issues affecting Seattle's pan-Asian International District. In 1976, the paper expanded to an eight-page monthly publication. The scope of coverage also expanded to include cultural aspects of the International District, including arts, history, current political trends, and the need for bilingual services and programs serving the elderly and the new immigrants.

In 1978, the paper acquired its own nonprofit, tax-exempt corporation status, and began functioning under a board of directors that reflected the diverse interests of Asian and Pacific Islander community groups. In 1981, the paper went to a semimonthly publication format with an accompanying increase in the number of regularly paid staff. This change allowed the paper to expand its scope of coverage to include issues of interest to Asian Americans throughout the United

States. By 1992, the paper had become a twelve- to thirty-two-page semimonthly publication with special sections focusing on arts, book reviews, college and university student concerns, and in-depth coverage of developments in the International District. It continued to give voice to the culture and concerns of the Asian American community, not only in Seattle but also nationally.

International Hotel controversy (1968-1977): Decade-long struggle that centered on whether Asian immigrant workers were entitled to low-rent housing (the International Hotel) in a city area targeted for redevelopment. The International Hotel was a three-story, 155-room residential hotel located in downtown San Francisco that offered low-rent housing to elderly Filipino and Chinese men and to working-class families. From the first eviction notice, issued in 1968, to the actual eviction on August 4, 1977, the hotel represented a battle between real estate developers on one side and the Filipino and Chinese community on the other.

With the expansion of the city's financial district, Manilatown was rapidly disappearing. The International Hotel was one of the last remnants. Hotel tenants paid between fifty and eighty-five dollars per month rent for single rooms, with shared toilets, showers, and cooking facilities on each floor. Retired single elderly Filipino and Chinese men who worked as seamen, busboys, and Alaskan cannery workers lived at the hotel. Others were transient tenants. The hotel functioned as a microcommunity offering a support system to those who lived there.

Four Seas Investment Corporation, an overseas-based company, bought the hotel from Walter Shorenstein in 1972. Four Seas purchased the surrounding land parcels and planned to replace the hotel with a commercial structure combining condominiums, retail space, and underground parking. Four Seas' development plans, however, met stiff opposition from the International Hotel Tenants Association. Tenants refused to move and called on the community for support.

Thousands of activists throughout the Bay Area responded to the tenants' call for support. The International Hotel Support Committee was formed and sponsored regular demonstrations. Demands were made to the city government to purchase the hotel from Four Seas using the power of "eminent domain." Under then-Mayor George Moscone the city refused to pay the $1.3 million price tag on the hotel and rejected the plan.

On the morning of August 4, 1977, four hundred police and sheriff's deputies on horseback or in fire trucks and police vehicles confronted the two thousand supporters who had formed a human barricade in front of the hotel, and they carried out the eviction order. As of March of 1993 the site of the International Hotel was still an excavated hole in the ground as negotiations continued between developers, community land use advocates, and the City Redevelopment Agency.

International Longshoremen's and Warehousemen's Union, Local 142: Hawaii's largest local labor union, with a membership in 1993 of about twenty-eight thousand. The International Longshoremen's and Warehousemen's Union (ILWU) has evolved and diversified from its original involvement in longshoring and agriculture to conform to the changing economy of the islands. Membership in Local 142 is divided roughly into four industrial groups: longshoring, agriculture (sugar, pineapple, macadamia nuts), tourism, and miscellaneous industries. The union operates statewide.

When the ILWU began to organize in Hawaii in the 1930's, the economy was dominated by a group of interlocking corporations known as the "BIG FIVE." The sugar-pineapple planters had maintained control over the labor force by importing different nationality groups and positioning them against one another in opposition. Union disputes with employers were conducted along ethnic lines and were rarely if ever successful.

The ILWU mitigated this ethnic obstacle, expressing its view in its constitution: "First to unite in one organization, regardless of religion, race, creed, color, political affiliation or nationality, all workers. . . ."

The Japanese attack on Pearl Harbor, December 7, 1941, and the imposition of martial law in Hawaii the same day, ended union organization on the plantations.

Later the ILWU sent organizers into the sugar and pineapple plantations. By 1944 organizing was completed. The ILWU won numerous National Labor Relations Board (NLRB) elections covering thousands of sugar workers.

In the same year, an ILWU-led Congress of Industrial Organizations (CIO) Political Action Committee (PAC) elected a majority of labor-backed candidates in the lower house of the Hawaii Territorial Legislature and enough candidates in the upper house to prevent vetoes of labor-sponsored bills. A number of antilabor laws were repealed and a "Little Wagner

Act" was passed to extend NLRB coverage to agricultural workers.

In 1954 the ILWU-led PAC helped the Democrats win a majority in both houses of the Territorial Legislature, marking the beginning of the enactment of a whole body of social legislation.

Successful industry-wide strikes in sugar in 1946, in pineapple in 1947, and in longshoring in 1949 established the ILWU in those major industries. The ILWU then went on to organize the remaining Big Five subsidiaries.

International Society for Krishna Consciousness

(ISKCON): Indian religious movement. Known popularly as the Hare Krishnas, the ISKCON is the first group to propagate successfully a traditional form of Indian devotional religion (*bhakti*) in the West. Though the Hare Krishnas are sometimes erroneously identified as a modern "cult," their practices of ecstatic chanting and worship descend directly from the teachings of Caitanya Mahaprabhu, a revered Bengali saint, and have theological roots in the epics and *Puranas* of ancient and medieval India.

The teachings of the ISKCON were brought to New York City in the mid-1960's by A. C. Bhaktivedanta Swami Prabhupada. Prabhupada found his first converts among the bohemian artists, musicians, and spiritual seekers who would soon be labeled "hippies." The young followers were drawn to the devotional chanting of the Hare Krishna mantra and to the absolute values and philosophical certainty that Prabhupada offered. Prabhupada gradually trained his devotees, eventually numbering in the thousands worldwide, to follow the rules of dress, hairstyle, diet, etiquette, and hygiene that govern the daily lives of pious brahmins in India. Devotees' exotic appearance and behavior led to the ISKCON being charged with "brainwashing." These charges, however, are largely dismissed by psychologists and scholars of religion.

The Hare Krishnas believe that the soul is eternal, indestructible, and immaterial. The supreme lord of the universe is Krsna, and the proper goal of human life is to render service to krsna (in his various forms), going to death to live forever with him on his spiritual planet. Selected Indian sacred texts are interpreted literally, which gives the ISKCON a fundamentalist tone; however, some ISKCON practices, for example initiating Western devotees as brahmins, are seen as liberal innovations by Indian traditionalists.

In the 1970's, the Hare Krishnas were attacked for their aggressive, and sometimes illegal, fund-raising practices. After the death of their founder, abuses grew as the eleven American and European devotees appointed as leaders struggled to cope with the responsibilities and temptations of power. Several leaders, or gurus, deviated seriously from ISKCON teachings and were excommunicated. By the late 1970's, ISKCON's greatest growth was in Latin America and India, although during the 1980's many Indians living in the West joined the ISKCON, a trend likely to continue.

Internment camps: U.S. government camps under the administration of the Justice Department used to house Japanese American evacuees during World War II. The internment camps were distinct from the RELOCATION CENTERS administered by the WAR RELOCATION AUTHORITY (WRA). The government reserved the internment camps for those individuals deemed to be the most dangerous to the United States and the war effort. (See JAPANESE AMERICAN INTERNMENT.)

Interracial marriage: Intermarriage, among the various Asian American peoples and between Asians and non-Asians, is a major factor shaping Asian American society.

Rates and Reasons. Rates of Asian outmarriage have varied enormously, depending on the Asian ethnic group, time, part of the country, generation removed from Asia, and other factors. Among the first-generation immigrants of almost all Asian groups, intermarriage was typically low—perhaps two to five percent among the first wave of Chinese, Japanese, and Korean immigrants in the late nineteenth and early twentieth centuries. Since these were all predominantly male populations and few Asian women were available, one might have expected quite a few Asian immigrant men to look for non-Asian mates. Yet several factors pushed this development in the opposite direction. In most Western states where Asians lived in large numbers, there were laws forbidding marriages between white people and people of color. Even where interracial unions were not formally outlawed, they were still opposed and punished by the white majority. In addition, intermarriages were infrequent because the Chinese, Korean, and Japanese immigrant men did not have much social contact with people of other races; these men tended to work in racially segregated crews and live in segregated camps and neighborhoods.

The main factor inhibiting intermarriage, however, was not white racism or lack of contact but Asian reluctance to marry people who were not from their own country. Most Asian immigrant men saw themselves as sojourners rather than settlers. Many already had wives waiting for them back in Korea, Japan, or China. Moreover, both Japanese and Korean cultures stressed the purity of their peoples and the undesirability of mixture. Chinese and Japanese national ideologies projected a sense of the superiority of their own peoples and the inferiorities of all others (including each other). Among the immigrants, the disposition against outmarriage even barred union with people who were from other parts of their homelands: Someone from Canton was loathe to marry a person from Shanghai, and a person from Hiroshima felt uncomfortable marrying someone from Okinawa. The gossip system in each ethnic community kept track of people who associated with foreigners and punished and ostracized the small number of intermarriers and their children. This meant that intermarriages were even less common in places such as the West Coast, where there were strong ethnic communities, than further east, where the Asian population was more spread out and surveillance and ostracism were harder to maintain.

The exceptions to the low rate of intermarriage were the Chinese immigrants in Hawaii, Filipinos there and on the U.S. mainland, and the small community of Asian Indians in California. In each of these three cases, the rates of outmarriage were higher. In Hawaii, intermarriage was commonly accepted by many groups (the Japanese were the major holdout from the islands' ethnic mixing). Many Chinese immigrant men married Hawaiian women in the early years of the plantation system, and most Chinese in the state today are part Hawaiian, as are most Hawaiians part Chinese. In rural California, Asian Indian men mixed with Mexican women—the outmarriage rate was almost 100 percent. Under American law, Filipinos throughout the United States were treated somewhat differently than other Asians, and as many as 90 percent of

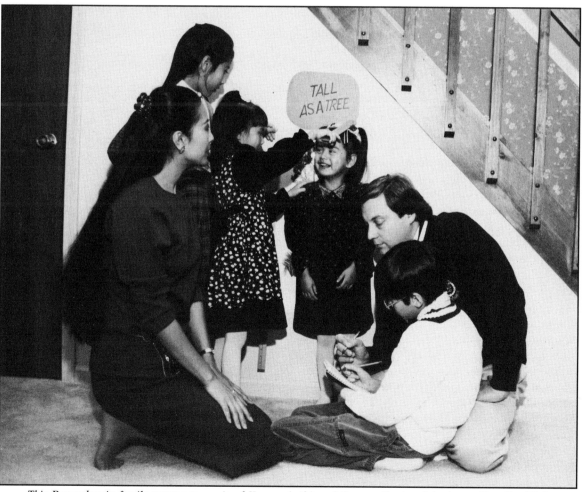

This Pennsylvania family represents a mix of Korean (wife) and German (husband) heritage. (Don Franklin)

Rates of Asian Outmarriage

Group	Early Percentage	Later Percentage
Asian Indian	98% (1913-1949)	18% (1980)
Chinese	10% (1950's)	26% (1979)
Filipino	90% (1950's)	24% (1980)
Japanese	less than 5% (1920's)	50% (1980's)
Korean		18% (1980)
Vietnamese		12% (1980)

their marriages were to non-Filipinos. For these three groups, as for the others described above, in the first generation nearly all outmarriages were to non-Asians, not to members of other Asian nationalities. There was no notion of a pan-Asian ethnic identity.

Outmarriage increased at a moderate rate in the second generation—to perhaps ten percent by Nisei and nearly that by second-generation Chinese Americans. The barriers that whites erected against Asians were still strong in the 1930's and 1940's when these generations came to marriageable age, and the ethnic communities were still adamantly opposed to intermarriage. The Nisei began to lose the intranational regional distinctions that had shaped immigrant marriage choices, but such boundaries continued to circumscribe Chinese American marital choices. Intermarriage continued at a high rate in the Filipino second generation; most of the second generation was mixed, and they tended to marry outside the community. The other Asian groups did not have a substantial second generation until much later.

Intermarriage rates by American-born Asians increased sharply in the 1960's and exploded in the 1970's and 1980's. This can be explained by the confluence of three social forces. First, there was a general increase in racial tolerance in American society as a result of the Civil Rights movement and other postwar developments. As it became less acceptable for Caucasians to express racism openly, and as Asians and other people of color took more prominent public roles, Asians became more attractive to Caucasians as potential marriage partners. Second, the Chinese, Japanese, and Filipino populations reached the third and fourth generations. For all American immigrant groups, there was a large increase in outmarriage during those generations. Third, the Asian American movement intentionally blurred the lines between the different Asian nationalities. Individuals began to think of themselves as Asians in addition to thinking of themselves as Japanese, Chinese, or whatever. These decades saw a sharp increase in intermarriages between the various Asian nationalities.

Gender Issues. One striking feature of outmarriage by nearly all Asian groups is the lopsided gender pattern. Among first-generation Filipinos, Asian Indians, or Chinese in Hawaii, the population was so overwhelmingly male that outmarriage was almost exclusively by males. Yet in the second generation and beyond, in all the Asian Groups, Asian women outdistanced Asian men when it came to outmarriage. This has much to do with the images of Asian women and men put forth by white American popular culture, such as movies and advertising. Asian men were cast in such media as either sinister or unmanly, while Asian women were pictured as submissive and alluring. The gender disparity also had something to do with family pressures, at least among the Confucian-influenced cultures such as Japan, China, Korea, and Vietnam. Frequently, families expected much of their sons, es-

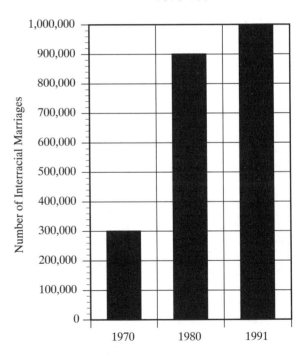

Interracial Marriage in the U.S., 1970-1991

Number of Interracial Marriages (y-axis, 0 to 1,000,000)
Years: 1970, 1980, 1991

Percent of Interracial Marriages, 1991
All Americans: 2%
Asian Americans: 17%

Source: William O'Hare, "America's Minorities: The Demographics of Diversity." *Population Bulletin* vol. 47, no. 4 (1992).

Founders of Downtown Community TV in Chinatown, New York, Keiko Tsuno and husband Jon Alpert. (Hazel Hankin)

pecially the eldest. Pressure to avoid intermarriage or any other embarrassing situation was stronger for young men than for their sisters. There is some evidence that, under more moderate racial ideologies from the 1970's onward, the gender disparity began to decline.

The outmarriage rates for third- and fourth-generation members of the older Asian groups are higher than those of more recent Asian immigrants. The numbers were lower for Vietnamese and the second wave of Koreans, because these were recent immigrants, but they were higher than they had been for Chinese or Japanese fifty or seventy-five years before. And more Vietnamese and Korean women married out than did men from these groups.

Intermarriage and Ethnic Identity. Intermarriage has implications for Asian American ethnic identities. Some groups that have fairly high rates of outmarriage—Chinese, Koreans, and Asian Indians, for example—continue to maintain highly distinct group identities and cohesion. In each of these three groups, population numbers and culture are reinforced by

Japanese American Outmarriage in Los Angeles County, 1924-1972

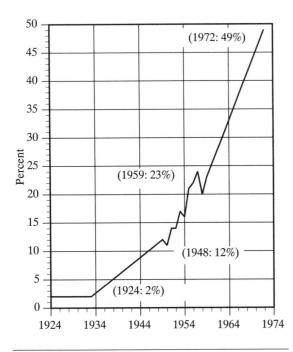

Percent

(1972: 49%)

(1959: 23%)

(1948: 12%)

(1924: 2%)

Source: Harry H. L. Kitano and Roger Daniels, *Asian Americans: Emerging Minorities.* Englewood Cliffs, N.J.: Prentice Hall, 1988.

regular infusions of new immigrants. For such groups, a high rate of outmarriage is not incompatible with continued ethnic vitality. For Filipinos the picture is more mixed, because the population is more mixed; The early immigrants heavily intermarried, and the post-1965 wave of immigrants seems to be intermarrying at a higher rate than some other Asian groups. For Japanese Americans the situation is more extreme—only a minority of Japanese Americans after the 1980's were marrying other Japanese Americans. These particular individuals were a fourth-generation group with only small numbers of new immigrants entering the country. The future of this group's ethnic identity in America seemed in doubt.

For many Japanese Americans (and potentially for other Asian groups), by the 1990's the survival of the group seemed to depend on finding a way to incorporate the large numbers of part-Asians into their community life. Some Asians pursued a different tactic toward group vitality: redefining the group in pan-Asian terms. This embrace of a larger Asian American identity was broadly political and not designed specifically to cope with the difficulties posed by intermarriage, but it had intermarriage implications. In fact, it implied an increase in what would formerly have been termed intermarriage, as some Chinese, Koreans, Vietnamese, and so forth began to define themselves as members of one group and to marry one another. The 1980's and 1990's also saw the rise of an assertive new set of Asian Americans: people of mixed ancestry, who asserted their right to inclusion as Asian Americans; as members of their various Asian nationality groups; and at the same time as possessors of other, non-Asian ethnic identities.—*Paul Spickard*

SUGGESTED READINGS: • Cretser, Gary A., and Joseph J. Leon, eds. *Intermarriage in the United States.* New York: Haworth, 1982. • Kikumura, Akemi, and Harry H. L. Kitano. "Interracial Marriage: A Picture of the Japanese Americans." *Journal of Social Issues* 29 (1973): 67-82. • Kitano, Harry H. L., Wai-Tsang Yeung, and Lynn Chai. "Asian-American Interracial Marriage." *Journal of Marriage and the Family* 46 (February, 1984): 179-190. • Lee, Sharon M., and Keiko Yamanaka. "Patterns of Asian American Intermarriage and Marital Assimilation." *Journal of Comparative Family Studies* 21 (Summer, 1990): 287-305. • Leonard, Karen Isaksen. *Making Ethnic Choices: California's Punjabi Mexican Americans.* Philadelphia: Temple University Press, 1992. • Posadas, Barbara. "Crossed Boundaries in Interracial Chicago: Pilipino American Families since 1925."

Amerasia Journal 8, no. 2 (1981): 31-52. • Root, Maria P. P., ed. *Racially Mixed People in America*. Newbury Park, Calif.: Sage Publications, 1992. • Shinagawa, Larry Hajime, and Gin Yong Pang. "Intraethnic, Interethnic, and Interracial Marriages Among Asian Americans in California, 1980." *Berkeley Journal of Sociology* 33 (1988): 95-114. • Spickard, Paul R. *Mixed Blood: Intermarriage and Ethnic Identity in Twentieth-Century America*. Madison: University of Wisconsin Press, 1989. • Sung, Betty Lee. "Chinese American Intermarriage." *Journal of Comparative Family Studies* 21 (Autumn, 1990): 337.

Inu: Japanese term literally meaning "dog." In the camps where Japanese Americans were interned by the U.S. government during World War II, *inu* was a term of abuse applied to internees who were perceived by some of their fellow internees to be informants or collaborators or, more loosely, too complaisant in dealing with the camp authorities. Suspected *inu* were frequently harassed and beaten; personal and political agendas often played a part in such accusations.

Irons, Peter (b. Aug. 11, 1940, Salem, Mass.): Scholar and activist. An attorney, political scientist, and constitutional scholar who has combined a distinguished academic career with a lifelong commitment to political activism, he played a leading role in the landmark *coram nobis* cases, *Korematsu v. United States* (1983) and *Hirabayashi v. United States* (1988). Irons is the author of *Justice at War: The Story of the Japanese American Internment Camps* (1983); in addition, he edited *Justice Delayed: The Record of the Japanese American Internment Camps* (1988), which presents transcripts from the cases.

The son of a nuclear engineer who resigned in protest from his job with the Atomic Energy Commission after J. Robert Oppenheimer was denied a security clearance in 1954, Irons was educated at Antioch College (B.A., 1966), Boston University (Ph.D., 1973), and Harvard Law School (J.D., 1988). He served more than two years in prison for resisting the draft during the Vietnam War. (Ultimately his conviction was overturned, and he received a pardon from President Gerald Ford.) Irons is a professor of political science at the University of California, San Diego, where he also directs the Earl Warren Bill of Rights Project.

Irons provoked controversy in 1993 with the publication of *May It Please the Court*, a book and six audiocassettes, edited by Irons and Stephanie Guitton, consisting of recordings of open arguments in twenty-

Peter Irons played a leading role in the landmark cases Korematsu v. United States *and* Hirabayashi v. United States. (Asian Week)

three key Supreme Court cases. By releasing this material, Irons violated a routine agreement he had signed to obtain access to the tapes in the National Archives. Some scholars were sharply critical of Irons, while others applauded his courage, contending that the restrictions on the tapes—which were taken from open sessions, not closed deliberations—are illegitimate.

Irwin, Robert Walker (1844, Copenhagen, Denmark—1929): Government official and immigration recruiting agent. Irwin was active in business ventures in Japan, served as Hawaiian consul-general to Japan, and was one of the main architects of the systematic immigration of Japanese to Hawaii.

Irwin was the son of William Irwin, a former member of the U.S. House of Representatives, who was then serving as U.S. Charge d'Affaires in Copenhagen. Robert Irwin first went to Japan in 1866 as an agent for the PACIFIC MAIL STEAMSHIP COMPANY in Yokohama, which was beginning regular transpacific shipping service. Later (in 1873) he helped some prominent Japanese businessmen establish Senshu Kaisha, an import-export company, and through acquaintances met Inoue Kaoru, who later served as Japan's minister of finance and foreign minister.

Senshu Kaisha underwent various changes, finally emerging as Mitsui Bussan Kaisha (Mitsui Trading Company) in 1876. Irwin was the main figure in foreign trade, which centered around rice, silk, and tea in exports and around ammunition, wool, and fertilizer in imports. In 1882 Irwin married Takechi Iki.

Irwin first became involved in Hawaiian affairs when he was appointed Hawaiian consul-general to Japan in 1880, partly because of his close connections with (now foreign minister) Inoue. Irwin later helped work out arrangements between the governments of Hawaii and Japan for new Japanese immigrants to go to Hawaii, mainly to supply the great need of the American sugar planters for a reliable source of workers for their rapidly expanding enterprise.

The Mitsui Company helped Irwin with recruitment in Yamaguchi (Inoue's native prefecture), sending employees there to recruit, as well as sending supplies to the immigrants in Hawaii, handling their financial affairs, and running immigration advertising in a company newspaper.

Irwin meticulously attended to nearly every detail of the immigration process, personally accompanying the first ship carrying Japanese immigrants to Hawaii in 1885. In 1893 he returned to Hawaii to try to resolve problems that had arisen with the immigration system and to work to obtain for Japanese immigrants the same rights and privileges accorded to other foreigners in Hawaii. In his promotion of enlightened racial attitudes toward Asians, Irwin was several decades ahead of his time.

Irwin, Wallace (1876, Oneida, N.Y.—Feb. 14, 1959): Journalist, humorist, and novelist. Under the pseudonym "Hashimura Togo," Irwin published a series of letters in *Collier's Weekly*. The letters, composed in fractured English and recounting stereotypical Japanese behaviors, were supposedly the work of a Japanese American schoolboy. They became so popular that several books of these letters also appeared. Irwin also wrote *Seed of the Sun* (1921), a novel about Japan's efforts to make California one of its colonies. The work was cited by anti-Japanese movement agitators as evidence of the need for exclusion.

Irwin attended Stanford University from 1896 to 1899 before being employed by the *San Francisco Examiner* and later the *Overland Monthly*. He began writing the Togo letters while living in New York in the early 1900's. *Letters of a Japanese Schoolboy* (1909) was the first of the three volumes published.

Ishigo, Estelle (July 15, 1899, Oakland, Calif.—Feb., 1989): She studied art in Los Angeles, where she met Arthur Shigeharu Ishigo, a San Francisco-born Nisei and aspiring actor, whom she married on August 28, 1929. In order to stay with her husband when people of Japanese descent were being forcibly relocated away from the American West Coast, she became one of the few Caucasians who voluntarily submitted to internment. At HEART MOUNTAIN relocation center, she did hundreds of sketches and water color paintings of life behind barbed wire. She was the subject of an Academy Award-winning documentary, *Days of Waiting* (1990), directed by Steven OKAZAKI.

Islam: Major world religion. Islam was developed by Muhammad ibn Abdulla in Arabia in the seventh century. Predicated on Judeo-Christian traditions—indeed, the *Injil* (Gospel) of Jesus, the *Zabur* (Psalms) of David, and the *Torah* of Moses as well as the messages of Muhammad were believed to have been derived from the same divine writing, *Mother of the Books*—Islam is seen by its adherents as the completion or fulfillment of those traditions. An uncompromisingly monotheistic faith that united and strengthened the Arab world and vastly enriched Arab culture, Islam brought a large part of the globe under its sway.

Indeed, while Arabia was the cradle of Islam, and while in the minds of many people Islam is associated primarily if not exclusively with the Middle East, fewer than 200 million of the world's approximately one billion Muslims are Arabs. There are more Muslims in Central Asia, South Asia, and Southeast Asia than in any other region. Estimates of the number of Muslims in the United States vary considerably. The *1993 Britannica Book of the Year*, for example, estimates the 1992 Muslim population of North America at about 2.85 million, while many American Muslims and scholars of Islam offer much higher estimates. According to John Esposito, for example, in a chapter on Islam in *World Religions in America: An Introduction* (1994), edited by Jacob Neusner, "There are five million Muslims now living in America."

Muhammad. According to tradition, Muhammad (b. August 20, 570 C.E.) probably began his encounters with the Divine in 610 and by 613 had become become convinced that he was God's messenger (*rasul Allah*). For ten years he spoke publicly about his visions and revelations. *Il-Allah*, he said, was One and Almighty, who had sent Muhammad as His *nabi* (Prophet) to warn of the impending Day of Judgment, when the faithful would be praised and the unbelievers punished.

Chinese Muslims participate in a parade on Muslim World Day in New York City. (Frances M. Roberts)

Initially most residents of Mecca, except his own family and some people among the lower classes, paid little attention to Muhammad and even held him in some contempt. In fact, after the death of his wife and his uncle in 619, Muhammad faced the wrath of his own clan and was forced to solicit support from the people of the nearby town, al-Taif, though to no effect. In 622 he emigrated to Yathrib (some two hundred miles to the north of Mecca). The emigration of the Prophet is called the *Hijra* ("severing of relationship"), and thereafter Yathrib came to be known as the City (*madina*) of the Prophet, Madinat al-Nabi. The formation of the Muslim community (*ummah Muslimah*) dates to the year of the *Hijra*, as does the beginning of the Islamic lunar calendar. At Madina, Muhammad presided over a federation of nine clans, including that of the emigrants (*muhajirun*) from Mecca. By 630, Mecca and other parts of Arabia were conquered by the Muslims.

The Caliphate. Muhammad's death in 632 brought about the regime of the caliphs (*Khalifa rasul Allah*, "representative of God"). Under the first four "Rightly Guided Caliphs" (*al-Rashidun*)—Abu Bakr, Umar, Uthman, and Ali—from 632 to 661, Islam was spread by conquest as well as peaceful missionary work. During the period from 661 to 750, under the Umayyad caliphate (named after Umayyad Muawiya), with its headquarters in Damascus, the borders of the Islamic world extended to the Pyrenees in the west and the Indus River in the east.

The Abbasid caliphate (begun by Abdulla and named after his father, Abbas), with its headquarters in Baghdad (from 762), ruled over a vastly enlarged *ummah*, comprising diverse ethnic, linguistic, and cultural groups that had converted to Islam. The Abbasid centuries (750-1258) were marked by the greatest achievements of Islamic civilization. The Abbasid caliphate spawned a number of protocaliphates during c. 850-c. 1055: the Umayyads in Spain, the Alids in Morocco, the Kharijites (a schismatic purist sect of Baghdad) in eastern Algeria, and the Daylamites and the Buyids in Iran. The Abbasid caliphate was destroyed by the Monguls in 1258. The name of the caliphate survived as a religious institution, inspiring

Muslims pray at a mosque in India. (Library of Congress)

the Khilaphat movement in the Middle East and South Asia after World War I.

A second wave of military conquest was begun in the fourteenth century by Turkic peoples who had migrated from central Asia to Iran and Asia Minor and been progressively Islamicized over a period of several centuries. One of these groups, the Ottomans (Osmanli), destroyed Byzantine Constantinople in 1453 and established Muslim rule in large areas of southeastern Europe, maintaining it until well into the nineteenth century. The Islamic invasion of Europe left important vestigial groups of Muslims in Spain, Sicily, Bosnia, Bulgaria, and Albania.

From the eighteenth century onward, the Western forces of nationalism shattered the traditional concept of Islamic community and unity and provoked rebellion against Ottoman oppression as well as against European imperialism. On the one hand, a consciousness of national identity led to the concept of *ummah Arabiyyah*, "the Arab nation." On the other hand, the foundation of sovereign states after World War I together with social and political modernization seemed to destroy the idealized unity of Islamic culture, leading to the development of the Muslim World League (*al-rabita-al-Islamiyyah*) and of fundamentalism that harked back to the authentic Islamic bases of government and society.

Sunni and Shia. A significant division within the *ummah* occurred during the caliphate of Ali (656-661), cousin as well as son-in-law of the Prophet. As one of "The People of the House," Ali and his party (*shiat Ali*) claimed that the Prophet had mandated his cousin to be his successor. Ali was eventually assassinated by a secessionist group, the Kharijites ("those who went out"), and his partisans came to be known as *Shia* (also Shii or Shiite). The majority of the early Muslims, led by Ali's rival Muawiya, the Umayyad governor of Syria, became *ahl al-Sunnah*, the *Sunnis*, claiming to be the depositories of correct and orthodox practice and theory. Today, about 85 percent of the world's Muslims are Sunni, while Shia make up about 15 percent.

The Quran. According to tradition, the Quran ("recitation"), initially a written report of Muhammad's revelations, was systematically and finally written down during the caliphate of Uthman (644-656). It comprises 114 *suras*, which vary in length from a few *ayats* (verses) to more than two hundred. Muhammad's familiarity with the Christians of Syria and the Jews of Madina led him to regard Islam as the legitimate continuation of these earlier monotheistic faiths. Not only does the Quran acknowledge that "our God and your God is one" (29.46), but also Islam incorporated some religious practices of pre-Islamic Arabia.

The Quran, the fundamental Book of Islam, con-

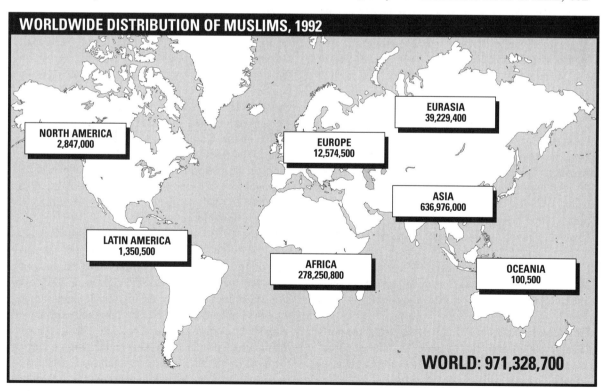

WORLDWIDE DISTRIBUTION OF MUSLIMS, 1992

NORTH AMERICA
2,847,000

LATIN AMERICA
1,350,500

EUROPE
12,574,500

EURASIA
39,229,400

AFRICA
278,250,800

ASIA
636,976,000

OCEANIA
100,500

WORLD: 971,328,700

tains, *inter alia*, detailed instructions for the Islamic way of life, the so-called Five Pillars of Islam: *shahada* (confession of faith), *salat* (five daily ritual prayers), *zakat* (almsgiving), *sawm* (daytime fasting in Ramadan), and *hajj* (pilgrimage to Mecca). There are two additional "pillars"—*ibada* (service to or worship of God) and *jihad* (exertion in the way of God). The *ummah* is held together and regulated by the *Sharia* ("the way" or law, derived from the Quran), *sunnah* (practices), and *hadith* (*logia*) of the Prophet.

The Quran teaches that God the Creator is One, and that angels carry out His decisions and communicate with humans through the Prophets. It often enjoins the faithful to reflect on God's providential designs and signs in cosmic, natural, animal, and human affairs. It informs all people of their *fitra* (true nature) as created beings, which should enable them to submit and be thankful to God and thus realize not only the divine *tawhid* (unity) but a unified *ummah* as well. Those who reject God by committing *shirk* (idolatry or a habitual pursuit of material pleasure and power), reject their *fitra* also. According to the Quran, "there is no compulsion in religion" simply because "the straight path of righteousness has been made clearly distinct from the crooked path" (2.256). Though a person can freely reject his or her *fitra*, this freedom thus exercised will lead to that Day of Judgment, "a Day on which human beings would be like so many scattered moths, . . . [and] he whose deeds are lighter in the balance will have the Abyss for abode" (101.4-9).—*Narasingha P. Sil*

SUGGESTED READINGS: • Ali, Ahmed, tr. *Al-Quran: A Contemporary Translation*. 1984. Rev. ed. Princeton, N.J.: Princeton University Press, 1988. • Endress, Gerhard. *An Introduction to Islam*. Translated by Carole Hillenbrand. New York: Columbia University Press, 1988. • Esposito, John. "Islam." In *World Religions in America: An Introduction*, edited by Jacob Neusner. Louisville, Ky.: Westminster/John Knox Press, 1994. • Maududi, Abul Ala. *Fundamentals of Islam*. 1975. 7th ed. Lahore, Pakistan: Islamic Publications, 1986. • Rahman, Fazlur. *Islam*. 1966. 2d ed. Chicago: University of Chicago Press, 1979. • Schimmel, Annemarie. *Islam: An Introduction*. Albany: State University of New York Press, 1992. • Watt, William Montgomery. *Muhammad, Prophet and Statesman*. 1961. Reprint. Oxford: Oxford University Press, 1964.

Islamabad: Capital of PAKISTAN, situated in the north. "Islamabad" means "city of Islam" or "city of peace." About 350 square miles in area, the city contained a population estimated at 360,000 in 1983.

Issei: The first generation of Japanese immigrants, particularly to countries such as the United States, Canada, and Brazil. The vast majority of Japanese immigrants came to Hawaii and the West Coast between 1885 and 1924. The GENTLEMEN'S AGREEMENT (1907-1908) greatly reduced immigration of Japanese laborers; during the same period, however, many wives and children of immigrants were allowed to enter. Much more severe restrictions on Japanese immigration were imposed by the IMMIGRATION ACT OF 1924, with significant long-term consequences for the evolution of the Japanese American community.

The History of Immigration. The early immigrants were overwhelmingly male and came mostly from Hiroshima, Yamaguchi, Fukuoka, Kumamoto and other southwestern prefectures in Japan. The new Meiji state implemented land taxes and draft systems that placed a heavy burden on the farmers. These increasing economic pressures forced small farmers to leave their farmland or to become tenants of the landlords. After 1885, when the Meiji government changed its policy toward the emigration of contract laborers in response to the plight of farmers, a sizable number of young males emigrated to the United States to start a new life. Many worked on plantations in Hawaii. Others became laborers in the agricultural, railroad, and mining industries on the West Coast, with long hours and low wages.

Between 1886 and 1899 approximately 80,000 Japanese immigrated, and by 1900 they formed nearly 40 percent of the population of Hawaii, constituting the single largest ethnic group in the islands. A large number of women, including picture brides, immigrated to Hawaii and the mainland. This infusion of women encouraged the Issei to settle down permanently in the United States rather than returning to Japan. The Issei women worked alongside their husbands in agricultural labor or small family businesses. Although by 1920 the Japanese population exceeded 100,000 on the mainland, Japanese Americans remained a tiny minority.

By the 1930's the Issei had established their economic status in small businesses and in labor-intensive agriculture. Despite their contribution to the economy, however, they were denied the right to U.S. citizenship. In order to survive in this hostile environment, the Issei built a cohesive ethnic community for mutual support. Issei from the same prefecture formed a *kenjinkai*, which provided financial and emotional support for noncitizens who were exempted from social welfare benefits. The Issei founded churches, Buddhist

Issei in the U.S., Selected Characteristics, 1900-1920

Residence

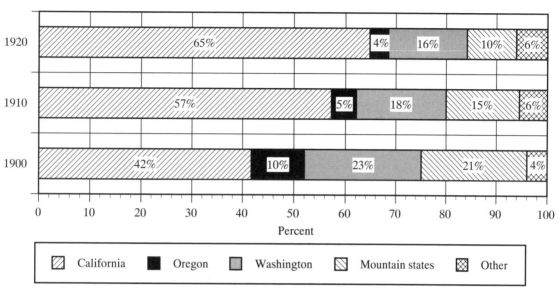

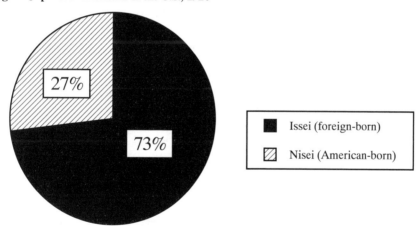

Percentage of Japanese Americans in the U.S., 1920

Source: Roger Daniels, *Asian America: Chinese and Japanese in the United States Since 1850.* Seattle: University of Washington Press, 1988.

temples, community centers, and Japanese-language schools to transmit Japanese culture and language to their American-born children. The TANOMOSHI, rotating credit associations, helped the Issei to accumulate resources to start their own businesses. The Issei also organized job-related associations such as gardeners' associations or farmers' associations to aid newcomers, to fight against discrimination, and to protect their occupational interests. Women, who were often ex-

cluded from male-dominated organizations, formed *fujinkai*, women's associations for mutual exchange.

The Anti-Japanese Movement. From their arrival the Issei had to contend with prejudice and discrimination in which racial and economic motives were often intertwined. The efficiency and productivity of the Japanese in farming began to threaten American farmers. Beginning in 1913, California and a number of other states enacted ALIEN LAND LAWS to prevent Japanese from leasing and owning land. An organized anti-Japanese movement lobbied for immigration restrictions and other discriminatory legislation.

Since the Meiji government had implemented a universal primary education system, most Issei had an average of eight years of schooling. The Japanese immigrants were thus considerably well educated and often were able to recognize exploitation. Contrary to the stereotype of submissive Japanese, the Issei successfully organized a series of strikes, often in alliance with other oppressed ethnic groups, when they faced racial discrimination.

Nevertheless, decades of discrimination—both blatant and subtle—created a climate in which injustice on a much larger scale became imaginable and even seemed quite reasonable to those who perpetrated or merely condoned it.

Wartime Internment. Following the Japanese attack on PEARL HARBOR in December, 1941, the entire Japanese population on the West Coast was uprooted and incarcerated in RELOCATION CENTERS. In all, about 120,000 Issei and Nisei—the first generation born in the United States—were interned. (The Japanese in Hawaii escaped mass internment.)

The internment had a devastating effect on the Issei, whose hard-earned houses, businesses, and land were confiscated all at one moment. Japanese-language schools, community centers, and Buddhist temples were closed and Japanese newspapers banned. In the camps, communal living conditions in crowded barracks made it difficult for Issei parents to socialize their children in the Japanese way. The Issei fathers lost their authority as their children became increasingly Americanized through social activities organized by churches and schools in the camps.

Further, the loyalty test included in questionnaires given to the internees in 1943 (see LOYALTY OATH) provoked considerable generational conflicts within families and the Japanese American community as a whole. Many Issei, because of their past experiences of racism, believed that answering no to the questions would keep family members together and prevent their sons from being drafted by the U.S. Army. By contrast, a majority of the Nisei tried to prove their loyalty or hoped to be allowed to leave the camps by answering yes.

In December, 1944, when persons of Japanese ancestry were allowed to return to the West Coast, many Issei were reluctant to leave the camps because of anxiety about confronting hostility in the outside world. They were too old to start their economic struggles all over again. Their old ethnic community, which had provided security, support, and meaning in their lives, was totally destroyed. The Issei lost economic power and authority in the community. Moreover, the large extended families characteristic of the Issei in the prewar years were gradually replaced by the smaller nuclear families of the Nisei. Thus, both the Issei-dominated patriarchal family structure and their ethnic communities eventually disappeared.

The Postwar Period. The McCARRAN-WALTER ACT OF 1952 granted the alien population the right to naturalization. At last, the Issei were able to obtain American citizenship. This increased the number of prospective Japanese voters and strengthened the political power of Japanese Americans.

Fearful of the reaction from the Caucasian community if they spoke out, most Issei tried to repress their traumatic memories of internment and the devastating losses they suffered. Beginning in the 1970's, however, as younger generations of Japanese Americans increasingly became aware of the profound injustice of the incarceration, a grass-roots redress movement developed. In 1980 the presidential COMMISSION ON WARTIME RELOCATION AND INTERNMENT OF CIVILIANS (CWRIC) was established to investigate the causes and outcomes of the wartime internment of Japanese Americans. It concluded that the internment was based on wartime hysteria and racial hostility and was therefore unjust. Finally, the CIVIL LIBERTIES ACT OF 1988 granted every surviving Japanese American internee $20,000 as compensation for the internment.

The Issei's legacy from old Japan—their work ethic, their family values, and their strong sense of obligation and commitment to the group—remains as the core of Japanese American culture, to be transmitted to future generations.—*Machiko Matsui*

SUGGESTED READINGS: • Daniels, Roger, Sandra C. Taylor, and Harry H. L. Kitano, eds. *Japanese Americans: From Relocation to Redress.* Rev. ed. Seattle: University of Washington Press, 1991. • Ichioka, Yuji. *The Issei: The World of the First Generation Japanese Immigrants, 1885-1924.* New York: Free Press, 1988. • Kimura, Yukiko. *Issei: Japanese Immigrants in Hawaii.* Honolulu: University of Hawaii Press, 1988. • O'Brien, David J., and Stephen S. Fujita. *The Japanese American Experience.* Bloomington: Indiana University Press, 1991. • Ogawa, Dennis M. *Kodomo No Tame Ni: For the Sake of the Children, the Japanese American Experience in Hawaii.* Honolulu: University of Hawaii Press, 1978. • Wilson, Robert A., and Bill Hosokawa. *East to America: A History of the*

Japanese in the United States. New York: William Morrow, 1980.

Itliong, Larry Dulay (Oct. 25, 1913—1976, Delano, Calif.): Labor organizer. Though his accomplishments have been overshadowed by those of Mexican American labor leader César Chávez, Itliong laid the foundations for the successful union movement among California's agricultural laborers. Aware of the poor wages and harsh conditions endured by his Filipino coworkers, Itliong convinced farmworkers in the early 1950's to act collectively to improve their situation. In 1956, he founded the Filipino Farm Labor Union (FFLU) and fought for the union's official recognition as a legitimate bargaining agent for farmworkers. Support from the powerful AFL-CIO paved the way for Itliong to organize field workers under the banner of AGRICULTURAL WORKERS ORGANIZING COMMITTEE (AWOC). Itliong's efforts succeeded when the AWOC initiated the Delano grape strike against grape growers in California's San Joaquin Valley in 1965. Members of the National Farm Workers Union (NFWU) led by Chávez joined the strike, and workers were elated when one of the largest vineyards in the valley recog-

Larry Itliong organized the Agricultural Workers Organizing Committee in California. (Filipinos: Forgotten Asian Americans by Fred Cordova)

nized Chávez's organization as the workers' sole bargaining agent. The AWOC and NFWU merged to form the United Farm Workers (UFW) Organizing Committee in 1966. Itliong served as vice president of the UFW until 1971, when he resigned in order to turn his attention to other activist causes.

Ito, Robert (b. July 2, 1931, Vancouver, British Columbia, Canada): Actor. A Japanese American, he gained his greatest exposure as supporting character Sam Fujiyama, a medical examiner in the NBC series *Quincy, M. E.* (1976-1983), an hour-long drama about a mystery-solving doctor of forensic medicine.

Iu Mien: Highland tribal minority group residing in the mountains of southern China and in the northern tier of Southeast Asia. In China the Iu Mien (Mien) are called "Yao," a term by which they are normally identified in anthropological literature published before 1975. The Mien are among the most highly Sinicized (subject to Chinese cultural influence) of all the tribal peoples of Southeast Asia. They have selectively adopted elements of Chinese writing, Taoist religious ritual, and social structure. Yet at the same time they have always struggled to maintain a unique cultural identity in the face of strong Chinese pressure for cultural assimilation. Contemporary Mien populations include approximately 2.5 million in China, 300,000 in Vietnam, 25,000 in Thailand, 25,000 in Laos, and a small but untallied number in Myanmar (formerly Burma). The Mien refugee population in the United States in 1993 is estimated at approximately 15,000.

The Mien reside in some of the most geographically inaccessible regions of Asia. Most of their villages are located far from roadways, schools, hospitals, or government services of any kind. Of the several nations of Asia where Mien refugees are found, Laos is the most remote. The only landlocked nation in Southeast Asia, Laos (which has a population of about four million) is the poorest country in the region and the most ethnically diverse nation in Southeast Asia. Sixty distinct ethnic groups are found in Laos, ranging from the majority Lao (54 percent) to groups such as the Mien, thought to comprise less than 2 percent of the population.

Mien Village Life. The Mien are traditionally a people adapted to life in remote regions. They are slash-and-burn farmers who carve farms out of tropical forests. As migratory agriculturalists, they traditionally chop down the forest, allow the cut wood to dry for several months where it has fallen, and then burn the dead trees and branches shortly before the onset of monsoon rains. The ash from the burned trees fertilizes the soil, enhancing productivity for the first year of planting. After a few years, Mien farmers must again move to a new area, opening up the forest and planting rice, corn, and vegetables on highland slopes.

Mien villages typically consist of twenty to forty houses, rarely exceeding populations of two hundred people in total. Mien farmers are intimately familiar with the surrounding jungle. Significant diet supplements are gathered from wild jungle produce; game is also taken, oftentimes with homemade, single-shot rifles. The Mien were the last of several tribal groups to migrate to Southeast Asia from China over the past five hundred years. They occupied the most inaccessible lands and the areas that were the most difficult to farm. The land available to the Mien consisted of parcels neglected by earlier migrating groups as too remote and too difficult to cultivate. Nevertheless, the Mien are among the most successful of highland Southeast Asian farmers, acute in the prediction of weather conditions, diligent and knowledgeable in the planting and production of crops, and successful in establishing viable satellite villages.

Mien in Modern History. Ancient Chinese annals dating to the Tang Dynasty more than one thousand years ago make reference to Yao (Mien) minority villages on the periphery of Chinese civilization. When France moved to establish a colonial presence in Cambodia, Laos, and Vietnam in the mid-nineteenth century, the Mien first came into limited contact with the Western world. After World War II (1939-1945), some Mien were recruited by the French to join in the French effort to retain control of Laos and Vietnam by force of arms.

In 1958 and 1959, American secret agents were sent to northern Laos to recruit tribal operatives. The Mien were the first of the highland peoples to commit to Central Intelligence Agency (CIA) operations in the area, accepting weapons, training, and guidance from a small group of Americans inserted deep into the Laotian hinterland. Mien special-operations groups conducted cross-border reconnaissance missions in Yunnan Province, China. The most adept Mien soldiers were provided advanced training at U.S. bases in Thailand, forming the core of a force that engaged the Communist Pathet Lao army in northern Laos. American support for the Mien in this struggle extended from 1958 through 1975. During this time, the Mien were forced to evacuate their traditional Laotian homeland

in the Nam Tha and Muong Sing areas, rallying to more secure government-controlled regions near the Mekong River.

Mien Refugees in the United States. As a result of their contributions to the U.S. war effort in Indochina (1958-1975), Mien residents of Laos were left in a vulnerable position after the United States withdrew from the region in early 1975. Mien villagers speak a separate language, wear a distinct folk costume, practice a different religion, and reside in easily identifiable villages. The Mien were universally loyal to the defeated Royal Lao Government, allied closely to the American government. As allies of the defeated side in the Laotian civil conflict, the Mien were subject to surveillance, harassment, and persecution as communist forces consolidated their administration in Vientiane, the capital of Laos.

In 1975, many Mien began to flee from Laos, crossing the Mekong River border dividing the kingdom of Thailand from the newly established Communist regime, the Lao People's Democratic Republic. Perhaps as many as thirty thousand Mien fled Laos between 1975 and 1985. Some found safe haven and a new life in remote Mien villages within Thailand, escaping periodic sweeps by Thai border police. Most Mien, however, were brought to refugee camps administered by the United Nations (UN). The camps became overcrowded as more and more highland refugees from Laos fled in the wake of the American withdrawal and the increasingly bitter conflicts between the new regime and its erstwhile enemies.

Although a handful of Mien leaders and their families were brought to the West Coast of the United States in 1976 and 1977, it is apparent that the U.S. government at first hesitated to begin a mass transfer of Mien villagers to the United States. The Thai government, however, threatened to force Laotian and Cambodian refugees pouring across its borders back into their homeland by military means unless they were quickly accepted for resettlement by second countries of asylum. Between 1978 and 1981, at least ten thousand Mien were transported to the United States, most to the West Coast. Never in U.S. immigration history had so many people from so remote a country with so little preparation been so quickly transferred to U.S. shores.

Adaptation Issues. Mien communities in the United States are concentrated in California. The largest Mien settlement is in Sacramento, thought in 1993 to number approximately three thousand. Nearby in the vicinity of San Francisco reside another three thousand

Mien American man completes work on a ritual drum, Oakland, California, 1981. (Eric Crystal)

Mien baby wears cap showing traditional needlework, Oakland, California, 1984. (Eric Crystal)

Mien. Adaptation to life in the United States has been difficult for multigenerational Mien families. Older people have become increasingly isolated. Unable to speak English, drive, or become productively employed, many Mien elders have become homebound. Middle-aged Mien refugees have adapted selectively. Some have found stable employment, purchased homes, and begun the transition to becoming a first generation of Mien Americans; others have remained, after a decade, dependent on transfer payments and increasingly marginalized within American society. A broad and widening culture gap separates young Mien Americans, either born or largely educated in the United States, from their parents and grandparents, who have spent most of their lives in highland Southeast Asian farming communities. Some Mien young people have excelled in school, enrolled in four-year colleges and universities, and entered the professional workforce. Others, acceding to parental wishes, have married early, dropped out of high school, and remained partially or permanently unemployed.

The Iu Mien are the most traditionalist of the Southeast Asian refugees to have been resettled in the United States since 1975. They have brought with them their strong kinship system and family values, their traditional religious beliefs, their intricate arts of embroidery and silver-jewelry making, and their concern for the maintenance and sustenance of their unique highland village tradition. Only time will tell whether this small, geographically concentrated refugee community will successfully negotiate a stable and prosperous future as a new component of Asian America.—*Eric Crystal*

SUGGESTED READINGS: • Butler-Diaz, Jacqueline. *Yao Design of Northern Thailand.* Rev. ed. Bangkok, Thailand: The Siam Society, 1981. • Crystal, E., and K. Saepharn. "Highland Southeast Asian Community and Culture in a California Context." In *Minority Cultures of Laos,* edited by Judy Lewis. Rancho Cordova, Calif.: Southeast Asia Community Resource Center, Folsom Cordova Unified School District, 1992. • Lemoine, Jacques. *Yao Ceremonial Paintings.* Bangkok, Thailand: White Lotus, 1982. • *Moving Mountains.* Video. Feather & Fin Productions, 1991.

J

JACL. *See* **Japanese American Citizens League**

Jade magazine: One of the first glossy Asian American magazines, published from 1974 until 1984.

Jainism: Indian philosophy and religion. The Jains fascinate many in the West, perhaps because their strict asceticism stands in sharp contrast to materialistic notions of comfort and progress. Though they constitute less than 1 percent of India's population, the Jains have been surprisingly influential in the modern world, especially through their teachings on *ahimsa* (nonviolence), which were brought to the global public by Mahatma GANDHI and Martin Luther King, Jr.

History. Western scholars attribute the founding of the Jain religion to Vardhamana Mahavira (a title meaning "Great Hero"), a northeast Indian prince of the sixth century B.C.E. Traditional Jain sources, however, claim that Mahavira simply reformed and systematized the teachings of an earlier group of ascetics known as the Nirgranthas. According to Jain sources, Mahavira was a young prince with a wife and daughter when he renounced his possessions, becoming a forest-dwelling ascetic. After practicing severe self-denial for twelve years, he became omniscient and enlightened, a "Jina" (Conqueror) and a "Tirthankara" (ford maker), one who had rediscovered the path to salvation and was capable of leading others to it. Mahavira taught for thirty years and was quite successful as a religious leader, before performing his final austerity: starving himself to death.

In the centuries following Mahavira's death, the Jain movement spread into eastern and northwestern India. Its stern teachings of self-denial and moral restraint appealed mostly to monks and nuns, especially since salvation was thought to be impossible for lay followers. The two main divisions of the Jain faith developed at this time; the Digambaras and Shvetambaras split over disagreements concerning monastic practice and the spiritual status of women, though they later became separated geographically as well.

In the early centuries of the medieval era, the Jains received support from several Indian dynasties and experienced corresponding periods of growth and cultural influence. The rules for lay members were developed as the movement made converts among the masses and began to rely upon the support of the growing Jain community. By the twelfth century, however, Jain expansion was curtailed by competition from Hindu devotional movements and ISLAM. In the modern period, the Jain religion is largely passed on within families; conversion is possible but not common.

Doctrines. Jain doctrines are based on logic and experience, and they explicitly reject the Vedic teachings that define Hindu "orthodoxy," though many traditional Indian concepts and practices are found in modified form in the religion. The doctrines of the Jains have remained remarkably constant over time; the two major Jain sects agree on nearly all points of doctrine, differing mostly on minor practices and on the scriptures that they accept.

The Jains believe that the universe is eternal and uncreated, passing through cycles of six hundred million years, each cycle comprising a period of decline followed by a time of improvement. At the beginning of each period, human beings are huge, moral, and long lived; at the end of the process of decline, they are slow-witted dwarfs, living short, brutish lives. In each period, there are twenty-four Tirthankaras; Mahavira was the last in the modern period, for humanity is currently about forth thousand years from the lowest point of decline. When human beings reach the bottom, the world will gradually begin to improve; after another forty thousand years, things will be back to the present level. In shape, the universe resembles an enormous human body. The modern world is at the waist, graded heavens are above, and hells are underneath. Gods are believed to exist, but they have no influence over the evolution of souls.

Like the universe, souls (*jivas*) are eternal and uncreated. All souls are essentially alike, omniscient and ecstatic, though they differ in their degree of entanglement in matter. Jains attribute *jivas* to natural objects. KARMA is understood by Jains to be a subtle form of matter that clings to the *jiva*, obscures its naturally blissful omniscience, and quite literally weighs it down, trapping it in the cycle of reincarnation. Enlightenment, the ultimate goal of the Jain religion, is achieved when all traces of *karma* have been worn off the *jiva* and it shines with its natural ecstatic omniscience. Then, when released by death of the body, the *jiva* will rise to the top of the universe, where it will reside for eternity in self-sufficient bliss. Most Jains believe that only male ascetics are capable of being liberated. Lay followers and nuns hope to earn rebirth as monks.

Practices. Study, meditation, fasting, and self-denial all serve to eliminate the deposits of KARMA, past, present, and future. The "three jewels"—right faith, right knowledge, and right conduct—provide the intellectual and ethical underpinnings for Jain spiritual life. Since travel stimulates desires, most Jains avoid pleasure trips; the first instance in recorded history when a Jain monk left India was in 1970. The most pernicious *karma* comes from killing, so virtually all Jains are total vegetarians and take great care to avoid injuring any life, no matter how small. For this reason, Jains often sweep the ground before each step; they also wear gauze face masks to prevent the destruction of tiny insects and dust particles.

Over the centuries, Jain lay followers have adopted many of the ritual practices of their Hindu neighbors, even offering temple worship to images of the Tirthankaras and Jain saints—despite their belief that liberated souls do not care about, or interfere in, the modern world.

Modern Significance. There are several reasons why the Jains' influence is greater than their small numbers might suggest. From medieval times, Jains have taken great interest in literature, both sacred and secular. Merit was earned by copying and preserving ancient writings; many early Indian texts exist today only because of these efforts. Jains are still active in writing and publishing.

The practice of nonkilling (*ahimsa*) has led most Jains to abandon farming, taking up urban careers in business and manufacturing instead. This fact, coupled with their limiting of desires, has, somewhat paradoxically, made the Jains one of the wealthiest, best-educated groups in India. GANDHI's understanding of nonviolence was strongly influenced by the friendship and support he received from Jain industrialists.

Perhaps because they believe all souls are similar, the Jains have egalitarian tendencies that have led them to fund social welfare work, founding hospitals and clinics for animals as well as people.

Although some scholars have questioned whether the austere asceticism of the Jains can survive in affluent urban contexts, Jain vitality appeared strong in the 1980's. Westerners looking for models of ecological sanity are also finding inspiration in Jain teachings.—*Scott Lowe*

SUGGESTED READINGS: • Chitrabhanu, Gurudev

Shree. *Twelve Facets of Reality: The Jain Path to Freedom.* New York: Dodd, Mead, 1980. • Jaini, Padmanabh S. *The Jaina Path of Purification.* Berkeley: University of California Press, 1979. • Kumar, Acharya Sushil. *Song of the Soul.* Blairstown, N.J.: Siddhachalam, 1987. • Stevenson, Margaret. *The Heart of Jainism.* London: Oxford University Press, 1915.

Jaisohn, Philip (So Jae-pil; Oct. 28, 1866, South Cholla Province, Korea—Jan. 5, 1951, Philadelphia, Pa.?): Physician and activist for Korean independence. Born into a wealthy Korean family, So Jae-pil completed his early education in Seoul before being sent to Japan to receive military training. In 1884, he returned to Korea and participated in the short-lived Kapsin coup staged to reform the country's political leadership and throw off Japanese control. When the coup leaders were forced out of power, So fled to Japan before emigrating to the United States. Obtaining work as a delivery boy in San Francisco, So began to learn English in order to further his education. He eventually enrolled at Lafayette College in Pennsylvania before completing medical studies at Johns Hopkins Medical School in 1895.

After receiving his medical degree, So returned to Korea, where he became an adviser to King KOJONG, established the Independence Association to help organize those individuals who wished to free Korea from Japanese influence, and founded a newspaper called *Tongnip Sinmun* (*The Independent*). His newspaper was first printed in a Korean vernacular script known as HANGUL as well as in English and eventually was printed in separate language editions. So's paper was particularly known for its support of political reforms and social reforms, including the emancipation of Korean women. Many figures who later gained prominence in the independence movement, including Syngman RHEE, got their start as activists in So's Independence Association. Troubled by So's activities in stirring up opposition to its policies, the Korean government stopped publication of the paper, disbanded the Independence Association, and ordered the organization's members to be arrested.

In 1898, So fled to the United States and settled in Philadelphia. Sometime after his arrival, he was married to a young American woman, and he changed his name to Philip Jaisohn after becoming a naturalized citizen. Continuing his participation in the struggle for Korean independence, Jaisohn lent his leadership skills to the task of organizing support for this cause

Korean independence activist Syngman Rhee (shown here) once belonged to the nationalist coalition founded by Philip Jaisohn. (AP/Wide World Photos)

among Korean immigrants in the United States. In the wake of demonstrations held in Korea in 1919 (known as the MARCH FIRST MOVEMENT) and their brutal aftermath, Jaisohn called for a KOREAN LIBERTY CONGRESS to be held in Philadelphia's Independence Hall from April 14 through 16, 1919, to rally greater support for the independence movement among sympathizers in the United States. During the three-day congress, delegates passed a ten-point resolution that included the demand that the League of Nations recognize Korea as independent from Japan. After the congress adjourned, Jaisohn was appointed to publicize activities on behalf of independence through the Bureau of Korean Information. When Korea was officially liberated from Japanese rule at the conclusion of World War II, Jaisohn was invited to return to his homeland to serve as an adviser to American occupation forces from 1945 through 1948. After completing this assignment, he returned to the United States, where he died in 1951 at the age of eighty-four.

Jallianwala Bagh incident (April 13, 1919): Firing by British troops on Indian protesters, killing many of them. Jallianwala is a rectangular open space surrounded on three sides by building walls and located in a residential district of AMRITSAR in the PUNJAB. At this spot, an estimated 379 unarmed Indians were killed and 1,137 were wounded by the British troops. This incident is described in the report of the Hunter Committee, appointed to investigate it.

The passing of the notorious Rowlatt Act (named after its framer, Sir Sidney Rowlatt, and aimed against "seditious conspiracy" among Indian nationalists) on March 18, 1919, was followed in April by *hartal* (closure of all business enterprises) throughout India, under the aegis of Mahatma GANDHI's campaign of noncooperation with the British. The Amritsar *hartal* was particularly violent because of the arrest of two popular local leaders, and consequently some Britishers were assaulted and a few killed by the rioting mob.

The Punjab governor, Sir Michael O'Dwyer, called in Brigadier General Reginald Dyer, commander of the Jullunder Brigade, to restore order. On Sunday, April 13, Dyer banned all public gatherings in the city. Upon learning that an assembly of the people was scheduled in Jallianwala Bagh that afternoon, he marched his Gurkha and Baluchi force of some ninety riflemen and swordsmen across the only entrance to that walled field and ordered them to shoot, without a word of warning to the crowd of more than ten thousand men and women assembled there to celebrate a

Hindu festival and possibly to hold a peaceful demonstration demanding the release of their arrested leaders. The ten-minute firing resulted in 1,516 casualties

The massacre shocked even many moderate Indians and some British liberals. On May 30, Rabindranath TAGORE resigned the knighthood conferred upon him after he received the Nobel Prize in Literature in 1913. The atrocity left its perpetrator unrepentant. Testifying before the Hunter Committee, General Dyer acknowledged that "I could have dispersed them without firing . . . but I was going to punish them." The Jallianwala Bagh incident intensified the moral outrage as well as the determination of the Indian freedom fighters, now led relentlessly by Gandhi, who would liberate India a generation later.

Jan ken po: Japanese game for children using the hands to make the shapes of paper, rock, and scissors. It is played within the Japanese American community as well.

Jan Ken Po Gakko: Japanese American cultural enrichment program founded in 1976 to provide learning experiences to enable fourth-generation children to "take pride in themselves and their community, and to strengthen their self-esteem as Japanese Americans." This summer program, financed exclusively by parents and community donations, offers Japanese-language instruction; provides field trips to increase occupational career choices; and teaches Japanese philosophy and values through games, arts, and crafts.

Jang, Jon (b. Mar. 11, 1954, Calif.): Pianist and composer. A highly original composer and performer of avant-garde jazz, Jang has fused diverse musical traditions—particularly Asian and African American—in works that also reflect his political commitment.

Jang's father came to the United States from China at the age of eighteen. A chemical engineer with a doctorate from the University of Minnesota, he was killed in a plane crash in 1956. Jang grew up in Whittier and Palo Alto, California. He received a scholarship to attend Oberlin Conservatory in Ohio, where he received a bachelor's degree in music.

Among his many compositions are *Tiananmen*, a piece for jazz orchestra which premiered on June 4, 1992, the third anniversary of the TIANANMEN SQUARE INCIDENT, and *Concerto for Jazz Ensemble and Taiko (Reparations Now!)*, which reflects on the INTERNMENT of Japanese Americans during World War II and the eventual triumph of the REDRESS MOVEMENT; it is available on Jang's album *Self Defense* (1992). Jang's other albums include *Jang* (1982), *Are You Chinese or Charlie Chan?* (1983), *Jangle Bells* (1988), and *Never Give Up!* (1989). As the leader of the Pan Asian Arkestra, he has toured the United States, Canada, and Europe. A fuller account of Jang's life and work can be found in Wei-hua Zhang's "Fred Ho and Jon Jang: Profiles of Two Chinese American Jazz Musicians," *Chinese America: History and Perspectives* (1994): 175-199.

Jao, Frank (b. June 15, 1949, Hai Phong, North Vietnam): Real estate developer. Regarded as the developer of Little Saigon in Westminster, California, he served as a translator in the South Vietnamese army and came to the United States in 1975 to escape the Communist regime. He has chaired the Bridgecreek Group, a company he founded in 1978, and has developed more than $250 million worth of commercial and residential properties, including his biggest development, Little Saigon's Asian Garden Mall.

Japan: An island nation that lies off the eastern edge of the Asian continent. It is surrounded on the east by the Pacific Ocean, on the south by the East China Sea, on the west by the Sea of Japan, and on the north by the Sea of Okhotsk. The country's 145,883 square miles of total land area contained a 1992 population of about 124.4 million people. The capital and largest city of Japan is TOKYO, on the island on HONSHU.

Geography. The four main islands of Japan are HONSHU, KYUSHU, Shikoku, and HOKKAIDO. Because of the warm Black Current that bathes the eastern coast of Japan, the climate is temperate. Other geographic features of Japan include abundant rainfall, mountainous terrain, sparsity of arable land, and lack of natural resources such as such as petroleum and iron ore.

Japan also lacks grazing land except in the northern

Mount Fuji, at an elevation of 12,385 feet the tallest peak in Japan. Its beauty and spiritual significance have made it the subject of countless poems, songs, and paintings throughout the centuries. Fuji is located about sixty miles west of Tokyo. (Japan Air Lines)

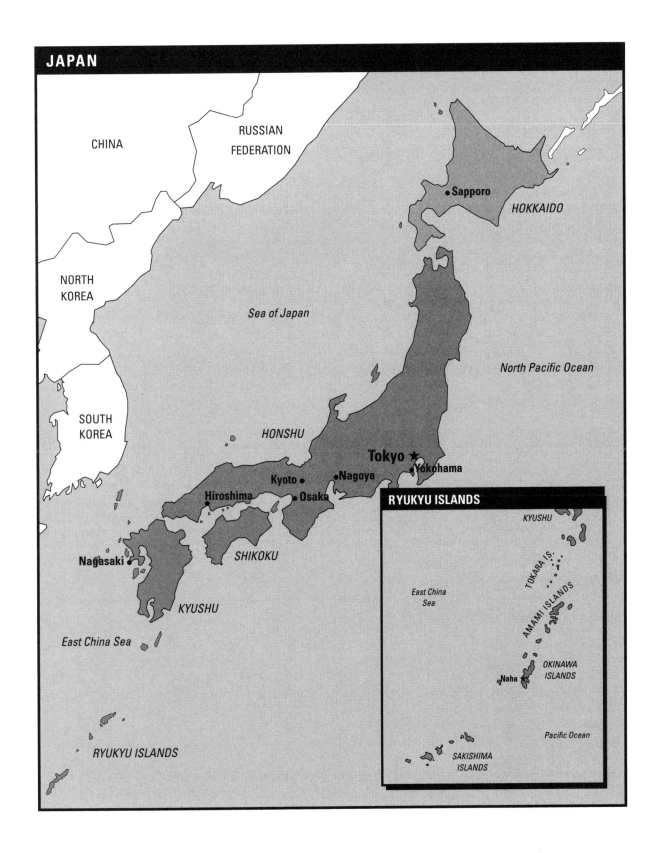

JAPAN

CHINA

RUSSIAN
FEDERATION

Sapporo

HOKKAIDO

NORTH
KOREA

Sea of Japan

North Pacific Ocean

SOUTH
KOREA

HONSHU

Tokyo ★

Kyoto

Nagoya

Yokohama

Hiroshima

Osaka

Nagasaki

SHIKOKU

KYUSHU

East China Sea

RYUKYU ISLANDS

RYUKYU ISLANDS

KYUSHU

TOKARA IS.

East China
Sea

AMAMI ISLANDS

OKINAWA
ISLANDS

Naha

Pacific Ocean

SAKISHIMA
ISLANDS

Kamakura Daibutsu (Great Buddha) towers in calm repose inside the walls of the Kotokuin Temple about thirty miles southwest of Tokyo. At almost forty feet high and weighing some ninety-three tons, the bronze statue is Japan's second largest Buddha figure. The edifice that once housed the figure was destroyed by a tidal wave in 1495. (Japan Air Lines)

island of Hokkaido, and while this has limited Japan's ability to produce sufficient meat for its people, it has made Japan a seafaring nation in search of fish. Japan is one of the world's leading fishing nations, and the seas provide the major source of protein for the Japanese people.

The combination of the seas and the nearby mountains and the sharp contrast between the two have blessed Japan with many scenic spots, which are often small in scale and intimate, giving the impression that the islands have a special affinity with nature.

People of Japan. The Japanese belong to the Mongoloid people. Yet the origins of the Japanese are still unclear. Based on archaeological evidence, ethnological studies, and historical records, scholars conjecture that various peoples came to Japan at different times and from different regions in the prehistoric period. The earliest settlers were the Ainu, who were proto-Caucasoids, characterized by their hairiness of face and body. They used to inhabit most of the Japanese islands but gradually lost their land to later peoples and were eventually vanquished and assimilated by them. As a result, only a small number of Ainu have survived, and while most of them live in the northern island of HOKKAIDO, they are in danger of losing their distinctive cultural heritage.

In general there are two major strains of Japanese ethnicity: the northern and the southern. Japan's geographic proximity to the Korean peninsula strongly suggests the early flow of peoples from northeast Asia to Japan by way of KOREA. These peoples represent the so-called northern strain. The southern strain consists of peoples from such regions as south China, Southeast Asia, and the South Pacific. There is no clear-cut answer to explain why these peoples came to Japan, but once they arrived, regardless of their diverse origins, they blended with one another, becoming a culturally homogeneous people.

History of Early Japan. The development of civilization in Japan was profoundly influenced by its neighbor, CHINA, the center of one of the oldest civilizations in the world. Many advanced ideas from China were introduced to Japan by way of KOREA, and Chinese sources provide the most reliable account of early Japan. According to official Chinese records, Japan is described as the land of Wa (Wo, in Chinese), consisting of some one hundred clans (*uji*). Some of these clan leaders had been in contact with China as early as the first century C.E. The Chinese records also mention the existence of primitive religious practices that involved extensive nature worship. Later these practices

were combined with the worship of the emperor as the descendant of the sun goddess and came to be known as SHINTO (way of the gods). Shinto worship was to remain an essential feature of Japanese religious practices until the arrival of BUDDHISM in the mid-sixth century C.E.

While the higher civilization of China influenced the Japanese in the development of arts and literature, politically it fostered the trend toward unification and made the Japanese accept the Chinese concept of centralized bureaucracy and a permanent capital. As a result, Japan by 710 C.E. had founded a permanent capital, Nara, with its own elaborate but cumbersome central government.

The Chinese influence remained strong until the mid-tenth century, when the Japanese, having absorbed Chinese civilization, began to develop a culture of their own, one reflecting the highly refined lifestyle of the aristocratic society in the capital.

Development of Feudalism. Japan's experimentation with the Chinese concept of centralized bureaucracy was superficial at best. Social conditions in the two countries were so different that in the late twelfth century, Japan broke away from the Chinese political pattern and developed a feudal system ruled by a leader of the warrior (samurai) class, who received the title of "SHOGUN" (generalissimo) from the emperor. Essentially it was a system of military dictatorship in which the warrior class constituted the ruling elite. The shogun confirmed the title and distributed the fiefs (land) to his retainers (vassals) and in turn demanded unswerving loyalty from them.

Feudalism in Japan lasted for almost seven hundred years, until about the mid-nineteenth century, when the TOKUGAWA shogunate, the last of the feudal regimes, collapsed in 1867.

Modern Japan. The MEIJI RESTORATION (1868-1912) marks the beginning of modern Japan. A small group of young, ambitious, and able former warriors of lower rank from the southwestern fiefs assumed leadership in 1868 and began to modernize Japan. By the end of the nineteenth century, Japan had become a modern nation-state; having defeated China in the Sino-Japanese War (1894-1895), Japan also became an imperialist power in possession of colonies abroad.

The first half of the twentieth century saw Japan's rapid growth as an empire, marked by the rise of militarism and culminating in the second Sino-Japanese War (1937-1945) and World War II (from 1941 to 1945) against the United States and the Allied forces.

Japan's defeat in the war was followed by seven

A view of Tokyo's famous Ginza district at night. (Japan Air Lines)

years of occupation by the Allied Powers. Under the direction of General Douglas MacArthur as the Supreme Commander for the Allied Powers (SCAP), Japan was demilitarized and democratized, and by 1952, when the Allied occupation had come to an end, Japan was on the road to democracy and economic recovery.—*B. Winston Kahn*

SUGGESTED READINGS: • Hall, John W., and Richard K. Beardsley. *Twelve Doors to Japan.* New York: McGraw-Hill, 1965. • Keene, Donald, ed. *Anthology of Japanese Literature: From the Earliest Era to the Mid-Nineteenth Century.* New York: Grove Press, 1955. • Nakane, Chie. *Japanese Society.* Berkeley: University of California Press, 1970. • Reischauer, Edwin O. *Japan: The Story of a Nation.* 4th ed. New York: McGraw-Hill, 1990. • Reischauer, Edwin O. *The Japanese.* Cambridge, Mass.: The Belknap Press of Harvard University Press, 1977. • Sansom, G. B. *Japan: A Short Cultural History.* Rev. ed. New York: Appleton-Century-Crofts, 1962.

Japan, occupation of (Aug., 1945—Apr., 1952): American troops occupied Japan almost immediately after the fighting ended in World War II. General Douglas MacArthur was appointed Supreme Commander for the Allied Powers (SCAP). He and his staff determined and implemented policy.

The SCAP did not govern the Japanese people directly but operated as a superstructure over existing governmental structures, issuing directives through Japanese officials.

Initially SCAP reforms had two aims: demilitarization and the establishment of democracy. Japanese troops were disarmed and the armed forces disbanded. Overseas troops were repatriated, and Japan was stripped of her empire. War criminals were tried and punished.

Convinced that democratic reforms would transform Japan into a peaceful, cooperative nation, the SCAP initiated a series of reforms aimed at providing a sound base for a democratic society. Some 200,000 officials, deemed antidemocratic, were dismissed. Reforms in education curriculum emphasized democracy and civil rights. A new, more democratic constitution was drafted and, after considerable wrangling, was approved by the Diet (legislature) in 1947. The 1947 constitution placed sovereignty in the hands of the people; the emperor became merely the "symbol of the state." The new laws established a popularly elected two-house parliamentary system, with the majority party governing and the cabinet responsible to the lower house. Article 9 renounced the use of war and forbade the maintenance of military forces.

Occupation authorities attempted to expand economic opportunity by breaking down the internal links of the giant *zaibatsu* firms and reducing them to individual competing enterprises. The SCAP actively encouraged the formation of labor unions. In the countryside the land of absentee or wealthy landowners was virtually expropriated and sold on easy terms to ordinary farmers.

The Cold War caused the Americans to adopt the so-called reverse course. The objective now was to promote Japan as a successful Asian capitalist democracy as a counterweight to Communist regimes in the Soviet Union and China. By 1949 the *zaibatsu* were allowed to regroup, Communists were expelled from unions, and Joseph Dodge became economic czar, implementing a deflationary program to provide economic stability.

On October 8, 1951, the United States concluded the peace treaty with Japan, and the occupation ended on April 28, 1952. Some 100,000 U.S. troops remained in Japan in accordance with security treaties attached to the peace treaty.

Japan, opening of: Opening of ports in the 1850's, bringing 250 years of Japanese seclusion to an end. From the early 1600's, Japan's ruling TOKUGAWA family had kept the country closed to foreigners, limiting international dealings to a few Chinese ships and one Dutch ship in Nagasaki each year. In the early 1800's, however, as Tokugawa family rule grew weaker and Western activity in East Asia increased, several foreign attempts were made to reestablish relations with the island nation.

All such efforts were rebuffed until 1853, when Commodore Matthew C. PERRY arrived just south of the Edo capital with several ships and requested that the Japanese government commence relations with the United States. He returned for an answer the following year, and the Japanese, concluding that isolation was

no longer feasible, signed the TREATY OF KANAGAWA (March 31, 1854), which opened two ports and provided for the exchange of diplomatic representatives. Shortly thereafter, Great Britain, France, and Russia also concluded treaties.

An important result of Japan's opening was the signing on July 29, 1858, of Japan's first commercial treaty, negotiated by the American representative Townsend HARRIS. This treaty was followed by similar agreements with the European nations, Japanese missions to both Europe and the United States, the opening of new ports, and a gradual increase in the volume of trade between Japan and other nations.

Another result was political turbulence. Unable to convince many of the samurai elite of the necessity of opening the country, the Tokugawa government now found itself increasingly under attack. A powerful movement, called SONNO JOI (revere the emperor, expel the barbarians), began to form, agitating—often violently—for the overthrow of the Tokugawa house and the restoration of power to the imperial family, who had been mere figureheads during the Tokugawa years. The opposition movement spread from young, out-of-power samurai to more powerful domain leaders in the 1860's, partly because of the Tokugawa impotence in dealing with the demands of this new age. In 1868, the restorationists succeeded in toppling the Tokugawa regime and setting up a new government under the nominal leadership of the boy emperor, MEIJI. It was during his reign (1868-1912) that Japan transformed itself into a military power and saw the beginnings of immigration to the West.

Japan bashing: The (mostly American) criticism of Japanese trade practices, which are supposedly anticompetitive and unfair. The Japanese word for this is *Nihon-tataki* (knocking Japan), although often the nativized version of the English loanword phrase—*Jyapan-basshingu*—is used instead. The word became current in Japan around 1984, referring to the very vocal responses of Americans as the value of the Japanese yen increased, the U.S. balance of trade fell, and Japanese high-technology electronic industries captured many North American markets. "Japan bashing" also became a popular buzzword in the United States, especially as used by those sympathetic to Japan to accuse American critics of making Japan a scapegoat.

The reasons for Japan bashing by many Americans are complex and varied. Most, however, fall under one of the following eight areas of concern.

Economic Hardships. American economic hard times have no doubt instigated some feelings of resentment toward Japan harbored by Americans. In the 1950's, when the imprint "Made in Japan" was synonymous with goods of poor quality, Japan was no threat to the American way of life. As the Japanese economy strengthened—and as many bastions of American economic dominance, such as automobiles or television, lost ground or collapsed entirely—Japan became more an economic enemy than a political ally.

Good Politics. Japan bashing often makes good campaign rhetoric, especially for politicians representing depressed economic areas. Accusations of unfair Japanese business practices, coupled with claims of overly generous American trade policies, strike a familiar chord among constituents who are out of work or underemployed. During the 1992 U.S. presidential primaries, for example, almost every candidate publicly challenged Japan on the issue of its burgeoning economic power and influence. Most implied that the U.S. trade deficit was, for the most part, caused by unfair Japanese trade practices.

Worker/Management Disputes. There has always been an adversarial relationship between workers and management in the United States. In the 1980's and 1990's, Japan has been conveniently used by both sides in American labor disputes. U.S. managers point to the famous high productivity of Japanese laborers and claim that by comparison American workers are lazy and spoiled. Thus, American workers tend to believe that Japan is a nation of workaholics. In contrast, the U.S. labor movement points to the high salaries, special perks, and job switching typical of American executives, which are unheard of in Japan. Japanese executives are said to live only for the greater good of the company, while American managers are selfish and greedy. American managers, then, see their Japanese counterparts as new economic "samurai," whose only motivation is to win the international business war.

The Symbolic Presence of Japanese Power in the United States. Unlike companies or investors from other nations, the Japanese seem to have a special symbolic presence in the minds of many Americans. Americans worry when Japanese realtors make purchases such as the Rockefeller Center or the Exxon Building, even though these were very profitable business transactions for American concerns. Japanese automobile manufacturing plants in Ohio, Tennessee, and Illinois are often seen as symbols of disappearing American economic vitality and know-how.

To most Americans, if a British conglomerate wants to buy an American newspaper, or if the (Dutch) Shell Oil Company opens another gas station, this is generally unspectacular business news. Yet when Matsushita bought MCA/Universal Studios, it made national headlines. Americans worry that Japanese own American recording companies and would even have bought a major league baseball team had that been made possible.

Canadian and European companies have substantially larger investments in the American economy than do the Japanese. Yet Japanese investments and ownership—and the presence of Japanese manufacturing plants—are often taken as demonstrations of alien power (or, conversely, demonstrations of American weakness).

Anti-Asian Racism. There is no doubt that many Americans are still racist, or that this accounts for at least some of the Japan bashing found in the media and political speeches. Even positive stereotypes of Japanese ("they are cooperative and hardworking") can become negative ("they are conformist robots").

Japan and Its Role in the Modern World. There is a feeling among many politicians and average citizens that Japan has been negligent in fulfilling its duty as a world leader and international superpower. This became most pronounced in the early 1990's, when Japan refused to send a military contingent to Saudi Arabia during Desert Storm. Ironically it is the American-authored Japanese constitution of 1945 that forbids the placement of the Japanese Self Defense Forces outside the country.

Lingering World War II Resentments. There is a feeling among some Americans that Japan has not yet truly confronted its wartime past. Aside from the fact that the PEARL HARBOR attack was premeditated and unannounced, many feel that Japan has not acknowledged its responsibilities for the death and destruction caused by WORLD WAR II. To many Americans the causes and consequences of the war are clear-cut, and Japan has not felt sufficiently guilty. To them, Japan bashing, then, is nothing more than a justifiable reminder that the Japanese lack an American-style sense of fairness.

The "Rising Sun" Conspiracy As Depicted in Popular and Academic Culture. The issues and fears of the war have not been forgotten by many Americans. To them, Japan is still an imperialist power bent on taking over much—if not all—of the world. This time Japan threatens to take economically what it could not achieve militarily half a century ago.

A scene from Rising Sun, *one of several American feature films that have incited public accusations of a perceived anti-Japan backlash in the United States.* (Museum of Modern Art)

These fears are often found in the popular media. Novels and television shows—but most effectively big-budget films with famous stars such as Michael Douglas and Sean Connery (as seen in *Black Rain* (1989) or *Rising Sun* (1993), for example—show inscrutable Japanese plotting to undermine the strength of the West. Whether it is via computer sabotage, industrial espionage, or economic terrorism, Japanese businesspeople and government officials are often depicted as little more than quasi-gangsters fully committed to helping Japan win this second round of World War II.

Some American academics and economists make similar arguments, though in less sensational ways. They claim that Japan is truly a different kind of economic entity, quite unlike anything seen in the world previously. American free-market capitalism, they claim, is no match for Japan, with its special relationships between business and government. The rhetoric these critics use is also alarmist, and some predict an economic (if not actual) war between the two countries.

A Response to Japan Bashing. While some of the above points contain an element of truth, Americans would be wise not to believe them too emphatically. First, there is no such thing as "*The* Japanese." As in the United States, there is great diversity of opinion among individual Japanese people; special interests and factions—very often with quite different agendas—are as prevalent in Japan as in any nation anywhere. There is no Japanese behemoth, bent on world domination, with a single consensus on how to do it. Second, the belief that America practices free trade while Japan has closed markets is, at best, exaggerated. No nation has a completely free market; America has hundreds of barriers and quotas, such as limitations on Asian textile imports, sugar from Haiti, or even ice cream from Jamaica. At the same time, the United States heavily subsidizes many of its own products—farm commodities, for example—and also pressures foreign countries to buy American products—including cigarettes. Third, American companies long believed that the American-style way of doing business was the only way. (For example, the company with the lowest price will have the greatest share of the market, everything in a contract must always be put in writing, and so forth. They failed to realize that in Japan (and many other Asian nations) personal relationships and a long past history of dependable service are as important as price. Even American marketing strategies were often inept. For example, it was only in the late 1980's that American auto manufacturers finally designed cars with steering wheels on the right side for use in Japan. Americans need to be careful not to use a foreign nation as a scapegoat for their own financial difficulties. Blaming Japan for the many problems of the American economy will not only hurt U.S.-Japan cultural and political relations but also distract Americans from facing the real economic crises—the national debt, health care, unemployment, to name only a few—that must be solved in the immediate future.—*James Stanlaw*

SUGGESTED READINGS: • Asahi Shimbun, ed. *The Pacific Rivals: A Japanese View of Japanese-American Relations.* New York: Weatherhill Asahi, 1972. • Ishinomori, Shotaro. *Japan, Inc.: An Introduction to Japanese Economics (The Comic Book).* Translated by Betsey Scheiner. Berkeley: University of California Press, 1988. • Morrow, Lance, et al. "Nation: America in the Mind of Japan." *Time* 139 (February 10, 1992): 16. • Shutt, Harry. *The Myth of Free Trade: Patterns of Protectionism Since 1945.* New York: Blackwell, 1985. • Van Wolferen, Karl. *The Enigma of Japanese Power.* New York: Alfred A. Knopf, 1989. • Vogel, Ezra. *Japan As Number One: Lessons for America.* New York: Harper Colophon, 1979.

Japan Foundation (JF): Nonprofit foundation in New York City dedicated to improving relations between Japan and the United States, founded in 1972. The group, also known as Kokusai Koryu Kikin, arranges for intercultural and educational programs between Japan and various other countries; provides financial support to individuals in social science and humanities to conduct research in Japan; and offers support programs to U.S. institutions for educational programs on Japan-related research.

Japan Pacific Resource Network: Nonprofit international educational organization based in Tokyo, Japan, and Berkeley, California, founded in 1985. The group, formerly known as the Japan Resource Center, provides translation and consultation services; offers Japanese-language classes, exchange programs, and student internships; conducts research and hosts forums on employment and civil rights issues; promotes activities that encourage interethnic and cross-cultural network building; and houses a resource center for reference materials.

Japanese American Citizens League (JACL): Nisei organization. Since the 1960's the JACL, founded in Seattle in 1930, has been the most important organization of NISEI (second-generation Japanese Americans). It is noted both for its collaboration with the U.S. government during World War II (1939-1945) and for its part in the movement for REDRESS of World War II-era grievances in the 1970's and 1980's.

Beginnings. The JACL had several short-lived beginnings: in San Francisco in 1919 as the AMERICAN LOYALTY LEAGUE (ALL); in Fresno in 1923 under the same name; in Santa Barbara as the ABC (American Born Citizens) Club; and in Seattle in 1921 as the Seattle Progressive Citizens League. These organizations avoided the word "Japanese" in their titles because they developed at a time when white Americans were forcibly trying to Americanize immigrants from all nations and were about to stop Japanese immigration entirely. From the start, these progenitors of the JACL emphasized the American citizenship of the Nisei generation, loyalty to the United States, and disavowal of connections with Japan. They were, in fact, organizational attempts to manifest the second generation's sense of separation from their ISSEI (first-generation) parents and their independence as Americans. At the time of these early foundings, however, few Nisei had reached adulthood, and even those who had were dependent on the Issei generation for their livelihood.

The younger generation was barely more independent by 1928, when James Y. SAKAMOTO, a blind ex-prizefighter and pugnacious journalist, brought the Seattle Progressive Citizens League back to life. That same year, San Francisco lawyer Saburo KIDO founded the New American Citizens League. Representatives of these two clubs met and decided to form a loose federation called the National Council of Japanese-American Citizens Leagues and to hold a national convention in Seattle in 1930. Thus, the JACL was born, though it barely survived infancy. That first national convention attracted only a hundred Nisei, three-quarters of them from the Seattle area. The meeting consisted of little more than the flag salute and some patriotic speeches about the virtues of unhyphenated Americanism (the hyphen in "Japanese-American" was quickly dropped from the league's title). For the next decade, the JACL was a tiny, moderately rightwing civics club, ignored by most Japanese Americans, who were bored by its political slant. It grew slowly but was not a force in Japanese communities until the 1940's. Some JACL members stated a desire to lead their ethnic communities, but they, like other Nisei, were dominated by the immigrant generation.

World War II. All that changed with the coming of World War II. In 1941, with war between the United States and Japan imminent, the JACL hired its first full-time staffer, a bright, energetic Nisei from Utah named Mike MASAOKA. Together with KIDO, who by now was the league's president, Masaoka undertook an aggressive campaign to recruit new members and publicize his generation's Americanism. He wrote and distributed widely the "Japanese American Creed," a paean to middle-class Americanism. Masaoka and Kido met whenever possible with powerful white Americans, including elected officials and intelligence agents. It is widely believed that Masaoka and Kido gave the names of Issei community leaders to the Federal Bureau of Investigation (FBI) and Naval Intel-ligence, to be arrested if war came, but the two men died without admitting it.

War did come on December 7, 1941. In the next few weeks, Issei leaders were rounded up and put in CON-CENTRATION CAMPS. The JACL, as the largest organization run by Japanese Americans who were U.S. citizens, stepped into the breach and counseled cooperation with the government. Throughout the winter of 1942, as hysterical fears of Japanese Americans were building among the white population, Masaoka, Kido, and other JACL leaders tried in vain to create a patriotic image for the Nisei generation. By spring, it was clear that both they and the Issei would be going to concentration camps. The JACL helped design the camps and helped organize the transition.

Once the Japanese American population was concentrated behind barbed wire, the JACL lost its power.

In the wake of the forced evacuation of Japanese Americans that began in early 1942, national JACL leaders called an emergency meeting at the organization's San Francisco headquarters to pledge their full cooperation. League president Saburo Kido (second from right) declared the loyalty of Japanese Americans to the United States. To his right is league secretary Mike Masaoka. (Pacific Citizen)

Other Japanese Americans resented the JACL's collaboration with the U.S. government and took out their frustrations on the collaborators. The vicious beating of Kido at the POSTON camp was the extreme, but the JACL fell from power in all the camps during that period, as other Japanese Americans took the lead.

The U.S. government subsequently removed Kido and other key JACL leaders from the camps. Masaoka received special dispensation and was never incarcerated. Those leaders formed a remnant that took up residence in Salt Lake City, published the JACL newspaper *PACIFIC CITIZEN*, and lobbied the American government on behalf of their patriotic, assimilationist vision for Japanese Americans. Their most desperate wish was for a way to demonstrate their loyalty to the United States. That wish met fulfillment in the JACL's only triumph during World War II when its leaders convinced the American government to form the all-Nisei 442ND REGIMENTAL COMBAT TEAM and to subject the Nisei to military draft. The 442nd Regimental Combat Team and some smaller Nisei units fought heroically, took enormous casualties, and—in the eyes of JACL leaders, some other Nisei, and many whites—vindicated the JACL's collaboration policy. In the camps, the issue of army service was the subject of agitation and strife.

Postwar Influence. When the war ended, the Issei generation did not reclaim the leadership of Japanese American communities. Yet it took the JACL several years after the war's end to regain the pinnacle of community power that it had held briefly in 1942. Japanese Americans emerged from the war scattered and demoralized. Communities in West Coast cities did not reform until the 1950's, and it took longer for prewar community institutions—from businesses to churches to language schools to the JACL—to resume their importance. The Issei's primary institutions, the JAPANESE ASSOCIATIONS and *KENJINKAI* (prefectural associations), never reasserted their prewar preeminence. Gradually, from the 1950's through the 1970's, the JACL established itself as the paramount organization of Japanese Americans.

In the early postwar years, the JACL's prime theater of activity was not West Coast Japanese communities but the corridors of power in Washington, D.C., where Masaoka was sent as a lobbyist. His major achievement in that role was to aid the passage in 1952 of the MCCARRAN-WALTER ACT. This law made it possible, for the first time, for the Issei to apply for U.S. citizenship. It also allowed a tiny number of Japanese to immigrate for the first time since 1924, even as it enshrined racism at the heart of American immigration law and surrendered to fear-mongering during the McCarthy era by legalizing CONCENTRATION CAMPS for "subversives." Masaoka and the JACL also succeeded in obtaining token compensation—less than

Multicultural panel at San Francisco State College in 1961 sponsored by the JACL as part of its national effort to dispel stereotypes about various religious, racial, and ethnic groups in America. (Pacific Citizen)

ten cents on the dollar—for wartime property losses of some Japanese Americans, opening the service academies to Japanese Americans, and overturning California's ALIEN LAND LAWS, which had kept the Issei from owning real property.

The JACL moved its national headquarters from Salt Lake City back to San Francisco, but its activities in the West Coast communities, where most Japanese lived, were mainly social in the 1950's and 1960's and did not involve the exercise of community leadership. In fact, the JACL as a national organization was dominated by Nisei from Utah, Washington D.C., New York, and other regions far removed from the centers of Japanese American life and culture. That began to change with the rise of a third generation, the SANSEI (those having Nisei parents), in the late 1960's and 1970's.

These younger people were as far removed from the worldview of MASAOKA and KIDO as those men were from their Issei parents. Mainly postwar baby boomers, their politics shaded gently toward the radicalism of many African Americans, Chicanos, and other ethnic groups. On questions such as combating poverty, confronting racism, and opposing the Vietnam War (1965-1975), they were far to the left of the JACL old guard and Masaoka's designated successor, a conservative Utah Sansei named David Ushio. Ushio's tenure as JACL director was brief, from 1972 to 1976, during which time the generational and political power struggle nearly tore the JACL apart.

After that contentious time, however, the league increasingly took on the complexion and concerns of the younger generation. Starting in 1978 and continuing through the 1980's, the new JACL took an active, if not leading, role in the ultimately successful drive to gain REDRESS—an apology and monetary compensation—from the U.S. government for the concentration camp episode. Its officers, both local and national, forged stronger links with other Japanese community institutions, and they began to go beyond their own community to express solidarity with the grievances of African Americans and Latinos as well as other Asian Americans. By the 1980's, the JACL had arrived at a position of community leadership similar to that to which its founders had aspired. It did so, however, on the basis of a program that those founders would never have endorsed.—*Paul Spickard*

SUGGESTED READINGS: • Daniels, Roger, Sandra C. Taylor, and Harry H. L. Kitano, eds. *Japanese Americans: From Relocation to Redress*. Rev. ed. Seattle: University of Washington Press, 1991. • Hosokawa,

Bill. *JACL in Quest of Justice*. New York: William Morrow, 1982. • Masaoka, Mike, and Bill Hosokawa. *They Call Me Moses Masaoka*. New York: William Morrow, 1987. • Spickard, Paul R. "The Nisei Assume Power: The Japanese American Citizens League, 1941-1942." *Pacific Historical Review* 52 (May, 1983): 147-174.

Japanese American Courier: English-language newspaper launched by James Y. SAKAMOTO in Seattle's Nihonmachi in 1928. As the first mainland newspaper specifically targeted at NISEI readers, the *Japanese American Courier* addressed many of the issues confronting the Japanese American community, including the problem of balancing the competing demands of Japanese identity and American society. As an influential member of Seattle's Japanese American community, publisher Sakamoto went on to help establish the JAPANESE AMERICAN CITIZENS LEAGUE (JACL) and became the organization's second national president. The weekly *Japanese American Courier* continued publication until 1942, when the forced evacuation and INTERNMENT of all persons of Japanese ancestry living on the West Coast halted publication of the paper.

Japanese-American Creed (1940): Statement of Japanese American loyalty to the United States, written by Mike MASAOKA of the JAPANESE AMERICAN CITIZENS LEAGUE (JACL) during World War II. As the U.S. government considered entering the war to stem the tide of Japanese military aggression, the sentiments of Japanese living in the country became an issue of some concern. The creed was written to allay such fears. It was essentially an expression of loyalty to the United States and a pledge to uphold the ideals of American democracy, freedom, and fair and equal treatment of all individuals.

Japanese American Curriculum Project (JACP): Nonprofit educational corporation founded in 1969. The JACP is devoted to building pride and a more positive self-image among all Asian Americans, both children and adults. It also seeks to expose the general public to educational and historical materials that will enhance its awareness of Asian American history, culture, and literature.

The JACP originally was organized to provide curriculum materials that tell the story of the Japanese American CONCENTRATION CAMPS of World War II from the viewpoint of the internees themselves. These materials included pamphlets, audiovisual materials, and some books, three of which are *Little Citizens Speak* (1970), *Wartime Hysteria: The Role of the Press in the Removal of 110,000 Japanese Americans During World War II* (1970), and *Japanese American Journey: The Story of a People* (1985).

In time the JACP began selling books and other materials to the public. It has become the most complete outlet for Asian American educational materials in the United States, serving homes, schools, and libraries by means of an annual annotated catalog and a retail store. The organization also conducts projects aimed at boosting the image of Asian America. Most of the services provided by the JACP are extended without charge.

Awards received include a 1989 citation by San Francisco Nikkei in Education for outstanding service in education; a citation in 1993 as being one of the top ten Bay Area companies, as selected by the Community Career Education Center, San Mateo; and a Special Service Award for advancing Asian American studies, presented by the Association for Asian American Studies in 1993.

Japanese American Evacuation and Resettlement Study (JERS): Broad-based sociological research project conducted by the University of California, Berkeley, and focused on the Japanese American assembly and RELOCATION CENTERS of World War II. With the cooperation of the WAR RELOCATION AUTHORITY (WRA), the project was designed to collect and evaluate data gathered from observing and interviewing evacuees in the various camps. This information would reveal what conditions inside the camps were like and would enable JERS staff to assess the internment's overall impact—for example, how the forced mass migration affected the internees psychologically and socially and the West Coast economically. The study, begun in the spring of 1942, was initiated and directed by Berkeley sociologist Dorothy Swaine Thomas. She was assisted by a team of university professors recruited from various academic disciplines. Under their supervision, a group of Berkeley students was to enter the many camps to amass the data specified. A short while later, in 1943, an office was established in Chicago to study the movement of former internees from the camps to the cities of the Midwest and the East.

Among the difficulties encountered in carrying out the project were the risks to personal safety to which the fieldworkers were exposed. Inside the compounds,

Thomas advised the fieldworkers to conduct their research under cover of secrecy, lest the inmates begin to suspect them of being government informants, a potentially dangerous position for any of the fieldworkers. Information gathering was especially dangerous in the more volatile camps, such as the TULE LAKE relocation center in northern California, which the JERS ultimately chose as a focal point.

From the reams of data amassed from such a large-scale research effort, several books on the internment experience were published. *The Spoilage* (1946), coauthored by Thomas and Richard S. NISHIMOTO, describes the camp experiences of those prisoners classified as "disloyal" to the United States and consequently segregated at Tule Lake. *The Salvage* (1952) tells of the Japanese Americans who left the relocation centers to resettle chiefly in the Midwest. *Prejudice, War and the Constitution* (1954) traces the history of anti-Asian racism in the western United States and the motivations behind the internment. Morton Grodzins' *Americans Betrayed: Politics and the Japanese Evacuation* (1949), published by the University of Chicago Press over Thomas' vociferous objections and threats of legal action, explains how California political and business interests may have influenced the government's decision to intern the evacuees. Also collected were numerous journals, diaries, biographies, field reports, and assorted other documents assembled by JERS staffers. Much of this material is archived in the Bancroft Library at Berkeley.

Japanese American Evacuation Claims Act of 1948: Legislation intended to provide compensation to Japanese Americans for loss of property as a result of their removal and incarceration during World War II. While the act resulted in the payment of approximately $38 million in claims between 1950 and 1965, when the last claim was settled, it was ill-conceived and inefficiently administered. The total amount paid represented only about one-tenth of the fair market value of the property in question at the time of the incarceration. As a result of restrictions and bureaucratic delays, many Japanese Americans who had suffered significant material losses were insufficiently compensated or not compensated at all.

Japanese American internment: The Japanese American internment during World War II was one of the most catastrophic abuses of the Constitution ever to occur in the United States. Approximately 120,000 Japanese Americans were forcibly removed from their

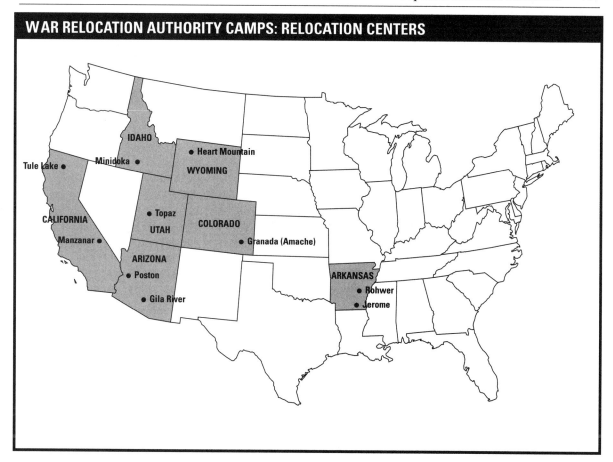

WAR RELOCATION AUTHORITY CAMPS: RELOCATION CENTERS

homes and detained in United States CONCENTRATION CAMPS solely on the basis of race. Of the Japanese Americans detained, approximately two-thirds were American citizens by birthright while the remaining one-third were immigrants barred from naturalization.

Background. The Japanese American internment during World War II was part of a long history of anti-Asian exclusion that began with the CHINESE EXCLUSION ACT OF 1882, which prohibited Chinese laborers from entering the United States. In 1885, Japanese workers replaced the Chinese and were initially welcomed as part of the work force. They were a good source of cheap labor and were viewed as being very industrious. Soon, however, their fortunes began to change like those of the Chinese who had arrived before them. White workers hated the Japanese because they worked for lower wages. Employers hated them because, like the Chinese before them, they started to organize and demand higher wages. In short, the fate of Japanese immigrants started to look strikingly similar to that of the Chinese immigrants before them.

In 1907 and 1908, a series of notes, collectively known as the GENTLEMEN'S AGREEMENT, were passed between Japan and the United States. Japan agreed to stop issuing passports to new immigrants who wished to go to the United States as laborers. Japanese laborers who had already spent time in the United States would be permitted to return there, and passports could be issued to spouses and other family members as well. In essence, the Gentlemen's Agreement demonstrated two things. First, it showed America's hatred for people of Japanese descent. Second, it showed the emergence of Japan as a world power following a resounding victory over Russia in the RUSSO-JAPANESE WAR (1904-1905). Whereas the Chinese were "excluded," the Japanese were allowed to bring their families to live with them in the United States like "gentlemen."

Additional measures were also taken against Japanese Americans after the Gentlemen's Agreement. California's ALIEN LAND LAW OF 1913 prohibited Japanese immigrants from owning land. In 1922, the CABLE ACT was passed to discourage American citizens (particularly the NISEI, the American-born children of Japanese immigrants) from marrying "aliens

Using photographs, news clippings, and letters, a Japanese American woman reviews the historical record regarding the internment. (Michael Yamashita)

ineligible to citizenship" by revoking their citizenship if they chose to do so. In the same year, the Supreme Court decision in the case of *Ozawa v. United States* closed the door on any chances the ISSEI (first-generation Japanese immigrants) had to become naturalized American citizens. The IMMIGRATION ACT OF 1924, which virtually sealed all immigration from Asia, was the final message to the Issei that their future in America did not hinge on themselves but rather on their American-born Nisei children.

Intelligence Operations. The 1931 Japanese invasion of Manchuria sent fear into the Japanese American community living in the United States. Both the Issei and adult-age Nisei realized that diplomatic relations between the United States and Japan could become further strained if Japan continued on its imperialist course. If the two nations went to war, they knew from past experience that they were potential casualties.

According to historian Bob Kumamoto, intelligence surveillance of the Japanese American community was in place by 1932. All aspects of Japanese American life were studied and filed for documentation. Organizations with cultural significance such as Buddhist churches and JAPANESE-LANGUAGE SCHOOLS were particularly viewed with suspicion, as were business associations, farmers, and fishermen.

As Japan's imperialist aggression advanced in Asia, intelligence operations on Japanese Americans increased in the continental United States and Hawaii (a U.S. territory since 1898). By 1934, officials in the Office of Naval Intelligence (ONI) believed that Japanese Americans were secretly practicing military maneuvers to assist Japan in acts of sabotage on the West Coast of the United States. The next year, the ONI suspected Japanese Americans of drug trafficking in an attempt to destroy the effectiveness of the U.S. military. All of these reports were unfounded.

By 1937, diplomatic relations between the United States and Japan were so marginal that the idea of CONCENTRATION CAMPS for Japanese Americans was raised by both Lieutenant General George S. Patton and President Franklin D. Roosevelt. The situation grew ominous as Japan invaded China. In 1939, war was imminent as the United States placed a full embargo on shipments to Japan. Surveillance on Japanese Americans was stepped up another notch and centralized with the joint cooperation of the ONI, the Federal Bureau of Investigation (FBI), and the Army's G-2 division.

By early 1941, more than two thousand Japanese Americans were under government surveillance, classified into three groups. Group A people were the so-called "known dangerous" because of their affiliations with Japanese cultural institutions and their positions of leadership in the Japanese American community. Those in group B were considered to be

Virtually every facet of Japanese American life was analyzed by U.S. intelligence gatherers in the prewar period. This photograph shows a Japanese fishing village in Southern California. The rows of dwellings on either side house Japanese fishermen and their families. (California State Library)

Japanese American Population Under War Relocation Authority
Control, Selected Statistics, 1942-1946

Total population under WRA control: 120,313
Residents of the forbidden zone eligible for imprisonment or internment, March-October, 1942: 117,116
Residents of the forbidden zone actually imprisoned or interned, 1942-1946: 110,723
Persons who migrated out of the forbidden zone voluntarily, March-October, 1942: 5,000

Source in 1942

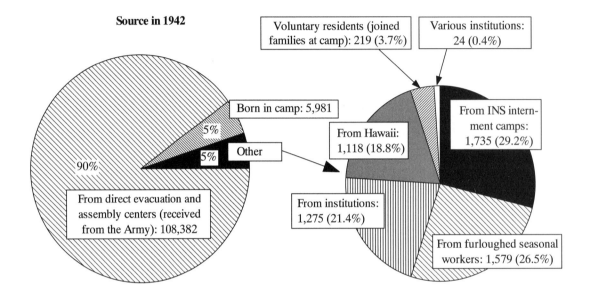

Voluntary residents (joined families at camp): 219 (3.7%)

Various institutions: 24 (0.4%)

Born in camp: 5,981

5%

Other

5%

90%

From direct evacuation and assembly centers (received from the Army): 108,382

From Hawaii: 1,118 (18.8%)

From INS internment camps: 1,735 (29.2%)

From institutions: 1,275 (21.4%)

From furloughed seasonal workers: 1,579 (26.5%)

Dispersed by 1946

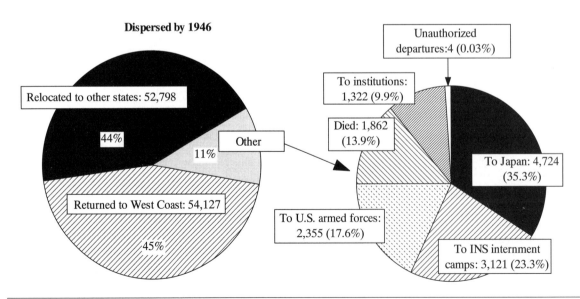

Unauthorized departures: 4 (0.03%)

To institutions: 1,322 (9.9%)

Relocated to other states: 52,798

Died: 1,862 (13.9%)

44%

Other

11%

Returned to West Coast: 54,127

45%

To Japan: 4,724 (35.3%)

To U.S. armed forces: 2,355 (17.6%)

To INS internment camps: 3,121 (23.3%)

Source: Roger Daniels, Sandra C. Taylor, and Harry H. L. Kitano, eds., *Japanese Americans: From Relocation to Redress.* Salt Lake City: University of Utah Press, 1986.

potentially dangerous, but more information needed to be gathered on them. Group C individuals were those considered to have "pro-Japan" inclinations and were supposedly operating very close to espionage networks. Nevertheless, it should be noted that by October of 1941, no concrete evidence was found by the FBI that Japanese Americans participated in any fifth column activity. This corroborated reports from the ONI that Japanese Americans, in general, were loyal to the United States and that Japan's espionage activities did not involve organizing fifth column work.

In October and November of 1941, State Department Special Representative Curtis B. Munson conducted an investigation of the Japanese American population on the West Coast and Hawaii. He observed Japanese American activities and interviewed members of the U.S. intelligence community and came back with the same conclusions as the FBI and ONI: There was no Japanese "problem" on the West Coast or Hawaii. His twenty-five page report was shared with the State, War, and Navy departments as well as the Executive Branch—all to no avail. (See MUNSON REPORT.)

After Japan bombed PEARL HARBOR on December 7, 1941, the fate of Japanese Americans was practically sealed. Within the next forty-eight hours, the FBI arrested 1291 Japanese from the "ABC" list as well as some German and Italian nationals. With this sweep, the FBI was convinced that all of the potential saboteurs were in custody and that no further action needed to be taken. Because of the tensions of the war, however, they were soon overruled. On February 19, 1942, more than two months after the bombing of Pearl Harbor, President Roosevelt signed EXECUTIVE ORDER 9066, which allowed the War Department to designate military areas from which any person could be excluded. This order was the basis for the forced removal of Japanese Americans from the West Coast and into CONCENTRATION CAMPS.

Causal interpretations. A number of historians have attempted to determine who was primarily at fault for the incarceration of Japanese Americans and why it was allowed to happen. Most scholars agree that the incarceration was wrong and that the U.S. government and the military had no proof to justify their argument of "military necessity" to intern Japanese Americans. Most academics also agree that several people or branches of government were at least partially responsible for the internment. Everything else, however, is up to historical interpretation.

One of the earliest interpretations to appear was the "interest group theory," which placed primary blame for the internment on anti-Japanese pressure groups who stood to profit from the Japanese American incarceration. First advanced by journalist Carey McWilliams and later by Yale law professor Eugene Rostow, the interest group theory received its most thorough treatment from Morton Grodzins in his book *Americans Betrayed* (1949). Grodzins not only blamed traditional anti-Japanese groups such as the NATIVE SONS OF THE GOLDEN WEST and the American Legion but also focused in on agricultural and business interests who would benefit from the lack of competition from Japanese Americans. Grodzins theorized that local, state, and federal politicians acquiesced to the pressure groups because 1942 was an election year and people were fearful of being voted out of elected office.

In 1954, Jacobus tenBroek, Edward N. Barnhart, and Floyd W. Matson attempted to debunk Grodzins' and other theories that were popular at the time in their book *Prejudice, War and the Constitution.* In short, they argued that none of the previous theories effectively connected the actions of certain groups with the timing of policy decisions made by the military and the government. In their conclusion, they placed primary blame on the general public—in particular the people on the West Coast. According to tenBroek, Barnhart, and Matson, widespread fear and anger brought on by World War II and the bombing of PEARL HARBOR, reinforced by a long history of anti-Asian agitation, led to the incarceration of Japanese Americans in CONCENTRATION CAMPS. The military, President Roosevelt, the War Department, and the Supreme Court also shared in the blame, but their role was secondary.

Michi WEGLYN, a Nisei who was interned in one of the concentration camps during World War II, developed the "hostage theory" in her 1976 book *Years of Infamy.* Basically, she put direct blame for the internment on the U.S. government. She theorized that the government regarded people of Japanese ancestry living in the Western Hemisphere as potential hostages to be used for ransom or a prisoner exchange with Japan. Weglyn documented the extradition to the United States of Japanese residents living in Central and South America (particularly Peru) and stated that the agreements with these nations had their origins in the State Department and were carried out by the Justice, War, and Navy Departments. Weglyn believed that this scenario best explained why all of these government departments chose to ignore intelligence information contained in the MUNSON REPORT.

Peter Irons in *Justice at War* studied the inner work-

Astride her family's belongings, a Japanese American child awaits shipment to the Santa Anita assembly center. (National Japanese American Historical Society)

ings of the military and Roosevelt's cabinet and laid the blame for the internment primarily on key government bureaucrats. In Irons' view, many in the government were at fault, but several people shared more of the blame than others. To start, Irons identifies Army Provost Marshall General Allen GULLION as the one person in the military most dedicated to putting Japanese Americans in concentration camps. Irons describes Karl Bendetsen, who was hired by Gullion to be a liaison between the War Department and General John DEWITT, as the architect of the internment, while John MCCLOY of the War Department is faulted for his determination in pushing for the exclusion program even though he knew Japanese Americans were no threat to the United States and that their acts were unconstitutional. General DeWitt bore the responsibility for capitulating to pressure put on him by Gullion and McCloy and for carrying out the exclusion pro-

gram. In short, many in the government and the military were responsible for the exclusion through either their rabid determination or acquiescence.

Justice Department Camps. Unknown to many casual observers of the Japanese American internment, two types of camps were actually in operation in the United States during World War II. One type was administered by the government's WAR RELOCATION AUTHORITY (WRA) and the other by the Immigration and Naturalization Service (INS) under the Justice Department. The vast majority of the more than 120,000 Japanese Americans incarcerated were interned in the WRA camps, while approximately 7,000 were detained in the Justice Department camps.

The Justice Department camps—or internment camps, as most scholars refer to them—were reserved for those individuals the government deemed to be the most dangerous to the United States and the war effort.

Japanese Americans arrested in the FBI "ABC" sweeps fit into the dangerous category: Issei business leaders, Japanese language school teachers, and so on. All were arrested and detained on the flimsiest of evidence and had two things in common: their knowledge of the Japanese language and their leadership position in the Japanese American community. Their imprisonment transferred leadership to the much younger, ill-prepared Nisei generation.

Among the internment camps administered by the Justice Department were CRYSTAL CITY, Texas; SANTA FE, New Mexico; Fort Stanton, New Mexico; Fort Missoula, Montana; Fort Lincoln, North Dakota; Kenedy, Texas; and Kooskia, Idaho. The best known and largest camp was the one at Crystal City. Besides Japanese Americans, Crystal City also held German and Italian nationals and Japanese extradited from Peru.

After the war ended, the camps gradually were closed and the prisoners released. Crystal City was the last to close, on February 27, 1948. In many ways, the cases of the Japanese Peruvians and other Japanese extradited from Central and South American countries were perhaps the most tragic of all those held in the Justice Department camps. After the war, they were rejected by their home countries and threatened with deportation to Japan, a country many of them had never seen. Fortunately, with the help of attorney Wayne COLLINS, many of them were allowed to stay in the United States and eventually become naturalized citizens.

War Relocation Authority (WRA). The WRA was created as a civilian agency by Executive Order 9102 on March 18, 1942, to administer the exclusion of Japanese Americans from the West Coast. The idea for the agency came at a meeting among President Roosevelt's top advisers on February 27, 1942. With EXECUTIVE ORDER 9066 behind them, they needed someone or some department to implement the so-called "evacuation" of Japanese Americans. Since

Japanese American Population, Nativity, and Residence, 1940

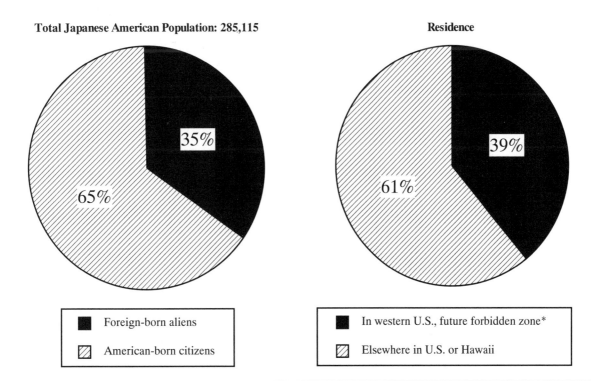

Total Japanese American Population: 285,115

35%

65%

■ Foreign-born aliens

▨ American-born citizens

Residence

39%

61%

■ In western U.S., future forbidden zone*

▨ Elsewhere in U.S. or Hawaii

Sources: Roger Daniels, Sandra C. Taylor, and Harry H. L. Kitano, eds., *Japanese Americans: From Relocation to Redress.* Salt Lake City: University of Utah Press, 1986. Roger Daniels, *Prisoners Without Trial: Japanese Americans in World War II.* New York: Hill and Wang, 1993.

* Includes California, western Washington and Oregon, and part of Arizona.

none of the departments wanted the responsibility, Attorney General Francis BIDDLE suggested the creation of a civilian agency; and thus the WRA was born. Milton Eisenhower was the first director, but he resigned after three months, largely because he disagreed with the plan to incarcerate Japanese Americans. Dillon S. MYER replaced him and stayed through the closing of the camps after the war.

The WRA camps were located in isolated areas (usually deserts) and were surrounded with barbed wire and armed guards. The barracks used to house the inmates were small and poorly constructed quarters unsuitable for the climate and inappropriate for family living. In general, the conditions were dreadful, but the Japanese Americans made the most of what was a very bad situation. In total, ten camps were administered by the WRA: MANZANAR and TULE LAKE in California, POSTON and GILA RIVER in Arizona, GRANADA (also known as Amache) in Colorado, TOPAZ in Utah, HEART MOUNTAIN in Wyoming, JEROME and Rowher in Arkansas, and MINIDOKA in Idaho.

Life in Camp. Life in the WRA CONCENTRATION CAMPS, euphemistically referred to as "RELOCATION CENTERS," was bearable for some and a living hell for others. The WRA had strict rules and a very skewed definition of a "loyal" American. Those that followed the rules and enthusiastically carried out the WRA program of assimilation, such as the leaders of the JAPANESE AMERICAN CITIZENS LEAGUE (JACL), were rewarded with special privileges. Those who disagreed with the WRA, complained about camp conditions, or demanded their rights as American citizens were labeled as "disloyal" or "troublemakers" and were severely punished.

In December of 1942, a "riot" broke out at MANZANAR in which at least ten people were injured and two killed by the military police. The disturbance centered around the beating of suspected *inu* ("dog"; that is "informant" or "collaborator") and JACL leader Fred Tayama by other camp inmates. Harry Ueno, a camp cook and WRA critic, was arrested and charged with the beating. While Ueno was in jail at the Inyo County facility, crowds assembled, demanded his release, and made plans to punish other suspected *inu*. When the crowd did not break up, the military police used tear gas and then fired into the unarmed mob.

Inmates of the Tule Lake camp, February, 1945. (National Japanese American Historical Society)

Tayama and other JACL leaders were rushed out of the camp for their own safety while a number of suspected "troublemakers" were removed from the camp. This incident served as a microcosm of events to follow concerning the underlying tensions in the concentration camps.

In February of 1942, the War Department and the WRA administered a questionnaire designed to distinguish the so-called "loyal" internees from those who were "disloyal." Two questions in particular served as the litmus test. QUESTION 27 asked if they were willing to serve in the armed forces. QUESTION 28 asked whether they would swear unqualified allegiance to the United States and forswear any allegiance to the Japanese Emperor or other foreign power. Those that answered "yes-yes" passed the test and were eligible for the military draft or resettlement outside of camp, while those who answered "no" to either question were deemed "disloyal" and were segregated to the TULE LAKE camp.

The loyalty questionnaire had a number of problems, most of them related to the wording of the questions. For example, many NISEI had trouble answering question 28 in the affirmative because it implied that they, American-born citizens, once had allegiance to the Emperor of Japan. For the ISSEI, question 28 had different consequences. If they answered "yes," they would be renouncing the only citizenship they were allowed to have since they were ineligible for naturalization in the United States. In essence, they would become stateless people.

There were other problems with the questionnaire as well. To start, many of the draft-age Nisei had difficulty believing that they would be asked to serve in the military while they were still interned behind barbed wire. As a means of protest, many answered "no-no" to the questions and were segregated to Tule Lake.

Military Service and Resistance. Once the registration of draft-age Nisei was completed, the army diligently recruited volunteers from the mainland and Hawaii to serve in the newly created all-Nisei 442ND REGIMENTAL COMBAT TEAM (RCT). In Hawaii, where Japanese Americans, in general, were not incarcerated in CONCENTRATION CAMPS, nearly 10,000 volunteered for the 442nd, and more than 2,600 were accepted. On the mainland, however, only about 1,200 out of a possible 23,000 draft-age Nisei in concentration camps volunteered, and only 800 were accepted into the army.

The heroics of the 442nd RCT and the 100TH INFANTRY BATTALION from Hawaii were many. They liberated the towns of Bruyeres, Belmont, and Biffon-taine and rescued a Texas battalion, which was under fire and caught behind enemy lines. The rescue of the "LOST BATTALION" was particularly costly: 211 men were saved, but more than 800 Nisei from the 100th Infantry Battalion and the 442nd perished in the mission. In total, the 442nd saw 225 days of combat and participated in the most dangerous, sometimes suicidal, missions. They suffered the highest casualty rate in the war: more than 700 were killed in action while the wounded numbered over three times the strength of the unit. Their record in battle was nothing short of remarkable; they proved by their actions how wrong the government had been to doubt their loyalty.

While the 442nd RCT chose to prove their loyalty to their country by serving in the military, others chose to show their version of Americanism by fighting for their constitutional rights. Three Japanese American individuals, Fred KOREMATSU, Minoru YASUI, and Gordon HIRABAYASHI, challenged the curfew and exclusion orders to restore their constitutional rights. Though all three lost their cases, they fought all the way to the Supreme Court and forced the government to justify the internment of Japanese Americans.

At the HEART MOUNTAIN concentration camp, a group calling itself the Fair Play Committee (FPC) also invoked the Constitution while protesting the drafting of Nisei into the military while they were still detained behind barbed wire. (See HEART MOUNTAIN FAIR PLAY COMMITTEE.) Because of their actions, eighty-five Nisei men refused to be inducted into the military until their rights as American citizens were fully restored. For this, they were arrested and sentenced to three years in prison. In addition, seven leaders of the FPC were tried for sedition and sentenced to Leavenworth Federal Penitentiary. Later, in 1946, their convictions were overturned on appeal. As for the draft resisters, President Truman pardoned them on December 24, 1946.

Release. On December 17, 1944, one day before the Supreme Court determined in the Mitsuye ENDO case that the WRA could not detain citizens deemed to be loyal, the War Department announced that the release of Japanese Americans from the CONCENTRATION CAMPS would begin on Janaury 2, 1945. At long last, Japanese Americans had their freedom restored but still faced a frightening and uncertain future. They had no homes to return to and no jobs awaiting them. In short, everything they had built for themselves before the war was gone. They had to start all over again from scratch. For older ISSEI, the task was nearly impossible. Some opted for suicide rather than face what

Gordon Hirabayashi appealed to the U.S. Supreme Court, and in 1988 the Court vacated his decades-old conviction for violating the government-imposed curfew orders. (AP/Wide World Photos)

seemed to be insurmountable odds. Others tried to rebuild, but never achieved the prominence they once enjoyed. Clearly, the future belonged to the younger people, who could better adapt to life after camp.

If anything is to be learned from the internment, it should be that the exclusion and detention of Japanese Americans in concentration camps was not a "mistake." It was a carefully planned policy devised by the government and upheld by the U.S. Supreme Court in the cases of Fred Korematsu, Minoru Yasui, and Gordon Hirabayashi. As law historian Peter Irons has noted, the government knew that its actions were unconstitutional and needed to find justification for the exclusion. Government officials concocted the "military necessity" defense of their program and either ignored or altered documents which contradicted their argument. In short, the U.S. government betrayed the very principles for which Americans were fighting and dying in World War II.—*Glen Kitayama*

SUGGESTED READINGS:

• Commission on Wartime Relocation and Internment of Civilians. *Personal Justice Denied*. Washington, D.C.: Government Printing Office, 1982. The Commission on Wartime Relocation and Internment of Civilians (CWRIC) was a government-appointed body that studied the internment of Japanese Americans. *Personal Justice Denied* is the report they wrote after conducting public hearings on the matter and doing close to three years of research. This comprehensive work was the basis for their recommendation of redress for Japanese Americans.

• Daniels, Roger. *Asian America: Chinese and Japanese in the United States Since 1850*. Seattle: University of Washington Press, 1988. Daniels is one of the leading authorities on Japanese Americans. In *Asian America*, he tells the history of Chinese Americans and Japanese Americans in the United States from the 1850's to the 1980's. The section of the book covering World War II is excellent.

• Drinnon, Richard. *Keeper of Concentration Camps*. Berkeley: University of California Press, 1987. Richard Drinnon wrote this very sarcastic biography on Dillon S. Myer to document the inner workings of a racist bureaucrat who implemented cruel policies as director of the War Relocation Authority during World War II and later as director of the Bureau of Indian Affairs. A fascinating and entertaining work.

• Grodzins, Morton. *Americans Betrayed: Politics and the Japanese Evacuation*. Chicago: University of Chicago Press, 1949. Grodzins was one of the researchers in the Japanese American Evacuation and Resettlement Study (JERS), a project conducted inside the concentration camps by academics with the cooperation of the WRA. This work, published over the objections of JERS director Dorothy Swaine Thomas, studied the rationale behind the internment.

• Hosokawa, William. *JACL: In Quest of Justice*. New York: William Morrow, 1982. Bill Hosokawa is a journalist and longtime JACL member. In this work, he chronicles the long history of the JACL and attempts to restore the group's legacy as a civil rights organization.

• Irons, Peter. *Justice at War*. New York: Oxford University Press, 1983. While doing research for this study of Japanese American internment cases, Irons, a legal historian, made discoveries that led to the vacating of the wartime convictions of Fred Korematsu, Minoru Yasui, and Gordon Hirabayashi. *Justice at War* is essential reading for anyone interested in the decision-making process of the government during World War II.

• Kumamoto, Bob. "The Search for Spies: American Counterintelligence and the Japanese American Community 1931-1942." *Amerasia Journal* 6, no. 2 (1979): 45-76. Kumamoto was a doctoral student at UCLA when he conducted this groundbreaking research.

It is a very intelligent look at the government's surveillance of the Japanese American community before and just after the United States entered World War II.

- TenBroek, Jacobus, et al. *Prejudice, War and the Constitution*. Berkeley: University of California Press, 1954. This book was written with the encouragement of Dorothy Swaine Thomas of JERS to discredit the views articulated by Morton Grodzins in *Americans Betrayed*. It contains valuable information for those wanting to study the causal interpretations of the internment.

- Weglyn, Michi. *Years of Infamy: The Untold Story of America's Concentration Camps*. New York: William Morrow, 1976. A classic in Japanese American history. Weglyn, a former camp interneé with no training in history, accomplished what no one else had done before. She gave new importance to the Munson Report, articulated the hostage theory, and provided a voice for the alleged "troublemakers" in camp.

Japanese American literature: Japanese American literature includes works by writers of Japanese descent who either live in the United States as permanent residents or are U.S. citizens.

History. Although Japanese immigration to the United States and Hawaii began at the end of the 1860's, Japanese immigration did not become substantial until the period between 1890 and 1910. The literature produced by Japanese Americans in this period was mainly in the form of logs, diaries, journals, and chronicles in Japanese. Many ISSEI (first-generation Japanese immigrants to the United States) did not feel the need to learn English. They were not allowed to become U.S. citizens, and many had come with the intention of returning to Japan when they had saved enough money.

Some Issei wrote poems using traditional Japanese verse forms, such as *tanka, haiku,* and *senryu*. The poems were published in Japanese-language newspapers on the West Coast.

Japanese American literature started to take shape with the emergence of NISEI (second-generation) writers. Some Nisei spoke both Japanese and English fluently. Besides serving as a bridge between their parents' Japanese culture and American culture, many Nisei writers also took on the responsibility of making the Japanese American voice heard in what Japanese American poet and critic Lawson Fusao INADA calls "the Occidental world of mainstream American literature."

In his introduction to the 1985 edition of Toshio MORI's *Yokohama, California* (1949), Inada echoes William Saroyan by naming Mori "the first real Japanese-American writer." Inada also calls *Yokohama, California* "the first real Japanese-American book." *Yokohama, California* is a collection of short stories. In the book Mori creates a fictional community to explore the richness of Japanese American culture from the 1930's to the early 1940's. Mori's style is as colorful as his sense of humor is amusing.

Internment and Its Impact on Japanese American Literature. During World War II, more than 110,000 Japanese Americans, mostly on the West Coast, were forced to leave their homes and were interned in camps by the U.S. government. Two-thirds of the Japanese Americans incarcerated were American citizens. The ordeal of internment is vividly recorded in Mine OKUBO's pictorial book, *Citizen #13660* (1947). While the early writings of Japanese Americans focused mainly on describing their struggles in learning how to survive in a foreign culture, after the war Japanese American writers shifted their attention to the injustices endured during the war.

John OKADA's *No-No Boy* (1957) presents an accurate depiction of the complicated feelings behind a Japanese American's struggle between his loyalty to his parents and his problematic relationship with America. The book not only examines why some Japanese Americans refused to join the army and swear unqualified allegiance to the United States during the war but also takes a realistic look at the lingering effects of internment on the Japanese American community in the postwar period.

The postwar period in Japanese American literature also saw the emergence of a large group of women writers. Hisaye YAMAMOTO spent three years at POSTON, the Colorado River relocation center, during the war. Yet Yamamoto did not stop writing. She published some of her works in the relocation center newspaper, *The Poston Chronicle*. After Yamamoto returned to the West Coast in 1945, she started publishing stories. In "Seventeen Syllables," "The Brown House," and "Yoneko's Earthquakes," Yamamoto explores both intercultural and intracultural conflict. "The Legend of Miss Sasagawara" is a story about the internment experience, and "Las Vegas Charley" describes how World War II and the internment camp have changed an Issei's life. Some of Yamamoto's stories are collected in *Seventeen Syllables and Other Stories* (1988).

Jessica Saiki grew up in Hawaii. Her *Once, A Lotus Garden* (1987), a collection of short stories, is set in the Japanese American community in Hawaii. The stories describe what many Japanese Americans went through before and during World War II. Saiki's depictions of the conflict between traditional Hawaiian/Japanese culture and the modern American lifestyle of the 1930's and 1940's are very poetic.

Japanese American Renaissance. Japanese American literature in the 1980's and early 1990's, as part of the ASIAN AMERICAN RENAISSANCE movement, is reaching a new height. Many SANSEI (third-generation Japanese Americans) are continuing the tradition begun by the Nisei writers. These Sansei writers are incensed by what happened to their grandparents before World War II and what happened to their parents during the war. Besides demanding that the U.S. government redress the injustice done to Japanese Americans, they have also started a movement to search for what Sansei writer David MURA calls the "lost center" within their souls.

Playwright and poet Velina Hasu Houston, daughter of an African American man and a Japanese woman, and son Kiyoshi Houston. Her plays' frequent themes include racism, culture clash, and ethical responsibility. (Peter Martin)

Garrett Kaoru HONGO, David Mura, and Dwight Okita are some of the new voices in Japanese American literature. Hongo's *Yellow Light* (1982), a collection of poems, was nominated for a Pulitzer Prize. Mura's poems collected in *After We Lost Our Way* (1989) intermingle the voice of anger with that of hope. Mura has also published a semiautobiographical travelogue, *Turning Japanese* (1991). The book is about his visit to Japan in 1984. Okita is a playwright, poet, journalist, and poetry video producer. His new book of poetry, *Crossing with the Light*, was published in 1992.

R. A. SHIOMI shuttles between Vancouver, Seattle, San Francisco, and New York City. Shiomi was born in Toronto and studied at the University of Toronto and Simon Fraser University. His is one of the leading voices in Japanese American theatrical productions. His plays *Yellow Fever* (pb. 1984), *Once Is Never Enough* (pr. 1985), and *Rosie's Café* (pr. 1987) were produced both by the ASIAN-AMERICAN THEATRE COMPANY, San Francisco, and by the PAN ASIAN REPERTORY THEATRE Off-Broadway.

The Japanese American Renaissance has not shown any sign of losing momentum. Its development will help build the United States into a culturally diverse society.—*Qun Wang*

SUGGESTED READINGS: • Bruchac, Joseph, ed. *Breaking Silence: An Anthology of Contemporary Asian American Poets.* New York: Greenfield Review Press, 1983. • Chan, Jeffrey Paul, Frank Chin, Lawson Fusao Inada, and Shawn Wong, eds. *The Big Aiiieeeee! An Anthology of Chinese American and Japanese American Literature.* New York: Meridian Books, 1991. • Cheung, King-Kok. *Articulate Silences: Hisaye Yamamoto, Maxine Hong Kingston, Joy Kogawa.* Ithaca, N.Y.: Cornell University Press, 1993. • Hsu, Kai-yu, and Helen Palubinskas, eds. *Asian-American Authors.* Boston: Houghton Mifflin, 1972. • Kim, Elaine H. *Asian American Literature: An Introduction to the Writings and Their Social Context.* Philadelphia: Temple University Press, 1982.

Japanese American National Library (JANL): Private, nonprofit research library founded in San Francisco in 1969. The library, which is open to the public, contains a wide range of documents pertaining to the Japanese American experience. It serves as the national repository for REDRESS material.

Japanese American National Museum (JANM): Private, nonprofit institution founded in 1985 for the purpose of chronicling the Japanese American experience.

The museum, which is located in the renovated Nishi Hongwanji Buddhist Temple in the Little Tokyo section of Los Angeles, opened its doors in April, 1992.

Plans for the museum had begun ten years earlier, when Bruce T. Kanji, president of Merit Savings Bank and later to become founding president of the JANM, met with Young Oak Kim, a Korean American war hero who served as an officer in the famed Japanese American 100TH INFANTRY BATTALION during World War II. Kanji and Kim formed a committee which began to raise funds and support within the community.

The museum's opening exhibit, "Issei Pioneers: Hawaii and the Mainland, 1885-1924," paid tribute to the first generation of Japanese Americans.

Japanese American press: As large numbers of mostly literate Japanese immigrants began arriving on the West Coast of the United States and in Hawaii in the late nineteenth century, the need for Japanese-language newspapers soon became apparent. For these new arrivals, the press was a means of education and of communication with other immigrants. Both local and international news was directly relevant to their lives abroad.

Early Years. For the Japanese American community, gathering news from Japan was a slow process—by steamer that took five days or more to reach Hawaii and twelve days to reach the Pacific Coast—until the 1920's, when cable and wireless technology enabled the news to cross the Pacific faster than ever before. Airmail service later helped to reduce the cost of news-gathering.

The earliest Japanese-language newspaper overseas, *Shinonome Zasshi* (dawn magazine), was published in 1886 in San Francisco. Handwritten, it consisted of local news, editorials, and columns on politics, economics, and culture. Copy was written with special ink on coated stock, then rubbed over a gelatin surface. No more than twenty legible copies could be duplicated by this method. The mimeograph, capable of producing hundreds of copies, was a more popular method as the twentieth century began. A good hand in writing Japanese on the stencil was all that was required.

The first Japanese newspaper in Hawaii, the *Nippon Shuho,* was started in 1892 to expose corruption in the Japanese section of the Hawaiian immigration bureau. The publication changed hands often and in 1906, with a complete change in editorial policy, became the major Japanese voice, the *Nippu Jiji.* There were as many as seven Japanese dailies in the Hawaiian Islands and

ten on the U.S. mainland at this time. They flourished through the 1920's, when many short-lived publications were expressing opinions about community issues. It was a colorful period for the immigrant press.

Increasing Sophistication. A modest Japanese newspaper in print needed at least 500,000 pieces of type. A tabloid page consisted of nearly 8,000 typefaces and spaces, each hand-picked by the compositor, who stood before a bank of trays with at least 5,000 different square-shaped Japanese characters (a selection of type for the Roman alphabet and Arabic numerals would also be at hand). The first Japanese typeset newspaper, *Shin Sekai Shimbun* (new world), was started in San Francisco in 1894. Later it became *Shin Sekai-Asahi Shimbun* (new world sun) and after World War II was renamed *Hokubei Mainichi.* The more prosperous newspapers could afford to replace worn-out type with the newer Japanese Monotype.

Rise of Bilingualism and Nisei Influence. The ethnic press became bilingual in the late 1920's as the Nisei generation came of age. The first English section appeared in the *Nippu Jiji* on a regular basis in 1919 "to enable Americans to understand what was happening in the Japanese community, to acquaint the children born of Japanese parents in Hawaii with what was occurring in their own community and to promote better understanding between the Japanese and Americans." As other papers introduced English sections, these goals were widely shared.

In San Francisco, Kyutaro ABIKO, publisher of the NICHIBEI SHIMBUN, started a modest English section in 1925. He initiated a Sunday weekly the following year, offering space to aspiring Nisei wanting to be published—a pattern that was emulated by other newspapers. The literary sections in the early 1930's were noteworthy, especially those edited by Larry TAJIRI in the *Kashu Mainichi.* These were the so-called golden years of Nisei journalism.

In 1942, RAFU SHIMPO English editor Togo TANAKA recounted for the University of California Japanese Evacuation and Resettlement Study Project that the three Little Tokyo dailies "exerted an influence greater than is generally attributed to the press in American life." The vernaculars created attitudes and views on community events. There was a minimum of daily collaboration editorially between the Japanese and English sections. Differences were conspicuous in reporting international events. For example, the Japanese editors relied on *Domei News,* by then under control of Japanese military authorities. The English sections relied on wire copy, what appeared in the local press, or what arrived from the communities by mail or telephone.

In Seattle, ex-professional boxer James SAKAMOTO launched the first Nisei-owned publication, the JAPANESE AMERICAN COURIER—without a Japanese-language section. It ran from 1928 until 1942. The JAPANESE AMERICAN CITIZENS LEAGUE (JACL) started the PACIFIC CITIZEN in 1929; the newspaper had an itinerant publication history, moving from San Francisco, to Seattle, to San Francisco in 1940, then to Salt Lake City in 1942 because of the evacuation and internment of Japanese Americans on the West Coast. The paper moved to Los Angeles in 1952 and to suburban Monterey Park in 1993. Other Nisei-owned papers bloomed in the late 1930's but wilted because of the war.

While the war shut down the Japanese vernaculars for the duration of the conflict, there were a few scattered exceptions imposed by the U.S. government. A month after the PEARL HARBOR attack, the military governor in Hawaii ordered the bilingual dailies, the *Hawaii Hochi and the Nippu Jiji*, to resume publication. On the West Coast, the Army used the vernaculars to publicize its pending evacuation orders in Japanese.

In the World War II internment centers, camp newspapers were exclusively in English until the *Manzanar Free Press* demanded a Japanese section since Japanese was the mother tongue among the evacuated majority. Communication in the ASSEMBLY CENTERS had been hampered by the fact that Japanese-language material, except for the Bible and dictionaries, was contraband. In October, 1942, the Japanese editors were granted freedom to write any original article of their own choice. At first, they had to render "literal" English translations of Japanese articles and have them appear in the same issue. This requirement was eventually dropped.

End of an Era? As the Japanese-speaking population in the United States decreased, the vernacular dailies, one by one, were closing down or appearing only on a weekly basis. The rising cost of printing, a lack of advertising, a shortage of Japanese typesetters, and the growing popularity of radio and television contributed to the decline of the vernacular press. One of the first newspapers to close was the *Shin-Nichibei* in Los Angeles in 1966. The pioneer *Nippu Jiji*, renamed the HAWAII TIMES after Pearl Harbor, shut down the same year.

A 1972 survey by HOKUBEI MAINICHI suggested that the era of the vernaculars would end in the 1990's. In 1984, Harry H. L. KITANO, a sociologist at the University of California, Los Angeles (UCLA), observed:

"The Issei have had the Japanese language sections; the Nisei have the *Pacific Citizen*. The question is, will the younger generations support an ethnic press?"

In the 1980's, a Japanese-language business and commerce press developed in Los Angeles to serve corporate personnel from Japan on assignment in the United States. The international weekly edition of the *Japan Times*, printed in Tokyo and airmailed to U.S. subscribers, began publishing an edition out of Los Angeles. By 1990, satellite transmission had enabled major Tokyo newspapers to begin reporting their dailies out of New York. None of these publications, however, is considered part of the Japanese American press.—*Harry K. Honda*

SUGGESTED READINGS: • Hosokawa, Bill. *Nisei: The Quiet Americans*. New York: William Morrow, 1969. • Ichioka, Yuji. *The Issei: The World of the First Generation Japanese Immigrants, 1885-1924*. New York: The Free Press, 1988. • Oda, James. *Heroic Struggles of Japanese Americans*. North Hollywood, Calif.: J. Oda, 1980. • Stroup, Dorothy Anne. *The Role of the Japanese-American Press in Its Community*. Berkeley: University of California Press, 1960. • Tanaka, Togo. "The Vernacular Newspaper." Chapter 3 of an unpublished manuscript written in 1942. Bancroft Library, Berkeley. • United Japanese Society of Hawaii, Publications Committee, ed. *A History of Japanese in Hawaii*. Honolulu: United Japanese Society of Hawaii, 1971.

Japanese American Research Project (JARP): Established by the JAPANESE AMERICAN CITIZENS LEAGUE (JACL) in the 1960's for the purpose of producing a definitive history of the Japanese in America. In 1960, at the JACL's biannual national convention, the idea for the project began as the Issei History Project. Chairpersons were appointed by each chapter to raise money for what some people envisioned as a history book on Japanese Americans. Ultimately, however, that vision turned out to be very shortsighted. By 1962 more than $200,000 had been collected for the project, but the organizers had no clear idea what the scope of the project should be. T. Scott MIYAKAWA from Boston University was asked to assist in the matter and eventually became the project director of the newly named Japanese American Research Project. Miyakawa came up with three objectives for the JARP: The group should pursue an extensive sociological study on Japanese Americans, a written scholarly history of Japanese Americans should be part of the project, and archival materials, including oral histories, should be collected. Later a popular history on Japanese Americans was also added to the original three objectives. Through University of California, Los Angeles (UCLA) alumnus and JACL president Frank Chuman, the group found a home for the collection at the university's research library.

To fulfill the goals of the project, many books and studies have been published through the JARP, including *Nisei: The Quiet Americans* (1969) by Bill Hosokawa; *The Japanese American Community: A Three-Generation Study* (1981), coauthored by Gene N. Levine and Robert C. Rhodes; *The Economic Basis of Ethnic Solidarity: Small Business in the Japanese American Community* (1980), by John Modell and Edna Bonacich; *The Economics and Politics of Racial Accommodation: The Japanese of Los Angeles, 1900-1942* (1977), by John Modell; *Japanese Americans: Changing Patterns of Ethnic Affiliation over Three Generations* (1980), by Darrel Montero; *East Across the Pacific: Historical and Sociological Studies of Japanese Immigration and Assimilation* (1977), edited by Hilary Conroy and T. Scott Miyakawa; *The Bamboo People: The Law and Japanese-Americans* (1976), by Frank Chuman; and *Planted in Good Soil: A History of the Issei in United States Agriculture* (1992), by Masakazu Iwata.

In addition, the JARP houses the largest Japanese American archive in the United States, complete with oral histories, photos, and the personal papers of historic figures such as Karl YONEDA, Edison UNO, and Kyutaro ABIKO. This collection has been the basis for numerous scholarly articles, master's theses, doctoral dissertations, and books throughout the years.

Japanese American women: The first significant wave of Japanese female immigration into the United States began with the establishment of the GENTLEMEN'S AGREEMENT (1907-1908) and ended with the restrictive IMMIGRATION ACT OF 1924, which barred entry to all aliens who were ineligible to receive citizenship. These ISSEI women, many of whom came to the United States as "PICTURE BRIDES," bore most of their children between 1918 and 1940. The second generation, the NISEI, growing up in a stable ethnic community, formed a strong generational identity, especially through their INTERNMENT experience. After World War II a sizable number of Japanese women arrived with their American husbands, who had stayed in Japan largely for military service. These "war brides" formed another wave of Japanese female immigration. The daughters of the Nisei, the SANSEI

women, were born between about 1940 and 1960; they began to enter various professions in large numbers and to form a new identity of Japanese Americans.

Issei Women. Prior to the GENTLEMEN'S AGREEMENT, which severely limited immigration of Japanese laborers, the Japanese immigrant community, like the early Chinese community, was largely male. The 1900 census shows that there were about 1,000 women among 24,236 Japanese in the contiguous United States at that time. Of the women, 410 were listed as married; a significant number of the rest came as prostitutes from Japan's impoverished countryside.

While the Gentlemen's Agreement, in conjunction with the IMMIGRATION ACT OF 1907, greatly reduced the flow of adult male immigrants from Japan, wives and children of Japanese men already in the United States were allowed to enter. Many ISSEI men sought their brides through go-between arrangements involving the exchange of portraits by mail, which was then a common practice in Japan. Between 1908 and 1920—when the Japanese government, under pressure from the ANTI-JAPANESE MOVEMENT in the United States, ceased issuing passports to PICTURE BRIDES—thousands of Japanese picture brides arrived. By 1920, the number of Japanese women had increased to 38,303 out of a total Japanese population of 111,010 in the contiguous United States. These women came from farming and small entrepreneurial families in southern Japan, with social backgrounds similar to those of their husbands. On average they were ten years younger than their husbands and had similar levels of education, about eight years of schooling.

These pioneer Issei women had to struggle along with their husbands to survive with limited resources in a hostile environment. Raised in Meiji Japan, where the ideology of "good wives and wise mothers" was imposed under the patriarchal extended family system, they maintained traditional practices such as self-devotion, self-sacrifice, hard work, submissiveness, modesty, and quietness. Since the Issei community was built exclusively by men, following the Japanese custom of male dominance in the public sphere, women were excluded from public meetings, associations, and dinners. Issei women were visible in the public sphere only through their supportive roles as wives and mothers.

Issei women, however, created their own space through *TANOMOSHI-KO* (ROTATING CREDIT ASSOCIATIONS), handcraft clubs, *tanka-kai* (poetry clubs), and *FUJINKAI* (women's associations). These segregated women's groups provided Issei women with a place

Educational Attainment, Labor Status, and Occupation of Japanese American Women, 1990

Education of Women 25 Years or Older	
	Percent
High school graduate	29%
Some college or associate degree	28%
College graduate	21%
Advanced or professional degree	7%
Total high school graduate or more	85%

Women 16 Years or Older	
	Percent
In labor force	56%
(Unemployed	3%)
Not in labor force	44%

Employed Civilian Women 16 Years or Older

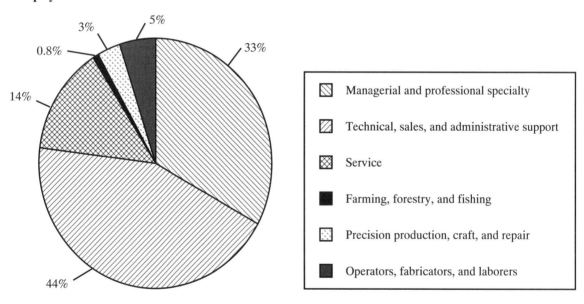

Managerial and professional specialty

Technical, sales, and administrative support

Service

Farming, forestry, and fishing

Precision production, craft, and repair

Operators, fabricators, and laborers

Source: U.S. Bureau of the Census, *1990 Census of Population: Asians and Pacific Islanders in the United States,* 1993.

for meeting one another, sharing their common experiences, and preserving their ethnic identity. These associations also enabled Issei women to transmit Meiji Japanese values, such as the importance of education, cleanliness, politeness, diligence, and honesty, to their children. Thus women served as guardians of Japanese culture and ethnicity.

Issei women worked alongside their husbands in farms, family-owned small businesses such as boardinghouses and laundries, and Japanese-owned stores in the Japanese community. Many Issei women worked in domestic service. They worked mainly in informal

sectors with low wages and long hours, at jobs which required little in the way of formal skills and no English fluency. Recognizing the extremely limited opportunities available to them, Issei women stressed education, hoping for a better future for their children.

Nisei Women. Because of their parents' similar backgrounds and occupational status, most Nisei women share common values and clear generational experiences. While their Issei parents expected them to follow the traditional stereotype of Japanese femininity, the Nisei became increasingly exposed to the dominant culture through their school and church activities. In the 1930's young urban Nisei, like their contemporaries in the larger society, were inspired by the ideal of "romantic love." In cities most Nisei women went to public high schools; many took commercial courses, and some went to business colleges. Although the sons' education took priority in most Japanese families, Nisei women were considerably better educated than the general female population. In 1940, in the eighteen-through-nineteen age group, 54 percent of Japanese American females versus 38 percent of the general female population were in school.

Despite their American education and fluent English, however, Nisei women found that their options were almost as limited as those of their immigrant mothers. White-collar jobs were closed to them except in a limited number of Japanese firms. A significant percentage of Nisei women in the workforce were employed in domestic service. Racial and ethnic barriers blocked upward mobility of even well-educated Nisei women.

The wartime INTERNMENT experience made a significant impact on Japanese American women's lives.

For many Issei women, communal life in camps provided a relief from heavy housework chores. Some of them learned English for the first time. Young Nisei women had opportunities to work in clerical jobs, nursing, teaching, health care, and social work in camp administration. Women strived to hold the family together for survival in the harsh camp environment. Nisei women were also among the Japanese Americans stranded in Japan during the war. They were closely watched by Japanese police and forced to do translating and interpreting services for the Japanese military. Upon returning to the United States after the war, some were made scapegoats for their "antipatriotic" activities. Prosecution of Iva Toguri d'Aquino (see TOKYO ROSE) is a case in point.

Postwar Change. A general change in the economic structure and the breakdown of racial and gender barriers in the postwar period caused a remarkable change in Japanese American women's status. Well-educated urban Nisei women entered white-collar professions for the first time. The Civil Rights movement raised the political consciousness of Nisei women, who had

Japanese American women pound the taiko *drums during San Francisco's Cherry Blossom Festival.* (Michael Yamashita)

Male-to-Female Ratio of Japanese American Population, 1870-1990

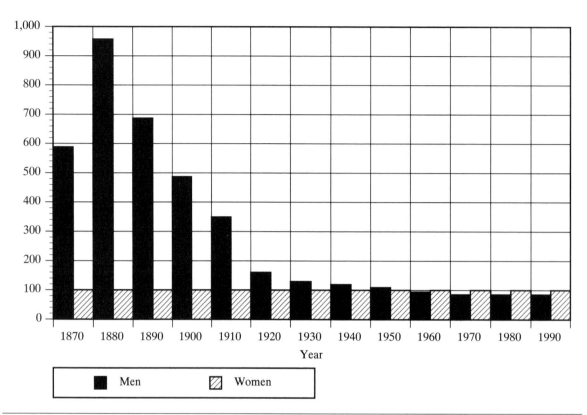

Sources: Herbert Barringer, Robert W. Gardner, and Michael J. Levin, *Asians and Pacific Islanders in the United States.* New York: Russell Sage Foundation, 1993. U.S. Bureau of the Census, *1990 Census of Population: Asians and Pacific Islanders in the United States,* 1993.
Note: Data show number of Japanese American males per 100 Japanese American females.

previously engaged only in auxiliary activities in Nisei male-dominated political organizations. In the struggle for American citizenship for the Issei, Nisei women played a crucial role, distributing information, leading workshops, and writing letters to legislators. Michi WEGLYN's document of the internment experience, *Years of Infamy* (1976), raised awareness of the issue of Japanese American INTERNMENT and contributed to the REDRESS campaign. Hundreds of women testified about their camp experiences for the COMMISSION ON WARTIME RELOCATION AND INTERNMENT OF CIVILIANS (CWRIC). Their testimony helped to bring about the passage of the CIVIL LIBERTIES ACT OF 1988.

Most SANSEI women, coming from urban and suburban environments, are college-educated. They have entered previously closed professions and established themselves in careers. They have become the most structurally assimilated group among Asian and Pacific islanders. More than 50 percent of Sansei women

have married non-Japanese. At the same time, there is an emerging tendency to learn Japanese language and culture. Many Sansei and YONSEI (fourth-generation) women share a political consciousness of themselves as Asian Americans.

Contrary to the myth of the MODEL MINORITY, Japanese American women are not free from the subtle racism built into American society. Nisei women workers are disproportionately employed in the public sector, while being underrepresented in the private sector. Few Japanese American women are found in the top-ranking positions in government and industry, in part perhaps because they are often considered to be passive and nonassertive. To confront and overcome such stereotypes is a lifelong struggle for Japanese American women.—*Machiko Matsui*

SUGGESTED READINGS: • Glenn, Evelyn Nakano. *Issei, Nisei, War Bride: Three Generations of Japanese American Women in Domestic Service.* Philadelphia:

Temple University Press, 1986. • Nakano, Mei. *Japanese American Women: Three Generations, 1890-1990*. Berkeley, Calif.: Mina Press, 1990. • Sone, Monica. *Nisei Daughter*. Boston: Little, Brown, 1953. • Weglyn, Michi. *Years of Infamy: The Untold Story of America's Concentration Camps*. New York: Morrow, 1976. • Yamamoto, Hisaye. *Seventeen Syllables and Other Stories*. Latham, N.Y.: Kitchen Table—Women of Color Press, 1988.

Japanese Americans: These individuals are an ethnic minority in the United States made up of immigrants from Japan and their descendants. The experience of Japanese Americans has been shaped by events and circumstances in Japan and the United States, as well as by the particular measures this ethnic group has taken to respond to discrimination. The history of their life in America includes the major period of immigration, from 1868 to 1924; the period of settlement and community development, from 1924 to 1941; the incarceration of more than 120,000 Japanese Americans (including citizens as well as aliens) during World War II, when America was at war against Japan; the postwar recovery and movement for REDRESS and reparation for Japanese Americans placed in the CONCENTRATION CAMPS; and life for Japanese Americans as they approach the twenty-first century.

Immigration. With the beginning of the MEIJI era in 1868, Japan reversed the policy of isolation it had followed for more than two hundred years, opened itself to the ideas and technologies of the Western world, and relaxed its restrictions against emigration. Large-scale immigration to Hawaii and the continental United States began in 1885 and continued until 1924. This first generation of immigrants, the ISSEI, were mostly young, single men who came from farming backgrounds and saw themselves as SOJOURNERS—temporary residents hoping to make their fortunes, help their families, who were experiencing economic hardship, and return to their homeland with their wealth.

During this period 200,000 Japanese went to Hawaii and 180,000 immigrated to the continental United States. In part this mass movement of young male workers out of Japan was a response to difficult economic conditions in Japan. It also served to fill a need for laborers in Hawaii's sugar plantations, and on the continent it was a solution for the shortage of cheap labor following the CHINESE EXCLUSION ACT OF 1882.

Upon arrival at their destinations, the young laborers found conditions to be far worse than they had expected. Plantation laborers in Hawaii were not free to work the land at their own pace. They were awakened in the morning by the plantation siren and herded by company foremen and company police to the fields. Most of the regimented work was harsh and exhausting. In addition to facing the difficulties of a new language and a strange culture, Japanese immigrants found that their three-year contracts made them servants to the plantation system.

In the continental United States, Japanese immigrants were concentrated in the West Coast states, especially California. Like the Chinese immigrants before them, the Japanese experienced intense resentment and discrimination. They were the objects of racial slurs, spitting, stone throwing, vandalism, and arson. During the early years most of the men worked as migratory laborers in agriculture, railroads, and canneries. For the most part, they had to endure physically fatiguing work and poor living conditions.

With its new international orientation, the Japanese government was concerned that its emigrants be honorable representatives of Japan. To ensure this, the government established review boards to see that emigrants were healthy and literate and also promoted the emigration of Japanese women in order to avoid the temptations common to a bachelor society, such as prostitution, gambling, and drunkenness. Because few bachelors could afford the time or expense of returning to Japan for formal social customs involving engagement and marriage, many men used the photo marriage (*shashin kekkon*), or picture-bride, practice. The traditional custom of arranged marriages and the exchanging of photographs as part of the pre-meeting process lent itself well to the needs of Japanese immigrants in America. Men sent information about themselves, with their photographs, to go-betweens in Japan, and negotiations were concluded with the parents of eligible daughters. Marriages in Japan were legal as long as the name of the bride was entered in the family registry of the groom. A wedding ceremony was not required.

By 1920, when Japan terminated the emigration of PICTURE BRIDES, more than 22,000 Japanese women had emigrated. For many the disappointments of their new life began at the immigration station when they met their husbands, who were not always as they appeared in their photos. Often, too, prospective husbands exaggerated their talents and social and financial circumstances. Life for women on the plantations and farms was characterized by physical hardship and poverty. The women felt isolated and lonely in a strange land where customs, language, food, and cloth-

Japanese American Statistical Profile, 1990

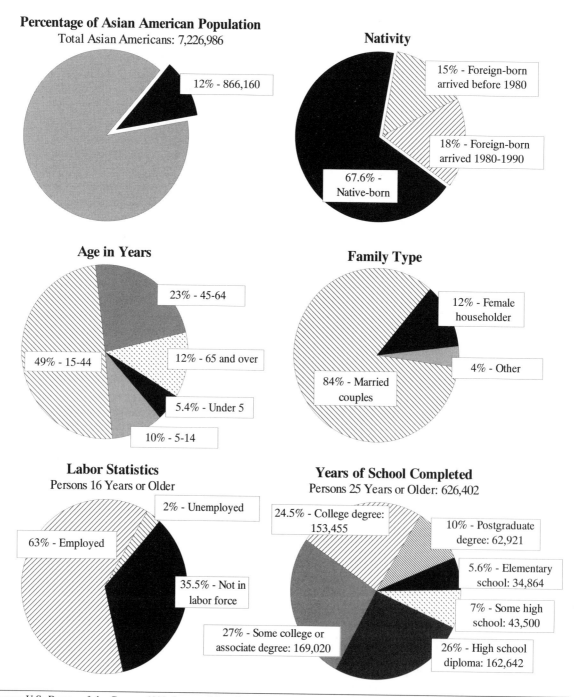

Percentage of Asian American Population
Total Asian Americans: 7,226,986

12% - 866,160

Nativity

15% - Foreign-born arrived before 1980

18% - Foreign-born arrived 1980-1990

67.6% - Native-born

Age in Years

23% - 45-64

12% - 65 and over

49% - 15-44

5.4% - Under 5

10% - 5-14

Family Type

12% - Female householder

4% - Other

84% - Married couples

Labor Statistics
Persons 16 Years or Older

2% - Unemployed

63% - Employed

35.5% - Not in labor force

Years of School Completed
Persons 25 Years or Older: 626,402

24.5% - College degree: 153,455

10% - Postgraduate degree: 62,921

5.6% - Elementary school: 34,864

7% - Some high school: 43,500

27% - Some college or associate degree: 169,020

26% - High school diploma: 162,642

Source: U.S. Bureau of the Census, *1990 Census of Population: Asians and Pacific Islanders in the United States,* 1993.

ing were alien to their own culture. They were, moreover, totally dependent on husbands who viewed women as their subordinates.

Anti-Japanese Movement. Because of the strong anti-Chinese racism during the later decades of the 1800's, Japanese immigrants suffered the legacy of the "YELLOW PERIL"—a fear on the part of Caucasians that Asians would invade their society and take over the dominion of the white man. For ISSEI who started in migrant occupations, agriculture provided the best chance of advancement. Individuals who began as ordinary laborers could progress to contract farming and eventually work their own land. Although this often meant working land that others viewed as unsuitable for raising crops, their efforts were productive. This

---

Occupation

Employed Persons 16 Years or Older	Percentage
Managerial and professional specialty	37%
Technical, sales, and administrative support	34%
Service	11%
Farming, forestry, and fishing	3%
Precision production, craft, and repair	8%
Operators, fabricators, and laborers	7%

Income, 1989

Median household income	$41,626
Per capita	$19,373
Percent of families in poverty	3%

Household Size

Number of People	Percentage
1	28.0%
2	31.0%
3	17.6%
4	16.0%
5	5.6%
6	1.6%
7 or more	0.7%

Source: U.S. Bureau of the Census, *1990 Census of Population: Asians and Pacific Islanders in the United States,* 1993.

---

ability to be successful in farming, however, contributed to the increase of anti-Japanese sentiment and resulted in numerous efforts to prevent the Japanese from becoming a part of American society.

One of the strongest sources of opposition to acceptance of the Japanese was the labor unions. Arguments for excluding Japanese from unions were based on the idea that Japanese were from such an alien culture that they could not be Americanized. Other government and fraternal groups in California joined the ANTI-JAPANESE MOVEMENT. In 1906 the San Francisco Board of Education directed that Japanese children be sent to segregated schools, along with Chinese and Korean children. The government of Japan quickly issued a protest to Washington, D.C., and President Theodore Roosevelt forced the San Francisco officials to back down. The trade-off for this concession was a promise that Roosevelt would negotiate an understanding with Japan, whereby the Japanese government would cease issuing passports to Japanese laborers to immigrate to the United States. This executive agreement, the so-called GENTLEMEN'S AGREEMENT (1907-1908), did not keep a number of women from migrating and led to a continuing increase of the Japanese American population.

ALIEN LAND LAWS were passed in the California legislature in 1913 and 1920 making it illegal for Japanese to own real property. These discriminatory laws, which soon spread to other states, were founded on the fact that Japanese immigrants were ineligible to become naturalized U.S. citizens. In 1870, when Congress amended the naturalization law to permit "persons of African nativity or descent" to become citizens, Asians were deliberately excluded from eligibility. Thus, until 1952, Japanese immigrants, like all Asian immigrants and unlike all other immigrants, could not become U.S. citizens, although their American-born children were citizens by right of birth.

The Issei did not accept such discrimination passively. In 1914, for example, Takao Ozawa filed an application for U.S. citizenship but was denied. In 1922 the U.S. Supreme Court upheld the decision of the district court that Ozawa was not entitled to naturalized citizenship because he was not of the Caucasian race. The final restriction to Japanese immigration came in 1924, when Congress passed a general immigration law that prohibited entry of any aliens ineligible to citizenship. The dominant message to Japanese immigrants was one of exclusion and racial discrimination.

The Early Japanese Community. While struggling

with the ostracism of American society, the Issei retreated to their ethnic community to develop resources and organizations in order to meet their own social and material needs. The entry of Japanese into agriculture and the arrival of Japanese wives changed the SOJOURN-ERS into settlers. In this setting men and women alike called upon the values of endurance and forbearance (*GAMAN*) and of persistence and tenacity (*genbaru*) to swallow their anger and survive the hardships of their lives. Instead of fighting the outside world, they turned their energies to family and community building.

Submerging individual interests to the interest of what is best for the group is another Japanese value that served the Issei well. The ability to cooperate and organize collectively made it possible to establish a network of economic, social, religious, educational, and humanitarian institutions that worked to support the lives of the Japanese. An example of such a practice was the development of ROTATING CREDIT ASSO-CIATIONS (*TANOMOSHI*), a common economic fund to which people regularly contributed. This fund was available to its members for making major family purchases or for financing the start-up or expansion of a small business. At a time when obtaining credit in the larger society was highly improbable, Japanese counted on the trust between members of the community to underwrite financial investments. This trust was based on the strong commitment to meeting obligations in order to uphold family honor.

The family was the primary source for transmitting traditional Japanese values. Issei women had been raised in the MEIJI era, when their role as women was to nurture members of the family and serve their husbands and sons, who were responsible for bringing honor to the family name. Each person acted in terms of clearly prescribed roles and responsibilities, and although life was harsh for the immigrant family in America, the emphasis on duty, obligation, and *gaman* contributed to the stability of the household. Even when husbands were gamblers or drunkards, women held the family together for the sake of the children.

The household (*ie*) became an asset to economic adaptation. Children were raised with a strong sense of family obligation, and they worked along with their parents at home and in the family business. As Japanese immigrants gathered in farm towns or in isolated sections of large cities, such as Seattle or Los Angeles, they engaged in activities such as meetings, picnics, and fundraising events sponsored by churches (both Buddhist and Christian), JAPANESE-LANGUAGE SCHOOLS, prefectural organizations, and the Japanese

The Reverend S. Naito and family of the Buddhist Church of Sacramento, 1934. (Sacramento Archive and Museum Collection Center)

Association of America. These events served to develop community ties. Although such activities reinforced the outside view that Japanese were incapable of assimilating and were loyal only to the emperor of Japan, the ethnic community activities had begun in response to hostility on the part of the majority society. As it became clear that the Issei would not be accepted into American society, Japanese immigrants placed their hopes on the future of their children, the NISEI.

The Nisei. The Japanese consider success in education as the primary way to achieve status and to bring honor to the family and the race. Japanese immigrant parents hoped the combination of U.S. citizenship and educational achievement would allow their offspring, the Nisei, access to economic opportunities that had been denied to the Issei. They encouraged their children toward educational achievement using the values familiar to them: being diligent in their studies, respecting authority, and doing their best. As good Japanese children, the Nisei followed their parents' wishes, and in so doing, they also became good Americans. By participating fully in the public educational system, the Nisei learned about the American values of freedom and democracy. They pledged allegiance to the American flag, spoke the English language, and learned about American sports, styles, and customs. In the process they became Americanized.

To be a Nisei meant being both Japanese and American. Nisei spoke English at school and with their friends, but Japanese was the language spoken at home. They celebrated Japanese Boys' Day and Girls' Day and observed New Year's Day Japanese-style, and they also celebrated Christmas and the Fourth of July. They were expected to do well in public school, but many were also sent to Japanese school after the regular school day or on Saturday. The Nisei wanted to be fully American, but they had also internalized many of their parents' Japanese values.

For Nisei on the West Coast, the duality of their lives was made worse by the fact that in spite of their very American behavior, they were not accepted by the majority society as Americans. They were called "Japs" and told to go back to where they had come from. They were not allowed to sit in the same section as white persons at theaters or to swim in public pools. Although they were U.S. citizens, they were still restricted from buying homes in many areas. The harshest blow to their efforts was that in spite of their exceptional educational achievements, the Nisei were not able to obtain the professional jobs for which their college training had prepared them. Having been trained at prestigious universities to become engineers, architects, attorneys, and schoolteachers, many Nisei graduates found themselves cut off from employment opportunities in the majority society. College-educated Nisei often worked as gardeners or in businesses and service jobs within the Japanese community.

Although the Nisei were frustrated and discouraged, they, like their parents before them, turned to Japanese community groups and organizations to adapt to a discriminatory American society. They formed their own sports leagues, church groups, dance clubs, and civic organizations. The most influential of these groups, in terms of mobilizing toward acceptance in American society, was the JAPANESE AMERICAN CITIZENS LEAGUE (JACL). The JACL sought to educate the larger society about the achievements of Japanese Americans. At the same time, within the Japanese community, the JACL emphasized patriotism as the key to acceptance, urging Japanese Americans to demonstrate their loyalty and worthiness as real Americans.

The experience of race relations and economic opportunity for the Nisei in Hawaii was markedly different from that of their counterparts on the continent. By the start of the twentieth century, the Japanese were the largest ethnic community in Hawaii, and the total number of Asians on the islands outnumbered the white population there. Japanese in Hawaii were "LOCALS." The Nisei in Hawaii eventually moved into skilled trade jobs and professional positions, especially in public institutions such as the schools. By the early 1940's, Japanese represented 37 percent of Hawaii's population, and they were widely accepted as valuable members of the island community.

World War II and the Incarceration of Japanese Americans. When the forces of Imperial Japan attacked PEARL HARBOR on December 7, 1941, the lives of Japanese Americans on the West Coast changed dramatically. In the early weeks of 1942, public outrage at the attack and fear of invasion by a successful Japanese military took the form of heightened anti-Japanese hysteria. Decades of anti-Japanese hatred and the economic threat of successful Japanese farmers created public pressure on the U.S. government to remove the Japanese living on the Pacific Coast. On February 19, 1942, President Franklin D. Roosevelt signed EXECUTIVE ORDER 9066 empowering the military command to remove Japanese Americans on the West Coast into fenced, guarded compounds, euphemistically called "RELOCATION CENTERS."

This mass incarceration of Japanese Americans—altogether, more than 120,000 were interned during World War II—into concentration camps in remote areas of the country has been described as the most tragic event of Japanese American history and an example of the failure of the U.S. Constitution to protect the civil rights of American citizens. Under the pressure of wartime hysteria, the leaders of the country failed to uphold democratic values. Instead, "military necessity" was used as an excuse to ignore information and withhold facts from the judiciary, the Congress,

Japanese American farm laborer, Nyssa, Oregon, 1942. (Library of Congress)

and the American people. Japanese Americans were aware of the history of rampant racism in the legal and social institutions of the United States; they believed there was no choice but to comply with the government.

The experience for the Japanese in Hawaii was considerably different. In spite of pressure from the War Department in Washington, D.C., to remove all Japanese from Oahu, General Delos EMMONS, as military governor of Hawaii, insisted that Japanese workers were indispensable to the economy and to the defense operations of Hawaii. He interned only those Japanese who constituted a potential threat to the country. His rational leadership and the widespread support for his stance by Hawaii's politicians, public officials, business community, and press saved the Japanese on Hawaii from the indiscriminate incarceration experience imposed on West Coast Japanese Americans.

Most of the Issei community leaders on the continent were interned by the U.S. Federal Bureau of Investigation (FBI) immediately after Pearl Harbor, and the representative organization for the Nisei, the JACL, decided to prove Nisei patriotism by cooperating with the orders of the military. JACL leaders also encouraged Nisei to prove their loyalty by joining in the war effort. When participation in the armed services was opened to Nisei, two units of all-Japanese American troops, the 442ND REGIMENTAL COMBAT TEAM and the 100TH INFANTRY BATTALION, composed of men from Hawaii and the continent, distinguished themselves in the European theater and became the most decorated units in American military history. Some five thousand Japanese Americans in the MILITARY INTELLIGENCE SERVICE (MIS) also performed important roles in the Pacific theater, earning praise from their superiors.

Although most Japanese Americans followed an accommodating mode, the unfair policies of the government brought forth a few citizens who challenged these injustices. Minoru YASUI in Oregon, Gordon HIRABAYASHI in Washington, and Fred KOREMATSU in California refused to follow the military orders. Each was arrested, convicted, and sent to prison. All three cases were reviewed by the Supreme Court—and their convictions were upheld on the basis of military necessity. In 1943, when the government required internees to answer loyalty questionnaires, one of the questions asked if draft-age males would be willing to serve in the U.S. armed forces. Although most Nisei answered yes, a large number of Nisei refused to cooperate with the draft, protesting that by having to be in camp they were being treated like enemy aliens rather than as American citizens.

Impact of the Camps. Japanese American families and businesses suffered economic losses that were devastating. In addition, the infrastructure that the Issei had worked so hard to develop in businesses such as agriculture and fishing was destroyed. Prewar Japanese communities were scattered, and upon leaving camp many Japanese Americans dispersed to the Midwest and the East Coast. The tight, close-functioning family unit was also broken in the camps. The authority of the Issei father was undermined, and children and teenagers ate meals with friends in camp rather than together as a family. Perhaps the most devastating effect of the concentration camp experience was the psychological impact on loyal, patriotic Japanese Americans. The accommodating, hardworking behavior of Japanese Americans was based on the belief that loyalty and good work would eventually be recognized by American society. The decision for mass incarceration was a deep betrayal by the government of the principles of democracy and fair play that Japanese

Government-enforced closure of a Japanese American business in Los Angeles' Little Tokyo, April, 1942. The note up top indicates that this family is being removed to the Manzanar relocation camp in the Owens Valley, California. (National Archives)

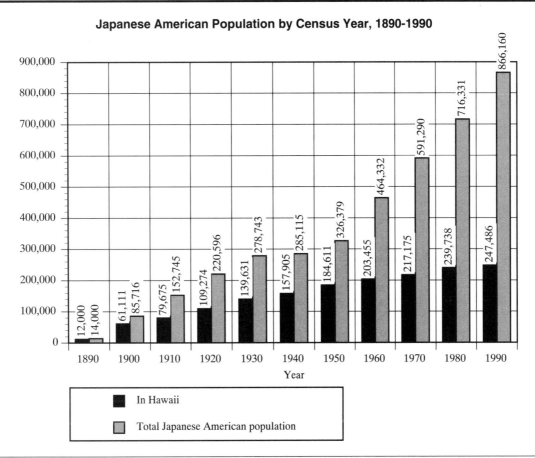

Japanese American Population by Census Year, 1890-1990

In Hawaii

Total Japanese American population

Sources: Fred S. Rolater and Jeannette Baker Rolater, *Japanese Americans.* American Voices series. Vero Beach, Fla.: Rourke Corp., 1991. Susan B. Gall and Timothy L. Gall, eds., *Statistical Record of Asian Americans.* Detroit: Gale Research, Inc., 1993.

Americans practiced. The sense of being dishonored was so painful, most victims of the camp experience did not allow themselves to acknowledge their feelings. The main psychological defense against the experience was a denial of its impact and an outward striving to be super-patriotic, acceptable Americans.

Postwar Recovery. The opportunity to succeed as Americans was realized in the period following World War II. After an initial period of tension and fearfulness immediately upon release from the camps, Japanese Americans found structural changes that allowed them to achieve success. The most dramatic change occurred in the area of occupational opportunities. In the economic boom following World War II, Japanese Americans found that they were able to use their education and skills to move into professions and civil service positions that had been closed to them before the war.

The defeat of Japan markedly diminished the fear of Japanese as a threat. Reports of the heroism of the 442ND REGIMENTAL COMBAT TEAM and the 100TH INFANTRY BATTALION in service to America also contributed to more favorable attitudes toward Japanese Americans. These changes were reflected in legal decisions. In 1952, the ALIEN LAND LAWS were declared unconstitutional by the California Supreme Court; in the same year, the McCARRAN-WALTER ACT was passed, allowing the Issei to become naturalized citizens. The increase in Japanese American citizens in Hawaii contributed to a growing leadership of Japanese Americans in the political arena there. By the mid-1970's, 50 percent of Hawaii's state representatives and senators were Japanese Americans. Japanese Americans were appointed heads of important departments, held top elected offices in the state, and were elected to the U.S. House of Representatives and Senate.

Social barriers against Japanese Americans were also lowered. ANTIMISCEGENATION LAWS were voided, and in the 1970's, the outmarriage rate among Japanese in Los Angeles County was 60.6 percent. By the 1970's

Top 10 Types of Businesses Owned by Japanese Americans in Los Angeles, 1958

Type of Business	Number
Private contract gardening	5,070
Apartments and hotels	250
Grocery stores and markets	129
Laundries and dry cleaners	65
Gas stations	60
Insurance agents	54
Dentists	46
Real estate agents	44
Florists	34
Accountants	24

Source: Fred S. Rolater and Jeannette Baker Rolater, *Japanese Americans.* American Voices series. Vero Beach, Fla.: Rourke Corp., 1991.

Japanese Americans were seen as a success story, and their achievements as a group were widely acknowledged and admired. While the new image of Japanese Americans as a MODEL MINORITY was an improvement on the old racist stereotypes, and while it served to reassure the majority society that America is indeed a country where minorities can succeed if they work hard enough, it too was a stereotype, a distorting oversimplification, and as such it has been rejected by many Japanese Americans and other Asian Americans to whom it has been applied.

Redress and Reparations. The silence of many internees about the camps was disturbed in the days of the Civil Rights movement of the 1960's when the SANSEI (third-generation Japanese Americans) began asking their parents about the camp experiences. As part of the widespread ethnic awareness movement, the Sansei sought to find pride in the Japanese roots their parents had painfully tried to put aside. This questioning within the context of the Civil Rights movement helped Japanese Americans to consider the idea of REDRESS—a way to rectify the wrongs committed against them during World War II. It was not easy to unite the Japanese American community to support this idea, but, once again, the persistence and collective organizational skills so characteristic of the Japanese moved the JACL and other community groups to seek an apology and monetary compensation from the U.S. government. The political sophistication and skill of Japanese American politicians in Washington were invaluable in guiding the timing and strategy. In 1981 and 1982 a congressional fact-finding commission, the COMMISSION ON WARTIME RELOCATION AND INTERNMENT OF CIVILIANS (CWRIC), held hearings to take the testimony of more than 750 persons in several major cities throughout the country. The outpouring of individual stories was an immensely cathartic experience for Japanese Americans, who had repressed their experiences for thirty years. The mass of evidence collected led the commission to conclude that the incarceration had been the product of "race prejudice, war hysteria, and failure of political leadership." To atone for the injustice that was done, the commission recommended a payment of $20,000 each to all living internees and an apology from the U.S. government.

Redress bills to implement the commission's recommendation were submitted, and because of the combined work by grassroots organizations, Washington lobbyists, and Japanese American legislators in the House and Senate, the CIVIL LIBERTIES ACT OF 1988 was passed and signed into law by President Ronald Reagan.

Contemporary Issues. The successful completion of the REDRESS MOVEMENT shows that Japanese Americans exist as a strong, vital ethnic community. Although Japanese Americans are no longer constrained to live in one geographic neighborhood, a sense of community is maintained through recreational and social organizations, religious and community service institutions, and Japanese American professional associations. A commitment to preserve the customs and history of the group is seen in events such as yearly *O-BON* festivals celebrated both in Hawaii and on the continent and in the establishment of the JAPANESE AMERICAN NATIONAL MUSEUM. The community has also responded to the issue of caring for its elderly Issei and Nisei. Because the American social structure is not conducive to several generations living in the same household, Japanese Americans have developed a number of retirement facilities and convalescent homes where residents can share common experiences, interests, and food preferences.

The efforts of the Sansei to reclaim their ethnic identity in the 1960's and 1970's contributed significantly to the establishment of ASIAN AMERICAN STUDIES programs in a number of universities throughout the United States. The concept of a pan-Asian approach to studying the experience of Asians in America, seeking funding for programs, and organizing for political purposes has affected the Japanese American community of the 1980's and 1990's, so that many of its efforts and activities are now shared with other Asian groups.

At the same time, the significant economic growth of Pacific Rim countries and Japan's status as a major power has increased economic tensions, and again the Japanese are being seen as a threat to American economic power. The large influx of Asian immigrants since the IMMIGRATION AND NATIONALITY ACT OF

Japanese Agriculture in California, Selected Characteristics, 1900-1940

Acreage Operated

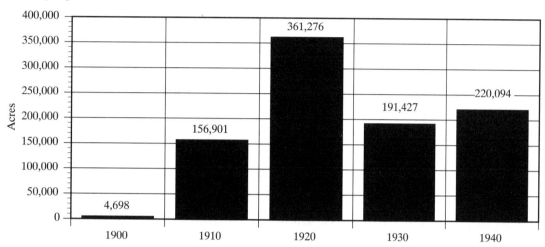

Percentage of Japanese Farm Owners, Managers, and Tenants

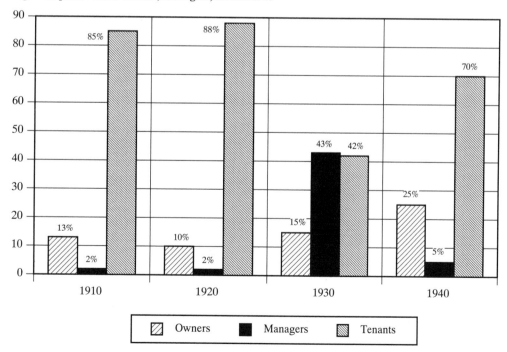

Sources: Gary Okihiro and David Drummond, "The Concentration Camps and Japanese Economic Losses in California Agriculture" in *Japanese Americans: From Relocation to Redress,* edited by Roger Daniels, Sandra C. Taylor, and Harry H. L. Kitano. Salt Lake City: University of Utah Press, 1986.

Japanese American students at the University of California at Davis. (Ben Klaffke)

1965 has added to an increase in racial tensions. Because many Americans do not discern distinctions between the various Asian groups, resentment toward any Asian group leaves all Asians vulnerable to attack. The U.S. Justice Department notes a rise in anti-Asian incidents since the 1980's. Hate crimes against Asians include vandalism, harassment and intimidation, physical attacks, and killings.

A coalition of Asian American community and professional groups has been responding to institutional policies, statements by public figures, media images, and news events that contribute to discrimination against Asians. The quiet, accommodating approach of earlier Japanese Americans is no longer useful. The response of Japanese Americans in the twenty-first century will reflect a people who are clearly confident about their rights and status as American citizens.—*Amy Iwasaki Mass*

SUGGESTED READINGS:

• Daniels, Roger, Sandra C. Taylor, and Harry H. L. Kitano, eds. *Japanese Americans: From Relocation to Redress.* Rev. ed. Seattle: University of Washington Press, 1991. The three editors, respected scholars on the internment of Japanese Americans, have drawn together a comprehensive account of the wartime relocation of Japanese Americans. The book was originally inspired by the International Conference on Relocation and Redress in March, 1983, during the earlier stages of the redress movement. The revised edition provides a fitting update on redress achieved.

• Hazama, Dorothy Ochiai, and Jane Okamoto Komeiji. *Okage Sama De: The Japanese in Hawaii, 1885-1985.* Honolulu: Bess Press, 1986. A comprehensive history of the Japanese in Hawaii which conveys a sense of their distinctive ethnic identity. Throughout the experience of the Japanese there is a strong feeling of "Okage sama de," or "I am what I am, thanks to. . . ." The phrase conveys the ingrained sense of appreciation that is so much a part of the Japanese heritage.

• Hosokawa, Bill. *Nisei: The Quiet Americans.* New York: William Morrow, 1969. Hosokawa, a Nisei journalist, was editor of the *Heart Mountain Sentinel* during World War II and was associated with the *Denver Post* for many years. A historical account of the Japanese in America, the book pays particular attention to the Nisei. The title reflects the Model Minority perspective on Japanese Americans that was prevalent in the late 1960's.

• Ichioka, Yuji. *The Issei: The World of the First Generation Japanese Immigrants, 1885-1942.* New York: Free Press, 1988. Historian Ichioka, a second-generation Japanese American born in California, writes a carefully documented history of the Issei in America. The author uses details from archival Japanese-language sources to show the living and working conditions of these immigrants and the context of intense racism they encountered.

• Kitano, Harry H. L. *Japanese Americans: The Evolution of a Subculture.* 2d ed. Englewood Cliffs, N.J.: Prentice-Hall, 1976. Professor of sociology and social welfare at UCLA, Kitano is an internationally recognized expert on Japanese Americans and on race relations. This was the first definitive book on Japanese Americans, and it provides a broad historical and sociological perspective on the Japanese American experience.

• Nakano, Mei. *Japanese American Women: Three Generations, 1890-1990.* Berkeley, Calif.: Mina Press, 1990. Nakano has been a longtime activist in the Japanese American community in Northern California. Her book reflects a new phenomenon, inspired by the feminist movement—a history of Japanese American women as told by women. The reader will gain a strong sense of the values that have sustained and motivated Japanese American women during a century of turmoil and change.

• O'Brien, David J., and Stephen S. Fugita. *The Japanese American Experience.* Bloomington: Indiana University Press, 1991. Drawing on the authors' study of Japanese American ethnicity, the book explains the history of the Japanese in America in terms of the discrimination they faced, their ability to organize collectively, and their success in retaining ethnicity while becoming structurally assimilated. Includes a number of good tables on demographic data.

• Ogawa, Dennis, M. *Kodomo No Tame Ni: For the Sake of the Children.* Honolulu: University Press of Hawaii, 1978. In this book, Ogawa, professor of the American studies department at the University of Hawaii, traces the history and cultural growth of Japanese Americans in Hawaii and provides the reader with a powerful feel for Japanese Americans achieving identity as "locals" in a multicultural society. Each chapter includes documents and articles by scholars, residents, public officials, and clergy that provide illuminating insights.

• Weglyn, Michi. *Years of Infamy: The Untold Story of America's Concentration Camps.* New York: William Morrow, 1976. Weglyn, a talented theatrical costume designer, grew up in California and was interned at the Gila River relocation center. Her book has become a classic, as it was the first publication to document clearly the unconstitutional action by the U.S. government against Japanese Americans during World War II. A thorough, compelling study.

Japanese Americans in Hawaii: The initial wave of Japanese immigration to Hawaii started in 1868, the year of the MEIJI RESTORATION, and ended with the restrictive IMMIGRATION ACT OF 1924. These immigrants' American-born descendants constitute more than 90 percent of Hawaii's Japanese American population today. In 1990 the 247,000 residents of Japanese ancestry made up 22.3 percent of Hawaii's total population and 29 percent of the Japanese American population in the entire United States.

History of Immigration. In 1868, 147 Japanese, including 6 women, were brought to Hawaii as contract laborers for sugar plantations. They were recruited from the Tokyo and Yokohama areas by an American, Eugene VAN REED. Because of the ill treatment and harsh working conditions they experienced, many

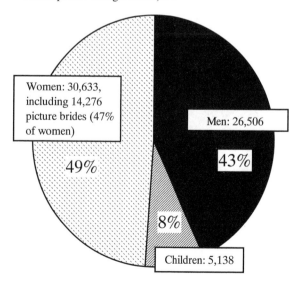

Japanese Immigration to Hawaii During "Yobiyose Jidai" (Period of Summoning Kin), 1908-1924

Total Japanese immigrants: 62,277

Women: 30,633, including 14,276 picture brides (47% of women) 49%

Men: 26,506 43%

Children: 5,138 8%

Source: Yukiko Kimura, *Issei: Japanese Immigrants in Hawaii.* Honolulu: University of Hawaii Press, 1988.

eventually returned to Japan. In part as a result of this failed attempt, the Meiji government imposed strict controls on labor emigration, rebuffing several Hawaiian envoys who sought the resumption of contract-labor immigration from Japan.

In 1885, however, following an agreement between Japan and the Kingdom of Hawaii, massive immigration of Japanese contract laborers to Hawaii began. There was a great labor shortage on Hawaii's burgeoning sugar plantations, which had prompted recruitment of Chinese laborers before the influx from Japan. For a variety of reasons, there was dissatisfaction with the Chinese, in part because they typically left the plantations after their first contract expired to find better employment and more humane working conditions. In addition, the Chinese were not welcomed by the Native Hawaiians, who preferred the Japanese. At the same time, a rural depression in Japan provided a motive for temporary immigration. As a result, from the impoverished countryside in southern Japan, immigrants were brought to Hawaii to replace Chinese laborers. In the period of the government-sponsored immigration (1885-1894), 29,069 immigrants arrived in Honolulu aboard twenty-six ships.

In the following fifteen years, 125,000 Japanese, mostly male, were recruited by private emigration companies. Although many returned to Japan or left for employment on the U.S. mainland after the completion of their three-year labor contract, about 61,000 remained in 1900. They formed 40 percent of the Hawaiian population, the single largest ethnic group in Hawaii, which by then was an annexed territory of the United States.

U.S. immigration policy played a major role in shaping the growing Japanese American community in Hawaii. The IMMIGRATION ACT OF 1907 prohibited Japanese who had been issued a passport to Hawaii, Canada, or Mexico from entering the continental United States. The purpose of this act was to bar secondary migration by Japanese laborers from Hawaii to the United States. Far more significant, however, was the IMMIGRATION ACT OF 1924, which excluded virtu-

Japanese store in Honolulu, circa 1895-1910. (Library of Congress)

Percentage of Japanese Americans in Hawaii, 1900-1990

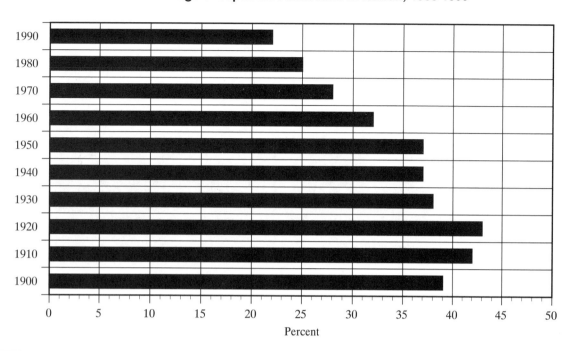

Sources: Norris Hundley, Jr., ed., *The Asian American: The Historical Experience.* Santa Barbara: Clio Press, 1974. U.S. Bureau of the Census, *1990 Census of Population: General Characteristics, United States,* 1992.

ally all immigration from Japan to the United States, including Hawaii. This act ended the major period of Japanese immigration.

The pioneer ISSEI, the first generation of Japanese immigrants, worked in flourishing sugar plantations with long hours and the lowest wages of all plantation workers. Women worked alongside their husbands in the field. They made up most of the wage-earning women in Hawaii. A labor commission report of 1900 stated that "Japanese wives almost without exception engaged in work outside their homes." Women also tended to the needs of unmarried men in the Japanese community. By establishing families in Hawaii, Japanese immigrants began to see themselves as permanent members of Hawaiian society.

Despite their significant contribution to Hawaii's sugar economy, Japanese settlers, along with immigrants from other Asian countries, were excluded from obtaining citizenship and from participating in political affairs. Nevertheless, they continued to fight for their rights. Japanese plantation workers began organizing strikes to demand higher wages and improved working conditions. In 1909 more than 7,000 Japanese workers walked off their jobs on all of Oahu's planta-

tions. In 1920, Japanese and Filipino unions organized a strike against six plantations on Oahu. The strike, which lasted five and a half months, was ultimately unsuccessful, but it was noteworthy as the only multiethnic strike on the sugar plantations prior to World War II.

The Japanese were increasingly seen as a threat to the dominant English-speaking Caucasian community. In 1928 a young Nisei kidnapped and murdered a son of the vice president of a plantation company. This incident aggravated the tension. The execution of the accused (who was suspected to be insane) revealed the racial inequality under Hawaiian law. Increasing pressures from the Caucasian community resulted in eliminating JAPANESE-LANGUAGE SCHOOLS in the 1920's. In 1922 the Palama Japanese Language School filed a petition against this injustice. Five years later the U.S. Supreme Court finally declared the elimination unconstitutional.

Wartime. When Japan attacked PEARL HARBOR on December 7, 1941, there were nearly equal numbers of men and women among the 158,000 Japanese Americans that formed 37 percent of Hawaii's population. A majority were American citizens, including 26.6 per-

Japanese sugar plantation laborers, Hawaii, circa 1890. (Hawaii State Archives)

cent of the adult population. Most Japanese had left the plantations and moved to the cities, forming large Japanese communities. The Japanese operated nearly 50 percent of the retail stores in Hawaii. Given Hawaii's strategic importance, this large Japanese population became a serious concern for the military. Pearl Harbor provoked extreme tension and brought the undercurrent of anti-Japanese sentiment to the surface. Nevertheless, there was a marked contrast between the government's treatment of Japanese Americans in Hawaii and on the West Coast of the mainland.

On Hawaii, Japanese who were considered sympathetic to Japan were arrested and interrogated. JAPANESE-LANGUAGE SCHOOLS, Buddhist temples, and community centers were closed. Eventually about 1,100 Hawaii Japanese, nearly all Issei, were sent to the continental United States to be incarcerated in RELOCATION CENTERS or INTERNMENT CAMPS. For the most part, however, Japanese Americans on Hawaii were seen not as a threat but as a vital asset. In contrast, virtually the entire Japanese American population on the West Coast was uprooted, relocated, and incarcerated.

At the time of the Pearl Harbor attack, there were more than 3,000 Japanese Americans in the U.S. armed forces. Soon after the United States entered the war, the policy toward the Nisei changed. Many recent Nisei inductees were discharged, and the Nisei were placed in the same draft classification as aliens, despite the fact that they were U.S. citizens by birth. As the war proceeded, however, the military had second thoughts. When the Nisei in Hawaii were permitted to volunteer for segregated all-Nisei units such as the 100TH INFANTRY BATTALION and the 442ND REGIMENTAL COMBAT TEAM, more than 10,000 enlisted. They had to prove their loyalty to a country that had denied them their rights as citizens. Their heroic performance gained national recognition and helped improve the status of Japanese Americans in the postwar period.

Postwar Period. After the war, NISEI and SANSEI, with their high level of educational attainment, began to enter professional and technical fields, including prestigious occupations such as medicine and law. The Japanese moved out of the areas of their ethnic concentration and increasingly entered the mainstream of the Hawaiian community. In the process of democratic transformation of the traditional racial hierarchy, they made dramatic inroads into Hawaii's politics. Before the war only a handful of Japanese Americans held responsible positions in local governments. The MCCARRAN-WALTER ACT OF 1952 granted aliens the right to citizenship through naturalization and increased the number of prospective Japanese supporters. In 1974, George ARIYOSHI, a Nisei, was elected governor of Hawaii—the state's first governor of Asian ancestry, and the first governor of Asian ancestry in the United States. In the 1980's about half of the senators and representatives in the Hawaii state legislature were Japanese Americans. They also held many executive positions in labor unions, local governments, and judiciary branches.

Every aspect of Hawaiian life shows Japanese American influence. Although more than 40 percent of the state's Japanese Americans married non-Japanese in the 1980's, they still preserve many elements of Japanese culture. The custom of gift exchange is widespread. Buddhist monks are called for funerals. Japanese influences are evident in homes, gardens, decor, and fabrics. Japanese food has become a part of the Hawaiian diet. The tea ceremony, the art of flower arranging, the martial arts, and Bon festivals are but a few of the aspects of Japanese culture that have become popular among the general population. The Japanese language is widely taught in high schools as well as colleges and universities in Hawaii. Moreover, Japanese Americans in Hawaii proudly maintain traditional Japanese values, such as an emphasis on education, close-knit family ties, politeness, and diligence—values which their immigrant ancestors brought from Meiji Japan.—*Machiko Matsui*

SUGGESTED READINGS: • Hazama, Dorothy O., and Jane O. Komeiji. *Okage Sama De: The Japanese in Hawaii, 1885-1985.* Honolulu: Bess Press, 1986. • Kimura, Yukiko. *Issei: Japanese Immigrants in Hawaii.* Honolulu: University of Hawaii Press, 1988. • Moriyama, Alan T. *Imingaisha: Japanese Emigration Companies and Hawaii, 1894-1908.* Honolulu: University of Hawaii Press, 1985. • Ogawa, Dennis M. *Kodomo No Tame Ni: For the Sake of the Children.* Honolulu: University of Hawaii Press, 1978. • Okihiro, Gary Y. Cane Fires: The Anti-Japanese Movement in Hawaii, 1865-1945. Philadelphia: Temple University Press, 1991.

Japanese associations: Administrative bodies in the United States, empowered by the government of Japan through its U.S. consulates, that significantly affected the lives of Japanese immigrants in the United States before World War II. These organizations were authorized to process applications for proof of U.S. residency; for overseas travel and return; for draft deferment under Japanese law; and for the registration of marriages, divorces, births, adoptions, deaths, inheritances, and so forth. Arising principally for the purpose of complying with the GENTLEMEN'S AGREEMENT (1907-1908), the associations exercised considerable control over Japanese living in the United States.

The Gentlemen's Agreement, signed by the United States and Japan, was an American initiative to control the resident U.S. Japanese population and stem the tide of Japanese immigration. Under the treaty, the government of Japan agreed to stop sending laborers to the U.S. mainland. It also agreed to undertake mass registration of all Japanese living in the United States. All valid registrants were to be issued certificates of proof of U.S. residency. Only those Japanese laborers holding them would be eligible to stay in the country, thus helping to enforce the treaty's exclusionary purposes. The burdensome task of enforcing compliance with the registration order and assigning the residency certificates fell to the Japanese consulates.

To execute the order more efficiently, the Japanese consul-general in San Francisco asked the newly formed Japanese Association of America (founded in 1908) for help. That association, operating under a different name, had previously been a central agency formed primarily to respond to anti-Japanese agitation. The organization, assisted by a band of smaller groups (which later became the basis for the local associations), agreed to handle the processing of not only U.S. residency applications but also the various other certificates issued by the consulates. The processed applications (other than for registration, which was now to be evaluated solely by the associations) then went to the consulates for approval or dismissal. Upon approval, the consulates issued the certificates requested. In exchange for such services, the associations were permitted to collect fees.

In time additional central and affiliated local associations were formed in other regions of the western United States to facilitate registration. These institutions formed part of a three-level administrative system of delegated authority. The consulates occupied the highest level. They directed the central associations, which composed the middle level and served as intermediaries between the consulates and the local associations while supervising the latter, the lowest level. Eventually, the processing of applications fell entirely to the local associations.

Given the scope of their power, the Japanese local associations exercised considerable control over the resident Japanese population. The consulates were authorized to issue certain documents to resident Japanese under the conditions set forth by the Gentlemen's Agreement and the laws of Japan; the consulates delegated to the associations the job of conducting preliminary screenings of all applicants for such papers. Only after securing the "endorsement" of a local association could an immigrant hope to be issued a passport to travel overseas and return to the United States. Certificates were also necessary to bring wives, children, parents, and other relatives to the United States on the return trip or to do so without traveling to Japan (the PICTURE-BRIDE practice, for example). These documents were, moreover, necessary for those wishing to file notice of draft deferment under Japanese law and to register marriages, births, and other vital statistics with authorities back home. The central and local associations were intertwined so that a person whose application had been rejected at one office would be unable to get it approved at another office. By such means the associations were able to cultivate an immigrant community acceptable to the larger American society, minimizing the influence of such undesirables as prostitutes and gamblers, whose applications were routinely denied.

The associations assisted Japanese in the United States in other ways as well. Those whose rights had been violated could expect help. Businessmen used the associations to gain access to ROTATING CREDIT organizations. Some associations formed cooperatives to assist Issei farmers and to represent them in labor disputes. Still others were agents of acculturation, urging the migrants to wear American clothing, to get a good education, to obey the laws, and to work hard and maintain a low profile in their communities.

The four central bodies in the United States were the Japanese Association of America, authorized by the San Francisco consulate to serve local associations in California, Nevada, Utah, Colorado, and Arizona; the Japanese Association of Oregon (founded in 1911), authorized by the Portland consulate to serve local associations in Oregon, Idaho, and Wyoming; the Northwest American Japanese Association (founded in 1913), authorized by the Seattle consulate to serve local associations in Washington and Montana; and the Central Japanese Association of Southern California (founded in 1915), authorized by the Los Angeles consulate to serve local associations in Southern California, Arizona, and New Mexico. Another association, the Pacific Coast Japanese Association Deliberative Council, was created to resolve issues common to Japanese aliens living·in both the United States and Canada; it comprised the four U.S. associations in cooperation with the Japanese Association of Canada from 1914 until 1929.

SUGGESTED READINGS: • Chan, Sucheng. *Asian Americans: An Interpretive History*. Boston: Twayne, 1991. • Daniels, Roger. *Asian America: Chinese and Japanese in the United States Since 1850*. Seattle: University of Washington Press, 1988. • Ichioka, Yuji. *The Issei: The World of the First Generation Japanese Immigrants, 1885-1924*. New York: The Free Press, 1988. • O'Brien, David J., and Stephen S. Fugita. *The Japanese American Experience*. Bloomington: Indiana University Press, 1991.

Japanese Buddhism: BUDDHISM, which originated in India in the sixth century B.C.E., was introduced into Japan in 538 C.E. via Korea and China. As a carrier of continental civilization, it not only brought the Buddha's teaching to Japan but also transmitted knowledge of art and architecture, astronomy, medicine, and calendar making; taught people irrigation methods, agriculture, and sericulture; helped build bridges, dams, roads, and wells; founded infirmaries, orphanages, leprosariums, and public bathhouses; sponsored special ceremonies to respect and release captured animals; and taught people to plant trees and build way stations, revere all life, and give proper burial rites to the dead. In periods of great Buddhist influence it contributed to a more humane society; for example, during the Heian period (794-1185), a span of almost four centuries, not a single recorded case of capital punishment exists.

Historically, Buddhism in the Nara period (710-784) prospered under imperial patronage, and it became an integral part of courtly life. Six schools of Buddhism were studied at the great monasteries of Nara, and the monks wielded great influence on the social and political life of the nation. The six schools included the scholastic traditions that originated in India: The Kusha and Jojitsu schools, the Ritsu school of monastic precepts, the philosophical schools of Sanron and Hosso, and the Kegon or Hua-yen school, which evolved in China. Perhaps the most significant was the Kegon school, with its headquarters at Todaiji, Nara, which was designated as the national church with branch monasteries in each of the provinces, establishing a vast network of interdependent and interconnected temples, symbolizing the unity of the state. A major influence of Buddhism on Japanese life was in the field of art, architecture, and aesthetics. While Buddhism was thus embraced by the upper classes, popularizers also spread the teaching among the masses. Strong state control of religion and lack of records, however, make it impossible to trace their activities.

In the Heian period, when the capital was moved from Nara to Kyoto, two more schools of Buddhism appeared, Tendai and Shingon, with their respective headquarters at Mount Hiei and Mount Koya. Both integrated the highest achievements of Buddhist phi-

Early photograph of a Buddhist congregation in Los Angeles. (Japanese American National Museum)

losophy with native traditions, laying the foundation for a Japanese Buddhism, distinct from those that characterized Indian or Chinese Buddhism. Buddhist ethos, customs, and rituals began to permeate Japanese cultural life, and Buddhism shaped the literary and aesthetic sensibilities of the major writers of the period, such as Lady Murasaki Shikibu, author of *The Tale of Genji* (c. 1004).

Japan experienced great social and political upheavals at the end of the Heian and the beginning of the Kamakura (1192-1333) periods. The age produced great religious figures, such as HONEN, SHINRAN, Dogen, and NICHIREN, who forged radically new interpretations of the Buddhist teaching to meet the spiritual needs of the time. They laid the foundations for such schools as Jodo, JODO SHINSHU, Soto Zen, and Nichiren. While the traditional schools of the Nara and Heian periods continued to prosper, the new movements generated large followings and in due time came to form the mainstream of Japanese Buddhism.

In the next period, known commonly as the Ashikaga or Muromachi (1338-1573), Japanese culture as it is known today began to take shape under Buddhist and native influences. They include the No theater, the arts of the TEA CEREMONY and floral arranging, native styles of painting and poetry, garden design, architecture, and calligraphy. While the schools originating in the Nara and Heian periods maintained their scholastic traditions, the new Buddhism of Zen, Jodo, Jodo Shinshu, and Nichiren began to take deep roots and to spread among various classes of people.

During the TOKUGAWA period (1600-1867) institutional Buddhism became strengthened as part of the social control imposed on the people by the government. SHINTO-based thought and Neo-Confucian ideology became dominant, and Buddhism as a creative force gradually declined in influence. Nevertheless sectarian Buddhist scholarship prospered, exegetical studies appeared in abundance, and the so-called temple schools provided education for the commoners, laying the foundation for universal education in the modern period.

With the MEIJI RESTORATION (1868-1912) Japan began its modernization process, absorbing various achievements of Western civilization. Its religious policy, however, favored Shinto as a state religion, leading to the suppression of Buddhism, which caused great consternation among the Buddhist leadership. Institutional Buddhism, however, fought back and was partially successful in regaining its position in society. Buddhist scholarship, influenced by Western scientific methodologies and utilizing PALI, SANSKRIT, and TIBETAN sources, advanced considerably. Today Japanese scholarship in Buddhist studies is among the highest in the world. Reflecting the turbulent changes through World Wars I and II, many so-called new religions appeared as offshoots of traditional Buddhist schools, some of which may eventually change the face of Japanese Buddhism in the years to come.

Traditionally Japanese Buddhism is divided into thirteen schools: Hosso, Kegon, Ritsu, Tendai, Shingon, Rinzai Zen, Soto Zen, Obaku Zen, Jodo, Jodo Shinshu, Yuzu Nembutsu, Ji, and Nichiren. Among Japanese Americans approximately 90 percent belong to Jodo Shinshu, and the remainder to the Shingon, Soto Zen, Jodo, and Nichiren schools. In the United States, however, there are a growing number of Vietnamese Buddhists, as well as Buddhists of the THERAVADA lineage from Cambodia, Laos, Thailand, and other Southeast Asian countries.

In spite of the great variety and variations among the schools, their central message may be summed up in the well-known verse: "Practice good, avoid evil, and purify the mind—this is the teaching of all the Buddhas." The injunction to do good and reject evil, however, is based on the "purity of mind." The impure mind is ego-centered, using others to satisfy one's desires and needs; in contrast, the pure mind is free of self-concern, always wishing the best for others. The practice of good, such as generosity, must be free of the egocentric impulse, and it must arise spontaneously as the most natural thing to do. In the act of pure giving, for example, Buddhism teaches that there must be no trace of self-centeredness—no giver, no gift, and no receiver. Good is practiced for the welfare of all beings, for as a part of the vast web of interrelationship and interconnectedness, it is the most natural and human thing to do. Life as interdependence is a fundamental tenet of Buddhism.—*Taitetsu Unno*

SUGGESTED READINGS: • Eliot, Charles. *Japanese Buddhism*. London: Routledge & Kegan Paul, 1969. • Shaner, David Edward. *The Bodymind Experience in Japanese Buddhism: A Phenomenological Perspective of Kukai and Dogen*. Albany: State University of New York Press, 1985. • Suzuki, Daisetz Taitaro. *Japanese Spirituality*. 1972. Reprint. New York: Greenwood Press, 1988. • Suzuki, Daisetz Taitaro. *The Training of the Zen Buddhist Monk*. 1934. Reprint. New York: Globe Press, 1991.

Japanese Chamber of Commerce of Southern California (JCCSC): An association of Japanese and American businesspeople and those interested in promoting the welfare of Japanese and Japanese American communities via business, cultural, social, political, and educational programs. Founded in 1951, the JCCSC fosters understanding and goodwill between the United States and Japan. It maintains close contact with the Japanese government and Japanese companies via personal meetings, the *keidanren*, and other Japanese Business Association publications in order to help Japanese and Japanese American businesses.

The governing board of directors consists of three distinct groups: Japanese corporations from Japan, Japanese corporations and individuals in the United States, and local non-Japanese corporations and individuals. Applications for paid membership must be approved by the board. In 1993 membership of individuals and corporations numbered 350. A membership directory is published every other year. Officers are elected by the board.

Restructuring in 1993 led to the formation of nine JCCSC committees. Four deal primarily with administration: membership, finance, legal affairs, and general administration. Three deal with commerce: business, agriculture, and public relations. Two deal with programs: culture, sports, and education and special events. Included in the last category are NISEI WEEK in Little Tokyo and a Japanese American scholarship fund.

The special events committee is responsible for the preservation of historical monuments including the JAPANESE AMERICAN NATIONAL MUSEUM and the overseas student exchange program. For three weeks every summer, the JCCSC sponsors twelve Japanese college students, each of whom has lost a parent in a traffic accident. The students come to the United States, live with American families, and study American culture. Other special events include spring and fall *Jokun* banquets at which the Japanese government confers awards upon Americans who have enhanced relationships between the Japanese and the Americans.

The most unique special events program is the *kansen kange*, a thank-you ship. Shortages in post-World War II Japan prompted Japanese Americans to send large quantities of foodstuffs, clothing, and other basic supplies. In remembrance of the assistance given then, the Japanese government sends the *kansen kange* each year with a crew of young senior-year cadets to Southern California and in collaboration with the JCCSC hosts a banquet for the Japanese American community.

Japanese "Chinese" restaurants: Restaurants serving Chinese food but catering primarily to Japanese American diners. Such establishments are most prominent in urban centers on the West Coast, such as Los Angeles, San Francisco, and Seattle. Oftentimes they can be found in unconventional locations such as bowling alleys. The inexpensive fare usually consists of standard menu choices—chow mein, fried rice, won ton soup, and beef with broccoli—prepared to suit Japanese American tastes.

Japanese Christianity: Christianity was introduced into Japan in 1549 when Roman Catholic priests arrived with Portuguese traders. After converting approximately three hundred thousand Japanese, the missionaries were forced to leave in 1639. The practice of Christianity was forbidden, and Japan closed its doors to the Western world, except for a small group of Dutch traders. The end of Japan's period of isolation in 1854 saw the return of Christianity, Roman Catholicism now sharing the mission field with Protestant and Orthodox Christianity. After an initial period of popularity, conversions leveled off in the mid 1880's, and the number of Christians in Japan has held at about one percent of the population. Japanese who emigrated to the United States register somewhat higher rates of conversion to Christianity. Japanese Americans also follow that trend, Protestants being more numerous than Roman Catholics.

Origins. Members of the newly founded Society of Jesus (Jesuits) were the first Catholic priests in Japan. They approached their conversion efforts by seeking permission of the DAIMYO (local lords) to preach. Because of the political unrest in Japan at the time, most early converts received less than two weeks of training. Eventually, Franciscans, Dominicans, and Augustinians joined the proselytizing efforts in Japan. The large numbers of Japanese converting to Christianity concerned Japanese officials, who began to feel uneasy about the double loyalty of the new converts,

Eighth-grade student at a Roman Catholic parochial school in the United States reads the Bible. Christianity was introduced in Japan in 1549 when Catholic priests arrived with Portuguese traders. (Robert Fried)

while also suspecting the missionaries of being agents of their governments, aiming toward an eventual takeover of Japan.

Persecution. The first order against Christianity was issued by the government in 1587, then again in 1614. Somewhere between four thousand and six thousand Japanese Christians died because of their beliefs. By 1639, all missionaries had been expelled, Christianity was strictly forbidden, and converts had three choices: to recant, accept execution, or go underground with their Christian practice. About a hundred thousand chose the last option and attempted to keep their faith alive underground.

Mid-Nineteenth Century Revival. When Commodore Matthew C. PERRY of the American Navy, through threat of force, convinced Japan to open again in 1854, it was not long before missionary activity followed, even though the ban against Christianity would not be rescinded until 1873. The first Roman Catholic priests were members of the Paris Foreign Mission Society (Société des missionères étrangères de Paris). Pockets

Into the 1990's, many Japanese Americans, including the Sansei and Yonsei (third and fourth generations), belong to Christian churches. (James L. Shaffer)

of *kakure* (hidden) Christians were found, descendants of the first Japanese Christians, whom the French missionaries sought to woo back to orthodox practice. Some thirty thousand Japanese, representing about half the *kakure* population, accepted the advances of the French missionaries, giving a big boost to the Catholic numbers of converts. Before the start of the twentieth century, several French religious orders of women sent missionaries to work with the priests. Protestant missionaries from the United States and Europe accompanied the government and business representatives, exerting influence on Japan's early modernization efforts. The initial activities of these missionaries centered on education as a means of proselytizing, their early converts coming for the most part from the ex-samurai class. Protestant Christianity came to be identified with the modern West, but by the mid-1880's

Japanese were beginning to look more toward Japanese culture for their religious needs. Christianity has remained influential in Japanese society despite its small numbers, Roman Catholics remaining the most numerous, followed closely by Protestants, with significantly fewer Orthodox Christians.

Japanese Americans. The majority of the Japanese who emigrated to the United States up to the 1920's claimed BUDDHISM and/or SHINTO as their religion. Once in the United States, however, conversions to Protestant Christianity were not uncommon. Because many of the early Protestant missionaries in Japan were from the United States, churches in California reached out to the new immigrants. The earliest efforts at evangelizing the Japanese immigrants came from the Methodist, Congregational, Presbyterian, and Baptist denominations. Although missionaries did not win large numbers to Christianity, those who did become Christians often acted as bridges between Japanese and American culture and also served in leadership positions in the community. The churches also offered possibilities of employment and a ready means of acculturation to American ways. Japanese women benefited from the women's groups, where they were introduced to American food, fashion, and politics. Initially, the ministers were Caucasian missionaries, but gradually the Japanese Christians developed their own all-Japanese congregations. As the second and third generations (NISEI and SANSEI) came along, the situation reversed itself, and the Japanese Christian churches provided a locus for learning traditional Japanese ways.

Conversions to Roman Catholicism were not as common as those to Protestantism. Perhaps one reason is that the United States did not have Catholic missionaries in Japan until the early twentieth century and therefore local churches did not reach out as quickly to the Japanese arriving on the West Coast. Serious efforts began in San Francisco in 1912, in Los Angeles in 1913, and in Seattle in 1922. As with the Protestant churches, the Catholic parishes served as a locus for the spiritual, cultural, and social needs of the immigrants.

The Japanese bombing of PEARL HARBOR in 1941 created a crisis situation for Japanese and Japanese Americans. The ISSEI (first generation) were Japanese citizens, ineligible for U.S. citizenship; remaining Buddhist made them suspect in the United States while converting to Christianity cut them off from their heritage. The fact that many white Americans saw Christianity as pro-American and Buddhism as pro-Japanese created enormous burdens for the Japanese and Japanese Americans. In the INTERNMENT CAMPS during World War II, one mode of peaceful resistance was the celebration of Japanese religious beliefs, whether the internee was Christian or Buddhist. Traditional Japanese religious practice allows for the intermingling of religious beliefs; being Buddhist does not preclude participation in Shinto or Christian rites.

Emphasis on maintaining ethnic group ties is important for Japanese Americans. This is seen in the third and fourth generations (Sansei and YONSEI). Many Japanese Americans retain ties to Christian churches and participate in church-related social, cultural, and athletic activities.—*Ann M. Harrington*

SUGGESTED READINGS: • Chan, Sucheng. *Asian Americans: An Interpretive History.* Boston: Twayne, 1991. • Dolan, Jay P., ed. *The American Catholic Parish: A History from 1850 to the Present.* Vol. 2. Mahwah, N.J.: Paulist Press, 1987. • Fugita, Stephen S., and David J. O'Brien. *Japanese American Ethnicity: The Persistence of Community.* Seattle: University of Washington Press, 1991. • Ichioka, Yuji. *The Issei: The World of the First Generation Japanese Immigrants, 1885-1924.* New York: Free Press, 1988. • Kitano, Harry H. L. *Japanese Americans: The Evolution of a Subculture.* Englewood Cliffs, N.J.: Prentice-Hall, 1969. • Petersen, William. *Japanese Americans: Oppression and Success.* New York: Random House, 1971.

Japanese contract farming: The occupational field to which the majority of Japanese immigrants gravitated was agriculture. In 1909 it is estimated that approximately thirty-eight thousand Japanese, mostly laborers, worked in farming in the United States. Almost 50 percent of male Japanese were still in some phase of agriculture on the eve of World War II (1939-1945). Many Japanese, particularly in California, progressed in stages from farm worker to contract farmer to sharecropper to land lessee to, finally, farm owner.

Contract farming was usually the first step above farm labor as it had minimal capital requirements. The ranch owner would furnish everything needed to run the operation except the wages to be paid to the farm workers. Usually the contractors would pay their laborers after being paid by the ranch owner. The contractors would buy provisions for themselves and their workers from Japanese merchants, who would extend credit. An important feature of the contract system was that the task of finding an adequate labor supply fell on the contractor. This was easier for the Japanese contractor who could secure Japanese crews through a Japanese labor contractor than it was for a white rancher.

Generally one or more Japanese would agree to an annual contract with a ranch owner to perform the necessary planting, watering, weeding, picking, packing, and so on for a set price per acre. The price that the contractor would receive for these services was set annually and was dependent upon such factors as the market for the particular crop, productivity of the plants, and labor conditions. Frequently, in subsequent years the contractor would be paid a set price per unit of output. As the landowner usually set the unit price based upon a low market price, the contractor would not receive the benefit of a rising market price. Often the earnings the contractor made were not much higher than those of a field worker. In many ways contract farming was similar to being an employee of the rancher. Inasmuch as most Japanese wanted the opportunity to earn more, sharecropping and leasing became more common arrangements. These arrangements, although containing greater risk, also provided greater incentives for high productivity.

Japanese dance. *See* **Japanese music and dance**

Japanese English: Term designating English spoken by Japanese people in Japan. Japanese English refers to the use of English vocabulary in standard Japanese speech. It does not refer to the inaccurate attempts of Japanese students to speak English.

The presence of English elements in the Japanese language is quite extensive. As many as five thousand English words are commonly in use, perhaps accounting for as much as 5 to 10 percent of the everyday vocabulary. Specialized topics such as automobiles, engineering, baseball, or contemporary fashion may contain substantially more loanwords.

While increasing contact with the West has encouraged the spread of English worldwide, the use of English loanwords in Japan is intended mostly for domestic consumption by Japanese among themselves. English loanwords do not necessarily render communication easier with foreigners. Indeed, many of these terms are coined in Japan and are not transparent, phonologically or semantically, for English speakers. For example, *dokuta sutoppu* (doctor stop) stands for a physician's prohibition on certain activities such as smoking; a *kurisumasu keki* (Christmas cake) applies to an unmarried woman older than twenty-five (presumably as unwanted as Christmas cake after December 25); and *Bajin Rodo* (virgin road), the title of a best-selling novel in the late 1980's, refers to the aisle a bride walks down in church. Statistics indicate that the English-based vocabulary items used in the Japanese language began steadily increasing after World War II (1939-1945), showing no sign of curtailment in the immediate future.

What is here termed Japanese English, however, should technically be distinguished from a number of English and Japanese pidgins that have been spoken since the mid-nineteenth century (even though they are sometimes covered by the same rubric). There have historically been at least three such cases: First, soon after the United States ended Japan's period of self-imposed isolation in the 1850's, a curious Japanese pidgin, ultimately in use for less than forty years, sprang up in Japanese seaports. Humorously called the "Yokohama Dialect," this simplified version of Japanese was used between foreign sailors, merchants, and residents and the local Japanese populace, mostly for economic transactions. Second, from the early 1900's, Japanese immigrants coming to Hawaii spoke a version of Pidgin English that was distinct from the other pidgins and creoles found in the islands. For the most part, this pidgin has been absorbed into the Hawaiian variety of English. Third, after World War II (1939-1945), a colorful pidgin often known as "Bamboo English" developed and was used between local Japanese and the United States military during the occupation. American involvement in other Asian military ventures caused much of this "Bamboo English" to spread for a while to other countries such as Korea, the Philippines, Thailand, and Vietnam.

Japanese Exclusion League of California: Anti-Japanese organization founded in San Francisco in September, 1920. Among those included on the league's membership rolls were representatives of the Native Sons of the Golden West, the American Federation of Labor (AFL), and the American Legion. Initially created to influence public and legislative sentiment against the Japanese presence in California, the group was replaced by the California Joint Immigration Committee following passage of the federal Immigration Act of 1924, which cut off further Japanese immigration to the United States.

Japanese Federation of Labor: Labor union established in 1916. The federation's primary purpose lay in advancing the ongoing effort to secure the favor of white labor unionists. Still, organized labor continued to discriminate against Asian immigrant laborers.

Japanese gardeners: Japanese immigrants and their descendants have been prominent in two types of gardening in the United States: vegetable (truck farming) and ornamental.

In the late 1800's discriminatory laws and attitudes forced many immigrant and ethnic Japanese from the cities of California and into rural occupations. Although these new rural residents were forced to settle on marginal lands, their industriousness made them successful.

Ironically their success led to accusations that they had taken the best land. Thus, by the early 1920's laws had been enacted to limit ownership, leasing, and inheritance rights of Japanese Americans. The Japanese American farmer responded by producing crops that, although labor-intensive, required little land or capital investment.

By 1941 Japanese Americans were producing nearly half of California's truck crops, including nearly all the green beans, celery, peppers, and strawberries; 50 to 90 percent of the artichokes, cauliflower, cucumbers, spinach, and tomatoes; and 25 to 50 percent of the asparagus, cantaloupes, carrots, lettuce, onions, and watermelons.

Following their forced internment during World War II, returning Japanese American farmers found it difficult to resume their vegetable-gardening businesses. Many of these displaced farmers, in addition to others who had been gardeners before the war years and many post-World War II Japanese immigrants, turned to contract gardening and nursery work for full-time employment.

Lawn care, tree and shrubbery trimming, and flower gardening were all important to many California homeowners, who provided steady work for the contract gardener. Like truck farming, gardening required little capital and allowed for individual creativity and independence. As demand for gardening services grew, so did salaries. People also grew to accept the notion that all people of Japanese ancestry were good gardeners.

In the 1960's approximately 75 percent of Japanese Americans working in Los Angeles were either operating garden-care businesses or working for one, although that figure dropped substantially as more higher-status job opportunities became available to Japanese Americans. The influence of Japanese gardeners on American residential landscapes remains widespread.

Japanese immigration to the United States: Japanese immigration to the United States, inaugurated in 1868—with the secret recruitment by the Tokyo-based Hawaiian trading commissioner and Hawaiian consul general in Japan of 148 Japanese contract laborers to work for three years in Hawaii's sugar plantations—began with an emigration *netsu* ("fever") to journey to the Hawaiian Islands and the United States as *dekaseginin* ("SOJOURNER" laborers). Their goal was to work temporarily in a foreign country in order to accrue enough monetary savings to purchase Japanese land or regain Japanese land lost due to debt in Meiji Japan. In the early twentieth century the purpose of Japanese immigration to the United States shifted from sojourning to a settling stage, a transition aided by the desire of Japanese agricultural contract laborers in Hawaii to become *dochyaku*, "to remain on the soil." This first wave of Japanese immigration, characterized by the efforts of ISSEI, first-generation Japanese immigrants,

Japanese Americans in Proportion to All Asian Americans in the U.S., 1980 and 1990			
1980		**1990**	
Total Asian Americans: 3,726,440 (1.5% of U.S. population)		Total Asian Americans: 7,226,986 (2.9% of U.S. population)	
Country of Origin	Percent	Country of Origin	Percent
China	21.6%	China	22.8%
Philippines	20.8%	Philippines	19.6%
Japan	**18.8%**	**Japan**	**12.0%**
Korea	9.8%	India	10.9%
India	9.7%	Korea	11.0%
Vietnam	7.0%	Vietnam	8.2%
Hawaii	4.5%	Hawaii	2.8%
Samoa	1.1%	Samoa	0.8%
Guam	0.9%	Guam	0.7%
Other*	5.8%	Other*	11.2%

Source: United States Department of Commerce, Bureau of the Census.

* "Other" includes but is not limited to Cambodia, Laos (including Hmong), and Thailand.

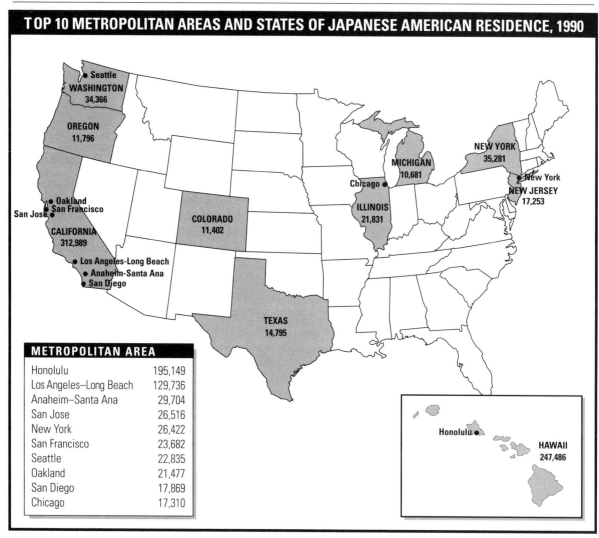

TOP 10 METROPOLITAN AREAS AND STATES OF JAPANESE AMERICAN RESIDENCE, 1990

METROPOLITAN AREA	
Honolulu	195,149
Los Angeles–Long Beach	129,736
Anaheim–Santa Ana	29,704
San Jose	26,516
New York	26,422
San Francisco	23,682
Seattle	22,835
Oakland	21,477
San Diego	17,869
Chicago	17,310

Source: Susan B. Gall and Timothy L. Gall, eds., *Statistical Record of Asian Americans.* Detroit: Gale Research, 1993.

to become *imin*, Japanese moving permanently to the United States, despite American discriminatory immigration policy designed to preserve "white" America, was followed by a second wave, much smaller than the first but not negligible, after the McCARRAN-WALTER ACT OF 1952 removed the virtual ban on Japanese immigration that had been in place since 1924 and made Japanese aliens eligible for naturalization.

While recent Japanese immigration to the United States is not insignificant relative to the total Japanese American population (17 percent of the Japanese American population in 1990 consisted of foreign-born who had arrived between 1980 and 1990), it has been quite small relative to immigration from many other Asian nations in the wake of the IMMIGRATION AND NATIONALITY ACT OF 1965. For example, between

1965 and 1984, 93,646 Japanese emigrated to the United States, a mere 3 percent of all Asian immigrants during that period. The recent low rate of Japanese immigration is a contributory factor to the reconfiguration of the Japanese American population in the United States: Between 1980 and 1990 the total Asian American population in the United States nearly doubled, from 3,726,440 (or 1.5 percent of the U.S. population) to 7,272,662 (or 2.9 percent of the U.S. population). The Japanese proportion of Asian Americans has dramatically decreased from 52 percent in 1960 to 11.7 percent in 1990. Moreover, in 1990, 68 percent of the Japanese American population were citizens by birth; third- and fourth-generation Japanese Americans (SANSEI and YONSEI, respectively) were for the most part not proficient Japanese speakers; and Japantowns or *Nihonmachis* were disappearing from the American urban scene due to the lack of an influx of new Japanese immigrants.

Japanese Emigration Policy, 1868-1908. Japanese émigrés to Hawaii recruited in 1868 by the Tokyo-based Hawaiian trading commissioner were termed GANNEN-MONO or "first-year men" after the fact that they had departed for Hawaii during the first year of the MEIJI RESTORATION. John Henry Schnell, a German merchant, encouraged 27 Japanese to emigrate to California in 1869 to found a silk farm. These two emigration efforts, however, were unsuccessful. The *gannen-mono*, recruited from the streets of Tokyo and adjacent Yokohama, were ill-suited to rural Hawaiian plantation life and eventually returned to Japan, their employers, the planters, paying for the expense; the Schnell-inspired WAKAMATSU TEA AND SILK FARM COLONY, located north of Sacramento, California, and

PRINCIPAL SOURCES OF JAPANESE IMMIGRATION

CHINA

RUSSIAN FEDERATION

NORTH KOREA

Sea of Japan

North Pacific Ocean

JAPAN

SOUTH KOREA

Tokyo ★

HIROSHIMA

OKAYAMA

YAMAGUCHI

FUKUOKA

WAKAYAMA

NAGASAKI

KUMAMOTO

East China Sea

Source: Sucheng Chan, *Asian Americans: An Interpretive History.* Boston: Twayne, 1991.

named for the original Japanese prefecture of its residents, soon collapsed without any trace of its settlers, save for a gravestone marked "Okei."

Difficulties associated with initial Japanese emigration to the United States convinced the Meiji government to regulate future contract-labor migration from Japan to Hawaii during the period 1885-1894. Japanese economic changes (resulting from the Meiji government's policy of financing its industrialization and militarization priorities through an obligatory annual fixed tax on land), Meiji government-instituted deflationary policies (resulting in a depression of rice prices), the growing realization among Japanese farmers that overseas emigration represented a significant alternative to lives governed by land tenancy and wage labor in Japan, and the inauguration of emigrant recruitment centered in the "emigrant prefectures" of southwestern Japan (Fukuoka, Hiroshima, Kanagawa, Kumamoto, Okayama, Wakayama, and Yamaguchi) contributed to the migrants' dream of striking it rich in Hawaii and returning to Japan as *kini kikyo* (wealthy persons).

Japanese contract laborers were told they could save 400 to 500 yen working on Hawaiian sugar plantations

Asian Immigration to the U.S. by Country of Origin, 1981-1988

Country of Origin	Immigrants	Percent of Total Asian Immigrants
Vietnam	549,462	28.6%
Philippines	374,523	19.5%
China*	343,607	17.9%
Korea	272,355	14.2%
India	200,038	10.4%
Thailand	48,188	2.5%
Pakistan	43,714	2.3%
Japan	32,669	1.7%
Indonesia**	9,319	
Tonga**	4,343	
Samoa**	2,147	
Guam**	5	
Other	41,458	2.2%

Source: United States General Accounting Office, *Asian Americans: A Status Report* (March, 1990).

* Inclusive of Hong Kong, Macau, and Taiwan emigration.

** Percent of total Asian immigrants less than 1.

over a three-year period at a time when the highest paid wage laborer in Japan, a roof tile maker, received in gross income just under eight yen a month. Possibly because of a triangular friendship between R. W. IRWIN, the Hawaiian consul in Japan; Meiji Foreign Minister Inoue Kaoru; and Masuda Takashi, head of the Mitsui Bussan trading company, the recruitment of Japanese contract laborers centered on Kyushu and southern Honshu (both Inoue and Masuda were from Yamaguchi prefecture) rather than the more financially depressed Tohoku region where displaced farmers migrated to the northern island of Hokkaido from northern Honshu island.

The Meiji government announcement in 1885 that it would accept 600 emigrant applications for Hawaii was oversubscribed by 27,000 applications. The first shipment of *KANYAKU IMIN* (government-sponsored contract laborers) arrived in Hawaii on February 8, 1885, aboard the ship *City of Tokyo* and numbered 944 emigrants. Between February 8, 1885, and June 15, 1894, the date of the last Meiji-government-sponsored shipment of contract laborers to Hawaii aboard the ship *Miike Maru*, 29,069 emigrants were sent to Hawaii by the Japanese government.

These Issei, however, sharply contrasted with the earlier "first-year men." The Meiji government exerted strong control over the "quality" of Hawaiian immigration. Aware that the Chinese were utilized as merely cheap labor in the United States, the Japanese government sought an emigration which would "maintain Japan's national honor." Overseas Japanese were regarded as representatives of the Japanese homeland, obligated to apply for passports and visas and chosen as hard-working laborers from agricultural prefectures rather than vagrants from the large urban centers of Tokyo and Yokohama. The Japanese consul in the United States, CHINDA SUTEMI, warned in 1891 that a failure to deny indigent Japanese emigration to the United States would result in the Japanese soon following "in the wake of the Chinese," a reference to the CHINESE EXCLUSION ACT OF 1882 and subsequent legislation barring Chinese laborers from immigrating to America.

Japanese emigration to Hawaii during the period 1885-1894 differed from the earlier Chinese immigration of contract laborers to the mainland United States in another important way: The Meiji government encouraged the migration of women to Hawaii. This encouragement occurred for a number of reasons: the effort by the central government to accelerate *fukoku kyohei* (a strong nation ready to oppose Western ex-

Asian Foreign-Born Population in the U.S. by Place of Birth and Citizenship, 1990

Country	Foreign-Born	Naturalized Citizen	Not a Citizen
Philippines	913,723	491,646	422,077
Korea	579,273	232,488	346,785
Vietnam	473,853	200,069	273,784
China	1,142,580	496,209	646,371
India	593,423	203,614	389,809
Japan	280,686	72,194	208,492

Source: U.S. Bureau of the Census, *1990 Census of Population: Asian and Pacific Islanders in the United States*, 1993.

pansion) meant that rural women became migratory wage laborers in urban centers; frequently emigration was an obligation not a choice for Japanese women as they became through marriage members of their emigrating husbands' families; the Emperor Meiji supported the importance of female education to Japanese society. Additionally, many Japanese women had their own reasons for going, not the least of which was "the dream of seeing America." Told by the Emperor Meiji that they "should be allowed to go abroad," Japanese women were encouraged to emigrate because the Meiji government assumed that Japanese female émigrés would bring stability to Japanese village life reproduced in Hawaii, avoiding the problems of an itinerant bachelor society such as the early, almost exclusively male Chinese American community. Between 1885 and 1894 Japanese women comprised 20 percent of the *kanyaku imin*.

Although cessation of Japanese government regulation of contract-labor emigration to Hawaii in 1894 did not stop the importation of Japanese prostitutes to the U.S. mainland, between 1894 and 1908, the beginning of enforcement of the so-called GENTLEMEN'S AGREEMENT between the American and Japanese governments restricting Japanese immigration to the United States, numerous Japanese women migrated to Hawaii as private contract laborers through emigration companies or as free laborers drawing upon their own personal resources to raise the 200 yen and more necessary for their voyage to Hawaii. Additionally, by 1920, the year that Japan terminated the practice, thousands of Japanese women had emigrated to the United States as PICTURE BRIDES.

Prior to the first meeting of prospective brides and grooms living at great distance from each other in Japan, it was customary for the couple to exchange photographs. This custom was extended across the Pacific to link by arranged marriages the increasing number of Japanese émigré males settling in the 1890's on the American West Coast, drawn there by the need for cheap labor in canneries, fishing, logging, meat-packing, the railroad industry, the salt-refining industry, and, especially, California's growing agricultural ventures, such as the YAMATO COLONY, founded in 1906, by Kyutaro ABIKO in the San Joaquin Valley near Livingston, California.

Discriminatory Regulation of Japanese Immigration. The immediate catalyst for American regulation of Japanese immigration to the United States mainland was the San Francisco school board's edict of October 11, 1906, requiring all Chinese, Japanese, and Korean children to attend an oriental school established as early as 1885 for Chinese students. The board's action, which affected 93 Japanese students, prompted a protest by the Japanese government describing the action as a denial of a treaty stipulation guaranteeing Japanese children in the United States equality of educational opportunity.

Publicly accepting Japanese immigration to the United States in his December 3, 1906, congressional message, President Theodore Roosevelt privately sought to limit it strictly, arguing that the newly acquired Hawaiian islands should be peopled with a "white population" indicative of "American Civilization." In the wake of the San Francisco school board's action, President Roosevelt issued an executive order forbidding remigration of Issei in Hawaii to the United States mainland. Roosevelt, together with his Secretary of State, Elihu ROOT, also entered into direct negotiations with the Japanese government to restrict Japanese immigration to the United States. The resulting GENTLEMEN'S AGREEMENT, consisting of a series

Japanese immigrating to America are examined by customs inspectors aboard the Shimyo Maru, *Angel Island, California, 1931. For millions of Asian immigrants, Angel Island, near San Francisco, was the initial point of entry into the United States.* (National Archives)

of diplomatic notes between the two governments in 1907-1908, was strongly mindful of the CHINESE EXCLUSION ACT OF 1882.

By the terms of the Gentlemen's Agreement, President Roosevelt obtained an understanding from the Japanese government that Japan would cease issuing passports to the United States to laborers who had not previously been there, a concession that California's governor, Henry Gage, and the white laborer-formed ASIATIC EXCLUSION LEAGUE had admonished the federal government to obtain, unsuccessfully until the San Francisco school board action. Roosevelt persuaded the school board to rescind its segregation order; in return, the Japanese government agreed to the use of self-imposed immigration quotas to restrict Japanese emigration to the United States. As a result of the Gentlemen's Agreement, Japanese immigration to the United States decreased by a third, from 108,163, or

.77 percent of all immigrants to the United States mainland between 1901 and 1907, to 74,478, or 1.11 percent of all immigrants to the United States mainland between 1908 and 1914. Brazil increasingly became the focus of Japanese immigration after 1908.

The Gentlemen's Agreement of 1907-1908 changed the characteristics of Japanese immigration to the United States dramatically. While the agreement's terms permitted Japanese already resident in the United States to send to Japan for PICTURE BRIDES, Japanese student émigrés to the United States more than doubled from pre-agreement numbers. The earlier male preponderance among Japanese migrants was sharply reduced. The agreement resulted in the increase of two-generation Japanese families in the United States as male migrants either traveled with their parents to America or joined parents already resident in the United States. A new "sub-generation" of

Issei arrived after 1908, defined largely by their continuing education in America, as post-agreement immigrants "were more likely than their predecessors to develop English skill . . . and more likely to read American periodicals." Eagerness to immerse themselves in American culture did not, however, free Japanese Issei immigrants from discrimination.

Between 1908 and 1924 Japanese immigrants to the United States faced increasing discrimination against their efforts to become naturalized citizens and own land. The number of Japanese immigrants to the United States between the Gentlemen's Agreement and the National Origins Act, 1924 was not large; an estimate for the total between 1911 and 1920 is 80,000. These immigrants became the target of overt white racism. Between 1907 and 1913, California constructed a law making the ownership of land by "aliens ineligible to citizenship" illegal. California State Attorney General Ulysses S. Webb declared this legisla-

tion essential due to the "race undesirability" of the Japanese. Status of Japanese immigrants relative to American citizenship was uncertain during this period. A 1790 United States naturalization law had restricted eligibility for naturalization to free white persons only. While Japanese immigrants submitted petitions for naturalization under terms of the Naturalization Act of June 28, 1906, the United States Supreme Court in *Ozawa v. United States* (1922) ruled that the 1906 act was restricted by prior congressional enactments; consequently Takao Ozawa, a Hawaiian resident and former three-year student at the University of California, and all other Japanese petitioners for American citizenship were declared ineligible because they were "clearly . . . not Caucasian." Clearly the naturalization issue begged the greater issue of the Japanese immigrants' assimilability into the United States, an immigration which had ended virtually with the "Ladies' Agreement" of 1921.

Japanese mother and daughter agricultural laborers, Guadalupe, California, 1937. Photograph by Dorothea Lange. (Library of Congress)

The apex of American discrimination toward Japanese immigration was the IMMIGRATION ACT OF 1924, otherwise known as the "National Origins Act." This act established a quota system for immigration based on the 1890 census. Each nation received an annual immigration quota equivalent to 2 percent of the foreign-born residents of that nationality living in the United States in 1890.

As it was, the national-origins quota system strongly favored immigrants from Northern and Western Europe. Still, that did not satisfy the anti-Japanese exclusionists, who succeeded in adding a clause specifically aimed at the Japanese, forbidding entry to "aliens ineligible to citizenship." The Japanese government viewed this clause as an abrogation of the Gentlemen's Agreement and its provision that the United States would not forbid Japanese immigration altogether. The Japanese government protest was to no avail. In virtually barring all Asians from immigration, Congress encouraged American employers to seek workers from the Philippines, then a U.S. territory. The Issei resigned themselves to devoting their energies to their daughters' and sons' (the Nisei) success in America *kodomo no tame ni* ("for the sake of the children"). Between 1925 and 1940 only 6,156 Japanese immigrated to the American mainland, constituting 0.03 of all immigrants to the United States during those years. Less than 50 Japanese had immigrated to the United States in 1925.

Post-World War II Japanese Immigration. The McCARRAN-WALTER ACT OF 1952 overturned the 1924 limits on Japanese immigration. Moreover, an estimated 25,000 Japanese war brides had arrived in the United States by the end of the 1950's. Japanese immigrants were also welcomed in the nonquota immigration categories of businessmen, consular officials, students, and tourists. Between 1948 and 1991, approximately 177,400 Japanese immigrated to the United States. Over a 43-year period this immigration was markedly smaller than a total for the peak years of

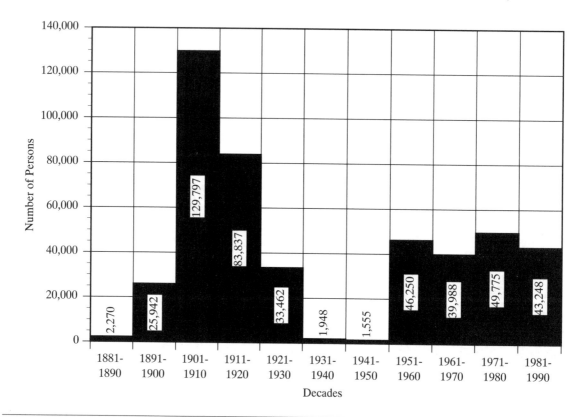

Japanese Immigration to the U.S. by Decade, 1881-1990

Source: Susan B. Gall and Timothy L. Gall, eds., *Statistical Record of Asian Americans.* Detroit: Gale Research, Inc., 1993.

Japanese American nursery worker, Oxnard, California. (Michael Yamashita)

Japanese immigration to the United States during the 17-year period between the GENTLEMEN'S AGREEMENT and the National Origins Act, 1907 to 1924. During the latter period approximately 267,838 Japanese immigrated, predominantly to the American West Coast states of California, Oregon, and Washington.

Passage of the McCarran-Walter Act was attributable in part to lobbying by Mike MASAOKA of the JAPANESE AMERICAN CITIZENS LEAGUE (JACL), a veteran of the Nisei 442ND REGIMENTAL COMBAT TEAM. While allowing new Japanese immigration, the McCarran-Walter Act retained the national-origins quota system. Japan's newly assigned quota was 185. However, other legislative measures, including the WAR BRIDES ACT OF 1945, permitted Japanese immigration to exceed the annual limit. In 1952, for example, 4,517 Japanese immigrated to the United States, followed by 2,393 in 1953. Moreover, the Issei—and the postwar Japanese-born immigrants—were eligible to become American citizens.

The IMMIGRATION AND NATIONALITY ACT OF 1965 (Public Law No. 89-236, 79 Stat. 911) further encour-

aged Japanese immigration to the United States by abolishing the national-origins quota system. This legislation, passed by the immigration-minded 89th Congress, still imposed numerical restrictions to limit immigration. The Eastern Hemisphere was given a total annual ceiling of 170,000 immigrants; no individual nation could exceed 20,000 quota immigrants annually. A seven-category preference system attached priority to immigrants with requisite skills, but more significant in terms of numbers was an emphasis on family reunification.

Post-1965 Japanese immigration differs significantly from early Japanese immigration. Skilled Japanese businesspersons represent a change from the Japanese agricultural workers of the past, although many are SOJOURNERS in their own fashion. SANSEI and YONSEI utilize the transient business-based immigrants, largely situated in Los Angeles and New York, to keep in contact with the homeland culture of Japan.

Two other American legislative enactments affected the configuration of Japanese immigration to the United States in the 1980's and 1990's: the Immigration Reform and Control Act of 1986 (IRCA) and the IMMIGRATION ACT OF 1990. IRCA created a two-step legalization process for unauthorized aliens (including Japanese) residing in the United States. Those aliens residing in the United States continuously since 1982 and unauthorized agricultural workers working on perishable crops in 1986 could apply for temporary resident status (first step) and permanent resident status (second step). Those eligible did so by 1991. Of the 11,028 Japanese immigrants to the United States in 1992, only 53 were admitted because of IRCA requirements.

The Immigration Act of 1990 (Public Law 101-649) occurred during a period when, due to economic expansion at home, the Japanese government was discouraging Japanese immigration to the United States. The Immigration Act of 1990, which has been described as "the most comprehensive change in [American] immigration law in more than 25 years," created two categories of immigrants subject to direct numerical limitation: family-sponsored and employment-based immigrants. Two new categories were added in 1992: legalization dependents and diversity transition immigrants. The former were spouses or children of persons gaining temporary or permanent resident status in the United States under IRCA, the latter natives of countries deemed adversely impacted by the Immigration and Nationality Act of 1965. Under the family-sponsored and employment-based preferences of the 1990 act, Japan, like other nations, was limited to 25,620 visas. In 1992, Japanese immigration to the United States ranked eighth as a contributor to the 356,955 Asian immigrants to the United States. Japan's contributions to the 1990 act's four new status categories were largest for employment-based preferences (3,203) and diversity transition (4,839). These two Japanese immigrant groups were the true successors to the Issei of an earlier day, individuals "seeking a challenge . . . they cannot find in the . . . confines of modern Japan," as described in *The New York Times* in November, 1977.—*Malcolm B. Campbell*

SUGGESTED READINGS:

• Barkan, Elliott Robert. *Asian and Pacific Islander Migration to the United States: A Model of New Global Patterns*. Westport, Conn.: Greenwood Press, 1992. Discusses post-1965 Japanese immigration to the United States within the context of contemporary Pacific Rim migration to the United States. Contains an excellent section on the impact of American immigration reforms, 1945-1985, on East Asian immigration to the United States.

• Ehrlich, Paul R., Loy Bilderback, and Anne H. Ehrlich. *The Golden Door: International Migration, Mexico, and the United States*. New York: Ballantine Books, 1979. While centered on Mexican migration to the United States, *The Golden Door* also includes an excellent discussion of the Gentlemen's Agreement of 1907, the Barred Zone Act of 1917, and the Immigration Act of 1924. Attributing American fear of the Japanese to xenophobia, the authors argue that American immigration policy ought to proceed from a "more complete" knowledge of the cultural and economic roles of immigrants.

• Espiritu, Yen Le. *Asian American Panethnicity: Bridging Institutions and Identities*. Philadelphia: Temple University Press, 1992. Focusing on the period from the 1960's to the 1990's, this pioneering study provides an excellent discussion of the development of bridging organizations and solidarities among ethnic groups of Asian ancestry. Espiritu notes that, prior to the 1960's, Asians in the United States often practiced "ethnic disidentification"; early Japanese immigrants, for example, sought to distance themselves from Chinese immigrants.

• Fawcett, James T., and Benjamin V. Carino, eds. *Pacific Bridges: The New Immigration from Asia and the Pacific Islands*. Staten Island, N.Y.: Center for Migration Studies of New York, 1987. A profile of Japanese immigration to the United States and to British Commonwealth nations in the post-1965 period. Readers will find the figures and tables assembled for this volume especially revealing of contemporary patterns of Japanese immigration to the United States within overall contours of East Asian and Pacific Islander emigration to the United States since the abolition of the national origin quota system.

• Fuchs, Lawrence H. *The American Kaleidoscope: Race, Ethnicity, and the Civic Culture*. Hanover, N. H.: Wesleyan University Press, 1990. Fuchs shows in rich detail how Japanese immigrants to the United States prior to World War II were viewed as unfit for full participation in American civic culture. How Japanese immigrants overcame discriminatory laws and attitudes is accented in *The American Kaleidoscope*, a must read.

• Hing, Bill Ong. *Making and Remaking Asian America Through Immigration Policy, 1850-1990*. Stanford, Calif.: Stanford University Press, 1993. Hing's focus is on the question of how U. S. immigration policies over the past 150 years have shaped the six largest Asian American communities: Chinese, Filipino, Japanese, Korean, Vietnamese, and Asian Indian.

• Jones, Maldwyn Allen. *American Immigration*. 2d ed. Chicago: University of Chicago Press, 1992. A useful introduction to the history of American immigration patterns and themes, including a brief overview of Japanese immigration. Jones's chapter, "New Sources of Immigration, 1860-1914," is especially informative.

• Moriyama, Alan Takeo. *Imingaisha: Japanese Emigration Companies and Hawaii, 1894-1908*. Honolulu: University of Hawaii Press, 1985. Essential reading for an understanding how the *imingaisha,* Japanese emigration companies, regulated the day-to-day lives of the "Imin," those Japanese emigrating to countries other than China and Korea for purposes of labor, in Hawaii during the period between the conclusion of Japanese-government-sponsored emigration to Hawaii and capitulation of the Japanese government to the so-called Gentlemen's Agreement of 1907-1908. Contains useful appendices and a note on sources utilized.

• Namias, June. *First Generation: In the Words of Twentieth-Century American Immigrants*. Rev. ed. Urbana: University of Illinois Press, 1992. This oral history collection contains the narrative of Natsu Okuyama Ozawa, who came to San Francisco, California, in 1924 from Japan to join her husband working then as a merchant. Subtitled "So the Big People Will Know," Ozawa's recollections as an Issei in America are eloquent testimony to the pleasures and, frequently, stresses her generation of Japanese immigrants endured in becoming "nice." Highly recommended.

• Takaki, Ronald. *Strangers from a Different Shore: A History of Asian Americans*. New York: Penguin Books, 1990. Grandson of Japanese immigrant plantation laborers on the Puunene Plantation, Maui, Hawaii, Takaki includes a vivid account of the nature and scope of Japanese immigration to the United States in this sweeping history of Asian Americans. Takaki's narrative is enriched by firsthand testimony, drawn both from the work of prominent writers and from a wide range of interviews and life histories.

Japanese in Brazil: The population of Japanese immigrants in Brazil, called the *colonia* by its members. Brazil is host to the largest community of Japanese and their descendants overseas. According to Japanese government statistics Japan contributed a total of about 250,000 immigrants to Brazil between 1908 and the 1980's. These immigrants had grown to be a population of more than 1.2 million Japanese Brazilians by 1992. Three-quarters of them live in the city and state of São Paulo.

Japanese migration to Brazil began in 1908, when contract laborers were needed to pick coffee on plantations in São Paulo. Formerly the harvest labor had been provided by European immigrants, who ceased coming to Brazil in anticipation of World War I. Representatives of Brazilian coffee planters approached Japanese diplomatic officials and requested immigrant labor. Japan investigated wages and working conditions on the plantations before signing a migration agreement. Brazil agreed to subsidize the immigrants' shipboard fares.

This pattern of contract labor immigration was followed by a period of colonization. In the 1920's and early 1930's Japanese emigration companies bought land in Brazil and divided it up into lots for sale to Japanese who planned to emigrate. These independent producers made significant contributions to the cooperative organization and technology of Brazilian agriculture.

The Japanese immigrants originally intended to return to Japan with savings accumulated in Brazil. The years of World War II, however, isolated Japanese in Brazil, and the poverty of postwar Japan discouraged return. In the meantime, most Japanese in Brazil had settled down and raised children and grandchildren in the host nation and were beginning to identify themselves as Brazilians of Japanese ancestry.

In the postwar years Japanese Brazilians followed a national trend of urbanization. Many left agriculture and chose life in São Paulo, where educational opportunities allowed their children to move into white-collar and professional fields.

In the 1980's at least fifty thousand Brazilians of Japanese ancestry returned to the land of their forefathers to work as temporary labor migrants, a curious reversal of the pattern set generations earlier.

Japanese in Canada: In the decade prior to World War I (1914-1918), Canada, under pressure from trade unions and elected officials in British Columbia, identified "a Japanese problem." The government's efforts at a solution involved restrictions on further immigration and denial of civil rights. During World War II (1939-1945), the government adopted a policy of removal of persons of Japanese origin from British Columbia and their dispersal across Canada. The attempt to deport Japanese Canadians after the war led to a public outcry and to a granting of civil and political rights in 1949. According to the 1991 census, there are 48,595 persons in Canada who identify their ethnic origin as entirely Japanese. Japanese constitute the

Japanese skiers at Lake Louise, Banff, Alberta, Canada. (Photo Search Ltd./Vern Minard)

fifth largest group of Asian origin in Canada, following Chinese (586,645), East Indian (324,840), Filipino (157,250), and Vietnamese (84,010).

Immigration. The first wave of Japanese immigrants, the Issei, arrived in Canada between 1877 and 1928. They were male peasants from fishing and farming villages in southern Japan, whose ocean passage was sometimes provided by large mining or railroad construction companies. By 1901 they numbered 4,738, nearly all of whom intended to return to Japan after earning some money as farmers, fishermen, or laborers. Accordingly, they made little effort to learn English or adopt local customs. Alarmed by their willingness to work long hours for low wages and their perceived inability to assimilate, British Columbians began to press the federal government to stop further immigration. Immigration, however, grew from 2,996 in 1906 to 8,196 in 1907. In September, 1907, a riot occurred in Vancouver in protest against this influx of Japanese. In 1908, under pressure from Canada, Japan restricted immigration of males to 400 per year but permitted wives to join their husbands. There were 10,000 Japanese Canadians in 1914, most of whom resided in British Columbia, with a few settling in Alberta. By 1919 Japanese Canadians held nearly half the fishing licenses in British Columbia. In 1928 Canada limited Japanese immigration to 150 persons a year. Canada banned all Japanese immigration in 1940 and did not allow it to begin again until 1967.

Denial of Civil Rights. The government of British Columbia did not want the Japanese to assimilate and passed a series of laws to force them to leave Canada. The province denied all persons of Japanese descent, even those born in Canada, the right to vote in both federal and provincial elections, excluded them from most professions, passed discriminatory labor legislation, and prohibited them from enlisting in the armed services. They could not run for political office at any level. In the 1920's the federal government attempted to limit the number of fishing licenses granted to Japanese. A 1925 British Columbia minimum-wage law effectively limited the number of Japanese employed in the lumber industry, and additional legislation forced them out of the mining and railroad construction industries. Despite the effort to deny them membership in the Canadian political community, by 1941 there were 17,225 persons of Japanese descent who had become citizens of Canada by birth or naturalization. Unlike their parents, the second-generation Nisei had no intention of leaving Canada, the country of their birth, and returning to the land of their ancestors.

Japanese Canadian novelist Joy Kogawa.

Internment. Following the Japanese attack on PEARL HARBOR and Hong Kong in December, 1941, the Canadian government impounded Japanese-owned fishing boats, arrested and confined a few Japanese whose loyalty was suspect, and closed the JAPANESE-LANGUAGE SCHOOLS. In February, 1942, the federal government ordered the removal of all persons of Japanese ancestry from the Pacific Coast. The government regarded these people as potential saboteurs and spies who could assist a Japanese invasion. The motivation, however, was as much hostility to the Japanese presence in British Columbia as it was concern with national security, since the Canadian military leaders opposed the removal. The pressure for exclusion came primarily from elected provincial officials, labor unions, and owners of small businesses. The government also justified the exclusion and internment on the grounds that Japanese Canadians needed protection from hostile white citizens. During the course of the war, no Japanese Canadian was charged with sabotage, espionage, or any act of disloyalty.

In 1942 the government removed 20,881 persons of Japanese descent, three-quarters of whom were Canadian citizens, and confined them in detention camps in the interior of British Columbia or on sugar-beet farms in Alberta and Manitoba. Most evacuees lived on government welfare benefits. The federal government sold off all the property of Japanese Canadians between 1943 and 1946. A suit challenging the forced sales brought by three Japanese owners was dismissed by the Exchequer Court of Canada in 1947. The federal

Flower shop worker, Granville Island public market, Vancouver, British Columbia, Canada. (Robert Fried)

government extended the disfranchisement of Japanese in 1944. In 1945 the government offered them the choice of free passage to Japan or relocation east of the Rocky Mountains. Most chose to move to Ontario, Quebec, or the prairie provinces. Because of the exclusion policy, Japanese Canadians now are scattered across Canada—a sharp contrast with their earlier concentration in Vancouver. Between 1942 and 1946, 5,510 Japanese Canadians settled in the prairies and 7,660 in eastern Canada.

In 1946 public opinion prevented the government from carrying out its plan to deport 10,000 Japanese Canadians. Both the Supreme Court of Canada and the Judicial Committee of the Privy Council in England sustained the power of the government to deport Canadian citizens of Japanese origin if it wished. In 1946, 3,964 persons migrated to Japan voluntarily. The Japanese population in Canada dropped from 23,149 in 1941 to 21,663 in 1951.

Gain of Civil Rights. In 1949 the federal government abandoned its policy of dispersal and exclusion and gave the Japanese in Canada the right to vote. Only about 1,000 Japanese, however, returned to their former homes in British Columbia. Following the report of a commission formed to investigate claims that the government sold Japanese Canadian property below market value, some Japanese owners received additional compensation after the war.

By 1971 the Japanese in Canada had become an urban people, with the largest concentration living in metropolitan Toronto. The third-generation Japanese Canadians, or Sansei, have become thoroughly assimilated, with 75 percent marrying non-Japanese. The

Canadian Japanese generally are more highly educated and earn higher incomes than their Caucasian fellow citizens.

In spite of vigorous lobbying efforts by the National Association of Japanese Canadians, the federal government refuses to acknowledge Japanese Canadians' grievances or to pay additional compensation to those interned during the war.—*Kenneth Holland*

SUGGESTED READINGS: • Adachi, Ken. *The Enemy That Never Was: A History of the Japanese Canadians.* Toronto: McClelland and Stewart, 1991. • Broadfoot, Barry. *Years of Sorrow, Years of Shame: The Story of Japanese Canadians in World War II.* Garden City, N.Y.: Doubleday, 1977. • Kogawa, Joy. *Obasan.* Boston: David R. Godine, 1981. • Sunahara, Ann Gomer. *The Politics of Racism: The Uprooting of Japanese Canadians During the Second World War.* Toronto: Lorimer, 1981. • Ward, W. Peter. *White Canada Forever: Popular Attitudes and Public Policy Toward Orientals in British Columbia.* Montreal: McGill-Queen's University Press, 1990.

Japanese in Peru: A small but viable Japanese immigrant community has inhabited Peru since the late 1890's. While numbering roughly seventeen thousand people by 1940, it represents less than 2 percent of Peru's population in the 1990's. During World War II the Peruvian Japanese endured hostility and discrimination, imprisonment, forced deportation to the United States, and the loss of their property. After the war these people, like other Japanese communities in the Americas, rebuilt their lives.

Japanese migration to Peru began in 1899, when agents for Peruvian sugar and cotton plantations recruited contract agricultural labor in Japan. These early connections between Japan and Peru were fostered by the development of steam passage across the Pacific and by economic dislocations in Japan resulting from Japan's industrialization and modernization.

Yet Japanese contract laborers began to drift away from the plantations whenever they could. By the 1910's some Japanese had saved enough money to lease sizable pieces of land and operate farms of their own. Others had filtered into Peruvian cities and found employment in various service occupations.

Because travel back to Japan was possible, Japanese males commonly returned to Japan for their wives and started families in Peru. Sensing that their interlude in Peru might be temporary, wanting to maintain cultural ties with other Japanese and with Japan, and being discriminated against and resented by Peruvians, the

Peruvian Japanese tended increasingly to congregate in urban areas. By 1940 approximately 80 percent of the Peruvian Japanese lived in the Lima-Callao metropolitan areas. Even in the cities they experienced problems, as indicated by the major anti-Japanese riots that erupted in Lima and Callao in 1940. Inspired by the security concerns of the United States, the Peruvian government saw World War II as an opportunity to solve its "Japanese problem." By attacking the economic and cultural viability of the Peruvian Japanese, and by offering to transport virtually all the Peruvian Japanese to the United States for wartime internment and forced repatriation to Japan after the war, the Peruvian government and citizens dealt severe blows to the Peruvian Japanese community.

On June 10, 1990, Alberto Fujimori, the son of Japanese immigrants, was elected president of Peru. Behind his campaign slogan of "Work, Honesty, and Technology," Fujimori, an unknown agronomist, defeated novelist Mario Vargas Llosa by capturing 56.5 percent of the vote.

Japanese internees from South America: During World War II Japanese residents or citizens of various South American countries who were deemed to be security risks by either the United States or its allies were sent to the United States for detention and possible repatriation to Japan.

In the 1930's the security agencies of the U.S. government were concerned about the presence of Japanese immigrant communities throughout South America. It was feared that enemy agents within these communities could transmit military information to Japan, mount some sort of attack on military installations, or even sabotage the Panama Canal. Accordingly, before December 7, 1941, the U.S. government began surveillance of South American Japanese communities and made plans to take into custody their leaders or those who seemed to be potential threats to American security.

Within weeks of the Japanese bombing of PEARL HARBOR, and with the full encouragement of the American government, various South American countries established programs ranging from close supervision of their Japanese populations to evacuation from sensitive areas to incarceration. Eventually some of the South American governments claimed that they could not effectively implement or afford the security programs that would satisfy U.S. military authorities in Panama or Washington, D.C. Therefore the United States accepted for internment on its territory several

thousand South American Japanese. Since the United States, with the approval of the Japanese government, had assumed the responsibility of repatriating to Japan the Japanese U.S. diplomatic corps and certain Japanese civilians from all the Americas, South American Japanese designated for return to Japan were also transported to and interned in the United States.

The South American Japanese were interned in camps operated by the Immigration and Naturalization Service (INS) of the Justice Department. During the war, in two separate operations a number of them were repatriated to Japan. When the war ended Washington tried to return the remaining South American Japanese to their countries of origin, but for the most part the governments of South America refused to take them back. Accordingly many of them were subsequently repatriated to Japan while a few managed to remain in the United States.

Japanese language: Japanese is the native language of more than 126 million people living in the (mostly monolingual) Japanese islands. According to 1990 figures it is one of the ten most commonly spoken languages in the world. Japanese is also spoken as a second language by many Korean and other immigrants living in Japan, as well as by a sizable number of people in former Japanese colonies such as Taiwan. Many people of Japanese ancestry living in Brazil, Peru, Hawaii, and other parts of the United States and Canada speak Japanese as a first or second language.

Japanese dialects are more diverse than those found in some other monolingual communities such as the United States. Some dialects are distinct to the point of almost mutual unintelligibility, while others differ only in accent, grammatical forms, or vocabulary. This dialect variability had implications for Japanese resettling overseas, as sometimes the "elegant" Kyoto-dialect speakers, "country farmer" KYUSHU-dialect speakers, or "rough" downtown Tokyo-dialect speakers would clash. Today a prestigious version of the Tokyo-dialect has become the semiofficial national language and is the version taught in schools and used in the media. Many Japanese, especially those in the work force, are bidialectical in both their local speech patterns and the standard language.

Historical Relationships. There is still much debate regarding the exact historical connections between Japanese and the world's other languages. It is certain that Japanese is not related to any of the Chinese languages, though the Chinese writing system was borrowed about fifteen hundred years ago. The four

	Sample Japanese Sentence							
Japanese characters	JAL	の	フライト	ナンバー	は	何番	です	か。
Script set	Roman letters	hiragana	katakana	katakana	hiragana	kanji	hiragana	hiragana
Transliteration	jaru	no	furaito	nambaa	wa	nan-ban	desu	ka
Sentence structure	Japan Air Lines	possessive marker	English loan: "flight"	English loan: "number"	topic marker	"what" + classifier	"is"	question marker
English translation	"What is the Japan Air Lines flight number?"							

languages spoken in the RYUKYU (Okinawan) ISLANDS are very closely related to standard Japanese but are unintelligible to speakers living on the four main Japanese islands. Korean and Ainu, the language of the people originally inhabiting the Japanese islands, show some distant affinities to Japanese, especially in terms of syntax. Many scholars now believe in a Japanese-Altaic connection, making Japanese distantly related to the Mongolian and Turkish languages, yet conceding some influence from the Austronesian languages of Southeast Asia, the Philippines, and Indonesia.

The Structure of the Japanese Language. The Japanese sound system is not radically different from English, and most Japanese consonants are generally pronounced in similar ways (with a few notable exceptions, such as the infamous Japanese blending of *r* and *l*). The five vowels are pronounced as in Spanish or Italian, though vowel length—how long one says the vowel—makes a difference in meaning (for example *ie* means "house," but *iie* means "no"). The Japanese sound system does not have the stress accent found in English, but it does often make distinctions regarding pitch. For example *HAshi* (chopsticks) differs from *haSHI* (bridge), as does *KAki* (oyster) and *kaKI* (persimmon).

The Japanese "spell" their language using a syllabary (symbols indicating vowels or consonant-vowel syllable units) rather than individual phonemes ("letters" or an alphabet).

In terms of grammar, Japanese is what linguists often call an "SOV" language: In Japanese the subject generally comes first in a sentence, followed by the object and other complements, and ending with the verb. This is the opposite of the word order in English, where verbs generally come in the middle of sentences, followed by objects and other phrases. This linguistic property has profound implications for the structure of Japanese. For example where English has prepositions that precede the word they modify, Japanese has postpositions coming after the noun ("Karen *kara*," literally "Karen from"). Another distinctive feature of the Japanese language is the use of special particles after words called "case markers" to indicate a particular word's part of speech.

The Japanese Writing System. For historical reasons the Japanese writing system is one of the most complex in the world. Ancient Japanese had no script until Chinese characters began to be borrowed in several waves starting in the sixth century. Because Chinese grammar and Japanese grammar are completely different, however, many adjustments had to be made to make the picture-based Chinese characters fit into a different, and somewhat inappropriate, Japanese syntax. For example Chinese verbs do not conjugate for tense; however, Japanese verbs (and even adjectives) change form depending on level of politeness, causality, and a number of other important conditions. New ways had to be devised to write these different grammatical features that were lacking in Chinese. The result of this was the two syllabary systems used to spell phonetically certain Japanese words, foreign names, and parts of speech that have no special characters.

Experimentation with the Japanese writing system has continued into modern times. The last major reform was in 1981, when the Japanese government decided that 1,945 *joyo* (or daily use) characters would be the only ones officially taught in school. Roman letters are also quite prevalent and are especially found in advertisements and the mass media.

Japanese Sociolinguistics. There are several ways that the Japanese language encodes social and cultural features in a manner quite different from English. For example Japanese has several grammatical techniques to indicate politeness, both toward the person being spoken to and for the person being spoken about. The famous suffix *-san* attached to proper names is only one simple means to indicate respect to the addressee.

There are also great differences between Japanese male and female speech patterns. Grammatical forms, choice of honorific expressions, and special words coming at the end of a sentence are all devices that are used to mark speech as masculine or feminine.

In Japanese there are also special ways to indicate in-group affiliations. For example in verbs of giving or receiving, a first-person speaker may use the same grammatical forms that, for example, his or her younger sister or friend would be required to use, indicating the speaker's psychological empathy with them.

Attitudes, Language, and Thought: The Alleged Difficulty of Japanese. Many Westerners believe that Japanese is a very difficult language for them to learn. Some famous Japanese linguists concur, claiming that Japanese is so different from any other language that it is almost impossible for even the most gifted foreigner to master. They believe that the mental and cultural world of the Japanese people can be encoded only by the Japanese language and that the linguistic reality depicted by the Japanese language applies only to Japan. Some have even argued in all seriousness that the Japanese brain is somehow fundamentally different from those of other racial groups.

Most Asian and Western linguists, psychologists, and anthropologists dismiss such claims, however, and believe that no language is any more complex or inferior than any other. Only the Japanese writing system presents a valid obstacle for most foreign students.— *James Stanlaw*

SUGGESTED READINGS: • Haradda, Tetsuo. *Outlines of Modern Japanese Linguistics.* Tokyo: Nihon University/Tateshina Publishing, 1966. • Kindaichi, Haruhiko. *The Japanese Language.* Translated by Umeyo Hirano. Rutland, Vt.: Charles E. Tuttle, 1978. • Miller, Roy Andrew. *The Japanese Language.* Chicago: University of Chicago Press, 1967. • Okutsu, Keichiro, and Akio Tanaka. *Invitation to the Japanese Language.* Tokyo: Bonjinsha, 1989. • Sugawara, Makoto. *Nihongo: A Japanese Approach to Japanese.* Tokyo: The East Publications, 1985. • Suzuki, Takao. *Japanese and the Japanese: Words in Culture.* Translated by Akira Miura. Tokyo: Kodansha International, 1978.

Japanese language on Okinawa: The Japanese PREFECTURE of OKINAWA, also known as the "Ryukyus," consists of more than one hundred islands, including the largest, Okinawa. More than 1.2 million people live in the RYUKYU ISLANDS, though it is less than nine hundred square miles in area.

The early inhabitants of the Ryukyus were racially and ethnically Japanese, probably coming to the islands from KYUSHU (in southern Japan) between fifteen hundred and two thousand years ago. By the twelfth or thirteenth century, however, the Okinawan rulers had consolidated the islands into kingdoms that considered themselves quite independent of the mainland. The *lingua franca* of the Ryukyu Islands was Shuri, a dialect of Okinawan spoken near Naha. Until the 1600's the Ryukyu Islands paid tribute to the Chinese emperor and carried on extensive economic and cultural exchange with Taiwan and the Asian mainland. This political and physical separation assured the continued divergence of the Ryukyu and Japanese languages. In the sixteenth century the sacred oral texts of the northern Ryukyu Islands of Amami Oshima and Okinawa were written down for the first time. Japanese warlords from Kyushu conquered much of the Ryukyus in the early 1600's, however, and after the SINO-JAPANESE WAR (1894-1895) the islands were officially annexed by the new Meiji imperial Japanese government.

Today there are four major Ryukyuan languages (though some claim as few as three or as many as five).

The Major Ryukyuan Languages		
Ryukyu Language	Major Dialects	Number of Speakers
North Ryukyuan/Amami Oshima	Amami	100,000
	Shodon	
	Nase	
Central Ryukyuan/Okinawa	Shuri	680,000
	Kikaijima	
	Okinoerabu	
	Saan	
	Tokunoshima	
	Nakajin	
	Iejima	
	Kudakajima	
Southern Ryukyuan/Miyako	Hirara	100,000
	Irabujima	
	Ikema	
Southwestern Ryukyuan/Yaeyama	Yonaguni	100,000
	Kobana	
	Kurojima	
	Sonai	
	Taketomi	
	Ishigakijima	
	Hateruma	

Note: The division of the Ryukyu languages into families and dialects is controversial. The two other main alternative hypotheses are: first, a three-language family consisting of Amami-Okinawa, Miyako-Yaeyama, and Yonaguni; and second, a three-language family consiting of Amami-Oshima, Okinawa, and Miyako-Yaeyama.

They are often named after the island complexes inhabited by their speakers: Amami Oshiman, Okinawan, Miyakoan, and Yaeyaman. Due to the physical separations of one community from another inherent in entities comprised of islands, there is extensive dialect diversity within each of these languages as well. Though similar in phonology, vocabulary, and syntax these languages are, for the most part, mutually unintelligible and are about as different as Spanish, Portuguese, and Italian.

The similarities between Japanese and Ryukyuan have led some linguists in Japan to wonder whether or not the Ryukyu languages should be considered as simply quite divergent Japanese dialects. For example there is evidence that the Ryukyu languages have retained several features of Old Japanese, such as some archaic verbal inflections. All the Ryukyu languages, however, are unintelligible to speakers of modern standard Japanese—as well as of most of the mainland Japanese dialects. If the Ryukyu languages are dialects of Japanese, they are certainly the most diverse and peripheral.

The American military occupied OKINAWA after World War II. In May, 1972, the Ryukyu Islands were officially returned to Japan by the United States. Most Okinawans, as well as many people in the outlying islands, are now bilingual. Standard Japanese is the language of instruction in the school system, government offices, and the media. The use of the Ryukyuan languages is likely to decline in the coming decades, especially on Okinawa, the cultural and political center of the Ryukyus and the island with the most contact with Japan proper. An Okinawan dialect of standard Japanese is developing. In the smaller remote islands, however, Ryukyuan languages will probably continue for some time.

Japanese-language schools: Supplemental schools established in the United States to teach Japanese language and heritage. The first school in Hawaii opened in 1892. By 1910 about seven thousand students were attending the Hawaii schools, increasing to more than twenty thousand in 1920. The first Japanese-language school in California opened in 1903. About seven hundred students were attending the California schools in 1913.

Hawaii enrolled so many students because of the large number of Japanese immigrants and their descendants living in a relatively small land area. For example, in 1920 there were about 110,000 Japanese in Hawaii, compared to about 72,000 in California, 17,000 in Washington, and 4,200 in Oregon.

During World War I (1914-1918), when German schools became targets of suspicion, opposition to Japanese schools grew. Beginning in 1920 the legislatures of Hawaii and California enacted laws to abolish the schools. In response the Japanese in Hawaii, led by Frederick Kinzaburo MAKINO and represented by attorney Joseph Lightfoot, took the issue to court. In 1926 the Ninth Circuit Court of Appeals, in *FARRINGTON v. TOKUSHIGE*, declared the Hawaii law unconstitutional, and the following year the U.S. Supreme Court upheld that decision. Together with several other Supreme Court cases, the *Farrington* decision negated anti-foreign language school laws in twenty-two states.

Opponents of Japanese-language schools argued that the schools impeded good American citizenship because they promoted Japanese culture and loyalty to Japan and interfered with learning English, a claim unsubstantiated by research. Supporters of the schools argued that the schools taught moral values that promoted good American citizenship, expanded job opportunities, and promoted family harmony by improving communication between parents and children. Despite claims made by both sides, the Japanese schools were generally ineffective agents of language and cultural transmission (most students did not achieve fluency in Japanese) because most NISEI were indifferent to the schools. Those who were interested in scholastic achievement placed their energies in the all-day public schools they attended.

Buddhist church school in Gardena, California. (Michael Yamashita)

Japanese-language school, Sacramento, California, circa 1910. (Sacramento Archives and Museum Collection Center)

With the outbreak of World War II (1939-1945), all Japanese-language schools were closed. In 1943 the Hawaii Territorial Legislature once again passed an antiforeign-language school law, which was challenged by the Chinese, who also maintained language schools. In 1947 the federal court declared the law invalid. Within months of that decision, Japanese-language schools reopened.

Japanese martial arts: Japanese methods of self-defense are developed from various ancient Asian fighting systems. The major systems of Japanese martial arts are karate, jujitsu, judo, and aikido. Other arts include sumo wrestling, kendo, kyudo, naginata-do, and iaido.

Karate. Karate, which means "empty hand," originated in OKINAWA. The Okinawans combined their unarmed combat style, te (hand art), with Chinese kung fu methods to form the art of karate.

Gichin Funakoshi, an Okinawan schoolteacher born in 1868, introduced karate to the Japanese. In 1912 he gave demonstrations to the Japanese Imperial Navy crews living at his school, and news of karate spread to Japan. In 1921 the emperor requested that Funakoshi teach in Japan, and soon, the first *dojo*, or training school, was established in Tokyo. The name of his

martial art was changed from Okinawan Te (Okinawan hand) into the Japanese characters for karate-do, or "way of the empty hand."

The number of karate schools and masters rapidly increased, leading to more than fifteen karate styles and millions of pupils throughout the world. Karate developed into a popular spectator sport, governed by the World Union of Karate Organizations. The first organized American karate association was opened by Japanese *sensei* (teacher) Oshima in Los Angeles in 1955.

In the United States a new form of karate sport, full contact karate, emerged. Unlike the traditional system, which forbids body contact, full contact karate participants wear Western-style boxing gloves, are allowed to hit one another, and compete in a boxing ring. Soon after its development, tournaments were shown on television, and the Professional Karate Association was founded. This American spectator sport has become very popular worldwide.

Karate is also a significant force in U.S. law enforcement. In the 1960's Hawaii became the first state to institute karate instruction for guards in penal institutions. By 1981 all U.S. law enforcement agencies had become familiar with Asian martial arts.

Karate Techniques, Methods, and Training. The basic techniques consist of focused blows delivered with the hand, foot, head, or knee. The *karateka* (one who studies karate) learns the basic techniques from his *sensei* in the *dojo*. The student practices with a partner or does *kata*, the performing of exercises against an

Karate practitioner breaks burning solid blocks. (Raymond J. Malace)

Karate workout at sunrise. Students practice the Sono-Ba-Zuki, or horse stance and punching. (Raymond J. Malace)

imaginary opponent. The pupil learns the power of the mind in harmony with the body. To release the power within, a *karateka* will perform *tamashiwara*, the breaking of hard materials with a blow using a part of the body, such as the head, fist, elbow, or fingertips.

Rank or proficiency is indicated by colored belts, with the black belt signifying the highest achievement. Within this rank, there are gradings called "dan." With the proliferation of various systems and styles throughout the world, there is no single standard of grading. The awarding of rankings can vary according to the school or teacher.

Jujitsu, Judo, and Aikido. Jujitsu, or "gentle art," was created from the Japanese art of sumo in 23 B.C.E. and is the forerunner of aikido and judo. Originally used in combat by the samurai, jujitsu came to encompass a wide variety of schools and techniques, including kicks, strikes, throws, trips, joint-locking, and swords. More than seven hundred schools of jujitsu existed in feudal Japan. In 1532 Takenuchi Hisamori systemized it with the founding of Takenuchi-Ryu.

Kano Jigoro, a Japanese educator, created judo (gentle way) by synthesizing various systems of jujitsu. In 1882 he began teaching judo, which basically uses throws and grappling.

In 1902 American President Theodore Roosevelt started studying judo. In 1909, in Los Angeles, a Japanese judo master opened the first American *dojo.* Judo, the sports form of jujitsu, was introduced as an Olympic sport in 1964 in Tokyo.

Aikido, or "way of all harmony," was created by Ueshiba Morihei in Japan in the late 1920's, in reaction to the physical emphasis in jujitsu. Using holds, locks, twists, and throws, the aikido artist uses an opponent's strength against himself or herself. Aikido aims for the unity of mind, body, and *ki,* the power within each person.

Other Systems. Sumo wrestling is indigenous to Japan. According to legend the first match occurred when the god Takemikazuchi defeated the leader of a rival tribe. The matches, which begin with a long prefight ritual based on the SHINTO religion, usually end in less than a minute. The contest is over when any part of the body, other than the soles of the feet, scrapes or

Pupils of a Japanese kendo school await their turn during a live public demonstration at a Japantown festival in San Francisco, California. In modern practice bamboo replicas are used instead of the original samurai swords. (Robert Fried)

Kendo swordsmen practice their art. (Raymond J. Malace)

lands on the surface of the *dohyo* (dirt mound). The Hawaiian Jesse Kahualua was the first non-Japanese to become a sumo champion.

Kendo, or "way of the sword," is a blending of spiritual values and technical skills. Although the samurai sword has been replaced with a bamboo sword called a *shinai*, kendo still requires intense fighting, intricate body moves, and powerful sword cuts and slashes.

Kyudo, or "way of the bow," is the Zen archery art that evolved from the ancient combative system of kyujutsu. Naginata-do is a popular women's sport that entered tournament competitions in the 1960's. The original naginata weapon, the foot soldier's short sword mounted on a pole, has been replaced with a bamboo replica. Iaido, the art of the quick draw sword, was developed by Hayashizaki Jinsuke in the mid-sixteenth century. A noncombative art, iaido has a Zen emphasis on ceremony and self-discipline.

Development in Europe and the United States. Near the end of the nineteenth century, Japanese immigrants to Europe and the United States began teaching systems of jujitsu and judo. The martial arts were not widely studied by Europeans and Americans, however, until after World War II. The American armed forces occupying Japan after 1945 studied techniques such as judo, jujitsu, karate, kendo, and aikido. When these soldiers returned home, they established martial arts schools and often invited Asian masters to teach in these schools.—*Alice Chin Myers*

SUGGESTED READINGS: • Donohue, John J. *The Forge of the Spirit: Structure, Motion, and Meaning in the Japanese Martial Tradition.* New York: Garland, 1991. • Hamada, Hiroyuki Teshin. *Spirit of Japanese Classical Martial Arts: Historical and Philosophical Perspectives.* Dubuque, Iowa: Kendall/Hunt, 1990. • Harrison, E. J. *The Fighting Spirit of Japan.* Woodstock, N.Y.: The Overlook Press, 1982. • Ratti, Oscar, and Adele Westbrook. *Secrets of the Samurai: A Survey of the Martial Arts of Feudal Japan.* Rutland, Vt.: Charles E. Tuttle, 1973. • Soet, John S. *Martial Arts Around the World.* Burbank, Calif.: Publications, 1991. • Williams, Bryn. *Martial Arts of the Orient.* New York: Hamlyn, 1975.

Japanese American kyudo archers perfect their skills. (Michael Yamashita)

Japanese-Mexican Labor Association: Labor union formed in 1903 in California. Though Asian immigrants and Mexicans provided the inexpensive labor that produced the monumental rise of the late nineteenth and early twentieth century agricultural industry in California, they were routinely denied adequate wages, bargaining rights, contracts, job security, or benefits by growers. The union formed in Oxnard when one thousand Japanese and Mexican sugar beet workers struck the American Sugar Beet Company. The union then applied for membership in the AMERICAN FEDERATION OF LABOR (AFL), but when the AFL, under the leadership of exclusionist Samuel GOMPERS, excluded the Japanese workers, the Mexican workers refused to join that organization. The Japanese-Mexican Labor Association stands as an example of interethnic cooperation in labor strife.

Japanese music and dance: Archaeological evidence and Chinese historical chronicles indicate that Japanese music dates back at least to the third or fourth century. Thus the antiquity of Japanese music rivals that found in Europe. Japanese music encompasses many forms and styles, from traditional religious chants and imperial court songs to modern film music and rock and roll. Today Japan supports two music cultures: a traditional variety based on ancient Japanese classical and folk elements and a second style originally influenced by Western music. The distinctions between these two forms are not always clear, however, and contemporary Japanese popular music seems to be, in many ways, a blend of both native and Western elements.

Traditional Classical Music. The earliest Japanese historical epics (around 700 C.E.) discuss the importance of music to Japanese culture. The sun goddess Amaterasu, the national deity of the country and the alleged founder of today's imperial family, hid in a cave, causing the whole world to turn dark. In order to entice her to come out, the minor gods performed lewd songs and dances. This primordial music is said to be the basis of *kagura* (gods' music, one of the oldest Japanese dance forms) and *saru-gaku* (monkey music), one of the precursors of No.

Traditional Japanese music of all kinds is often referred to as *hogaku*. The music that developed in the early imperial courts, however, is generally called *gagaku* (elegant music). Influenced from China and Korea, it consists of elements of both dance (*bugaku*) and orchestra (*kan-gen*). The *gagaku* orchestra itself consists of wind instruments (the *kan*) and plucked string instruments (the *gen*), with up to thirty musicians taking part. In the eighth century this style became institutionalized at the Nara court. Among the instruments employed were *koto* (zither or horizontal harp), *biwa* (tear-drop-shaped lute), *hichiriki* (short double-reed flute), *sho* (panpipes with seventeen reeds), and drums. The *bugaku* dances were performed at the great monasteries at Nara. Today *gagaku* and *bugaku* can still be found, though they have never been as popular as the other two famous classical forms, No and Kabuki.

No was originally popular entertainment but developed into an upper-class art form sponsored by the samurai. No was invented by Kannami Kiyotsugu and his son Zeami Motokiyo in the late fourteenth century under the third Ashikaga shogun. Combining elements of both *gagaku* and Buddhist chants, as well as poetry and highly stylized dance movements, No has little scenery but stresses elaborate costuming. No uses only four instrumentalists and a chorus of eight vocalists. There are more than two hundred No dramas in existence, and No is still popular among certain audiences today.

In the Edo-period towns of the prosperous seventeenth century, middle-class urbanites found a novel kind of entertainment. This new theater genre—Kabuki—grew out of elements of No, Shinto dances, the contemporary *bunraku* (puppet) theater, and current stories. Unlike the subtle and restrained No dance-theater, Kabuki is gaudy and spectacular. In addition to No instrumentation Kabuki adds the *shamisen* (a plucked three-string banjo) and several new drums, cymbals, gongs, and wooden clappers. Today Kabuki is one of the most popular of the classical Japanese theatrical forms.

Traditional Folk Music. While the imperial courtiers listened to *gagaku*, the aristocrats their No, and the townspeople their Kabuki, the rural farmers, fishermen, and laborers sang their *minyo* (folk ballads). Often these folk songs were accompanied by the *shamisen* banjo or the *shakuhachi*, a vertical, hollow bamboo flute. *Minyo* is the other main division of *hogaku* (traditional Japanese music). Sometimes the word *zokkyoku* is also used to describe folk music. Some, however, feel that *zokkyoku* songs differ from

Members of the Matayoshi koto *school of Hilo, Hawaii.* (Michael Yamashita)

Students of the Hayashi music school of Los Angeles, California, practice the traditional Japanese taiko *drums.* (Michael Yamashita)

minyo in that they are more earthy and profane and are often sung while drinking. Ballads about lost loves, good sex, or fine drink are thought to be *zokkyoku*, while songs sung during a planting or harvest are usually *minyo*.

In the late Edo period a narrative style of singing called *naniwabushi* (minstrel songs) developed, especially in the Osaka area. This was a mixture of solo storytelling along with songs accompanied by a *shamisen*. In some ways these songs arose from the musical preachings of the ascetic Buddhist mystics and monks (*yamabushi*) who wandered the mountains a millennium ago. The *naniwabushi* songs tell stories of simple justice, right and wrong, and good triumphing over evil.

In the early Meiji period, soon after Japan reestablished contact with the West in the 1860's, a new form of music called *enka* developed. *Enka* combined elements of *minyo* folk songs and epic *naniwabushi*, with Western musical scales and structures. Singers were often accompanied by Western instruments such as guitars or violins, and the subjects of their songs were contemporary social or political problems. *Enka* is often compared to American country-and-western music, as both have a distinctly nonurban flavor, similar topics, and origins in folk music. In the modern age *enka* became the music of choice for the Japanese *saraiman* (salaried man, or white-collar worker) as he sings with his friends after work in the bars. It became one of the most favored genres of popular music, especially with men and women over forty.

Contemporary Popular Music. Indigenous Japanese popular music (as opposed to music imported from the West) is generally known as *kayokyoku*. Though always having a steady following, the popularity of Japanese *enka* began to wane even before World War II (1939-1945). As the postwar generation of young people became a more significant record-buying force, *kayokyoku* became dominated by a lighter style of music. These were mainly Westernized made-in-Japan songs, or Japanese-style versions of Western pop music. This genre became dominated by very young *aidoru* (teen idol) singers, often with only brief moments of popularity.

Japanese dancers at a public exhibition in Southern California. (Unicorn Stock Photos/Ron P. Jaffe)

In the late 1970's there was a strong reaction against the "idol" singers. Proponents of this movement, known as "New Music," wanted to go beyond the artistically superficial and socially unsophisticated songs that dominated the popular music arena. Their music used more complex melodies and poetic lyrics and appealed to an older listener. Today anything that is not clearly *enka*, mainstream pop *kayokyoku*, foreign or Japanese rock, or imported or domestic jazz is considered to be New Music.

Since the 1930's, when sound motion pictures became widespread, another genre of popular music—*shudaika*, or the movie theme song—has also become important. Today commercial jingles and television *tema songu* (theme songs) are popular and can help determine the ultimate success of a film, television show, or product.

Rock and roll, both Euro-American and Japanese, is quite prevalent all over Japan. Though facing competition from imported bands, homegrown Japanese rock has been increasing in popularity. Subgenres such as New Wave or Techno-Pop command a devoted, if not huge, following. Many forms of American or British rock have their Japanese counterparts, though among the latter there are also some styles that are uniquely Japanese.

Western Music. In addition to rock and roll all other varieties of Western music are extremely popular in Japan. As of 1993 there were a half dozen symphony orchestras in Tokyo alone. Jazz and classical music seem to be even more popular in Japan than in the United States. There are many Japanese who are masters of Western music as well. Toshiko AKIYOSHI, Watanabe Sadao, and Matsui Keiko are world-class jazz artists well known in the West, as are classical musicians Takahashi Aki and Midori. Seiji OZAWA has won several Grammies conducting European and American orchestras, and Sakamoto Ryuichi received an Oscar for his film score for *The Last Emperor* in 1988. Takemitsu Toru is considered to be one of the most important symphonic composers of the twentieth century. Japanese companies such as Yamaha make some of the world's finest musical instruments.

The Meeting of Japanese and Western Music. Some

segments of Japanese popular culture, such as comics, or *anima* (animated science fiction films), have a devoted, if limited, audience abroad. Yet most styles of Japanese popular music—and their artists—are still virtually unknown outside the country. For example in 1990 the Japanese *aidoru* superstar Matsuda Seiko attempted to break into the American market singing a duet with one of the members of the highly popular New Kids on the Block. She met, however, with only marginal success. There have always been a few Western scholars interested in Japanese classical music as an academic discipline. It remains to be seen whether Japanese popular music will eventually find a place among the other European and American rock and ballad styles.—*James Stanlaw*

SUGGESTED READINGS: • Ernst, Earle. *The Kabuki Theatre.* New York: Oxford University Press, 1956. • Gunji, Masakatsu. *Buyo: The Classical Dance.* Translated by Don Kenny. New York: Weatherhill, 1970. • Japanese Classics Translation Committee. *The Noh Drama.* Tokyo: Charles E. Tuttle, 1960. • Malm, William. *Japanese Music and Musical Instruments.* Tokyo: Charles E. Tuttle, 1959. • Malm, William. "Some of Japan's Musics and Music Principles." In *Musics of Many Cultures: An Introduction*, edited by Elizabeth May. Berkeley: University of California Press, pp. 48-62, 1980. • Stanlaw, James. "Not East Not West, Not Old Not New: Trends and Genres in Japanese Popular Music." *The World and I* 4, no. 11 (1989): 622-633.

Japanese occupation of the Philippines (1942-1945): During World War II (1939-1945), Japan sought to incorporate the Philippines into its empire. Aided by Filipino collaborators, the Japanese invaders propagandized the population, stressing the need for Asian unity under Japanese leadership.

Once President Manuel QUEZON fled into exile, the Japanese established a new government through an alliance with members of the Philippine upper class. They imprisoned and executed uncooperative Filipinos and installed Jorge B. Vargas as chairperson of the Executive Commission, a puppet administration advised by a Council of State. The Japanese advised various departments, and Vargas ordered local organizations of ten-family units to implement commission programs.

Japanese authorities imposed political changes. Old parties were replaced by the Kalibapi, or Association for Service in the New Philippines. Inspired by Benigno Aquino, Sr., the Kalibapi sought to drum up support for the occupiers' policies. Hoping to influence Asian opinion and gain Filipino gratitude, Japan created the Preparatory Committee for Philippine Independence, which wrote a constitution and proclaimed the independence of a Japanese-sponsored republic in 1943. The Japanese also founded a military unit called the Makapili, or the Patriotic League of Filipinos, and pressured the new republic of José P. Laurel to declare war on the United States.

Japanese officials used newspapers and Filipino celebrities to spread their ideas. Discipline and thrift were encouraged. The populace was pressed to discard its psychological reliance upon the United States and was urged to restore its original culture. Nipponese propaganda pictured Americans as prejudiced and feeble, and the use of English was restricted. Japanese and Tagalog were made the authorized languages, and Japanese became required in all educational institutions.

The Philippine economy was merged with Japan's self-sustaining sphere through the Greater East Asia Ministry, an agency designed to assemble the assets of conquered areas. The Japanese gave priority to military needs, and rice was diverted from the archipelago's inhabitants in order to feed their troops.

Despite attempts at long-range planning, Japan's occupation of the Philippines was short lived. From the beginning, most Filipinos supported a guerrilla resistance against the Japanese until American forces liberated the islands in 1945.

Japanese ornamental horticulture: Japanese art form that comprises the creation of gardens, both open and enclosed; of miniature potted trees and shrubs (bonsai); and of flower arrangements (*ikebana*). These forms are all well-established horticultural arts in Japan, with their own formal principles, traditions, masters, and masterpieces. The various arts have as their basis the representation of the landscape of Japan and often inspire and allude not only to one another but also to the companion art of landscape painting.

Moreover these horticultural arts attach to certain plants and flowers a symbolic value. This includes associating the pine's evergreen quality with eternity, the early-blooming plum's with perseverance, and the bamboo's bending but not breaking before the wind with the virtue of strength in flexibility. All embody the belief that the whole of nature is present and can be evoked in its most minute parts.

An open garden incorporates faraway views into its design, utilizing the principle of *shakkei*, or "borrowed scenery." A small courtyard garden creates the impression in its viewers of being but a small corner or angle of a much larger totality. This whole-part relationship is even more compressed in the creation of bonsai (potted plant). It is also starker—and thus more powerful still—in its use of a single flower in bud (rather than in full bloom) in the flower arrangement that evokes the world of nature in the TEA CEREMONY.

In direct opposition to the tradition of Western art, Japanese art emphasizes the asymmetrical, the fragmentary, and the impermanent as ideal vehicles for expressing the larger world of natural flux, the feeling for the poignant beauty of passing things (*mono no aware*). In using nature to express nature, the Japanese horticultural arts demonstrate that the greatest art is that which is most seamlessly at one with natural processes, and in which the designer's hand is most invisible. They unfold a vision in which art and nature, rather than being antithetical to each other, embody and reveal the infinitely creative life of the cosmos.

Japanese restaurants and cuisine: Each culture produces a cuisine that is influenced by its climate and geography. In the case of an island country such as Japan, that is reflected in the wide range of fresh seafood eaten. An important principle underlying Japanese cuisine is that the natural flavor of fresh food should be preserved. Japanese cuisine provides a nutritious diet that is nevertheless low in fat content. Meals usually include delicately prepared vegetables, seafood, chicken or small portions of meat, and rice. Emphasis is placed on the symbolism and appearance of food, and ingredients are selected with attention given to the seasons and the balance of textures and colors. Care is also given to arrangement, garnishing, and placement of food on individual serving dishes. The characteristic features of Japanese cuisine are its freshness, simplicity, delicacy, and aesthetic qualities.

The Importance of Rice. Rice has been a fundamental part of Japanese culture and economy for more than two thousand years. It is the main staple of the diet and is served at most meals, although bread is increasingly substituted at breakfast. Japanese prefer a round, small-grain species of rice that is moist and sticky. The importance of rice is reflected in the use of separate words for cooked rice, called *gohan*, and uncooked

Sampling of Japanese cuisine. (Japan Information and Culture Center, Embassy of Japan)

Patrons at the Atomic Cafe, Los Angeles, California. (Michael Yamashita)

rice, which is referred to as *kome*. Because people believe that a meal is incomplete without rice, the word *gohan* is often used metaphorically as a term for "meal" itself.

Typical Foods and Ingredients. Together with rice, green tea and pickles made of cabbage, cucumbers, radishes, or other vegetables are basic components of most Japanese meals. When eating in a restaurant, a *teishoku*, or prearranged set meal, inevitably includes rice, pickles, tea, and one or more side dishes.

The use of some typical ingredients gives a characteristic flavor to Japanese food. Of special importance is *shoyu* (soy sauce), which is made from wheat or barley, soybeans, salt, water, and malt. A base for many soups and sauces is *dashi*, a clear broth made of dried kelp or bonito. *Miso* is fermented soybean paste made in red or white varieties and used in soups, sauces, and dressings. Japanese also eat many varieties of seaweed and algae, all of them rich in minerals and vitamins. Other typical ingredients or seasonings include *mirin* (sweet cooking rice wine), ginger root, white radish, *tofu* (soybean curd), rice vinegar, *katsuo-bushi* (dried

bonito shavings), and *wasabi* (green horseradish).

Two distinctive categories of food are *sashimi* and *sushi*. *Sashimi* are thin slices of raw seafood such as yellowtail, salmon roe, sea bream, tuna, sardine, flounder, scallop, or mackerel. *Sushi* refers to seasoned and vinegared rice prepared in rolls or mounds and topped with an assortment of items, including egg omelet, vegetables, char-broiled eel, prawns, or raw seafood. A third category of food is *nabemono*, one-pot dishes cooked at the table. One *nabemono* is *sukiyaki*, which is made with thin slices of beef, *tofu*, onions and other vegetables cooked in a sweet broth of soy sauce, *mirin*, and sugar.

Restaurants in Japan. There is great diversity in traditional restaurant types, ranging from intimate family-run businesses to extravagant inns that specialize in lavish dinners. *Soba-ya* (the suffix "-ya" means "restaurant") are noodle shops that sell a variety of inexpensive noodle dishes. Noodles are either served hot in a soup broth with various combinations of meat, fish, and vegetables or are served cold and accompanied by condiments and a sauce into which the noodles are then dipped. Dishes featuring seasonal fresh fish and vegetables are available at traditional restaurants called *koryori-ya* and *shokuji dokoro*. Very expensive restaurants serving Japanese haute cuisine, called *ryotei*, give customers an opportunity to dine in elegant Japanese-style surroundings in a private room. *Kissaten* are cafés that feature coffee, tea, and other beverages and desserts. Food can also be ordered in a variety of drinking establishments, such as the *nomi-ya*, which serve light selections and snacks.

In addition to Japanese-style restaurants, there are also authentic Chinese restaurants and *chuka ryori-ya*, restaurants that serve inexpensive Chinese food that has been modified to suit Japanese tastes, as well as many kinds of Western-style restaurants. A type of diner or cafeteria is the *shokudo*, which offers a mixed selection of Japanese, Chinese, and Western-style dishes.

Among the most-preferred eating places are specialty restaurants where one particular food or type of dish dominates the menu. One specialty restaurant is the *yakitori-ya*, where the main fare is skewered chicken grilled over a charcoal fire and brushed with a soy sauce-based glaze. A *tempura-ya* offers batter-coated fish and vegetables delicately deep-fried and served with a dipping-sauce. In a *robatayaki*, charcoal barbecue restaurant with a rustic atmosphere, individual orders of fresh seafood, vegetables, and meat are called out to the chefs, who grill the orders in front of the customers.

One famous type of specialty restaurant is the *sushi-ya*, a shop that features *sushi sashimi*. Customers may sit at counters of natural wood where the *sushi*-chef prepares fresh individual orders. A unique custom in the *sushi-ya* is the use of special words for everyday food items such as soy sauce and tea.

Japanese frequently eat out, primarily because restaurants are an enjoyable and convenient location for meeting and socializing with friends and coworkers. Numerous restaurants are found around any train or subway station, in and around shopping areas, in the basements of large buildings, and in department stores. Restaurants often display a *noren*, a short slitted curtain with the shop's name on it, which is hung over the doorway when open and pulled inside when closed. Cheaper restaurants exhibit wax models of the food they provide together with prices in display cases outside the entrance.

Japanese Restaurants in the United States. Japanese restaurants were at one time most common in Hawaii and California but nowadays may be found across the United States. In the 1980's, *sushi* restaurants reached a new level of almost faddish popularity among Americans. Many Japanese restaurants, perhaps the majority of them, specialize in one form of food such as *ramen*, *sashimi*, *tempura*, or *sukiyaki*. In addition, many restaurants feature Japanese chefs who prepare the food right at the customers' tables; the result is often both entertaining and delicious.—*Laura Miller*

SUGGESTED READINGS: • Belleme, John, and Jan Belleme. *Culinary Treasures of Japan.* Garden City Park, N.J.: Avery Publishing Group, 1992. • Japan Travel Bureau. *Illustrated Eating in Japan.* Volume 3 in *JTB Illustrated Books.* Tokyo: Japan Travel Bureau, 1989. • Sugano, Kimiko. *Kimiko's World.* San Francisco: Strawberry Hill Press, 1982. • Tsuji, Shizuo. *Japanese Cooking, A Simple Art.* Tokyo: Kodansha International, 1980.

Japanese sharecropping: Agriculture was the occupational field to which the majority of earlier Japanese immigrants were drawn. It is estimated that in 1909 approximately thirty-eight thousand Japanese, mostly laborers, were working on U.S. farms. Almost 50 percent of male Japanese were still employed in agricultural jobs at the start of World War II. The Japanese, particularly in California, progressed in stages from farmworker to contract farmer to sharecropper to land lessee to, finally, farm ownership.

In sharecropping, the landowner shared the profits with the sharecropper. If the landowner provided only the land, the two parties usually split the profits evenly when the crops were sold. If the landowner provided horses, tools, and other necessities, that individual's share was generally greater. If, however, the sharecropper provided these, then his or her share would be greater. The essential feature of sharecropping was that the ranch owner and the share tenant would share both the risks and the rewards. As the profits made by the sharecroppers were directly related to their productivity, the share tenant had a high incentive to be efficient and productive.

Sharecropping could, but did not necessarily, require a significant amount of capital on the part of the sharecroppers. This would be the case if the sharecroppers provided horses and tools. If the sharecroppers did not have sufficient capital for the subsistence needs of their families and their laborers, they relied upon credit advanced to them by Japanese or sometimes white merchants. As such loans were lucrative, there were few problems in securing the necessary credit. The share tenant was responsible for securing the necessary number of field laborers. This generally involved working with a Japanese labor contractor who had a Japanese crew. The sharecropper typically did not make final payment to these workers until first being paid by the ranch owner. The length of the share tenancy contract was dependent upon the crop and local conditions.

Japanese Women's Society of Honolulu: Japanese American organization dedicated to preserving culture and providing care for the elderly. The group offers scholarships in gerontology and by 1993 had raised more than $500,000 for Kuakini Hospital's home for the elderly since the home's establishment in 1954.

Japantown Art and Media Workshop: Grassroots community arts organization in San Francisco, California, founded in 1977. It is committed to preserving, producing, and promoting cultural materials that accurately depict the Asian American experience. The group sponsors an internship program for high school students; provides art and writing workshops, a graphic design service, and cultural shows and exhibitions; and was instrumental in the establishment of the Community Asian Art and Media Project in 1979 and the Ohana Cultural Center in 1985, both in Oakland, California.

Jati: SANSKRIT term for a subcaste group within the Hindu caste system. While *VARNA*, or caste, is a hereditary category that classifies people by type in a general or theoretical way, a *jati* is an actual group of people who have in common certain customs, language, and perhaps also a traditional occupation. The word literally means "birth," and there are in India more than twenty-five hundred *jatis*, or birth groups.

For example, the brahmin *varna*, or caste, is composed of dozens of brahmin *jatis*, each of which is to be found in a particular region of India, its members related to one another as in a clan and having their own customs. Some of the *jati* groups apparently originated as trade groups, and their members have the same occupation and pass down their trade secrets from father to son; these groups could be compared to the guilds of medieval Europe. While customs vary from one *jati* to another, a traditional arrangement often exists whereby males of one specific *jati* marry females of a particular *jati*, and vice versa.

Each *jati* is identified as belonging to one of the *varna* groups. The social status of a *jati* is dependent on the consensus of opinion of Hindu society as a whole regarding that groups' behavior. The status of a *jati* can change somewhat over several generations if society as a whole perceives the groups' behavior as more socially acceptable. A *jati*'s imitation of the practices of higher status groups such as brahmins, for example, by adopting vegetarian dietary practices results in a higher status for it. This process of a *jati* advancing in social status over a long period of time is known as "Sanskritization" and is a well-known phenomenon throughout India.

India's constitution, adopted in 1950 shortly after India achieved independence, declared illegal all forms of discrimination based on the social system of caste and *jati*. Many Indians, however, continue to describe themselves as members of one or another of the social groups called *jati*.

Jen, Gish (b. 1956): Novelist. Her first novel, *Typical American*, about the life of a Chinese immigrant family, appeared in 1991. She earned a B.A. degree from Harvard, attended Stanford Business School, and completed a degree from the Iowa Writers' Workshop. Her work has appeared in *The Atlantic* and *Best American Short Stories, 1988* (1988).

Gish Jen. (AP/Wide World Photos)

Jensen, Joan M. (b. Dec. 9, 1934, St. Paul, Minn.): History professor. A teacher at New Mexico State University, she is author of *Passage from India: Asian Indian Immigrants in North America* (1988), a pioneering account of the emigration of South Asian Indians to North America between 1870 and 1930. Her work marks the first thorough documentation of the Asian Indian immigrant experience in America. She attended the University of California, Los Angeles (UCLA), earning her Ph.D. degree in 1962.

Jerome: One of ten U.S. government camps under the administration of the WAR RELOCATION AUTHORITY (WRA) used to house Japanese American evacuees during World War II. The camps were officially designated as "RELOCATION CENTERS."

Jerome, which was operational from October 6, 1942, to June 30, 1944, was located in the Mississippi bottomlands of southeastern Arkansas and was remembered by its inhabitants for its ever-present mud. The camp, which consisted of Army barracks laid out in rows and columns, was located on land that President Franklin D. Roosevelt's New Deal had intended for use by dispossessed tenant farmers. The dimensions of the barracks were approximately 20 feet by 120 feet, with the interior of the buildings divided into four to six family apartments of about 20 by 20 feet. Jerome was one of the smallest camps administered by the WRA, housing about 8,500 people at its peak.

Though ringed by barbed wire and guarded by watchtowers and sentry posts, Jerome's Japanese American internees provided all the labor necessary to operate the camp. They established schools, operated a basic medical facility, published a camp newspaper, and conducted a variety of social services and recreational activities. Gardening was a popular activity for the internees. Through flowers, they could add color to their drab surroundings, and through vegetable gardens the meals at the camp's mess halls could be made more healthy and palatable. Life behind the barbed wire was never comfortable for the internees, but in camps such as Jerome the internees were not cruelly mistreated either.

The last of WRA camps to open, Jerome was the first to be closed, with operations ceasing in June, 1944. By then, about half its population had resettled in the Midwest and Eastern states. Its remaining population was transferred to active relocation centers.

Jiyu imin: Japanese phrase for those migrants who sailed from Japan to Hawaii from 1894 to 1908 as immigrant laborers recruited by private emigration companies, as opposed to Japanese government sponsorship. The *jiyu imin* are distinguished from the earlier *kanyaku imin*, who arrived in the islands between 1885 and 1894 under government contract. The total number of *jiyu imin* was about 125,000.

Jizo: Guardian deity of children. Jizo statues are found in Japan in parks and on the street.

Jodo Shinshu: Largest of the thirteen schools of Japanese BUDDHISM. Jodo Shinshu, to which the great majority of Japanese American Buddhists belong, is also called "Shin" and was founded in the thirteenth century.

The name Jodo Shinshu is derived from the writings of the Japanese Buddhist philosopher and religious reformer SHINRAN, who praised the legacy of his teacher, HONEN, as revealing the "true essence" (Shinshu) of the PURE LAND (Jodo) teaching. Shinran's descendants and followers organized an independent lineage to establish a school, later called Jodo Shinshu, with Shinran as its founder.

Jodo Shinshu has several unique qualities that were attractive to the laity: married clergy; rejection of meditative practice for recitative *nembutsu* (calling the name of Amida Buddha); emphasis on listening to the teaching; daily religious service at home; and becoming truly human through the working of Buddha's compassion. Through the efforts of Shinran's successors, the school spread throughout various parts of Japan, such as Fukui, Hiroshima, Yamaguchi, and various parts of Kyushu.

Many Japanese immigrants who came to Hawaii and the mainland United States in the later years of the nineteenth century came from these strongholds of Jodo Shinshu. Hence, the great majority of Buddhist temples established in the United States belong to Jodo Shinshu, which has two major branches: the Honpa Hongwanji (or Nishi) and the Otani Hongwanji (or Higashi).

It was the headquarters of Nishi Hongwanji that made a concerted effort to propagate Jodo Shinshu among the Japanese American population. Jodo Shinshu is represented on Hawaii as the Honpa Hongwanji Mission, with thirty-seven temples (as of 1989), and on the mainland as the Buddhist Churches of America, with about sixty independent temples, twenty-seven branch temples, and six less formally organized fellowships (as of 1994). The Buddhist temples have been major sources of spiritual sustenance in Japanese American life, especially during periods of anti-

Japanese persecution, including the wartime internment years. This support attests their vital contribution to Asian American history.

Joe, Kenneth (b. Aug. 14, 1923, China): Banker. Vice president and director of Sincere Federal Savings Bank in San Francisco, California, he served as editor of several major Chinese newspapers in Hong Kong and the United States and as dean of the Central Chinese School in San Francisco for twelve years. He is regarded as a "walking encyclopedia" of Chinese art and culture in the San Francisco Chinese American community.

Joe Boys: San Francisco Chinatown youth gang in the 1960's and 1970's. The group consisted of predominantly immigrant Chinese. It rivaled the WAH CHING (predominantly American-born Chinese) and Yu Li gangs for dominance in Chinatown. Their bitter turf war became national news when, on September 4, 1977, members of the Joe Boys entered the GOLDEN DRAGON RESTAURANT and began firing their guns into the main dining room. Although members of the Wah Ching had been the intended targets, seven innocent bystanders died. Years later the killers were finally brought to justice. The Joe Boys were led by Joe Chung Fong, an immigrant and a graduate of Galileo High School in San Francisco.

Johnson, Albert (Mar. 5, 1869, Springfield, Ill.—Jan. 17, 1957, American Lake, Wash.): Newspaperman and U.S. representative. Following a public-school education, Johnson became a successful journalist with a string of newspapers. After serving as managing editor of the *New Haven Register*, in 1898 he became news editor of the *Washington Morning Post* in the District of Columbia. In about 1909 he arrived in Washington State to assume leadership of the *Grays Harbor Washingtonian*, which he had recently purchased. He served as editor and publisher until 1934.

Johnson remained solely a newsman until 1912, when he won a seat in the U.S. House of Representatives. From the state of Washington, he went on to serve a consecutive twenty-year term, from 1913 until 1933.

Staunchly opposed to unrestricted immigration, in 1919 Johnson became chairman of the House Committee on Immigration and Naturalization. As chair he spearheaded the congressional drive of the 1920's to establish more severe limits on alien admissions into the United States. Particularly targeted for exclusion were the Japanese, who Johnson believed were an affront to American democracy and civilization.

In 1924 Johnson's strong nativist sentiments found their full expression. That year he introduced a congressional bill that was eventually signed into law as the IMMIGRATION ACT OF 1924 (National Origins Act). The act limited the number of yearly admissions to 2 percent of the nationals of a given country living in the United States in 1890. All Asian immigrant laborers were completely barred from entry. Johnson insisted that the new plan faithfully reflected the makeup of American society. As enforced, it all but completely eliminated Asian immigration into the United States.

Jones Act of 1916: Formally the Philippine Autonomy Act of 1916, announcing the U.S. government's intention to create an autonomous and independent Philippines. The act in essence relinquished all legislative power to the people of the Philippines and extended voting rights to them as well. Also incorporated into the new law was a bill of rights.

The Philippines had become a U.S. possession in 1898, following the end of the Spanish American War. A few years later, American authorities approved the establishment of the Philippine Commission as a legislative body; ostensibly created to give Filipinos a voice in government, it was instead effectively dominated by Americans. The Jones Act replaced the commission with a senate elected by the people.

Meanwhile, Francis HARRISON, the ruling American governor-general of the Philippines appointed by the U.S. president, moved quickly to integrate as many qualified Filipinos as possible into the Philippine civil service. By the end of his term of office, natives filled many of the top governmental posts.

The act remained in force as a de facto Philippine constitution until 1934, when it was superseded by the TYDINGS-MCDUFFIE ACT.

Jook Kock: Cantonese term referring to Chinese born in China, who are like bamboo stalks—that is, strong but flexible. (See JOOK SING.)

Jook Sing: Cantonese term referring to Chinese born in the United States, who are like hollow bamboo—that is, who are Chinese on the "outside" but not on the "inside." (See JOOK KOCK.)

Jordan v. Tashiro (1928): U.S. Supreme Court ruling that affirmed the right of Japanese aliens (the ISSEI) to establish and maintain hospitals in the United States. As a result, the Japanese Hospital of Los Angeles, later one of the most important Japanese hospitals, was incorporated in 1929.

A group of Issei physicians wanted to start a hospital in Los Angeles and so filed the necessary incorporation papers with the California secretary of state. The latter rejected their application on the basis that state laws prohibited Japanese aliens from leasing land for this purpose. The state court, however, agreed with the doctors and ordered that their request be approved.

The Supreme Court upheld the state court's decision. Authorization for the establishment of hospitals by Japanese aliens, it announced, was provided by the terms of the U.S.-JAPAN TREATY OF COMMERCE AND NAVIGATION (1911). According to the Court, those treaty portions defining the right of U.S. aliens to lease and occupy land in the course of conducting trade also encompassed the founding of hospitals on American soil. The state of California was therefore obligated to file the articles of incorporation as requested.

Judd, Walter Henry (b. Sept. 25, 1898, Rising City, Nebr.): U.S. representative. A Minnesota congressman from 1942 to 1962, Judd also worked as a physician, lecturer, and radio commentator. He was among the few American statesmen who knew China through personal experience.

After graduating from high school, Judd went to the University of Nebraska, earning his B.A. degree in 1920 and his M.D. degree in 1923. During World War I he served in the U.S. Army as a private and later as a second lieutenant. Between 1920 and 1924 he taught zoology at the University of Omaha. In 1924 and 1925 he served as traveling secretary of the Student Volunteer Movement in colleges and universities.

Judd's relationship with China began in 1925 when he arrived there as an American medical missionary. In 1925-1931 and 1934-1938 he carried out his work in various provinces in China.

In 1942 Judd won congressional election and became a member of the Seventy-eighth Congress. As a friend of China, he was responsible for the passage of the IMMIGRATION ACT OF 1943 (also known as the Magnuson Act), which repealed the CHINESE EXCLUSION ACTS in force since 1882. Sympathetic with the Chinese Nationalist government, Judd urged the U.S. government to extend more aid to China after PEARL HARBOR and was critical of the China policy of the Roosevelt Administration for what he saw as American ignorance and interventionism. In the late 1940's Judd became genuinely concerned with China's civil strife and regarded the Chinese revolution as part of the world communist movement. He headed the China bloc in Congress to pass the China Aid Act of 1948. In the Eightieth Congress, Judd voted for limiting the presidency to two terms and for the subversive activities control bill.

In 1962 Judd failed to get reelected to the Eighty-eighth Congress. Between 1963 and 1976 he worked for *Reader's Digest* as a contributing editor. Between 1964 and 1969 he gave frequent lectures and daily radio commentaries on U.S. domestic and foreign policy.

Judd married Miriam Louise Barber in 1932; their three daughters are Mary Louise, Carolyn Ruth, and Eleanor Grace.

K

K. & S. Company: Korean wholesale company established in 1928 in Los Angeles. One of the most prosperous fruit and vegetable wholesale businesses in Los Angeles' Korean American community, it was formed by two Korean students, Kim Yong-jeung and Song Chull (Leo Sung). Lacking funds to continue their education, the two left school in 1922 and worked as wholesale agents for the KIM BROTHERS COMPANY in Reedley, California. A few years later, they established the K. & S. Company, which became the supplier of most Asian-owned retail vegetable stores in the area.

Kachigumi (victory groups): Japanese term designating Issei groups in Hawaii during World War II united by a common belief that Japan would win the war. Driven by delusions of imperial Japan's invincibility, these underground groups maintained that Japan was indeed winning the war in the Pacific and would eventually emerge triumphant. They therefore devoted their efforts to resisting "false" reports of U.S. military victories over Japan and exhorting Hawaii's Issei population not to lose heart.

Even after Japan's unconditional surrender in August, 1945, some of these groups refused to accept defeat, becoming known as *kattagumi* (also meaning "victory groups," but with a shift to the past tense, implying that Japan had in fact won the war). They included the Kalihi Eight Corners Society, the Palama Rebirth Society, and the Eastern Brotherhood Society. After the Japanese emperor repudiated his claim to divinity on New Year's Day of 1946, however, many members of the *kattagumi* were persuaded that Japan had been defeated. By 1949, the overwhelming majority of Issei had accepted the outcome and stopped insisting that the U.S. government had somehow subverted the truth of a Japanese military victory. A handful, however, did not publicly acknowledge defeat for many years; the last *kattagumi* group in the Hawaiian Islands, the Hawaii Victory Society, did not officially dissolve until 1977.

Kadohata, Cynthia Lynn (July 2, 1956, Chicago, Ill.): Novelist and short-story writer. Kadohata is the daughter of June Akiko Kaita and Toshiro Kadohata. After she was born, the family moved to Arkansas, Georgia, and Michigan before settling in Los Angeles. There she enrolled in Hollywood High School but later dropped out and worked at a variety of jobs. After attending Los Angeles City College, she transferred to the University of Southern California, where she earned a degree in journalism.

Following a serious automobile accident in Los Angeles in 1977 that crushed her right arm, Kadohata moved to Boston, where her sister was living. As a child Cynthia had enjoyed writing and continued to write during her college years. Yet it was not until this post-accident period that she decided to try writing fiction. Surviving on the insurance settlement from the accident, supplemented by odd jobs earnings, she set a goal of producing one short story a month.

Kadohata soon began sending her stories to *The New Yorker* and *The Atlantic*. All were rejected until 1986, when *The New Yorker* bought "Charlie O" and, later, others. She also sold stories to *Grand Street* and the *Pennsylvania Review*.

Novelist and short-story writer Cynthia Kadohata. (AP/ Wide World Photos)

At this time, Kadohata began taking graduate writing courses at the University of Pittsburgh, and then at Columbia University. She eventually dropped out, but her literary career was on the upswing. In 1988 with the help of New York literary agent Andrew Wylie, she sold her first novel, *The Floating World* (1989). In 1991, she was awarded a prestigious Whiting Foundation Award and a grant from the National Endowment for the Arts (NEA). Her second novel, *In the Heart of the Valley of Love*, was published in 1992. Both books earned strong reviews from *The New York Times*, *Time*, *New York*, *Newsday*, and *Elle*. Her short story "Miracles in the Sky and on the Road" appeared in *The New York Times* on Christmas Day of 1992.

Kadomatsu: In Japan, a New Year's pine decoration placed at the entrance of the house. Its pine boughs symbolize longevity, its bamboo stalks prosperity, and its plum tree sprigs constancy—the hope that the new year will bring these qualities to the members of the household.

Kaeguk chinchwi: Korean phrase that means, "the country is open, go forward." It is associated with the laborers who left Korea to work on Hawaii plantations.

Kagawa, Lawrence (1904—1973): Insurance executive. First hired by the International Trust Company of Honolulu in 1923, Kagawa eventually left to assume a position with Occidental Underwriters of Hawaii in 1933. Following World War II, the company was the first insurance firm to stop the practice of charging Asians higher premiums, the first to employ Asians as agents, and the first to invest money in Hawaiian concerns. Company president until 1963, he was named chairman and chief executive that year, serving until retirement in 1970.

Kagiwada, George (b. July 4, 1931, Los Angeles, Calif.): Scholar. Kagiwada, who received a Ph.D. degree from the University of California, Los Angeles, in 1969, was professor of Asian American Studies at the University of California, Davis, until his retirement in 1993. A specialist in social adaptation theory, Kagiwada taught sociology at the University of Manitoba, Canada, from 1968 to 1970. He was the first tenured Asian American professor in Asian American Studies at Davis (1977).

Kagoshima: Prefecture located on the southernmost tip of Kyushu, the southernmost major island of Japan.

Kagoshima was the region of origin of many Japanese who emigrated to the United States from the 1880's to 1924, thanks to an agreement arranged by Robert Walker Irwin, whose friends, Japanese foreign minister Inoue Kaoru and importer Masuda Takashi—both from Yamaguchi Prefecture—suggested attracting laborers from the area. Irwin had been serving as consul general for the kingdom of Hawaii while simultaneously acting as a foreign advisor to the Japanese government.

Kahoolawe: Smallest of the eight major islands of Hawaii, with an area of 45 square miles of land rising from the sea to an elevation of 1,477 feet. This island is uninhabited.

Kahoolawe had several ancient names. Kanoloa or Kohe malamalama o Kanaloa Kahiki moe (sleeping Kahiki or homeland), and Hinelii (a variety of light rain typical to the island) are some of them. Kahoolawe is the legendary home of Kaumualii, the shark god and brother of Pele (the fire goddess). The island thrived as a fishing village, as an adz quarry site, and as a special place for *na kahuna* (religious priests and scholars). After 1200 C.E. Kahoolawe became a prominent navigational center for those voyaging between Hawaii and Tahiti. Kahoolawe's west point, Lae o Kealaikahiki, was a directional source for early navigators.

English captain James Cook first visited Hawaii in 1778. He described Kahoolawe as having no vegetation. In 1829 Queen Kaahumanu, favorite wife of King Kamehameha I, proclaimed that Catholics were to be banished to Kahoolawe. Historian Samuel Kamakau writes that Kahoolawe and Lanai served as penal colonies, Kahoolawe for men and Lanai for women. In 1853 Kahoolawe ceased to be a penal colony.

In 1850 the first lease for the island went to R. C. Wyllie. By 1884 more than nine thousand goats and twelve thousand sheep grazed on Kahoolawe, causing serious erosion problems. The Territorial Board of Agriculture proclaimed Kahoolawe a "forest reserve" but did not solve the erosion problem. By December, 1918, under a new ranch lease to Angus McPhee and Harry Baldwin, Kahoolawe Ranch had been formed and the island's goat population brought under control.

In 1941 Kahoolawe Ranch signed a sublease with the U.S. Navy allowing the Navy to build a dummy runway and fake aircraft for target practice. Ranching on Kahoolawe ceased after December 7, 1941 (the day of the Pearl Harbor attack), and the military took control. In 1952 Kahoolawe Ranch's lease with the Territory of Hawaii expired; in 1953 U.S. president Dwight D. Eisenhower issued an executive order reserving Kahoolawe for use by the Navy.

In 1976 many questioned the need for continued use of the island for live munitions training. The Protect Kahoolawe Ohana was formed that year to stop the bombing of Kahoolawe and force the U.S. Navy to comply with environmental, historic preservation, and religious freedom laws. As a result, Kahoolawe is now listed on the National Register of Historic Places in the United States.

In 1980 the U.S. Navy was mandated by court order to survey and protect historic and cultural sites on Kahoolawe, clear surface ordnance, begin soil conservation and revegetation programs, eradicate goats from the island, and limit ordnance impact training. The Protect Kahoolawe Ohana was acknowledged as caretaker for the island and was allowed access to the island for religious, educational, and scientific activities. Since 1980 more than three thousand people have visited Kahoolawe with members of the Protect Kahoolawe Ohana. In 1990 a presidential directive permanently halted bombing practice there.

Kaibal Hoesa: Korean organization established in 1902 to recruit Korean laborers to work on Hawaii's plantations. Also known as the Development Company, it was formed by David W. Deshler, who was a junior partner with the American Trading Company in Seoul. With the help of his hired interpreter, Kim Jae-ho, Deshler established branch offices of Kaibal Hoesa in Wonsan, Seoul, Pusan, and Chinnampo.

Kaisha: Japanese word for "company." *Kaisha* is an abbreviation of *kabushiki kaisha*, or joint-stock company, which corresponds to the corporation in the United States or the limited liability company in England. For example, *kaisha* are such Japanese corporations as Toyota, Honda, Mitsubishi, Tosha, and Matsushita. A typical Japanese *kaisha* is controlled by its shareholders, who exercise their power through the general meeting. The shareholders elect the members of the board of directors to oversee the management and operations of the *kaisha*. The board of directors is usually chosen from the top- and middle-level managers; the "inside" (from within the *kaisha*) directors comprise the president (*sacho*), the top executive director; the vice president (*fukusacho*), the executive director; the senior managing director (*senmu torishimariyaku*), who may be in charge of a large unit of the *kaisha*; the managing director (*jomu torishimariyaku*),

who is usually responsible for several departments or a division; and the ordinary director (*torishimariyaku*), who might be the second in charge of a division. Two or three directors from outside the *kaisha* may also be elected. These "outside" directors may, for example, be retired bank managers of the *kaisha*'s main bank.

Most *kaisha* have a system of standard rank, as follows: president, vice president, senior managing director, managing director, director, department head (*bucho*), section head (*kacho*), subsection head (*kakaricho*), foreman (*hancho*), and workers (*hira shain*).

Most *kaisha* provide lifetime employment to their employees, who are expected to stay with their *kaisha* until retirement. The practice of lifetime employment was instituted first by Matsushita Konosuke in his *kaisha* during the worldwide depression in 1929, giving his employees lifetime job security. In return, Matsushita obtained loyalty from his employees. The mandatory retirement age in the *kaisha* is normally set at fifty-five for male employees, but retirees may be rehired at lower salaries. Most *kaisha* in Japan encourage female employees to "retire" at the age of twenty-five or when they get married. Between 1967 and 1984, however, the number of female workers increased from ten million to fifteen million, which represented one-third of the work force in Japan. They generally perform clerical work, receiving about half the salary of the average male employees. The *kaisha* also provides its employees with fringe benefits including an annual bonus, which is worth four to six months' salary, hospital care, the use of health facilities, and even a hall for weddings.

The effective operations of the *kaisha* in Japan are reflected in the country's staggering economic success throughout the 1970's, 1980's, and early 1990's. In 1945 the *kaisha* sprang up amid a shattered, defeated country. Thirty-five years later, in the early 1980's, the *kaisha* surpassed U.S. manufacturers in the production of automobiles. Dentsu became the world's largest advertising firm. Other *kaisha* outproduced and outsold their American counterparts in electronic goods, including compact disc players, video tape recorders, cameras, televisions, stereos, calculators, and watches. In 1988 the ten largest banks in the world were Japanese, and four of the world's largest ten security firms were operated by the Japanese. In the meantime Matsushita built the world's biggest multinational electric home appliance industry. Nippon Steel outgrew U.S. Steel in size. Fuji Film became the principal competitor of Eastman Kodak, and Fujitsu and Hitachi were serious rivals of International Business Machines (IBM) in the field of mainframe computers. Japan's National Electronics Corporation (NEC) was racing Texas Instruments to become the world leader in semiconductor production.

After 1987 the Japanese trade surplus grew to more than $80 billion annually, of which more than $40 billion was tied to the United States. By the end of the 1980's, 40 percent of the total U.S. trade deficit stemmed from the imbalance in trade with Japan, making Japan the world's largest creditor nation and the United States the world's largest debtor nation. The United States' interest payments on its credit and debts quickly increased each year, making it more difficult to balance the deficit. In fact during the 1992 presidential election, one of the major issues debated by the American public was how to resolve the U.S. trade deficits.

What are the contributing factors for the spectacular success of the Japanese *kaisha*? For one thing, the *kaisha* won the loyalty and the lifelong commitment of the workers by providing them with many fringe benefits including lifetime employment and generous annual bonuses. Moreover the managers adopted the most effective techniques of production. For example they adopted the system of "quality control," through which they ensured the manufacturing of superior quality products. The application of the "just-in-time" technique eliminated the need for inventory in manufacturing plants. In this system the vendor would place the raw materials or component parts on the assembly line only when they were needed. Senior managers also encouraged their subordinates to take part in the decision-making process, in which suggestions of subordinates were often adopted. Furthermore managers took the long-range view in developing and marketing products. They would risk current losses for the sake of future gains. Foreign technology was purchased regardless of its cost, in the expectation that it would pay off in the long run. Lastly the *kaisha* received cooperation and positive support from the Japanese government. The latter offered subsidies, loans, tax relief, and tariff protection. It also assisted in obtaining needed resources, facilities, and technology.

Kakutani, Michiko (b. Jan. 9, 1955, New Haven, Conn.): Critic. Michiko Kakutani began her career as a journalist in 1976, the same year in which she received her bachelor's degree in English from Yale University. She worked first as a reporter for *The Washington Post* and then as a writer on the staff of *Time* magazine,

from 1977 to 1979. In 1979, she joined the staff of *The New York Times*, where she specialized in covering cultural news. In January of 1983, Kakutani became a book critic in the cultural news department of *The New York Times*, a position that she continues to hold. She has become widely known for her perceptive critical sense and her writing style. Kakutani is also the author of *The Poet at the Piano: Portraits of Writers, Filmmakers, and Performers at Work* (1988).

Kalakaua, David (Nov. 16, 1836, Honolulu, Hawaii—Jan. 20, 1891, San Francisco, Calif.): Hawaiian royalty. Kalakaua was educated at a special school for the children of Hawaiian chiefs and married Julia Kapiolani, granddaughter of the king of Kauai, in 1863. He served for thirteen years in the Hawaiian legislative assembly before being elected king of Hawaii on February 12, 1874, as successor to King Lunalilo, who had died without leaving a direct heir. During his reign, Kalakaua encouraged the government to reopen negotiations on a reciprocity agreement with the United States. The Reciprocity Treaty (1875) eliminated the American tariff on sugar, which, in turn, led to the rapid expansion of sugar production in Hawaii, produced new demands for immigrant labor, and resulted in the construction of an industrial infrastructure to meet the plantations' needs for irrigation and transportation. In exchange for lifting the tariffs, the Hawaiian government agreed not to grant special harbor privileges to any foreign powers. Kalakaua was also concerned about the impact of rapid industrialization on the islands' dwindling native population. In order to solve the labor shortage, Kalakaua traveled to Japan in 1881 and helped negotiate a new treaty to encourage immigration from Japan. Combining a great love of Hawaiian folklore and culture with interest in European architecture and arts, the "Merry Monarch" traveled throughout the world and enjoyed entertaining foreign visitors, among them Robert Louis Stevenson, in his elaborate Iolani Palace. Upset by expensive licensing schemes used to generate revenue for the government and concerned about the power wielded by cabinet adviser Walter Murray Gibson, American businessmen in Hawaii staged a bloodless revolution in 1887, adopted a new constitution to restrict royal authority, and forced the king to dismiss Gibson from his post. That same year, these businessmen also pressured Kalakaua to accept the demand that the United States be allowed to establish a coaling station in the previously neutral port of Pearl Harbor as a condition for renewing the Reciprocity

Treaty through 1894. Fatigued by these stressful events and suffering from the ill health to which many native Hawaiians were susceptible, Kalakaua traveled to California to recuperate but died at the Palace Hotel in San Francisco in 1891. Upon his death, Kalakaua was succeeded on the throne by his sister LILIUOKALANI, the last queen of Hawaii.

Kalbi: Korean entrée. It consists of short ribs marinated with soy sauce, scallions, sesame oil, sugar, and chopped garlic. When barbecued, it is called *kalbi gui*; when simmered, it is called *kalbi jim*.

Kamehameha Dynasty: The islands of Hawaii were ruled by individual chiefs prior to the arrival of English captain James COOK in 1778. By 1810 Kamehameha I, through conquest and political alliances, had united the Hawaiian Islands under one ruler, establishing the first dynasty of Hawaii.

Kamehameha I (c.1758-1819) or Kamehameha the Great, was born at Kohala on the island of Hawaii. "Kamehameha" means "the lonely one," for he spent his early years in hiding to avoid being killed by jealous chiefs. He spent his young adult life being trained as a warrior and later became keeper of the Hawaiian war god, Ku-kaili-moku. His unification of the Hawaiian Islands, begun in the 1790's and completed in 1809, and his strong leadership preserved Hawaii's independence during the critical years after first contact with traders and explorers from Europe and America. Kamehameha ruled until his death.

Kamehameha II (ruled 1819-1824), a son of Kamehameha I, was twenty-three years old when he became king. Queen Kaahumanu reigned as coruler. During his reign Christianity arrived, the traditional Hawaiian system of *kapu* (laws) lost authority, and the Hawaiian *heiau* (temples) and gods were abandoned. Sandalwood was the main article of Hawaiian commerce. The king and his wife, Queen Kamamalu, traveled to England in November, 1823. While in England the queen died in July, 1824, of measles. The king, grief-stricken, died a few days later.

Kamehameha III (ruled 1825-1854) was also a son of Kamehameha I. He reigned for thirty years, implementing critical changes in land ownership, with the *Mahele* (land division) (see GREAT MAHELE) and the *kuleana* reforms (allowing commoners to claim title to land), and in government, with the constitution of 1840 (the first written constitution for Hawaii). He also gave Hawaii its motto: *Ua mau ke ea o ka aina i ka pono* (the life of the land is preserved in righteous-

Christianity was brought to the Hawaiian islands during the reign of Kamehameha II. (Hawaii State Archives)

ness). He died in December, 1854.

Kamehameha IV (ruled 1854-1863), a grandson of Kamehameha I, was well educated, traveled widely, and preferred the British to the Americans. He established the Episcopal Church in Hawaii and his wife, Queen Emma, established St. Andrews Priory (a school for girls) in Honolulu. Sugarcane grew as an industry. His son, the young Prince Albert, died of a serious illness in August, 1862. Being in poor health and grief-stricken, the king died in November, 1863.

Kamehameha V (ruled 1863-1872) was the older brother of Kamehameha IV and was also well educated and traveled widely. He was a bachelor and left no heir. The growth of the sugar industry, a Reciprocity Treaty, annexation to the United States, and the 1864 constitution (limiting voting rights) were major issues of his reign. He was the dynasty's last great chief and died in December, 1872.

Kamehameha Schools (Honolulu, Hawaii): Private preparatory schools established by the will of Princess Bernice Pauahi BISHOP in the later nineteenth century. The Kamehameha School for Boys opened in 1887; the Kamehameha School for Girls opened in 1894; and both schools merged in 1961, becoming coeducational.

The Kamehameha Schools are funded by a land trust that originally consisted of 434,300 acres of land in Hawaii originating from the will of Bishop, great-granddaughter of Kamehameha I. The school system and the land trust that finances it are a single institution, The Kamehameha Schools/BISHOP ESTATE. The institution is presided over by five trustees who are appointed by the Hawaii Supreme Court.

The schools' mission is to perpetuate the legacy of Bernice Bishop through its educational system. This system assists and gives preference to children and youth of Hawaiian ancestry; fosters the development of their highest potential as effective participants in society; and provides as many meaningful opportunities as resources will permit. The total value of Kamehameha Schools/Bishop Estate at the end of 1992 was more than $1.3 billion. The legacy continues.

Kami: Objects of worship in the Shinto religion of Japan. Although the term often refers to gods or deities, it can include other forces that, by virtue of being superior or divine, are viewed with reverence. Creator spirits, ancestors, animals, plants, and rocks can all be exalted as *kami.*

Kana: System of written characters that represent the forty-eight syllables of the Japanese language. Japanese writing is based entirely on characters borrowed from Chinese writing, following the introduction of Chinese culture into Japan in the sixth century C.E. What was sufficient for written communication, however, was not wholly sufficient for spoken communication. The Japanese therefore eventually found it necessary to modify the existing script to enable it to express the sounds of words, rather than the meanings (as in Chinese). Because of this linguistic departure, *kana,* which originally meant "temporary, nonofficial, irregular writing," was created. It was distinguished from *mana,* "real or regular writing," which employed Chinese characters known collectively as *kanji.*

Although Japanese can be written using nothing but *kana* symbols, in practice the language combines characters from both *kana* and *kanji.* In Japan the two forms of *kana* are the *hiragana* and the *katakana,* which serve different purposes and differ stylistically. *Hiragana* is a cursive style with flowing strokes derived from Chinese characters. It is used when writing native Japanese words; verb inflections, adjectival endings, and other grammatical functions; and words that are of Chinese origin but that are not written using Chinese characters. By contrast, *katakana* is a square, angular, noncursive style and is used typically when writing foreign words.

Kanamori, Hiroo (b. Oct. 17, 1936, Tokyo, Japan): Seismologist. Kanamori is considered by many in the field to be the world's foremost expert in earthquake seismology. His father, a Japanese cabinet minister, opposed the militarists who came into power in the 1930's and was pushed out of the government in 1936, the year in which Kanamori was born. Kanamori earned his Ph.D. in 1964 at the University of Tokyo, where he remained to work at the Earthquake Research Institute. In 1972, after a stint at the Massachusetts Institute of Technology (MIT) in Boston, Kanamori began to teach geophysics at the California Institute of Technology (Caltech) in Pasadena, California. In 1990, he became the director of the school's Seismological Laboratory. Kanamori is known for his wide range of interests and his ability to apply his knowledge of earthquakes to other related areas. On November 17, 1993, he was named California Scientist of the Year.

Kanazawa, Tooru J. (b. Nov. 12, 1906, Spokane, Wash.): Journalist. Armed with a journalism degree from the University of Washington, Kanazawa was employed in 1932 by the *Rafu Shimpo,* a Los Angeles Japanese newspaper. In 1940 he moved to New York. During World War II, he served as a volunteer with the U.S. Army's all-Nisei 442ND REGIMENTAL COMBAT TEAM, and was awarded the Bronze Star for meritorious service. At the age of eighty-three, he published *Sushi and Sourdough: A Novel* (1989), based on his experiences growing up in the frontier gold-mining town of Juneau, Alaska, and the lives of Issei working in the salmon canneries there.

Kandodan brides: Marriage practice among Japanese immigrants, literally meaning "excursion brides." Many early Japanese immigrants to the United States were married in absentia to brides they had not met but knew only via photographs. After the "marriage," these "picture brides" were permitted to enter the United States as spouses of resident Japanese. Protests in the United States against this practice led the Japanese government to cease issuing passports to picture brides as of March 1, 1920. As an alternative, Japanese immigrants who could afford the round trip (most could not) returned briefly to Japan to take "Kandodan brides."

Kanemitsu, Matsumi (b. May 28, 1922, Ogden City, Utah): Artist. A Kibei Nisei, he returned to the United States in 1938 and lived in Utah and Nevada, where he toiled as a copper miner while working on his art. After service during World War II, he moved to New York City in the early 1950's, where he was influenced by artists such as Mark Rothko and Willem de Kooning and by Japanese brush painting. He moved to Los Angeles in 1964.

Kang, Connie Kyonshill (b. Nov. 11, 1942, Ham-hung, Korea): Journalist. One of the first Asian American women to break into mainstream print media, she cofounded the Korean American Journalists Association in 1985. She has written for the *Los Angeles Times*, *The Wall Street Journal*, *The New York Times*, *The San Francisco Chronicle*, and the *Korea Times*.

Kang, Younghill (May 10?, 1903, Song-Dune-Chi, Korea—Dec. 11, 1972, Satellite Beach, Fla.): Writer. He immigrated to the United States in 1921, attended college in Canada and at Harvard University, and became the first Korean-born comparative literature professor at New York University. His books include his autobiography, *The Grass Roof* (1931); *East Goes West* (1937); and *The Happy Grove* (1933). Recipient of Guggenheim and Le prix Halperine Kamnisty (1937) awards, he also fought for the rights of people of color in the United States.

Kang Youwei (Mar. 19, 1858, Canton, Guangdong Province, China—Mar. 31, 1927, Qingdao, Shandong Province, China): Scholar and reformer. Founder of one of China's first political parties, the Baohuanghui (Chinese Empire Reform Association), seeking to revive China at a time when the government had become weak and corrupt, Kang tried to unite Chinese throughout the world to come to the aid of their motherland. His party at one time dominated the Chinese communities of the United States, with branches located in cities and towns all across the country as well as in Hawaii.

Kang was born into a literary family, many members of whom served the Qing Dynasty as government officials. Kang himself did exceptionally well in the traditional literary civil service exams and seemed to have a promising government career ahead of him. He became radicalized by China's humiliations in the face of Western and Japanese encroachment, however, and by her loss of the Sino-Japanese War (1894-1895). Thereafter Kang worked for the radical reform of the dynasty. He also reinterpreted Confucianism to promote modernization and to suggest that the world would one day have only one government, dedicated to the good of all humankind.

Kang briefly gained influence at court under the Emperor during the Reform Movement of 1898, also known as the Hundred Days of Reform, but soon lost it when the ultraconservative Empress Dowager staged a successful coup d'état. Kang had to flee China to save his life. In 1899, while in Canada, he founded the Chinese Empire Reform Association, later known as the Constitutionalist Party. Within a few months, branches of the society sprang up in Chinese communities throughout the United States, with Kang as their leader.

Kang himself only rarely visited the United States. His longest and most notable visit was in 1905, at which time he had an interview with President Theodore Roosevelt. While there he worked to strengthen his party and to end the Chinese exclusion laws. Kang also learned enough about modern capitalism and joint-stock companies to help him and others launch several businesses in connection with his party, so as to improve party financing and show other Chinese how to compete in the modern business world. These businesses included hotels and Chinese-language newspapers in the United States.

After China underwent a republican revolution in 1911, Kang was finally able to return to his homeland. As a constitutional monarchist he soon found that he did not have much political influence. In 1917 he supported a short-lived movement to revive the Qing Dynasty. After the failure of the restoration Kang devoted himself primarily to his writing. Some of his ideas later influenced Mao Zedong and others. After Kang's death in 1927 he was given a state funeral and was buried near Shanghai.

Kanji: Chinese characters that the Japanese borrowed from the Chinese language, initially through the translation of the Buddhist scriptures. *Kanji* were introduced to Japan at different periods. In the past the ability to read Japanese books required a knowledge of no fewer than 3,500 to 5,000 Chinese characters along with the Japanese systems. The Japanese writing system is a mixture of *kanji* and the two types of *kana* syllabary, *hiragana* and *katakana*.

In 1866 Maejima Hisoka recommended wider use of the *kana* syllabary and a gradual lessening of the number of *kanji*. In 1923 Monbusho (of the Ministry of Education) compiled a list of 1,962 Chinese characters known as "*joyo kanji*" (Chinese characters for frequent use), but it was not adopted.

In 1946 the Japanese government announced an official list of 1,850 Chinese characters called "*toyo kanji*" (Chinese characters for general use). Among these, 881 were designated as *kyoiku kanji* (Chinese characters for educational use) and were published as a separate appendix: Grade 1 (1-46), Grade 2 (47-151), Grade 3 (152-338), Grade 4 (339-543), Grade 5 (544-737), and Grade 6 (738-881). In 1951 a special list of 92 additional *kanji* were added for use in personal names (*jinmeiyo kanji*).

In October, 1981, the 1946 *joyo kanji* list was replaced with a revised *toyo kanji* list. Some traditional characters were either simplified or reshaped. Thirty-seven characters for personal names were then added. Among these, 996 characters are to be studied in elementary and junior high schools. The Monbusho 1989 instruction guide for elementary schools lists 1,006 *kanji*: Grade 1 (80), Grade 2 (160), Grade 3 (200), Grade 4 (200), Grade 5 (185), and Grade 6 (181).

Generally speaking there are two main types of *yomi* (reading) for a single *kanji*. Onyomi is the Chinese version of the character from the original Chinese pronunciation. It is usually used in compounds. In addition to the *kanyoon* (derived pronunciation), there are also Go, Kan, and To pronunciations. The word "bright" is pronounced "mei" in *kanyo*, "myo" in Go, "bei" in Kan, and "min" in To. Kunyomi involves attaching Japanese meaning to the character and using Japanese pronunciation that often is a polysyllabic word. For example the word "mountain" is *san* in *on*, *yama* in *kun*; "fish" is *gyo* in *on*, *sakana* in *kun*.

Kanji are written according to the order of strokes. In traditional *kanji* dictionaries, *kanji* are arranged according to 214 *bushu* (radicals), written left to right, top to bottom, horizontal stroke before vertical stroke.

Kanreki: Party marking the sixtieth birthday, a milestone especially for Japanese men.

Kanrin Maru: Japanese war steamer that accompanied the USS *Powhattan* to San Francisco on March 29, 1860, on a mission of the Japanese Tokugawa government to learn about the United States and to establish diplomatic ties. During that year the shogunate, in an effort to modernize Japan, commissioned the nation's first overseas mission. The main purpose was to ratify a treaty between Japan and the United States. The other reason was to allow Japanese officials to get an idea of the outside world. In 1862 various missions were sent to Europe and Asia.

Kansas Camp: Korean military training center established in 1912. It was formed by Korean immigrants who had previously served in Korea's army and who were led by Park Yong-man, whose Korean Youth Military Academy, the first such training center, was founded in Hastings, Nebraska, in 1909. The purpose of these centers was to prepare for a military revolt against Japanese colonial rule in Korea. Similar camps were established in Claremont and Lompoc, California, and Superior, Wyoming.

Kanyaku imin: Contract migrants, Japanese who arrived in the New World with labor contract in hand. In the early period of Japanese immigration to Hawaii, the mainland United States, and Brazil, most Japanese signed labor contracts with agents of emigration companies, who in turn promised the labor to the owners of plantations in the host nations.

Kanyaku imin, also called *keiyaku imin*, were not the only type of immigrant to arrive in the Americas. There were also free migrants, called *jiyu imin*, who arrived without labor contracts. Workers who were sponsored by the Japanese government and those who were aided by Japanese emigration companies were contract migrants. They constituted the overwhelming majority in the early years of Japanese immigration to Hawaii, the mainland United States, and Brazil. In Hawaii most immigrants before 1900 had contracts.

A typical labor contract for Japanese immigrants in Hawaii in the 1890's specified the hours of work and wages paid to the immigrant and his wife. Contract laborers worked twenty-six days per month, ten hours per day if engaged in field labor and twelve if they worked in the mill or sugar house. The monthly wage, paid in gold coins, was twelve dollars and fifty cents for a man and seven dollars and fifty cents for his wife. The contract also specified the amount of subsidy paid for shipboard passage, the conditions on the plantation, holidays observed, and the details of any enforced savings. The contracts promised unfurnished lodgings, fuel for cooking, medicine, and medical attention.

The average contract in Hawaii expired in three

years. Immigrants were then faced with a choice between renewing the contract for another three years, moving on to the mainland, or returning to Japan. In Brazil the conditions of the early contracts made it difficult to save money. Many fled the plantations in violation of their contracts in order to escape mounting debt.

The Japanese were not the first to do contract labor in the Americas. In North America, Chinese were contract laborers before the arrival of the first Japanese immigrants. In Brazil, Europeans had done contract labor on the coffee plantations before the arrival of the Japanese.

Kao: Japanese term translated as "face"—and embodying the idea of the need to preserve one's honor and reputation in the eyes of not only family and friends but also the general public. The principle of *kao* is regarded highly in Japanese American communities.

Kaohsiung incident (1979): Clash between the Taiwanese government and demonstrators protesting the government's refusal to permit them to stage a political rally. The incident on December 10 involved numerous antigovernment activists who had gathered in Kaohsiung, Taiwan, to commemorate the United Nations Declaration of Human Rights. Many of the marchers, anticipating the government's reaction, were armed with wooden clubs for self-defense. The demonstration turned into a riot, and marchers attacked the police, injuring nearly two hundred, while the police used tear gas and force to control the crowd, injuring many.

The government arrested more than one hundred people. Those arrested included Huang Hsin-chieh, an opposition member of the national legislature and the publisher of *Formosa* magazine, an antigovernment publication; Shih Ming-teh, a well-known political activist and a staff member of *Formosa*; as well as most other members of the magazine's staff. Most of those arrested were soon released, but eight prominent leaders of antigovernment movement, including Shih and Huang, were held for trial before a military court on charges of sedition, a crime punishable by death. The government accused them of establishing *Formosa* as part of a plot to overthrow the government and deliberately inciting the demonstrators to attack the police as a violent means to that end.

The government interrogated the eight dissidents for about ten weeks without the aid of legal counsel. It then announced that they had completely confessed and that it would recommend clemency on account of their cooperation in the investigation. The defendants claimed that their confessions were untrue and were coerced from them only after long hours of questioning. The trial was observed by representatives of foreign human rights groups, family members of the defendants, and selected representatives of public-interest groups. On April 18, 1980, the court issued its verdict. All eight were convicted of sedition; Shih Ming-teh was sentenced to life in prison, Huang Hsin-chieh to fourteen years and each of the remaining defendants to twelve years.

Karaoke: A form of entertainment in which amateurs sing the words to recorded music. Karaoke is Japanese slang for "empty orchestra" or "orchestra empty of vocals." It is one of the most popular forms of entertainment in Japan and is regularly found in bars, restaurants, nightclubs, sight-seeing coaches, and at almost any entertainment establishment. The most frequent customers are common businesspeople who flock together after a day's work to relax and release stress at these places. It does not take much talent, just a little courage, for anyone to grab a microphone and sing along with the accompanying music aided by on-screen lyrics. Many Japanese who are usually shy in public quickly overcome their reservations and indulge in the fantasy of being a stage star. Off-key notes and the mistimings of amateur singers are tolerated by karaoke aficionados, who for the sake of camaraderie will even join in and help poor performers pull through their numbers. Because of the uplifting psychological effect and release from the intensity of Japanese life, karaoke has evolved into a Japanese national pastime as clean, inexpensive fun.

Karaoke had a modest beginning in the 1970's with audio cartridge tapes containing customized music tracks without the vocals. These tapes were played on eight-track players with a microphone input. In 1980 Japan Pioneer Electronic Corporation started to manufacture the karaoke laser disc player and karaoke music videodiscs. Nowadays karaoke media consists of audiotapes, compact discs (CDs), videotapes, and laser videodiscs. Patrons can sing along to music television (MTV)-style videos with high-quality instrumental accompaniment and background vocals and visuals. In 1988 karaoke entered the American market for commercial and private entertainment and quickly gained cross-cultural popularity. Karaoke is now found in American bars, nightclubs, and restaurants, and as the main attraction at private and commercial parties. The word karaoke has become part of the American vocabulary.

Karma: Fundamental term in Indian philosophy. Karma means "action," "performance," or "ritual act." It refers to the power produced by the actions of individuals and is believed to determine their fate in their next life.

The concept of Karma as a ritual activity was first adumbrated in *Satapatha Brahmana*, a Vedic exegetical text dealing with sacrifices and rites to be performed by priests. In the course of time, the Purva-Mimamsa philosophers viewed the priestly rituals in magical terms: Prescribed actions performed rightly could control the gods, whereas improper performance of the ceremony brought ruin to the performer. In this way, the concept of Karma was enlarged to designate a universal order governed by a metaphysical system of cause and effect. The Brahmanic notion of Karma as ritual was expanded by the Upanishadic philosophers to mean that action is an unavoidable concomitant of one's birth and being. Hence every action leads to a result. A corollary of this notion is that human beings' desires determine their will, which leads them to act, and their actions elicit appropriate results.

Hindu philosophers have always counseled against actions for material pursuits (that is, *pravritti*, or active activity) because such pursuits necessarily lead to dissatisfaction and thus to a cycle of rebirth (*samsara*). In order to liberate oneself from *samsara*, one must free oneself from the processes of Karmic law. Hence the Upanishadic philosophers urged people to perform meritorious acts (that is, *nivritte*, or passive activity), such as abnegation, abstinence, practice of yoga, or devotion (*bhakti*) to a personal god.

The notion of Karma has often been confused with destiny over which humans have no control. Thus, a Hindu is seen as a passive fatalist incapable of personal exertions. Actually, however, Karma is far from passive.

Kashiwahara, Ken (b. July 18, 1940, Waimea, Kauai, Hawaii): Broadcast journalist. He became the San Francisco bureau chief for ABC News in 1978, after working as anchor and reporter for radio and television stations in Honolulu and Los Angeles. He was graduated from San Francisco State University, where he received a B.A. degree in broadcast communications in 1963. He was ABC's correspondent in Southeast Asia in 1975 and was the Hong Kong bureau chief

Emmy-award winning broadcast journalist Ken Kashiwahara. (AP/Wide World Photos)

from 1975 to 1978. He won a national Emmy Award in 1986 for a segment on *20/20*, and, as a correspondent in Vietnam, was one of the last reporters to leave the country at the end of the war.

Katakana. *See* **Kana**

Katayama, Sen (1859, Okayama Prefecture, Japan—1933, Soviet Union): Labor unionist and Communist Party leader. After attending schools in Tokyo and working as a printer and lecturer, Katayama went to the United States in 1884 to study theology. He eventually earned a B.D. degree from Yale in 1895. Two years later, he went back to Japan and helped establish the country's first labor union. In the early 1900's, as a traveling recruiter and organizer for the Japanese Socialist Association, he visited San Francisco and Los Angeles and established offices there. Through 1915-1916, he organized the Japanese Labor Federation of America and started publishing a Socialist monthly magazine, *Heimin* (commoner). A few years later, in 1919, he helped organize the Communist Party of America. He fled to the Soviet Union in 1921 to escape government prosecution. He died there and was buried in the Kremlin.

Kava ceremony: Among the Samoan island cultures of western Polynesia, the ritual preparation, distribution, and drinking of the beverage *kava*. The ceremony is invariably associated with such occasions as village council meetings (*fono*), ceremonial visits of chiefs from other villages (*malaga*), and title installations (*saofai*). *Kava*, also drunk ceremonially in Fiji and Tonga, is nonalcoholic but does have some mild narcotic qualities. The drink is prepared by the village ceremonial maiden (*taupou*) by steeping pulverized or chewed pieces of *Piper methysticum* root in a prescribed amount of water until a cloudy, khaki-colored liquid is produced. It has been described by one anthropologist (Clellan Ford) as tasting "like the smell of a cedar lead pencil when it is sharpened."

Kava paraphernalia includes a carved wooden bowl eighteen inches in diameter with either four or twenty-four legs, a strainer of shredded hibiscus bast, and a polished coconut cup. While the *kava* is being prepared under the watchful eye of the village talking chief (*tulafale*), this orator will deliver a speech of welcome to the assembled chiefs and recount the mythological origin of the ceremony in poetic verse (*solo*). When he judges the *kava* ready (by its color), he will direct its distribution by the *taupou*, who will carry the cup to all titled chiefs in the order of their relative rank.

While there have been reports of soporific and even stupefying effects from *kava* consumption in Micronesia and Eastern Polynesia, this has not been observed in Samoa, where in a ceremonial context *kava* is consumed in small amounts and is consistently described as "producing nothing more than a tingling sensation in the mouth, a short-lived numbness of the tongue and a pleasant feeling which refreshes the body and sharpens the intellect."

The origin of the *kava* ceremony is unknown, although Samoans maintain that it was a gift from the god Tagaloa Ui. There is, however, some resemblance of the *kava* ritual to Soma rites of the ancient Indian Vedic religion, and it is conceivable that *Piper methysticum* and its attendant ceremonialism could have been carried into the Pacific by early migrants from Southeast Asia.

Kawabe, Harry Sotaro (1890, Maibara, near Osaka, Japan—1969): Businessman. After landing in Seattle, Washington, in 1905, he began taking English lessons and bought and managed a small business. Attracted by the booming economic prospects offered by Alaska, he traveled there in 1909 and worked at various jobs in regions dominated by railroad and mining interests. He eventually started a prosperous steam laundry business. Kawabe's internment in a relocation center during World War II took him away from Alaska, to which he did not return once the war had ended. Instead he went back to Seattle and over the next several decades acquired wealth in real estate and Japanese import/export. During the latter half of his life, he also worked to improve relations between the United States and Japan, for which he won public recognition. In 1965 he went back to Alaska to start a company that would supply Japan with needed natural resources.

Kawakami, Karl Kiyoshi (1879, Yamagata Prefecture, Japan—1949): Journalist. A socialist in his early student years (hence his adopted Western name, "Karl," for Karl Marx), Kawakami immigrated to the United States in 1901. After earning a degree in political science from the University of Iowa, he wrote for American periodicals, specializing in Japan and East Asian affairs. Becoming an outspoken advocate of Japan's foreign policy, Kawakami headed the Pacific Press Bureau, a news agency operated by the Japanese government, from 1914 until 1920. He was also the author of a number of books in English, including *American-Japanese Relations: An Inside View of Japan's Policies and Purposes* (1912) and *Asia at the Door: A Study of the Japanese Question in Continental United States, Hawaii, and Canada* (1914). In addition to promoting the interests of the Japanese government, Kawakami wrote extensively on behalf of Japanese immigrants in the United States. Emphasizing the ability of Japanese immigrants to become fully assimilated in American society (in contrast, he argued, to the Chinese), he was strongly critical of the increasingly harsh restrictions on Japanese immigration that culminated in the IMMIGRATION ACT OF 1924, and he called for the extension of naturalization rights to Japanese immigrants.

Kawakita v. United States (1951): U.S. Supreme Court ruling that affirmed the conviction and death sentence of an American-born Japanese tried for treason. Tomoyo Kawakita, a native Californian, spent time in Japan during World War II. While there he became an English-language interpreter for a Japanese mining company that used American prisoners of war (POWs) as laborers. In 1947, a year after returning to the United States, he was recognized by a former POW as one who had assisted the Japanese and was brought to trial in federal court for treason. The court, finding

Kawakita guilty, sentenced him to death, a ruling later upheld by the High Court. President John F. Kennedy later pardoned him, releasing him from Alcatraz penitentiary but barring him from ever returning to the United States.

Kawamura, Terry Teruo (1949, Oahu, Territory of Hawaii—1969): Vietnam War hero. While serving there he was attached to the 173d Engineer Company at Camp Radcliffe. During an enemy raid, he threw himself atop an explosive, killing himself but saving the lives of several others in his unit. His valor earned for him the United States' highest military honor, the Congressional Medal of Honor. One of 155 Vietnam veterans to receive this award, Kawamura was one of only 4 Japanese Americans ever to win it.

Kawano, Jack (d. 1984, Calif.): Labor organizer. The son of an Issei contract laborer, Kawano grew up in Pahoa on the island of Hawaii. At the age of fourteen, he left school in order to earn money as a laborer on the Hakalau Plantation. Dissatisfied with the conditions endured by plantation workers, he worked as a day laborer at various jobs until he found steady employment as a dock worker. Like other Asian American dock workers, he was excluded from membership in established unions. As a result, Kawano helped to found the Honolulu Longshoreman's Association. Unable to bargain effectively, the association merged with the mainland-based International Longshoreman's and Warehouseman's Union (ILWU) in October of 1937.

As an organizer for the ILWU, Kawano helped increase the union's rolls from 970 members in 1944 to some 30,000 members by 1947. A member of Hawaii's Communist Party, Kawano eventually dropped out of the party and lost influence over the ILWU in the wake of a dispute with mainland union leadership in 1949. Kawano traveled to Washington, D.C., in 1951 to appear before the House Committee on Un-American Activities, where he provided testimony regarding connections between the ILWU and the Hawaii Communist Party. His testimony eventually led to the arrest and conviction of the Hawaii Seven. Shunned by mainstream citizens and former union colleagues alike in the wake of his testimony, Kawano struggled to make a living in Hawaii. Eventually he moved to California, where he worked for many years at a Lockheed aerospace plant. He died in California in 1984.

KCB Radio: Radio station founded by KCB Incorporated on March 21, 1991. It is the FM counterpart to Radio Korea, an AM station established on February 1, 1989. Its programming, from music to news, is broadcast in Korean.

Kearney, Denis (Feb. 1, 1847, Oakmount, Cork County, Ireland—Apr. 24, 1907, Alameda, Calif.): Political leader and anti-Chinese agitator. Until his brief rise to fame as leader of the Workingmen's Party of California during the late 1870's, Kearney had had no significant involvement in politics. His earlier focus on his personal and business advancement gave no strong indication of his later participation in the anti-Chinese and prowhite labor activities of the late 1870's.

Kearney was orphaned at an early age, went to sea as a cabin boy, and eventually rose to the rank of first mate. In the 1860's he arrived in San Francisco and took work on the coastal steamers. In 1870 he married and began a family; in 1872 he began a drayage business; and a few years later he became a naturalized U.S. citizen. He was a moderately successful businessman, who, like other immigrants, identified strongly with the myth of the self-made man.

By the time of the emergence of the Workingmen's Party in the late 1870's, California was caught in a deepening depression. In San Francisco, unemployment and coinciding anti-Chinese sentiment among white workers and others was rising. In the summer of 1877 anti-Chinese riots broke out in the city. It was at this historical juncture that Kearney stepped from obscurity and into the political limelight.

In the fall, after the summer riots, Kearney and others began promoting the newly formed Workingmen's Party. The new party drew its main support from San Francisco's large white working class, many of whom were Irish immigrants like Kearney. Through the use of charismatic and demagogic rhetoric, Kearney propelled himself and the party into the public eye. At outdoor nightly rallies in working-class neighborhoods, Kearney attacked the Chinese as morally unfit, the lackies of the monopolies, and the curse of white labor.

The brief but intense anti-Chinese furor unleashed by Kearney and the Workingmen's Party eventually contributed to the enactment of the Chinese Exclusion Acts of 1882 and 1884. By the mid-1880's the Workingmen's Party was defunct, Kearney had returned to his business affairs, and California's traditional parties had absorbed much of Kearney's anti-Chinese rhetoric. Years later Kearney expressed disappointment with the white worker but continued to voice anti-Chinese as well as anti-Japanese sentiment.

Kearny Street Workshop: Artists' collective, founded in 1972, that serves as a base for Asian American writers, musicians, filmmakers, and photographers to develop innovative ways of expressing the wide-ranging experiences of Americans of Asian descent and of using various art forms to reflect the community. In one of its own publications, *Texas Long Grain* (1982), workshop members described the importance "of art, not as art for art's sake but as works more genuine and reflective of our people and our society."

The group's first location was a storefront on Kearny Street, in the INTERNATIONAL HOTEL, on the boundary between San Francisco's Chinatown and the financial district. In 1968 the hotel had become the focal point of an eventual nine-year struggle by low-income and elderly Chinese and Filipino residents to stay in their hotel rooms despite plans to raze the

June Kuramoto performed at the Thirteenth Annual Asian American Jazz Festival at the Kearny Street Workshop. (Asian Week)

building and replace it with a parking garage. That fight also inspired the works and exhibits of many of the workshop artists.

Other works published by the workshop include *Without Names* (1985), which focuses on works by San Francisco Bay Area Filipino writers; *October Light* (1987), *Winter Place* (1989), and *Trespassing Innocence* (1989), collections of poems by San Francisco writers Jeff Tagami, Genny Lim, and Virginia Cerenio, respectively; and *Larawan: Portraits of Filipinos* (1989), which includes essays and photographs by Lenny Limjoco (copublished with Likha).

One of the workshop's primary projects was the Angel Island Exhibit, which combined research about Angel Island—the port of entry for most Chinese immigrants to the United States from 1910 to 1940—with historical and current photographs and poetry of the immigrants. The exhibit was shown in several locations throughout the United States.

The workshop organizes and sponsors jazz festivals and visual arts exhibitions, theater performances, and lectures and arranges poetry and prose readings of works by Asian Americans. Members of the collective have also conducted classes through which they teach their skills and encourage other members of the community to find their own ways of recording their stories.

Keetley Farms: Farming colony in Keetley, Utah, that housed more than a hundred Japanese American evacuees who opted for "voluntary" resettlement during World War II. Under the authority of EXECUTIVE ORDER 9066, signed by U.S. president Franklin D. Roosevelt in early 1942, Japanese Americans living on the Pacific Coast were urged to move to inland regions of the country, away from certain zones that the government had designated as militarily sensitive. Less than five thousand evacuees chose "voluntary" resettlement; most were forcibly removed to the assembly and relocation camps. Among the former, Keetley Farms came to comprise the largest single group.

The new colony began to take shape largely through the efforts of Oakland produce merchant Fred Isamu Wada, who persuaded the tiny Utah town to authorize a lease for 3,500 acres of surrounding farmland. He then set about enlisting other evacuees. Moving in, however, was not easy. In the beginning, other communities in the immediate vicinity used various tactics, such as setting off dynamite, to discourage the resettlement, and the land to be farmed was rocky and uneven. Yet the farmers' hard work and diligence provided their subsistence and eventually helped to defuse a once-hostile situation. Most of the colonists returned to California when the war ended, although others stayed in Utah.

Keihin Bank: Officially the Kabushikigaisha Keihin Chokinginko, the primary bank for numerous Japanese contract laborers in the Hawaiian Islands, founded in 1898. The bank was originated through the collaboration of three of Japan's emigration companies. It was based in Tokyo and included four branches, one in Honolulu.

Keihin Bank gradually became a source of resentment to the laborers. U.S. immigration laws as of 1894 mandated that only those Japanese arrivals with at least one hundred yen in their possession could enter Hawaii upon landing. To do that, many applicants had to take bank loans before leaving Japan. Many migrants borrowed this money from Keihin Bank.

Repayment terms were harsh and unjust. The money was to be repaid almost immediately once the laborers had landed in Honolulu. Moreover, each borrower had to leave a deposit with the bank, all or part of which was forfeited if the laborer failed to complete his or her contract term of service. After fulfilling their contracts, the immigrants could retrieve their deposits—but only by asking for it in person at the Tokyo office. These terms allowed the bank to hold the laborers' money for the longest possible time, thereby accumulating the greatest interest on the money. It was not long before Hawaii's plantation laborers started calling for the bank's closure—a campaign undertaken by the Japanese Reform Association and the islands' Japanese press. Buckling under heavy pressure, Keihin Bank was forced to close in 1907.

Keiyaku-nin: Japanese term designating Japanese labor contractors. The *keiyaku-nin* would begin recruiting laborers in Japan after first striking an agreement with American employers willing to hire them. In America, the Issei, in particular, depended on these contractors when looking for work. Although frequently exploitative in their methods, the labor contractors formed a crucial link between immigrant laborers, who spoke little or no English, and their new employers.

Kenjinkai: Prefectural association formed by Japanese immigrants to America who came from the same town or area of Japan. These associations provided a sense of commonality and familiarity for settlers with the same dialect, culture, and history.

Importance. Originally, the *kenjinkai* was a category used by the Japanese government to identify geographical areas, similar to the way the designation of state is used in the United States. As a means of group identification, however, the *ken* (prefecture) took on greater significance in the United States than in Japan. It was beneficial for early Japanese immigrants to belong to these associations. The *kenjinkai* served a social function since the *ken* was the source of strong friendship bonds. The *ken* also provided another resource network besides the family. Those from the same *ken* were tied by a sense of obligation and mutual aid. For example, an immigrant would be more likely to patronize the business of another from the same *ken*. Thus, those immigrants from a small *ken* generally would not have as large a clientele as those from a large *ken*.

Immigration. Prefectural origins affected the pattern of immigration from Japan to Hawaii. Labor recruiters from Hawaii, with the assistance of Japanese officials and merchants, recruited laborers from specific prefectures in Kyushu and Honshu. Many of the Japanese laborers recruited to work under government contract in Hawaii from 1885 to 1894 came from Hiroshima and Yamaguchi prefectures on Honshu, the central island of Japan. Other prefectures included Kumamoto and Fukuoka on Kyushu, the southern island. Japanese immigrants who settled in Seattle, Washington, before World War II came from the southern prefectures of Japan: Hiroshima-ken, Okayama-ken, Yamaguchi-ken, Fukuoka-ken, Kumamoto-ken, Kagoshima-ken, Wakayama-ken, Shiga-ken, and Ehime-ken.

Immigrants from Okinawa, meanwhile, formed prefectural associations in Hawaii and on the mainland United States.

Many Japanese-owned or -associated hotels and boardinghouses were associated with particular prefectures. Moreover, many of the boardinghouses were way stations for labor contractors. The prefectural association provided social services, such as helping the thousands of Japanese displaced by the 1906 San Francisco earthquake. In 1909, there were twenty-seven *kenjinkai* in San Francisco.

Functions. The *kenjinkai* assisted the Issei, Japanese immigrants, in establishing social supports and mutual aid in America. The Issei and Kibei were active in these associations. The prefectural ties helped immigrants in a number of ways. For example, the custom of *koden*, of offering a sum of money at a funeral to the family of the deceased, or of forming a TANOMOSHI

California Japanese American prefectural organization or "kenjinkai" holds a meeting against the backdrop of the American flag. (Japanese American National Museum)

among *kenjinkai* members in order to provide a small loan were forms of mutual aid practiced by the Issei, particularly among prefectural members. Both customs were rooted in a strong sense of obligation and duty that the favor be repaid. Thus, a family is expected to reciprocate once it has received *koden* by giving *koden* to other *ken* members whose family members have died.

On the mainland United States, the Nisei or Sansei were not active in the *kenjinkai* as it drew largely from the immigrant generation, the Issei. In Hawaii, many Nisei joined the *kenjinkai* of their parents. The Issei, upon arrival in Hawaii or on the mainland, established locality clubs based on village and prefectural origin. The *kenjinkai* was the larger locality club. For example, a *kenjinkai* was established in San Francisco and in the East Bay in the San Francisco Bay Area. These organizations sponsored picnics, trips, memorial services for departed family members, and annual new year's parties. These associations provided kinship ties between the Japanese immigrants and their families. As a result, among the Nisei, the second generation,

marriages of family members from the same prefecture were typical.

The future of the *kenjinkai* appears to be limited as the membership has relied upon the Issei and Nisei. The importance of the *ken* was based on its functions as an intermediate level of social organization between the family and the community. In various communities Japanese Americans have formed self-help groups such as Kimochi in San Francisco and Yu-Ai Kai in San Jose, California, that bridge prefectural associations.—*Alexander Yamato*

SUGGESTED READINGS: • Ethnic Studies Oral History Project. *Uchinanchu: A History of Okinawans in Hawaii*. Honolulu: Ethnic Studies Program, University of Hawaii at Manoa, 1981. • Ichioka, Yuji. *The Issei: The World of the First Generation Japanese Immigrants, 1885-1924*. New York: Free Press, 1988. • Kitano, Harry H. L. *Japanese Americans: The Evolution of a Subculture*. 2d ed. Englewood Cliffs, N.J.: Prentice-Hall, 1976. • Miyamoto, S. Frank. *Social Solidarity Among the Japanese in Seattle*. Seattle: University of Washington Press, 1939.

Khalistan: Literally, the "land of the pure," one of the names used to describe a Sikh homeland in what is now part of the Indian province of Punjab. This sovereign political entity would be created by separation from India, resulting in full political autonomy.

Khalistan derives from Khalsa, "the pure," a group affiliation defined by Guru GOBIND SINGH, the tenth Sikh guru, in 1699. At this time, the Sikh community, having been founded by Guru NANAK in sixteenth century Punjab, was responding to increasing persecution at the hands of the Mughal emperors. Gobind Singh therefore cultivated defense readiness as a fundamental value for community preservation. In 1801 all of the Punjab (and Kashmir as well) came under the political authority of a Sikh ruler, Maharaja Ranjit Singh. Although the population of this kingdom, known then as the "Land of Five Rivers," was predominantly Muslim, both the Muslims and the Hindu minority lived in harmony with the Sikh rulers. After Ranjit Singh died, a new military threat emerged in the form of the BRITISH EAST INDIA COMPANY, which used troops from other areas of India and superior weaponry to conquer Punjab.

Although the struggle was intense, and thousands of Sikhs died to protect their new kingdom, the British noted their bravery and martial spirit and rapidly included Sikhs in the English policy of using Indian troops commanded by English officers. Concessions were made to accommodate Khalsa identity, and Sikh troops rapidly became an essential ingredient of the British Raj, especially after the Mutiny of 1857. Sikhs were also involved in the resistance movement, however, and soon after the AMRITSAR massacre of 1919, the Akali Dal (eternal party) emerged to reassert control of the Sikh temples.

Master Tara Singh campaigned for a tripartite division of the old Raj into India, Pakistan, and Khalistan, but the Punjab was divided between India and Pakistan in 1947, and massive migrations and massacres occurred. In subsequent years, violent confrontations and long periods of martial rule have continued in the Punjab. Indian politicians have debated constitutional recognition of Sikhism's separateness from Hinduism, and the degree of political autonomy that might or might not be granted. (See KHALISTAN DECLARATION OF INDEPENDENCE.)

Khalistan Declaration of Independence (1986): Culminating agitation that dates back to the drafting of the Indian Constitution in 1950, the Declaration of Khalistan, dated April 29, 1986, announced the formation of the Sikh state Khalistan, or "the land of the pure."

The Sikhs had been given the option of forming their own nation during India's independence in 1947 but instead elected to remain a part of India because of the assurances of equal and fair treatment from Mohandas Gandhi and Jawaharlal Nehru. Nevertheless, a constitution was adopted that categorizes Sikhs as Hindus. This failure to recognize the distinctiveness of the Sikh religion led to a great sense of betrayal felt by the Sikhs. The terms of the constitution were so offensive to the Sikh delegation that it refused to ratify it. To this day, no Sikh has ever signed the Indian Constitution.

During the next three decades, Sikhs felt a persistent pattern of discrimination against them, their language, and their state. The conflict came to a head on June 4, 1984, when the Indian government launched a bloody assault on the Golden Temple, the holiest shrine of the Sikhs, in which more than 10,000 Sikhs were killed. Many of these were innocent pilgrims to the shrine, including thousands of women, children, and elderly people. In addition, international human rights organizations reported horrifying violations of human rights by Indian soldiers before, during, and after the attack. The bitterness and insecurity that resulted from this savage attack—seen by many as an attack upon Sikhism itself—as well as the November, 1984, government-assisted pogroms in New Delhi, after the assassination of Indira Gandhi, led to a wider call for an independent Sikh nation.

Among the provisions outlined in the declaration is the peaceful transfer of power from the Indian government to the new state through negotiations, in order to avoid any unnecessary bloodshed. In addition, specific mandates are included in order to establish a truly egalitarian society. Discrimination on the basis of gender, race, religion, caste, class, and education is prohibited, and Sikhism is established as the official religion.

Khalsa: Sikh brotherhood of "the pure." Established by the last guru, GOBIND SINGH, in the Punjabi town of Anandpur Sahib, the Khalsa represents a community of equals with highest authority vested in the Sarbat Khalsa, or assembly of the entire Sikh people. In April, 1699, Gobind Singh initiated five chosen followers, the Panch Piaras, with a sugar-crystal water solution called *patasha*. Men adopted the surname "Singh" (lion) and women "Kaur" (princess), thereby eliminating former caste names. Infusing them with a spirit of purity and the boldness of a lion, Gobind Singh himself was initiated into the Khalsa along with some twenty thousand devotees. The initiation rite transformed a formerly pacific people into a militant brotherhood of crusaders. To them Gobind Singh gave discipline and structure distinguished by five outward "*K*'s": *kesh*, or unshorn hair, wrapped in a turban and an unshaven beard to signify saintliness; *kanga*, or a comb, to cleanse and maintain the hair and to signify the "combing" of evil from one's heart; *kara*, or steel bracelet, on the right wrist as a symbol of constraint and service; *kirpan*, or sword, as an instrument of offense and defense in the struggle for justice and against oppression and tyranny; and *kaccha*, or shorts, as active attire. The "5 *K*'s" remind a Sikh to behave exactly like the gurus and represent the visible symbols of his faith. The aim of founding the Khalsa was to build a nation of purified Sikhs who would be free from fear and selfishness, imbued with a sense of divine mission, and embodied with the highest ideal of manhood or womanhood. Although designed by Gobind Singh himself, the Khalsa was saluted by him as his own ideal and master. In it all men and women became equal regardless of status, race, or caste. It was to be the "guru" after Gobind Singh, the agency authorized to work in the name of the gurus and the guide to their teachings as found in the Adi Granth. The Khalsa represents the martial egalitarian religiosocial organization of Gurmat or Sikhism as a primary source of strength and unity.

Khalsa Diwan Society: Created in 1907 in Vancouver, Canada, this Sikh organization facilitated political organizing among South Asian immigrants of all religions. It also formed a link between all the members of the Sikh community.

Among the early religious concerns of the group was the preservation of the ideals of the Sikh religion, as they fought the influences in Canada that pressured the immigrants to shed their cultural identity and assimilate. The group also worked closely with political groups such as the United India League to protest the ban on new immigration from South Asia, including the families of those who had already settled in Canada.

Another chapter of the group formed in Stockton, California, and was instrumental in establishing the first American *gurdwara*, or Sikh temple. Formed in 1912, this is widely considered by historians as the most important of the organizations formed by South Asian immigrants in North America. The first meeting established the goals of the group: to provide for the welfare of South Asian immigrant students and laborers. By the end of May, 1912, the group had become

incorporated in California and had made progress toward acquiring land for a *gurdwara*. As in India, the Khalsa Diwan handled the management of the Sikh temples.

The establishment of a *gurdwara* was especially important for the community because it served as a center of political, social, and spiritual activity. Political discussions, including those on the liberation of India from the British, were often held there, making it a gathering point for the entire community. Functioning as it would in India, the *gurdwara* also provided a place to stay for those who needed it, as well as free meals for all. This stemmed from the principle of *seva*, selfless service of others, which is a primary aspect of the Sikh religion. The Sikh community worked together to build the *gurdwara* and to supply the free kitchen, tightening the bonds between themselves. Additionally, in the face of opposition (such as displays of hostility by white Canadians) ties within the entire South Asian community were strengthened by the protests in which they participated together.

Khan, Ali Akbar (b. Apr. 14, 1922, Shivpur, India, now Bangladesh): Sarodist. Along with his brother-in-law Ravi SHANKAR, he is known both for his artistic excellence and for a long-term commitment to sharing Indian classical music with new audiences. He studied sarod (a long-necked plucked, fretless lute with four melody strings, four drone strings, two rhythm strings, and fifteen resonating strings) with his father, Allauddin Khan, thereby inheriting a rigorous discipline and technical sophistication passed down through generations of musicians from the musical family of Tansen, a court musician to the Mughal emperor Akbar. Tansen is regarded as one of the founders of Hindustani (north Indian) classical music.

Khan's youth was spent in the village of Maihar. According to Shankar, Khan's father required his students to practice throughout most of their waking hours. Khan's performing debut came in 1936 in Allahabad, and his first professional position was as a courtier to the maharaja of Jodhpur during the 1940's. In the 1950's, he began performing abroad, and in 1956, he founded the Ali Akbar College of Music in Calcutta. In 1963, he received the Sangeet Natak Akademi award for Hindustani classical music.

While never forsaking the traditions of his artistic lineage, the *ustad* (or maestro) Khan has occasionally experimented in collaborations with musicians from other traditions, including jazz saxophonist John Handy III. He often closes his traditional solo recitals with a *ragamala* (garland of ragas), in which he includes quotations from European classical themes. He has also extended the Hindustani tradition through the creation of new ragas (classical melodic forms).

One of his most important contributions to the appreciation of Indian music abroad is his work as an educator. In 1967, he founded a second branch of the Ali Akbar Khan College of Music in San Rafael, California, and his son, tablaist Pranesh Khan, became the school's director. With his student George Ruckert, Khan is the co-author of *The Classical Music of North India* (1991), a 367-page introductory text. In 1991, he was awarded a MacArthur Fellowship. He is featured on numerous recordings spanning almost three decades.

Khan, Fazal Muhammad (1910, Punjab, India, now Pakistan—Apr. 28, 1972, Butte City, Calif.): Farmer and community leader. In spite of restrictive ALIEN LAND LAWS, Khan became a highly successful rice farmer in Northern California's Butte County. Khan, along with his partners and other Asian and South Asian farmers, has been recognized for his contribution to the growth and development of the rice industry in northern California.

Arriving in California in 1926 at the age of sixteen, Khan joined fellow South Asians from his native Punjab who had settled in the Sacramento Valley. He began working as a farm laborer in Sutter County in 1926. In 1929 he became the partner of two brothers, Babu and Naimet Khan, who had been rice farmers in neighboring Butte County since 1916. This partnership flourished, and eventually the Khans leased and later purchased in excess of four thousand acres of rice land, becoming one of the larger rice-growing operations in the northern Sacramento Valley.

The Khans' farming success was especially notable considering the adverse land ownership policies that affected Asian immigrants during the first few decades of the twentieth century. Khan and his partners were forced to lease land in the name of their attorney. When they later purchased their leased land, they again had to do so through their attorney. Khan and his partners were not able to hold their land in their own names until laws were passed in 1946 making South Asians eligible for naturalization and thereby eligible to own property. (See LUCE-CELLER BILL OF 1946.)

Khan, an active member of the California farming and business community, joined organizations such as the California Farm Bureau Federation, the World Affairs Council of Northern California, the California Chamber of Commerce, and the local Rotary Club. Additionally, as a prominent member of the pakistani American community, he led organizations such as the Muslim Association and the Pakistan-America Association. He was one of the founders of the Muslim mosque in Sacramento and served as its president.

In 1948 Khan revisited Pakistan and married Bashira Khan. Returning to California, they made their home on the farm near Butte City, which became a visitors' center for travelers from Pakistan. While guests at the Khan home included Pakistani educators, government officials, and students attending universities across the United States, Khan was particularly anxious to host Pakistani farmers and agricultural experts who might benefit from observing local agricultural practices and techniques. One of Khan's goals was to establish a farm in Pakistan where methods of rice cultivation and production could be demonstrated.

Khan, who had become a naturalized citizen of the United States, dedicated himself to enhancing the relationship between Pakistan and the United States. In 1968 the president of Pakistan presented Khan with a medal of honor for "outstanding service" to his community and country of origin.

Khan was active in farming and business until his death in 1972. The partnership with the Khan family (heirs to Babu and Naimet Khan, who were since deceased) remained intact until after his death. The respective Khan families, along with other South Asian American farmers, have continued to cultivate rice in the Sacramento Valley, which is one of the centers of rice farming in the United States.

Khan, Mubarak Ali (Mubarek Ali Khan): Activist and community leader. Founder of the India Welfare League, founder-president of the Pakistan Welfare League of America, lobbyist for Asian Indian naturalization rights, farmer, and community spokesperson, Khan and his associates gathered 5,000 signatures from U.S. citizens in support of Asian Indian naturalization rights.

As a youth in Allahabad, United Provinces (now Uttar Pradesh, India), Khan became involved in nationalist demonstrations against the British colonial government. He was forced to leave his home as a result of his political activities. He traveled first to Japan and then proceeded on to the United States in 1913. Khan settled in a farming community near Phoenix, Arizona.

In 1937, Khan founded the India Welfare League, which was based in New York City. The League assisted unemployed Asian Indians and advocated naturalization rights for immigrants from the Indian subcontinent. During the 1940's, Khan traveled between Arizona, New York, and Washington, D.C., promoting civil rights for Asian Indians. As one of the spokespersons from the immigrant community, Khan helped gain congressional support for legislation that allowed Asian Indians to become naturalized citizens.

After the passage of the LUCE-CELLER BILL OF 1946, Khan shifted his concern to the Indian subcontinent, which was soon to become independent. He supported Muslim demands for the separate nation of Pakistan, which would be created upon the withdrawal of the British colonialists. To present the case for a separate nation to the American public, he formed the Pakistan Welfare League of America.

Once Pakistan was created in 1947, Khan continued his efforts to promote understanding about South Asia. In 1949, Khan invited the first Pakistani ambassador to the United States, M.A.H. Ispahani, to visit Phoenix, Arizona. During this official visit, the ambassador met members of the local Pakistani American community, addressed business and civic organizations, and spoke on local radio programs. On the occasion of the ambassador's visit, Arizona governor Dan E. Garvey delivered a testimonial lauding Khan for his dedication to increasing understanding between the peoples of Pakistan and the United States.

Khmer: Ethnolinguistic majority of Cambodia, constituting about 94 percent of the population in 1993. In the early 1990's there were about 8 million Khmer in Cambodia, one million to 1.5 million in Vietnam, and 150,000 in Thailand. U.S. census data for 1990 indicates a resident population of about 150,000 Cambodians (under the census the latter are not broken down into their various ethnic subgroupings). The Khmer language springs from the Mon-Khmer family of Austroasiatic languages. Khmer culture, of which the twelfth century temple at ANGKOR WAT is a testament, is old and complex. The Khmer of Southeast Asia are predominantly Theravada Buddhists; their religious beliefs are also influenced by a mixture of pre-Buddhist animism and the use of magic to ward off evil spirits. South Asian Indian culture has strongly influenced Khmer arts, literature, and popular scientific thinking. (See CAMBODIAN AMERICANS as well as other entries under Khmer.)

Khmer-language schools: Many Cambodian American community organizations have attempted to stem

Khmer monk, Stockton, California, 1984. (Eric Crystal)

the tide of language loss among immigrant children by establishing Khmer literacy classes. Often these are organized through the local Cambodian Buddhist temple, the traditional centers of learning and literacy in Cambodia. Others are arranged through Cambodian American community organizations.

Such programs make use of literacy materials published either in the Cambodian refugee camps on the Thai-Cambodia border or within Cambodia itself. These materials are rarely bilingual, rendering them less effective for Cambodian American children. They are also printed on very poor quality paper, which makes them difficult to photocopy, and are unappealing to students accustomed to beautifully illustrated children's literature. Since funding is nearly impossible to find for such teaching programs, the latter depend largely on volunteer services provided by adult Cambodian Americans.

Khmer is a difficult language to learn to write because of a very complicated alphabet system. The system was devised by Buddhist monks from South Asia more than a thousand years ago, based on Indic scripts and modified to accommodate the vastly greater pho-

Street banners show examples of Khmer written language as Vietnamese troops leave Battambang, Cambodia, in 1985. (AP/Wide World Photos)

netic richness of Khmer, particularly in the realm of vowels. Literacy in Cambodia has never been overwhelmingly high and was greatly reduced during the Pol Pot period, so that parents of children in Khmer-language classes may not be in a position to assist their children with the lessons. Since Cambodian American children are linguistically and culturally disadvantaged in American schools, their scholastic burdens are already heavy. The addition of another intellectual hurdle (classes are usually taught using traditional Cambodian rote methods and ironclad discipline) is successful for only a relatively small percentage of students.

There are at least two major American institutions that offer beginning through advanced instruction in Khmer. One is Cornell University; the second is the Southeast Asian Summer Studies Institute, held annually on the campus of a university with a Southeast Asian Studies center or program. Other university programs in linguistics provide courses on Southeast Asian languages, including Khmer, among them the University of Chicago, the University of Hawaii, and the University of California, Berkeley.

Khmer literature: Khmer verbal arts comprise two overlapping categories: oral literature and written literature. Both categories are represented in ancillary art forms including sculpture, dance, song, ritual, painting, and drama.

Written literature. There are two methods of delineating the history of Khmer literature. Linguists adopt a three-period scheme based on language change consisting of Old Khmer (the period of inscriptions, from the seventh to the fourteenth century,), Middle Khmer (the period of manuscripts, from the fifteenth to the nineteenth century) and Modern Khmer (twentieth century). Historians and archaeologists divide the past into five periods: pre-Angkorean (before the ninth century), Angkorean (from the ninth to the fourteenth century), post-Angkorean (from the fifteenth to the eighteenth century), French Protectorate (nineteenth century) and contemporary (twentieth century). The "classic" period is considered by most to extend from the sixteenth to the nineteenth century.

The first surviving evidence of written Khmer is an inscription dated 611 C.E., using an Indic script from south India. Sanskrit, the language of Brahmanism and the ruling elite of India, was similarly the language adopted by the Khmer elite in government and religion until the end of the Angkor period. This exerted a major influence on the language that is still strongly evident today. Pali, a derivative of Sanskrit and the language of Theravada Buddhism, was brought to Cambodia in the fourteenth century and continues to influence the Khmer language today. Neologisms based on Pali roots were introduced into the language by the Buddhist Institute in Phnom Penh earlier in the twentieth century to accommodate modern concepts and technologies. Thai words adopted into Khmer often prove to be originally from Old Khmer, lost in the language until reintroduced via Thailand. In addition, European words, especially French and more recently English, have contributed to the modern Khmer vocabulary.

From the Angkor period, manuscripts were created in the Indian fashion on palm leaf using the scrimshaw technique, in which letters are incised with a sharp metal tool into the leaf and then dusted and rubbed with a dark substance to darken the letters. Also, manuscript paper was made from ground mulberry and *snay* shrub matter, usually painted black and lettered in white, but sometimes the reverse. These manuscripts were preserved in monasteries, especially in Battambang and Phnom Penh, as well as in private collections. The Buddhist Institute in Phnom Penh had 1,647 manuscripts in 1975. From the late nineteenth century, typesetting was introduced, and printed materials in French were circulated. The first literary text to use Khmer characters appeared in 1908. Khmer-language publishing remained limited until the late 1920's.

Texts. Among the most important religious texts to be published in the twentieth century are the *Tripitaka*, a set of three works in Pali: *Vinnayapitaka*, *Suttantapitaka*, and the less known *Abidhamapitaka*. These existed only in manuscript form until the Buddhist Institute published the entire work in 110 volumes, including a Khmer translation, from 1931 to 1968.

The Jataka stories of the earlier incarnations of Gautama Buddha are also well known in Cambodia, especially the last ten *Mahajataka* ("Great Jatakas"): the 50 extra-canonical Jatakas are especially popular, first published in the fifteenth to sixteenth century with many verse adaptations following.

There have been many religious texts published in the original Pali with Khmer translation and hermeneutical interpretations, called *samray*. These include such works as the *Traibhumi* ("Three Realms"), a Pali cosmological text on heaven, earth, and hell.

Didactic works, *cbap*, whether old or new, are short poetic texts memorized in the schools for teaching correct behavior.

Fictional literature is concerned primarily with topics of love and adventure. *Lbaeng* are poetic plays; *lbaek* are poetic stories. Folk stories, fables, and origin myths are called *roeung preng*, while *roeung* is verse fiction, as well as the basis of narrative dance and theater. Composed by monks and palace scholars, the oldest of these to be dated is *Roeung Khyong Sangkh*, "The Conch Shell Story," of 1729. This story is an adaptation of the forty-first (in the Khmer order) of the 50 Jatakas, also known as *Sangkh Thong* ("The Golden Conch"), *Suvarna Sankha Jataka*, or, in the dance version, *Preah Sangkh* ("Sacred Conch"). This story was originally a Khmer folktale of a golden-skinned boy, Preah Sangkh, born from a conch shell, who acquires magic powers from his demon stepmother. He disguises himself with black skin and calls himself "Ngo." Later, Preah Sangkh is identified as an earlier incarnation of the Buddha. In his blackened form he is chosen by a princess for marriage because she can see beneath his disguise. After a series of trials, culminating in a battle with Indra, he proves himself more worthy than any of the king's other sons-in-law.

Two great Khmer epics are also rendered in verse. The first, dating from 1620, is *Lbaek Angkor Wat*, "poem of Angkor Wat." It tells of the origin of the great temple city, designed by the celestial architect Pisnaoka (Visvakarma), who was sent to earth by Indra to build a palace for his son from a previous life, Prince Ketumala (Ketumealea). This story has been used as the subject of a classical dance drama by Cambodian American dancers. The second epic is the *Reamker I* (*Ramakerti*; "Composition on Rama"), dated from the sixteenth to the seventeenth century, the Khmer version of the Indian *Ramyana* epic. A second version, *Reamker II*, is considered to date from the eighteenth century. Like so many of the Jataka stories, this epic has also found a prominent place in the classical dance repertoire. It is also the principal source for the large shadow puppetry tradition, *sbaik thom*.

Forty historical inscriptions in the stone walls of Angkor Wat include the oldest dated Khmer verse writing: number 38, dated 1702 C.E. The historical chronicles (*raba ksatr*) are typically in two sections, an opening section derived from oral tradition concerning the period of mythological origins through the fourteenth century and a second section delineating the reigns of successive kings. The more recent chronicles are more discursive in style, while older ones are more concise.

Technical literature includes those texts that are memorized under the guidance of a master in such fields as astrology, magic, divination, ritual, or medicine.

During the colonial period, traditional literature continued to be refashioned, but new genres also were created, including the novel, dubbed *pralaom lok* ("pleasure for people"). The first, published in 1938, led to some 750 other works by 1972. Many foreign works were also translated, especially the French classics, but also some from Chinese epic literature. Some were serialized in magazine form.

All publishing appears to have ceased from 1975 until after 1979. With the decline in literacy effected during the Pol Pot period, ensuing government censorship, and the resulting lack of economic incentive to publish, very little has been produced since, with the notable exception of some fine poetry and plays. Instead, a video production boom seems to have swept the imaginations of the country's creative artists, largely trained at the University of Fine Arts. Some 157 video production companies were in operation in 1991, for the market within the country as well as abroad. Many of these are based on *roeung kun*, gung-fu stories, but with Cambodian features, also a popular form of fiction.

Oral Literature. As stated earlier, oral and written literature share many of the same materials. The folktales, legends, and Jataka stories from the written sphere provide materials for rural story-singers, accompanied by the long necked lute, *chapey veng*; similarly, many written works derive their materials ultimately from the lore of oral poets and narrators.

Song texts for the classical dance repertoire and for the wedding ceremony (*phleng kar*) remain mostly in oral tradition, although they may also be found in rare manuscripts and contemporary singers' notebooks. Modern technology is also being used to record and document these primarily oral forms.—*Amy Catlin*

SUGGESTED READINGS: • Carrison, Muriel P. *Cambodian Folk Stories from the Gatiloke*. Translated by Kong Chhean. Rutland, Vt.: Charles E. Tuttle, 1987. • Dy, Khing Hoc, and Mak Phoeun. "Cambodia." In *South-East Asia Languages and Literatures: A Select Guide*, edited by Patricia Herbert and Anthony Milner. Honolulu: University of Hawaii Press, 1989. • Jacob, Judith M. "The Short Stories of Cambodian Popular Tradition." In *The Short Story in South East Asia*, edited by Jeremy H. C. S. Davidson and Helen Cordell. London: School of Oriental and African Studies, University of London, 1982. • Jacob, Judith M. "Some Features of Modern Khmer Literary Style." In *South-East Asian Linguistics: Essays in Honour of Eugenie J. A. Henderson*, edited by Jeremy H. C. S. Davidson, R. H. Robins, and Helen Cordell. London: School of Oriental and African Studies, University of London, 1989. • Piat, M. "Contemporary Cambodian Literature." *Journal of the Siam Society* 63 (1975): 251-259.

Khmer Rouge: The popular term for a radical Communist group that led probably the most extreme revolution in world history. "It is conservatively estimated that between April 1975 and January 1979, over one million people—one in seven—died as a direct result of [Khmer Rouge] policies and actions," from execution, overwork, famine, and other causes, writes historian David Chandler. Materials such as the 1984 film *The Killing Fields* and *The Death and Life of Dith Pran* (1985) by journalist Sydney Schanberg have portrayed the regime's brutality.

Origins (1951-1975). "Khmer Rouge," like "Viet Cong," originally was a pejorative term. Prince Norodom Sihanouk, Cambodia's mercurial ruler from 1941 until a group of pro-American generals ousted him in 1970, labeled Cambodia's insurgent Communists *Khmers Rouges*, French for "Red Cambodians."

In September, 1960, a group including Saloth Sar (known as POL POT) met at the Phnom Penh railway station to form the Khmer Worker's Party. This meeting came to be considered the founding of the party that ruled Democratic Kampuchea from 1975 through 1978. In 1951 Vietnamese revolutionary leader Ho Chi Minh's Indochinese Communist Party had formed the Khmer People's Revolutionary Party to aid its own fight against French colonialism. "Later efforts to play down the 1951 meeting were meant to dissociate the Cambodian movement from its Vietnamese antecedents," writes Chandler.

General Lon Nol's corrupt Khmer Republic began declining in 1972. Secret bombing by the United States, described by journalist William Shawcross in *Sideshow: Kissinger, Nixon and the Destruction of Cambodia* (1986), had begun in 1969. In May, 1970, the United States and South Vietnam invaded Cambodia. "The invasion protected the U.S. withdrawal from Vietnam, but it probably spelled the end of Cambodia as a sovereign state," writes Chandler.

During 1973 the U.S. military dropped 250,000 tons of explosives on Cambodia, "a country that was not at war with the United States and that had no U.S. combat personnel within its borders." The bombing "probably halted the Communist forces encircling Phnom

Khmer Rouge soldier holds inquisitive news team at gunpoint in the film The Killing Fields. (Museum of Modern Art/Stills Archive)

Penh, even though some people have argued that it hardened the will of the surviving Communist forces," according to Chandler. The Khmer Rouge entered Phnom Penh on April 17, 1975, two weeks before the fall of Saigon heralded Vietnam's unification under the Communists.

The Killing Fields (1975-1978). The Khmer Rouge evacuated all of Cambodia's cities. "This brutal order, never thoroughly explained, added several thousand deaths to the approximately five hundred thousand in the [1970-1975] civil war," writes Chandler. "Reports reaching the West spoke of hospital patients driven from their beds, random executions, and sick and elderly people, as well as small children, dead or abandoned along the roads."

The new regime collectivized all property, abolished currency, instigated a border war with Vietnam, and ceased contact with all countries except the People's Republic of China. China supported Democratic Kampuchea as a geopolitical counterweight to Soviet-allied Vietnam. Offering no material incentives (except, notes Chandler, "The bizarre promise that every-

one would enjoy dessert on a daily basis" by 1980), the Khmer Rouge used "new people"—those who had not supported the revolution before 1975—in an attempt to triple rice production.

"The fact that ["new people"] were socially unredeemable was seen as an advantage," writes Chandler. "In a chilling adage recalled by many survivors, they were often told: 'Keeping you is no profit; losing you is no loss.'"

Many Khmer Rouge soldiers were very young. Dith Pran told Schanberg: "They took them very young and taught them nothing but discipline. Just take orders, no need for a reason. Their minds have nothing inside except discipline. . . . That's why they killed their own people, even babies, like we might kill a mosquito." In the early 1990's many soldiers were so young they remembered the party's time in power vaguely or not at all.

Civil War (1979-1991). Vietnam invaded Cambodia in December, 1978, and installed a client regime in Phnom Penh, Cambodia's capital. The Khmer Rouge and other groups fought the new government in a civil

Thai military patrol at work near the Cambodian border where fighting continues between Vietnamese troops and remnants of the toppled Phnom Penh regime. (AP/Wide World Photos)

war from 1979 to 1991. The United States, China, and Thailand gave them crucial help and support. After 1982 the resistance coalition, including the Khmer Rouge, were given a United Nations (UN) seat—the only government in exile so honored. "It was clear that China and the United States were willing to support this state of affairs as punishment for Vietnam's invading Cambodia, standing up to China, and defeating the United States [in the Vietnam War]," writes Chandler.

The October, 1991, Paris Agreement calling for UN-sponsored elections was signed by all four factions and several foreign governments, including the United States and Vietnam. The Khmer Rouge reneged on the agreement by refusing to turn over their weapons to the UN Transitional Authority in Cambodia (UNTAC). The government army also failed to disarm completely.   .

The May 1993 Elections. Afraid the government Cambodian People's Party (CPP) would win the May, 1993, elections, the Khmer Rouge boycotted the polls.

Instead FUNCINPEC, the royalist party led by Sihanouk's son Prince Norodom Ranariddh—allied during the civil war with the Khmer Rouge—won a slight plurality. Many considered the Khmer Rouge election boycott a tactical error and their subsequent call for inclusion in the planned new government a desperate attempt to regain lost political ground.

Though the election boycott had cost them political credibility, no one seemed sure of the Khmer Rouge's military power or how best to deal with them. In July, 1993, nominal faction leader Khieu Samphan said the Khmer Rouge were willing to join an integrated national army. (Pol Pot was believed to remain in overall control of the group.) The same month a visiting U.S. diplomat said her country would not support a government that included the Khmer Rouge, and China vowed it would give the latter no more military aid.

Sihanouk, now Cambodia's "head of state," abandoned plans to consider giving the Khmer Rouge an advisory role in the new government. He said "incessant" American warnings were driving him toward "a mental asylum." Sihanouk, who had briefly been the Khmer Rouge's figurehead head of state, also warned against "sweet words," saying that "we have already tasted the sweetness of the Khmer Rouge." In August, 1993, Ranariddh, now interim coprime minister with CPP leader Hun Sen, vowed to retaliate against further Khmer Rouge attacks, which continued sporadically. In an August 6, 1993, radio broadcast, the Khmer Rouge vowed to continue fighting until they were admitted into a new national government and army.

Postelection Prospects. Early in the civil war, "the Thai military fed, clothed, and restored to health several thousand DK soldiers [and gave them] arms, ammunition, and military supplies from China, ferried through Thai ports," according to Chandler. Thailand also harbored Khmer Rouge soldiers and leaders. Cross-border trade in gems, timber, and other products from areas of western Cambodia it controlled had helped fund the group. In September, 1993, the spokesperson for Thailand's military Supreme Command said Khmer Rouge soldiers who crossed the border would not be handed over to the new Cambodian government, which he continued to call a "fac-

tion." After the elections, the specter of continuing Thai economic and military cooperation with the Khmer Rouge remained a wild card in assessments of the group's ability to survive.—*Ethan Casey*

SUGGESTED READINGS: • Chandler, David P. *Brother Number One: A Political Biography of Pol Pot.* Boulder, Colo.: Westview Press, 1992. • Chandler, David P. *A History of Cambodia.* 2d ed. Boulder, Colo.: Westview Press, 1992. • Jackson, Karl D., comp. *Cambodia, 1975-1978: Rendezvous with Death.* Princeton, N.J.: Princeton University Press, 1989. • Schanberg, Sydney H. *The Death and Life of Dith Pran.* New York: Penguin Books, 1985. • Shawcross, William. *Sideshow: Kissinger, Nixon, and the Destruction of Cambodia.* London: The Hogarth Press, 1986.

Khmer special events: There are two types of special events traditionally celebrated by the Khmer: calendrical events and life-cycle events. To these may be added contemporary events such as fund-raisers for political parties or other organizations and anniversary celebrations for institutions such as businesses, schools, and community groups. In general, Cambodian Americans seem to enjoy producing and participating frequently

Oscar-winner Haing Ngor, who starred in The Killing Fields *went on to produce a documentary about Cambodian refugees.* (AP/Wide World Photos)

in such special events, which usually feature music and dancing.

Calendrical Events. The two most important annual events are New Year (*chol chhnam thmei*, "entering the New Year," when the sun enters the new zodiac sign) on April 12 or 13 and the Festival of the Ancestors (*prachum ben*, "gathering the offerings" for the souls of the dead), a two-week observation culminating in late September or early October. Exact dates are fixed each year according to the lunisolar Cambodian calendar.

Each New Year celebration features some visual representation of the animal associated with the year, from the original zodiac cycle of twelve animals as first noted in an inscription dated 992 C.E. A mound of sand (*phnom ksac*) may be erected, variously interpreted to represent Mount Meru, the center of the universe according to Indian cosmology; the celestial stupa in which the Buddha's hair was placed when he renounced his worldly life; or the grains of sand deposited individually by devoted Buddhists to absolve sin. Small altars may be placed at the cardinal and intercardinal directions to the divinities of space, with an

extra altar at the east for the god of hell, Yumoreac (Yama Raja).

Monks are invited on both occasions to a suitable hall where they lead the community in Pali chants from early to late morning. Special prayers and observations are made on each occasion by the lay clergy (*achar*). Before noon the monks are fed with the finest dishes cooked by each family, with major items such as roast pigs purchased by the community. After the monks depart, the remaining food is retrieved by the families to distribute among themselves and any guests present. All who enter the hall are expected to give a donation at the door to defray the costs of the event, which includes feeding everyone present, alms for the monks, payments for hall rental, and fees for musicians and dancers.

Following the feast, staged entertainment by local or visiting classical and folk dancers and traditional *pinnpeat* or *mohori* musicians may be offered. Traditional instruments may include the xylophone, *roneat*; gong circle, *korng vung*; oboe, *sralai*; lute, *takhe*; hammered dulcimer, *khimm*; fiddle, *tror*; fipple flute, *khloy*; drums, *sampho* and *skor thomm*; and hand cym-

Young Cambodian American dancer performs at Cambodian New Year festivities. (Claire Rydell)

As part of both the Cambodian New Year and Festival of the Ancestors, offerings of the finest foods are presented to the presiding Buddhist monks. (Eric Crystal)

bals, *chhing*. Special dances for the New Year include the story of Thomabal and Kabel Moha Prohm, who loses a riddle contest and must forfeit his head, which is then carried through the heavens by the goddess of the day of the week in which the New Year falls; *Trott* ("to break or cut off"), a folk dance representing a deer being sacrificed to expiate sin; and *Chung*, a singing game played with balls of cloth. These entertainments are followed by social dancing to modern bands playing the latest style of contemporary Khmer pop music. Social dancing style reflects both Cambodian *ramvung* ("circle dance") traditions as well as contemporary influences.

Life-Cycle Events. The wedding is the most elaborate life-cycle event and involves many different stages, shortened to two days from at least three in Cambodia. On the penultimate day, monks recite sacred scriptures and sprinkle lustral water on the engaged couple, who must bow from a specific seated position on the floor during the entire ceremony. A mistress of protocol supervises their costume and actions. The culmination occurs on the final day in the wedding ceremony, when the groom's procession walks to the home of the bride-to-be. The entire procession of musicians, groom, matchmakers (*meba*, "mother-father," or representatives of both the groom's and the bride's parents), best men, relatives, and guests bearing gifts are then seated in the living room to await the entrance of the bride. Musicians and singers entreat her to emerge with one of the many special songs sung for each stage of the wedding, in a unique repertoire and style called *phleng kar* (music for weddings). Cassette recordings are sometimes used when live musicians, always in heavy demand, are not available. The musical instruments used include the plucked and bowed strings, fipple flute, and small drums heard at the New Year, without the xylophones and gongs.

A lay priest (*achar*), uttering Pali verses and Khmer admonitions, presides over the ceremony, in which the bride and groom are feted as if they are queen and king, groomed and entertained by heavenly singers. These singers actually dance during the haircutting ritual while singing "Kat Sok" ("Cutting Hair") in which a lock of hair is cut from the bride and groom to honor them and to symbolize the preparation for a new life together. In the *baisey* (rice of the goddess) ritual, the family and guests pluck white threads from a tiered offering made of banana stalks and leaves. They tie these to the wrists of the couple while uttering good wishes. Another ritual is the circling of candles and *popil* (a spadelike form) around the couple numerous times.

At the end, areca palm blossoms are sprinkled on the couple as a symbol of fertility and of the value of the areca nut, an essential element in all stages of wedding negotiations. Humor is enjoyed during many segments of the ceremony, especially when the couple

A Cambodian couple is resplendent in their wedding finery. (Smithsonian Institution)

repairs to the bridal chamber to feed one another fresh fruits in a teasing game. The married couple then changes costume for at least the third time that day and rejoins their family and guests for the wedding feast, often held in a rented restaurant with live band and social dancing.—*Amy Catlin*

SUGGESTED READINGS: • Catlin, Amy. "Apsaras and Other Goddesses in Khmer Music, Dance, and Ritual." In *APSARA: The Feminine in Cambodian Art*, edited by Amy Catlin. Los Angeles: Woman's Building, 1987. • Commission des moeurs et coutumes du Cambodge. *Ceremonies des douze mois: Fetes annuelles cambodgiennes*. Paris: Centre de Documentation et de Recherche sur la Civilisation Khmere, 1985. • Commission des moeurs et coutumes du Cambodge. *Ceremonies privees des cambodgiens*. Paris: Centre de Documentation et de Recherche sur la Civilisation Khmere, 1985. • Smith, Jeffrey Merrill. *Cultural Comparison Chart: American and Cambodian Cultures*. Rev. Ed. Portland, Maine: Portland Public Schools, 1988.

Khmu: Tribal group from the highlands of northern mainland Southeast Asia. More than half a million in number, they straddle the national boundaries of northern Thailand, northern Laos, the southwest region of the People's Republic of China, and northwest Vietnam. Most live in the uplands of northern Laos and the Bolovens Plateau of the southern part of the country. Unlike the HMONG and MIEN, who traditionally live at the top of mountain ranges, the Khmu typically are found at middle-level elevations.

Following the end of the Vietnam War and the establishment of the (Communist) Lao People's Democratic Republic in 1975, more than 3,500 Khmu fled from Laos as refugees, most during 1978 and 1979. Of these, approximately 3,000 settled in the United States. Most Khmu settled in California, but there are also smaller communities in Boston, Seattle, and other parts of the country.

Distinct in language and customs from both the lowland Lao and the upland Hmong and Mien of Laos, the Khmu are sometimes classified together with other smaller middle-elevation tribal groups collectively referred to as the "Lao Theung."

Language. Khmu is a Mon-Khmer language belonging to the wider Austroasiatic language family. Northern Khmu, which includes many bitonal dialects, is spoken in northwestern Laos and parts of northern Thailand adjacent to the Lao border. Khmu living in other parts of Laos, as well as those in China and Vietnam, speak the southern nontonal form of Khmu.

Today most Khmu are bilingual or even multilingual. Khmu is spoken at home, the language of the country in which they live is used at school, and possibly other languages are employed for trading and market purposes.

Culture and Religion. Like many upland tribal groups, the Khmu practice swidden, or slash-and-burn, agriculture. Fields are cleared, burned, and planted with rice and other crops for one or two years and then left to become fallow. The group meanwhile moves to new ground, returning to the original plot after a number of years.

Recently the practice of swidden agriculture has come under attack from both the Lao and Thai governments. Many Khmu have been forced to relocate to the lowlands and form permanent settled villages, raising rice by the wet instead of the dry rice method. The Khmu also hunt, fish, and gather forest products such as bamboo for food and for housing, baskets, and other purposes.

While Khmu who have assimilated to Lao culture often become Buddhists, and a small number of Khmu have been converted to Christianity, most are animists. Shamans officiate at Khmu religious ceremonies, diagnose causes of calamities and recommend appropriate sacrifices to the spirits, and engage in healing ceremonies.

Khmu social structure is patrilineal, and family ties are strong. Family members belong to clans that are in turn classified into three major lineages. Khmu marry outside their own clan and ideally also outside their lineage. To marry within one's own clan would be considered incestuous. Elaborate arrangements of wife-giving and wife-taking take place between the clans. Khmu women are accorded relatively high status and must consent before being given away in marriage. Eligible young women command a good bride-price; if a young man's family is unable to come up with the required amount of money, customarily the young man will work for his prospective father-in-law until the bride-price is paid off. Even in the United States, Khmu refugees still follow traditional bride-price practices.

History. It has not been easy for historians to piece

Director of Lao-Khmu Association points out the homeland of the Khmu. (Ben Klaffke)

Khmu students participate in the Lao-Khmu Association educational programs. Today most Khmu are bilingual or multi-lingual. (Ben Klaffke)

together the Khmu past. The Khmu did not develop a writing system and have no early written records or historical inscriptions. According to their oral tradition, however, their history dates from the establishment of the Khmu domain of Muong Svaa during the first millennium C.E. Centered at the confluence of the Ou and Mekong rivers, the capital of Muong Svaa was located near where Luang Prabang stands today.

From the eleventh century onward, the Tai peoples, or the parent group from which the modern Lao and Thai derive, began migrating into mainland Southeast Asia from southern China and northwestern Vietnam, settling in valleys along the major rivers and their tributaries. Khmu groups already living in these areas either intermarried with and became assimilated into Tai culture or were forced into the mountains.

Although pushed to the periphery of Tai/Lao centers of power, the Khmu never lived in isolation. The Lao have always regarded the Khmu as the original inhabitants of Laos and have incorporated this recognition into origin legends and numerous local rituals. Over the centuries the Khmu also traded upland rice for lowland cloth, salt, and metal and continued to intermarry with the Tai/Lao, from whom they took many customs.

As the Tai/Lao came to dominate lowland polities, however, increasingly they treated the politically weak and fragmented Khmu as social inferiors. The Khmu were forced to pay ritual tribute or taxes to lowland rulers and were used as conscripted laborers. For years they were often referred to as "kha," or "slave," a pejorative term used by lowland Lao and Thai for upland peoples of the Austroasiatic language family.

Modern Situation. Even during the period of French colonial rule in Laos from the late nineteenth through the mid-twentieth centuries, the Khmu remained a subordinate people. The French interacted with Lao government officials and made no attempts to draw tribal peoples into the body politic or to provide them with education.

The Khmu were, however, swept up into the 1946-1954 Indochina War, which ended with the defeat of France at Dien Bien Phu in 1954. They also fought in large numbers in the Vietnam War that followed, both with the Vietnam-supported forces of the Communist Pathet Lao and with those of the Royal Lao government supported by the United States. Casualties ran extremely high. The Khmu strongholds of Sam Neua and Phong Saly in northeastern Laos sustained some of the worst bombing of the war. For some of the Khmu survivors, military service did, however, provide an opportunity for upward social mobility. Today several high-ranking military officers and government officials in the Lao People's Democratic Republic are Khmu, while many Khmu who fought on the Royal Lao government side and fled from Laos after 1975 are today carving out new lives for themselves and their families in the United States.—*E. Jane Keyes*

SUGGESTED READINGS: • Kunstadter, Peter, ed. *Southeast Asian Tribes, Minorities and Nations.* 2 vols. Princeton, N.J.: Princeton University Press, 1967. • LeBar, Frank M., G. C. Hickey, and J. K. Musgrave. *Ethnic Groups of Mainland Southeast Asia.* New Haven, Conn.: Human Relations Area Files Press, 1964. • Lewis, Judy, ed. *Minority Cultures of Laos: Kammu, Laua, Lahu, Hmong, and Mien.* Rancho Cordova, Calif.: Southeast Asia Community Resource Center, 1992. • Lindell, Kristina, Hakan Lundstrom, Jan-Olof Svantesson, and Damrong Tayanin. *The Kammu Year: Its Lore and Music.* Scandinavian Institute of Asian Studies: Studies on Asian Topics 4. London: Curzon Press, 1982.

Kiang, Peter Nien-chu: Scholar. Kiang is a graduate of Harvard College and the Harvard University Graduate School of Education, from which he earned his Ed.D. degree in 1991. An assistant professor at the University of Massachusetts, Boston, he teaches courses in multicultural education and Asian American Studies. He has published widely in his field, particularly in the areas of education and Asian Americans, minority and immigrant community development, and multicultural curriculum design. Kiang has also made several videos and sixteen-millimeter (16mm) films on the Asian American experience, including *Cahoon Hollow* (1979), an animated work that explored the legacy of the Vietnam War; the film was exhibited at the Asian American International Film Festival (AAIFF) in 1980. In 1980 he established, and until 1986 directed, the nationally recognized Asian American Resource Workshop, located in Boston, which sponsors educational, cultural, and community advocacy programs for Asian Americans throughout New England. Profiles on him have been published in the *Boston Globe* and *Boston Magazine*, and he has been quoted in *The New York Times* and *Time* magazine and interviewed by the *CBS Evening News* and ABC's *20/20.*

Kibei: Japanese Americans, usually Nisei, who returned to the United States after being sent by their parents to spend a portion of their childhood in Japan, often for purposes of education.

The Japanese term Kibei literally means "return to America," but it refers to those Japanese Americans sent to Japan in their youth who then returned to their immigrant parents in North America. Kibei were indistinguishable from those who returned to Japan for occasions such as the death of a relative, so it remains unclear how many kibei there were.

Kibei were more likely to be young men than young women. As many as one-fifth of Nisei males may have been Kibei. Usually the children selected to return to Japan were only part of a sibling set. In other words Japanese American families who sent children to Japan sent only one or two of their children. Some brothers and sisters remained in the United States or Hawaii.

Children selected were often the designated successors of their households. The parents wanted the successor to spend time in Japan so that he could learn the ways of the house and be known to the grandparents. Some parents were uncertain about the future in the midst of the exclusionist immigration policies enacted by the United States in 1908 and 1924, and they hoped their children would be familiar enough with the language and culture of Japan to return if necessary. Some children may have been sent to Japan to free their mothers of child-care duties for work in family businesses.

During incarceration in the camps on the American mainland, some Kibei were denounced to the U.S. government as possibly suspect in their allegiances by other Japanese internees who were anxious to prove their loyalty to the United States. Kibei had learned more about Japanese culture, including the spoken and written language, and were thought to be less acculturated in the American way of life.

As cultural symbols the Kibei epitomized the conflict experienced by many Japanese Americans who were torn between two cultures and forced by wartime events to choose one.

Kido, Saburo (1902, Hilo, Territory of Hawaii—April 4, 1977): Activist. Raised in Hawaii, he moved to San Francisco to study law at Hastings College of the Law, from which he was graduated in 1926. A founding member of the JAPANESE AMERICAN CITIZENS LEAGUE (JACL), he was elected president of the group in 1940. He played an instrumental role in developing the organization's policy of cooperation with the U.S. government during World War II concerning the Japanese American internment. While interned in the Pos-

Saburo Kido was a founding member of the Japanese American Citizens League. (Pacific Citizen)

TON relocation center, Kido was viciously beaten by fellow internees who regarded him as a collaborator. After the war he continued to play an active role in the JACL.

Kikuchi, Charles (1917—Sept. 25, 1988): Social worker and researcher. Born in the San Francisco Bay Area, Kikuchi was the son of an Issei barbershop owner and his wife. Rejected by his father at an early age, he was placed in an orphanage when he was eight years old. After graduating from high school in 1934, Kikuchi moved to San Francisco to attend college. Although he graduated from San Francisco State College in 1939, Kikuchi was unable to find suitable permanent employment. Like many other college-educated Nisei, he worked at a variety of menial, low-paying jobs.

In 1939, Kikuchi's important autobiographical essay, "A Young American with a Japanese Face," had been published anonymously in Louis Adamic's anthology, *From Many Lands*. Eventually he found work with the California State Employment Service as a survey taker, compiling responses for a survey on Nisei occupations. He enrolled at the University of California at Berkeley in the fall of 1941 to pursue graduate studies in social welfare.

After the Japanese attack on Pearl Harbor, Kikuchi was hired as a researcher for the Japanese American Evacuation and Resettlement Study, led by Berkeley sociologist Dorothy Swaine Thomas. He also began to keep a diary at this time. Kikuchi completed field surveys at the Tanforan Assembly Center, a temporary detention center in Northern California, and at the GILA RIVER relocation center in Arizona. In 1943, he began chronicling the resettlement of certain camp residents to new homes in Chicago. In 1950, after serving in the military, Kikuchi became a social worker with the Veterans Administration in New York, where he remained until his retirement in 1973.

A selection from Kikuchi's diary, *The Kikuchi Diary: Chronicle of an American Concentration Camp*, edited by John Modell, was published in 1973.

Kikuchi-Yngojo, Robert (b. Sept. 22, 1953, San Francisco, Calif.): Performing artist. The first Filipino American to introduce traditional *kulintang* gong music to California, he founded the San Francisco Kulintang Ensemble and codirected Eth-Noh-Tec, an Asian American organization dedicated to cultural performance and education. Fusing traditional and contemporary music and dance, his works have been featured in such movies as *Chan Is Missing* (1982), *Carved in Silence* (1988), and *Eat a Bowl of Tea* (1989).

Kim, Bok-lim C. (b. 1930): Scholar. She has written extensively on Korean American sociological experiences and history. Her books include *The Asian Americans: Changing Patterns, Changing Needs* (1978). In *Women in Shadows: A Handbook for Service Providers Working with Asian Wives of U.S. Military Personnel* (1981), she was a contributing author.

Kim, Charles (Kim Ho; May 25, 1884, Korea—Jan. 5, 1968): Business leader and philanthropist. Born Kim Ho, Charles Kim left Korea for the United States in 1914. Settling in California's San Joaquin Valley, Kim established the KIM BROTHERS COMPANY along with the help of his friend Kim Hyung-soon, better known as Harry Kim. Profits from their ventures into fruit cultivation and distribution as well as nursery management allowed the Kims to provide generous donations to the Korean American community. Charles Kim served as chairman of the United Korean Committee, a political organization dedicated to supporting the Korean government in exile during World War II, and was cofounder of the Korean Foundation, a charitable organization that provided scholarships to deserving Korean American students.

Kim, Elaine H. (b. Feb. 26, 1942, New York, N.Y.): Scholar. A professor of Asian American Studies at the University of California, Berkeley, and one of the first tenured Asian American women at a major American university, Kim is the author of *Asian American Literature: An Introduction to the Writings and Their Social Context* (1982), a pioneering work in its field. She coedited *Making Waves: An Anthology of Writings by and About Asian American Women* (1989) and *Writing Self, Writing Nation: A Collection of Essays on Theresa Hak Kyung Cha's "Dictee"* (1993).

Elaine Kim, Professor of Asian American Studies. (Asian Week)

A past president of the ASSOCIATION FOR ASIAN AMERICAN STUDIES, Kim has cofounded several groups, including ASIAN IMMIGRANT ADVOCATES and ASIAN WOMEN UNITED of California.

Kim, Ernie (b. Sept. 2, 1918, Manteca, Calif.): Ceramist. Born to early Korean immigrants, he was graduated from the Ceramics Craft Studio in Mountain View in 1955. He later became chair of the ceramics department at the San Francisco Art Institute and director of the Richmond Art Center. He is well known for his ceramic work and has received numerous awards.

Kim, Eugene Eun-Chol (b. May 5, 1928, Wonsan, Korea): Scholar. After immigrating to the United States in 1965, he became a professor of education and ethnic studies and program director of Asian American Studies at California State University, Sacramento. His publications include *American Mosaic: Selected Readings for America's Multicultural Heritage* (1993) and *Strangers to This Land: Interdisciplinary Perspective on Ethnic Studies* (1986). He has also coauthored *A Resource Guide for Secondary School Teaching: Planning for Competence* (1990).

Kim, Haeryen (b. July 14, 1948, Iri Chonpuk, Republic of Korea): Theater director, actor, and producer. After completing degrees in English literature and theater at Seoul's Korea and Chung Ang universities, Kim emigrated to the United States in 1985 and continued her theater studies at New York University. In 1988 Kim founded two Korean American theater companies in New York City. The Seoul Theatre Ensemble (STE) drew upon traditional Korean theater techniques and cultural themes; the Educational Theatre for Asian Teenagers (ETAT) utilized experimental theater techniques, such as oral histories, collaborative scriptwriting, improvisation, and audience participation. Both companies encouraged Asian American adolescents to find and speak in their own voices. Together the STE and ETAT constituted an umbrella organization, The Silk Road Playhouse, through which Kim produced intercultural works, including *America Far-Merica* (1988), *Joyness of the Youth* (1989), *Sesame Leaves . . . Sleepwalking in Korea* (1990), and *Peony* (1991). In 1992 Kim's company produced the dance drama *Deungsinbul*, about the self-immolation of a Korean monk, at the LaMama Experimental Theatre Club in New York City.

Kim, Hyung-chan (b. Nov. 4, 1938): Scholar. With his pioneering reference works and his studies of Asian Americans and the law, Kim has made a major contribution to Asian American Studies. A professor at Western Washington University, Kim received a B.A. from Hankuk University of Foreign Studies in Seoul, South Korea (1961), and B.A. (1964), M.A. (1965), and Ed.D. (1969) degrees from George Peabody College for Teachers. Kim's *Dictionary of Asian American History* (1986) was the first major reference work in the field of Asian American Studies. He edited *Asian American Studies: An Annotated Bibliography and Research Guide* (1989). His study *Asian Americans and the Supreme Court: A Documentary History*

(1992) was followed by *A Legal History of Asian Americans, 1790-1990* (1994). In addition, he has a number of other works to his credit as author, coauthor, or editor.

Kim, Illsoo (b. 1944): Scholar. Kim holds a Ph.D. degree from the Graduate Center of the City University of New York. He has worked extensively among the Korean community of New York. His books include *New Urban Immigrants: The Korean Community in New York* (1981), *The Koreans: Small Business in an Urban Frontier* (1987), and *Immigrants to Urban America: The Korean Community in the New York Metropolitan Area* (1991).

Kim, Jay C. (Kim Chang Joon; b. March 27, 1939, Seoul, Korea): Businessman and U.S. congressman. Kim, an only child, was born Kim Chang Joon to a Seoul restaurant manager and his wife. During the Korean War, the family home was destroyed, and Kim and his parents walked ninety miles to Taejon, pulling their belongings on a cart.

Kim returned to Seoul after the war to attend high school and begin college. After a stint in the military, he moved to the United States, enrolling in a California community college. He then transferred to the University of Southern California (USC), from which he earned bachelor's and master's degrees in civil engineering. He married Jung Ok (June) Kim in 1962, and the couple had three children.

After he was graduated from USC, Kim worked as a city engineer for the California cities of Ontario and Compton and earned a master's degree in public administration from California State University, Los Angeles. He also became active in politics, helping to found and serving as president of the KOREAN AMERICAN POLITICAL ASSOCIATION.

In the late 1970's, Kim used Small Business Administration (SBA) loans to form JayKim Engineers. By the mid-1980's, the firm had become highly successful, winning millions of dollars in government contracts. In 1985, he was named the SBA's small businessman of the year for the Los Angeles area. Yet his firm was also the target of criticism from auditors for alleged overcharges and lax bookkeeping.

In 1990, Kim ran a successful campaign for a seat on the Diamond Bar, California, city council. In 1992, running as a Republican candidate for the U.S. House of Representatives for the newly created 41st Congressional District, he became the first Asian immigrant to win election to the U.S. Congress; his election was

Congressman Jay C. Kim on the steps of the U.S. Capitol Building, Washington, D.C. (Korea Times)

widely hailed as a sign of the increasing importance of the Asian American community in Southern California. In 1994, however, the Federal Bureau of Investigation (FBI) and Internal Revenue Service (IRS) began a widely publicized investigation into Kim's finances as part of a probe into alleged violations of campaign-spending laws.

Kim, Kyu-sik (Jan. 27, 1881, Korea—1950): Activist. Adopted by an American missionary family, he came to the United States as a student in 1897. Because of Japan's colonial rule in Korea, he began a thirty-two-year exile in 1913, during which he served as foreign minister, education minister, and head of delegates of the Korean provisional government-in-exile in Shanghai. He returned to the United States in 1919 and chaired the Korean Commission to Europe and the United States until conflicts with Syngman RHEE caused him to return to China. There, in 1935, he was elected president of the Korean National Revolutionary Party, which established a branch in Los Angeles, in 1943. (See KOREAN NATIONAL REVOLUTIONARY PARTY OF LOS ANGELES.)

Kim, Randall Duk (b. Sept. 24, 1943, Honolulu, Territory of Hawaii): Actor. Of Korean Chinese descent, Kim forged a successful acting career playing title roles in Shakespeare's *Titus Andronicus* (1972), *Richard III* (1973; 1974-1975), *Pericles* (1974), *The Tempest* (1974; 1975-1976), and *Hamlet* (1976; 1978-1979) at theaters throughout the United States and filling major roles in stage classics by Goldoni, Brecht, Moliere, and Williams. Kim was critically acclaimed for his portrayals of Tam Lum (*The Chickencoop Chinaman*, 1972) and Fred Eng (*Year of the Dragon*, 1974) in the New York premieres of Frank CHIN's plays at the American Place Theatre. In 1977 Kim, Charles Bright, and Anne Occhiogrosso founded The American Players in Washington, D.C., later relocating the company to Spring Green, Wisconsin, where Kim continued to star in productions of Sophocles, Shakespeare, Marlowe, Chekhov, Ibsen, Moliere, and O'Neill for more than a decade. He returned to Hawaii in 1991 to continue working in the theater. Kim's approaches to acting are noted in Mary Maher's study *Modern Hamlets and Their Soliloquies* (1993) and Holly Hill's *Actors' Lives* (1993).

Kim, Richard E. (b. Mar. 13, 1932, Hamhung City, Korea): Novelist and educator. Born in the northern portion of Korea as Kim Eun Kook, Kim enlisted in the Republic of Korea (ROK) army at the age of eighteen. Serving as aide-de-camp to the commanding officer of the ROK 2nd Corps and as a liaison officer to the American commander of the U.S. Army 7th Division during the Korean War, Kim was eventually promoted to the rank of first lieutenant. In 1954 Kim emigrated to the United States. He attended Middlebury College in Vermont, where he graduated with a bachelor's degree in 1959. Kim continued his academic career at The Johns Hopkins University, earning his M.A. degree in 1960. He went on to earn two more master's degrees: an M.F.A. from Iowa State University in 1962 and an M.A. from Harvard University in 1963. Kim took a teaching position at Long Beach State College from 1963 to 1964. His first novel, *The Martyred* (1964), drew heavily on his wartime experiences. Set in Korea in 1950, the novel relates the experiences of a young Korean intelligence officer who is charged with investigating the murders of twelve Christian ministers by Communist troops in Pyongyang prior to that city's occupation by the ROK army. A thought-provoking work combining deep philosophical themes with elements of a traditional thriller, the novel was nominated for the National Book Award in 1964. Kim received a Guggenheim Fellowship for 1964-1965 and joined the staff of the English Department at the University of Massachusetts, Amherst, in 1964. *The Innocent* (1968), his second novel, was set in postwar Korea and traced the relationships of a group of men planning a military coup to overthrow the civilian government of South Korea. In 1970, Kim published a collection of autobiographical pieces entitled *Lost Names: Scenes from a Korean Boyhood*, which was reissued in a paperback edition in 1988.

Kim, Warren Y. (Won-yong Kim; Dec. 25, 1896, Seoul, Korea—Los Angeles, Calif.): Activist and community leader. Fleeing Korea, he came to the United States in 1917 to study law and government. Throughout his life he played an active role in the affairs of the Korean American community. He helped to establish the Korean Foundation, which gave scholarships to students of Korean ancestry, in 1957 and the Korean Center, which eventually became the Korean Association of Southern California, in 1963. Kim also held posts in the Korean National Association (KNA), a U.S.-based organization supporting the Korean independence movement. He wrote *Chaemi Hanin Osimnyon-sa* (1959), a fifty-year history of the Koreans in America.

Kim, Willa (b. Los Angeles, Calif.): Costume designer. Educated at Los Angeles' Chouinard Institute of Art, Kim made innovations in the field of dance costuming that have earned for her a permanent place in American theater history. Her use of stretch fabrics and unique approaches to fabric painting set standards for dance costuming. Kim's own designs have been seen at the Eliot Feld Ballet, San Francisco Ballet, Joffrey Ballet, Glen Tetley Dance Company, Harkness Ballet, American Ballet Theatre, and Alvin Ailey Dance Theatre. Since 1966, when she designed Edward Albee's *Malcolm*, her first Broadway production, Kim has designed for more than one hundred theatrical productions, ballets, operas, and television productions. In 1981 she received a Tony Award for best costumes for Duke Ellington's *Sophisticated Ladies* and an Emmy for her work on Michael Smuin's ballet version of *The Tempest*. She won her second Tony Award in 1991 for the musical *The Will Rogers Follies*. Kim continuously garnered a host of additional honors throughout her career, including Drama Desk Awards, *Variety New York Drama Critics' Poll Awards, and Obie Awards*.

Kim, Willyce: Writer. A Korean American poet and novelist who has written on lesbian themes, Kim is the author of several collections of poetry, including the chapbooks *Curtains of Light* (1971), *Eating Artichokes* (1972), and *Under the Rolling Sky* (1976). Her novels include *Dancer Dawkins and the California Kid* (1985) and *Dead Heat* (1988).

Kim, Yongjeung (b. Apr. 2, 1898, Kum-san, Korea): Publisher and editor. A student in 1922, Kim left his studies to become a wholesale agent for the KIM BROTHERS COMPANY. In 1928 he helped establish the K. & S. Company, which became one of the most prosperous wholesale businesses in Los Angeles' Korean American community. Kim was public relations director for the Korean National Association (KNA) from 1939 until 1943 and a member of the United Korean Committee in America from 1941 until 1943. During World War II he assisted the U.S. Office of War Information during its broadcasts to Korea and the Far East. As founder and president of the Korean Affairs Institute (Washington, D.C.), he published and edited *The Voice of Korea*. The monthly newsletter, published from 1943 until 1962, advocated the unification of Korea through neutralization.

Kim, Young Oak (b. 1918, Los Angeles, Calif.): Army officer. Widely acclaimed as one of the outstanding U.S. Army officers of World War II and the Korean War, Kim was one of the most decorated soldiers of his generation. Unlike the men of the Japanese American 100TH INFANTRY BATTALION with whom he served in World War II, Kim was of Korean ancestry.

Because of the limited career opportunities open to Korean Americans in the 1930's, Kim had left junior college to work as a butcher. Drafted as an Army private in January, 1941, Kim's intelligence and leadership skills were noted in basic training. Soon thereafter—much to his surprise—he received orders to attend Army Officer Candidate School, where he again excelled.

Commissioned in January, 1943, Kim's first assignment was with the newly formed 100th Battalion, still in training at CAMP SHELBY, Mississippi. Because the Japanese and Koreans were traditional enemies, Kim's commanding officers believed his assignment to the 100th a mistake and offered to have him reassigned. Kim refused the offer and took command of the Second Platoon, Company B, soon drawing up infantry training plans for both platoons of the company.

Upon arrival in Italy, Kim personally captured the

Highly decorated Korean American army officer Young Oak Kim. (The Korea Society/Los Angeles)

first three German prisoners of war taken by the 100th Battalion. He became battalion intelligence officer at the Battle of Cassino and soon rose to operations officer. Already awarded the Silver Star, he earned the Distinguished Service Cross (next in importance only to the Congressional Medal of Honor) at Anzio for crawling six hundred yards in the daylight to capture and return safely with two German soldiers, who later provided essential information about the German army's position.

Kim continued his military career following World War II. In 1952, as commander of the First Battalion, 31st Infantry Division, Major Kim was widely recognized as one of the most effective field commanders of the Korean conflict. Although distinguished by many more successes before his retirement, Colonel Young Oak Kim remains best known for his service with the Army's 100th Infantry Battalion during World War II.

Kim, Young-ik (b. May 15, 1920, Korea): Writer. Immigrating to the United States as a student, he became a naturalized citizen. His highly acclaimed short stories include "From Below the Bridge" (1958), "The Happy Days" (1960), "The Dividing Gourd" (1962), "The Blue in the Seed" (1964), "Love in Winter" (1964), and "The Shoes from Yan San Valley" (1970).

Kim Brothers Company: Wholesale agricultural business founded in 1921 by friends Charles Kim and Harry Kim in the town of Reedley near Fresno in California's San Joaquin Valley. In addition to establishing their own orchards, nurseries, and fruit-packing plants, the Kims expanded their company to develop new hybrid varieties of peaches, nectarines, and other fruit. Upon their retirement in 1962, they were able to sell the company for $1.4 million. During their stewardship of the company, the Kims used profits from numerous ventures, including the development of fuzzless peach varieties such as Le Grand and Sun Grand, to make substantial charitable donations in support of the Korean American community. Responsible for donating $10,000 toward the founding of Los Angeles' Korean Community Center, they were also instrumental in establishing scholarships through the Korean Foundation that enable students of Korean ancestry to pursue higher education.

Kim chee: Korean side dish. It is made of fermented Chinese cabbage, shredded radishes, dried red peppers, scallions, diced fresh garlic, and ginger.

Kim Il Sung (Kim Song Ju; Apr. 15, 1912, near Pyongyang, Korea—July 8, 1994, Pyongyang, North Korea): Political leader and official. Kim was the leader of the Communist regime and party in North Korea. He was born into a farming family. At age fourteen he moved with his family to Manchuria, where he joined the Korean Communist Party in 1931. The following year he became the leader of a small anti-Japanese guerrilla regime. His political involvements attracted the attention of Soviet military authorities. Through their connection, Kim went to the Soviet Union, where he was given training and served as an officer in the Red Army.

In 1945, after the end of World War II, Kim returned to his country as Soviet forces took over the northern part of Korea. Backed by the Soviet occupation authorities, Kim was thrust into a leadership position when, in 1946, the Soviets established a provisional government in northern Korea and put him at its head. By the end of the occupation in 1948, the Korean Workers Party, dominated by Soviet-trained Koreans, had established firm control and Kim became premier of the new Democratic People's Republic of Korea.

After 1948, Kim consolidated his power by eliminating rival factions and forming a coalition that assured a Communist domination of North Korea under his control. With Soviet backing, Kim started the Korean War (1950-1953) by attempting to conquer the South. Only Chinese intervention saved his regime. After the war, Kim embarked on programs of rapid reconstruction, industrialization, and military build-up. In 1956 Kim crushed opponents who denounced him and his policies. From that time his leadership was characterized by austerity and a growing cult of personality. By 1966 only members of his own faction of Manchurian Koreans remained at the top.

Kim became president of North Korea in 1972. As president he urged reunification of north and south, a proposal that in 1980 also included the withdrawal of U.S. troops stationed in South Korea. He also expressed his government's willingness to forge friendly relations with capitalist nations.

Although Kim made occasional conciliatory gestures toward South Korea and the United States, Kim's attitude toward them was generally hostile. Moreover, news of North Korea's nuclear capabilities, and the country's unwillingness to allow United Nations (UN) inspection of its nuclear facilities, have made the international community wary of North Korea's military intentions, while also alienating the United States and South Korea.

Kim Ku (1876, Hwanghae Province, Korea—June 26, 1949, Seoul, Republic of Korea): Government leader and political activist. Kim eventually served as the head of the Korean provisional government in exile and was an ardent anti-Japanese nationalist. Following the liberation of Korea in 1945, he played an active role in South Korean politics until his assassination by an officer of the Korean army.

A commoner by birth, Kim studied the Chinese Confucian classics as a child. In 1892 he became involved in the Tonghak movement's push for equality in Korean society and later its revolt against the Japanese occupation. He continued to work for and lead nationalist organizations in Korea through the March 1, 1919, independence uprising. That rebellion led to the establishment of the provisional government in Shanghai, China; in 1926 Kim became its prime minister and later its president. In 1930 he helped organize the Korean Independence Party and in 1936 the Korean Nationalist Party.

During World War II, and with Korea still under Japanese rule, Kim became a terrorist, twice attempting to assassinate the emperor. The right-wing Kim also formed Aeguktan (Patriots Corps) and sought cooperation with Chiang Kai-shek and his Chinese Nationalists.

Returning home in 1945, Kim worked with Syngman RHEE to achieve national unity and resist the Communists; the men later had a falling out and parted company. After the formation of the Republic of Korea (South Korea) in 1948, Kim headed his own revamped Korean Independence Party until his death. He published his autobiography in 1929.

Kim Ronyoung. *See* **Hahn, Gloria**

Kimm v. Rosenberg (1960): U.S. Supreme Court ruling authorizing the deportation of a Korean alien from the United States. Diamond Kimm left Korea and went to the United States to study in 1928. He chose to extend his stay when the Sino-Japanese War broke out in 1937. Having completed his term of study, instead of returning home he remained in the United States, where he found employment. Subsequently, U.S. immigration officials ordered his deportation.

Challenging the order, Kimm invoked a legal motion under which the government could suspend the order if Kimm could prove good moral character and was not associated with certain identified groups such as the Communist Party. When asked about his Communist affiliations, however, Kimm claimed the Fifth Amendment right against self-incrimination and declined to answer. The hearing officer chose to view the reply as a lack of evidence attesting good moral character and reinstated the deportation.

The Court on appeal concluded that the alien had the burden of proving issues of character and Communist association. The majority opinion affirmed the deportation decision. The dissent, however, argued that an alien's invocation of the Fifth Amendment should not be viewed as evidence pointing toward bad moral character.

Kimochi: Nonprofit senior service organization founded in 1971 in San Francisco, California, to provide care and support for Japanese American elders. The bilingual/bicultural organization began by assisting Issei, or first-generation Japanese American, elders in filling out social security forms and by providing nighttime escort services in San Francisco's Japantown. It later expanded to include a nutrition program, transportation, counseling, nursing home/hospital visitations, in-home support, and other recreational, educational, social, and cultural activities.

Kim-Shan Jit San-Luk (*Golden Hills' News*): First Chinese newspaper to appear in San Francisco. It was published weekly from April, 1854, until the end of 1858.

Kimura, Larry (b. June 17, 1946, Waimea, Territory of Hawaii): Educator and songwriter. Between 1982 and 1984 he served as president of *Punana Leo*, a Hawaiian immersion program in which students are taught academic subjects in Hawaiian. He began teaching courses in Hawaiian language and culture at the University of Hawaii, Hilo and has won several prestigious songwriting awards for his compositions in Hawaiian.

King, Jean Sadako (Jean Sadako McKillop; b. Dec. 6, 1925, Honolulu, Territory of Hawaii): Lieutenant governor of Hawaii, 1978-1982. King became the first woman in the state to hold this office. She served previously as state representative (1972-1974) and state senator (1974-1978).

King's father, William Donald McKillop, was a postmaster of Scottish descent, and her mother, Chiyo Murakami McKillop, was the daughter of Japanese immigrant coffee farmers. They married in the early 1920's, at a time when such intermarriages were rare.

King attended Japanese-language school along with

regular school. After graduating with a B.A. degree from the University of Hawaii in 1948, she earned an M.A. degree in history from New York University in 1953 and an M.F.A. degree from the University of Hawaii in 1968. She was married to James A. King from 1948 to 1972. They had a son and a daughter.

During the early 1950's the Republican Party controlled politics in Hawaii, as it had for the past half-century. Although her parents were Republicans, King decided to help bolster the fledgling Democratic Party because she agreed with its philosophy of greater political participation for Hawaii's large multiethnic population. She worked hard to enact affordable housing legislation and also labored for laws to allow the public to attend the meetings of government officials.

Disturbed about the rapid spread of urban sprawl at the expense of the natural environment during the 1960's, King questioned the pursuit of short-range economic benefits over long-range deterioration of the environment. As chairperson of the first Environmental Protection Committee in the state house and a parallel committee in the state senate, King worked tirelessly for laws to protect the environment. Two of the more important pieces of legislation enacted under her leadership were the Environmental Protection Act (1972) and the Shoreline Protection Act (1975).

Because King consistently placed principle above party loyalty, she never became part of the Democratic Party machine that came to dominate politics in Hawaii. After she ran unsuccessfully for governor in 1982, she retired from politics.

Kingman, Dong Moy Shu (Tsang King-man; b. Apr. 1, 1911, Oakland, Calif.): Watercolorist. Kingman has garnered international acclaim as one of the world's leading watercolor artists. His works are represented in permanent collections in Boston's Museum of Fine Arts, New York's Metropolitan Museum of Art and Museum of Modern Art, the Chicago Art Institute, the U.S. State Department, and many other galleries. In addition, he has executed murals for banks and hotels, illustrated children's books, and produced artwork for several films such as Lost Horizon (1973). Kingman was a Guggenheim Fellow in 1942-1943 and the (New York) Chinese American Planning Council's Man of the Year in 1981. The autobiographical *Paint the Yellow Tiger* was published in 1991.

Kingston, Maxine Hong (Maxine Hong; b. Oct. 27, 1940, Stockton, Calif.): Writer. Maxine Hong Kingston has played an instrumental role in introducing Asian American literature to the United States and in making Americans more aware of its achievements. In the middle of the 1970's, Kingston helped initiate a literary movement to reclaim Asian Americans' sense of history and identity by giving a voice to the voiceless and a name to the nameless. Kingston's writing style, use of language, and thematic concerns have not only strongly influenced the development of Asian American literature but also enriched the spectrum of American literature.

Biographical Notes. Both of Kingston's parents, Tom and Ying Lan (Chew) Hong, were first-generation immigrants from China. After receiving her B.A. degree from the University of California, Berkeley, in 1962, Maxine Hong married one of her Berkeley classmates, Earll Kingston, who was to become an actor. Their son, Joseph Lawrence Chung Mei, was born in 1964. In the same year Maxine Hong Kingston returned to Berkeley to study for a teaching certificate.

From 1965 to 1977, Kingston taught high school in both California and Hawaii to finance her interest in creative writing. After the success of *The Woman Warrior: Memoirs of a Girlhood Among Ghosts* (1976), Kingston was invited by the University of Hawaii in Honolulu to teach English and writing as a visiting associate professor. Kingston also served as the Thelma McCandless Distinguished Professor in the Humanities at Eastern Michigan University in Ypsilanti in 1986.

In the mid-1980's Kingston and her husband moved back to California, where Kingston began teaching courses at the University of California, Berkeley. They moved into a home in the Rockridge section of Oakland.

Publications. Kingston's first two books, *The Woman Warrior* and *China Men* (1980), culminate and conclude the first period in the development of Chinese American literature, a period distinguished by Chinese American writers' interest in using autobiographical approaches to portray their experiences and to identify their relationship with mainstream American culture. The form of autobiography was well suited to Kingston's attempt to define the Asian American experience through the study of family history, a history that interweaves facts, memories, stories, and legends.

The narrator in *The Woman Warrior* is a second-generation Chinese American. The book describes the narrator's relationship with her mother and her search for identity. The narrator's ability to identify with Fa Mu Lan, a legendary Chinese woman warrior who

Maxine Hong Kingston won the National Book Critics Circle Award for The Woman Warrior *and* China Men. (San Francisco Chronicle)

went to war for her senile father, is what bridges the gap between the past and the present, the real and the imagined, the visible and the invisible worlds, and between China and the United States. This narrative device delineates and accentuates the process of cultural suture which helps give shape to the narrator's true identity.

China Men chronicles the experience and sufferings of the first-generation Chinese male immigrants in the United States. As Korean American critic Elaine Kim observes, Kingston first conceived *The Woman Warrior* and *China Men* as an interlocking story. She decided to publish the two books separately, however, because of the fear that the men's stories "were anti-female and would undercut the feminist viewpoint." The narrative point-of-view in *China Men* is similar to that in *The Woman Warrior*, yet the female narrator's detached voice suggests both a physical and an emotional distance between the daughter and her male ancestors.

Kingston's third book, *Tripmaster Monkey: His Fake Book* (1989), was the writer's first attempt at fiction. The main character, Wittman Ah Sing, is a fifth-generation Chinese American who vacillates between the psychedelic culture of the 1960's and his interest in traditional Chinese literature. After Ah Sing loses his job as a salesperson, he devotes himself to introducing stories from Chinese classics into the American theater. In *Tripmaster Monkey*, Kingston continues her experiment with the use of language. She believes that the Chinese accents, cadences, and rhythms that she uses in her books help to enlarge the store of American English.

Kingston has also published poems, short stories, and articles in magazines and journals. Her collection of twelve prose sketches, *Hawaii One Summer*, was published in a limited edition with original woodblock prints and calligraphy in 1987.

Both *The Woman Warrior* and *China Men* won the National Book Critics Circle Award. Kingston's other accolades include the *Mademoiselle* Magazine Award for *The Woman Warrior* (in 1977), the National Education Association Award (1977), the Anisfield-Wolf Race Relations Award (1978), the Living Treasure of Hawaii designation (1980), the Stockton Arts Commission Award (1981), the Asian/Pacific Women's Network Woman of the Year Award (1981), and the California Council for Humanities Award (1985). Kingston has also been the recipient of a National Education Association writing fellowship (1980) and a Guggenheim Fellowship (1981).

Thematic Concerns. In Kingston's *The Woman Warrior*, there is a description of how the narrator once lost her voice as a child. The narrator did not speak English at home. She became silent when she had to speak English for the first time in kindergarten. After years of struggle the narrator finally managed to gain her voice back, but she could not free herself from being tormented by the sense of dumbness and shame.

The narrator in *The Woman Warrior* was born in the United States. Her silence is apparently occasioned not so much by her struggle with English as by her awareness of being different and by her feeling of inadequacy. The traumatic experience of alienation results from the narrator's not knowing how to cope with what African American writer W. E. B. Du Bois calls the experience of "double consciousness," a conflict that can potentially undermine the very sense of a person's identity.

The thematic power of Kingston's works may be lost unless they are read as social allegories. Mis(sing)-representation has now become a serious issue in the study of social and cultural diversity in the United States. Kingston's works convincingly suggest that to canonize the Asian American voice is to recognize the struggle behind *The Woman Warrior* narrator's cracked voice, to respond to her earnest call for understanding, and to avoid inflicting the same kind of pain on those who even now are experiencing "double consciousness."—*Qun Wang*

SUGGESTED READINGS: • Cheung, King-Kok. *Articulate Silences: Hisaye Yamamoto, Maxine Hong Kingston, Joy Kogawa*. Ithaca, N.Y.: Cornell University Press, 1993. • Kim, Elaine H. *Asian American Literature: An Introduction to the Writings and Their Social Context*. Philadelphia: Temple University Press, 1982. • Lim, Shirley Geok-lin. *Approaches to Teaching Kingston's "The Woman Warrior."* New York: Modern Language Association of America, 1991. • Ling, Amy. *Between Worlds: Women Writers of Chinese Ancestry*. New York: Pergamon Press, 1990. • Smith, Sidonie. *A Poetics of Women's Autobiography: Marginality and the Fictions of Self-Representation*. Bloomington: Indiana University Press, 1987.

Kishi, Kichimatsu (1880's—1956): Rice farmer. Kishi founded a large rice-farm colony in Texas—one of several operated by Japanese immigrants in the state during the first half of the twentieth century. Prior to emigrating, he studied business at a university in Japan. After serving in the Russo-Japanese War, he spent further time in Japan, eventually traveling to the United States with the intention of becoming a rice farmer. He chose a site near the now-extinct town of Terry, Texas (located in the southeastern region of the state, near the Gulf of Mexico), and purchased a 3,500-acre tract of land there in 1907.

As the state's largest Japanese producer of rice, Kishi and his farm prospered until 1916, when salt water leakage destroyed two rice crops. He and the Japanese who worked for him then successfully turned to other avenues such as truck farming, livestock, and oil drilling to sustain themselves and their operation. The colony prospered once again, and Kishi used some of his money to build a church and a school to benefit the local community.

As the Great Depression of the 1930's swept across the United States, however, Kishi could not meet his debts, and creditors seized all of his property in the fall of 1931. A little later, with the help of their son Taro, Kishi and his wife, Fuji, were able to resurrect the business on a much smaller scale. In 1982, a commemorative state historical marker was affixed to the site of the Kishi farm.

Kitagawa, Daisuke (Oct. 3, 1910, Taihoku, now Taipei, Taiwan—Mar. 27, 1970, Geneva, Switzerland): Author and clergyman. The son of a clergyman, Kitagawa attended Episcopal schools in Tokyo before leaving Japan to study theology in the United States. He continued his training at the University of Chicago's Divinity School and at General Theological Seminary in New York. Ordained as an Episcopalian priest in 1939, he was interned at the TULE LAKE relocation center in Northern California in 1942. From 1943 until 1944, he served as field secretary for the National Council of Churches' Committee on Japanese American Resettlement. Kitagawa spent the next decade in Minnesota as a pastor and church administrator. Between 1956 and his death in 1970, he worked for the World Council of Churches in Geneva and served his denomination in several posts at the national level. St. Paul's University of Tokyo, from which Kitagawa was graduated in 1933, awarded him an honorary doctor of divinity degree in 1962. His books include *Issei and Nisei: The Internment Years* (1967), based on his own experience, and a volume on the impact of Christianity on race relations.

Kitano, Harry H. L. (Haruo Kitano; b. Feb. 14, 1926, San Francisco, Calif.): Scholar. Kitano was born to Motoji and Kuo Yuki Kitano. During his early years he

Harry Kitano holds an endowed chair in Japanese American Studies at UCLA. (Asian Week)

lived in Chinatown in San Francisco, where his parents owned a hotel. Although he lived in a racially mixed neighborhood, his experiences were influenced mainly by the close-knit local Japanese community. In San Francisco many recreational activities such as use of public parks and swimming pools were denied to persons of Asian ancestry.

After the onset of World War II and while attending Galileo High School, Kitano was evacuated along with thousands of other Japanese Americans to TOPAZ in Utah, one of ten relocation centers administered by the WAR RELOCATION AUTHORITY (WRA). His father, whom the family would not see for several years, had been interned earlier as a prisoner of war.

Kitano earned several degrees at the University of California, Berkeley: a B.A. degree in 1948; an M.S.W. degree in 1951, and Ph.D. degree in 1958. He began his career as a psychiatric social worker and child guidance consultant for the Child Guidance Clinic of the San Francisco Unified School District (1954-1958) and as a caseworker for the International Institute of San Francisco (1953-1961).

Kitano became an assistant professor at the University of California, Los Angeles (UCLA) in 1958, earning his full professorship in social welfare and sociology in 1972. In 1990, he accepted an endowed chair in Japanese American Studies at UCLA.

Kitano has traveled extensively as a visiting professor: to the University of Hawaii, Manoa, 1971; International Christian University, Tokyo Study Center, Tokyo, Japan, 1972-1973; University of Bristol, England, 1979; and Yamaguchi University, Yamaguchi, Japan, 1992.

Since 1959 Kitano has contributed more than sixty articles to professional sociological journals dealing with child rearing, housing, achievement, racism, mental illness, stereotypes, interracial marriage, alcohol, immigration, and geriatrics. Among his publications are *Japanese Americans: The Evolution of a Subculture* (1969; 2d ed. 1976), *American Racism: Exploration of the Nature of Prejudice* (1970, with Roger Daniels), *Race Relations* (1974; 4th ed. 1991), *Japanese Americans: From Relocation to Redress* (1986; Rev. ed. 1991, edited with Roger Daniels and Sandra C. Taylor), and *The Japanese Americans* (1987).

Kitano has been honored for outstanding community volunteer service by the Los Angeles Human Relations Commission (1979) and was chosen as the Japanese American Citizens League's Nisei of the Biennium (1982) and Nikkei of the Year (1983).

Knights of Labor: Founded in 1869 by a Philadelphia garment worker, Uriah S. Stephens, as the Noble Order of the Knights of Labor, the first nationwide labor union in the United States. It began as a secret organization with an elaborate semireligious ritual. Unlike the National Labor Union, which limited its membership to white skilled workers, the Knights adopted a policy of inclusion, opening its doors to skilled and unskilled workers, men and women, white and black alike (but no Chinese). The organization was in fact the first general labor association to urge the organization of women. It abandoned its secrecy in 1879 when Terrence V. Powderly assumed leadership.

Like other early workingmen's organizations, the Knights focused on the "bread-and-butter" issues such as higher wages and shorter hours. It was thus strategically opposed to strikes while interested in arbitration and compromise. Ironically, in 1884 and 1885, its membership swelled to 700,000 by riding over the tide of strikes against the Union Pacific and Wabash railroads.

While condemning the wage system, leading Knights attempted to improve workers' lots through a policy of collective entrepreneurship. "The aim of the Knights—properly understood—is to make each man his own employer," Powderly asserted. Such a policy achieved limited success between 1884 and 1886, during which the Knights' cooperatives increased to 135. In a time of industrial consolidation, however, it became increasingly difficult for workingmen's cooperatives to compete with large corporations.

As the Knights rose to power in labor union circles, they began a campaign of strenuous opposition against the Chinese in California. The Knights, including nonwhite members, agitated powerfully for Chinese exclusion. Even after passage of the CHINESE EXCLUSION ACT OF 1882, the group continued to push for complete exclusion, urging its members to take part in activities against the Chinese. Events finally culminated in the Wyoming Rock Springs riot (1885), in which white miners burned down the local Chinatown, killed twenty-eight Chinese, and drove the rest out of town.

After 1886, the influence of the Knights of Labor ("Noble Order" had earlier been dropped from the name) declined drastically. In that year, the Knights participated in a strike against American financier Jay Gould's southwestern system of railroads that ended in disaster. It received an even heavier blow from its implication in the Haymarket Affair in Chicago. Unable to dissociate itself from anarchist activities, the Knights lost members who were unwilling to confront employers and the government. In addition, skilled workers left the Knights for the rising craft and trade unions that served their needs better. By 1890, the Knights' membership had plummeted, and Powderly resigned. Its position among industrial workers was quickly taken by the better-organized American Federation of Labor.

Knights of St. Crispin: Nineteenth century shoemakers' trade union that reorganized in the 1870's on an anti-Chinese basis and agitated for the New York state legislature to consider banning Chinese laborers. Chinese workers broke this union's 1870 strike at a North Adams, Massachusetts, shoe factory.

Knox, Frank (Jan. 1, 1874, Boston, Mass.—Apr. 28, 1944, Washington, D.C.): U.S. Secretary of the Navy. Appointed secretary by President Franklin D. Roosevelt in 1940, he prepared an official report following the bombing of Pearl Harbor by Japan. Before releasing it, he implied that Hawaiian Japanese had spied on U.S. military facilities and assisted Japanese Fifth Column (sabotage) activity. Although the report provided no evidence of espionage or sabotage, his statement helped build the belief among the American public that Japanese Americans were spies.

Ko: A Japanese principle, brought to the United States by immigrants, meaning filial duty.

Kochi, Shinsei Paul (Feb. 27, 1889, Nakijin, Kunigashiragun, Okinawa Prefecture, Japan—Dec. 20, 1980): Writer and community leader. An only son, he taught school for awhile, then left Japan to see the world. He eventually reached Los Angeles, where he worked as a gardener. During this time he also wrote for various publications. When the United States entered World War II, Kochi was sent to HEART MOUNTAIN relocation center in northwestern Wyoming. Despite the mass evacuation, Kochi supported the United States' role in the war. When the government began allowing resettlement in other parts of the country, he seized the opportunity. Working in Nebraska, Kochi published accounts of his life on the outside and urged other internees to leave the camps.

Kochi went to New York in 1943 and found a job with the Office of Strategic Services (OSS), a post that took him to various regions of Asia, where he was able to observe the effects of war firsthand. Back in the United States he set about organizing relief efforts on behalf of Okinawa and writing articles to publicize conditions there. For five years he published a newsletter, *Kyuen News* (relief news). Later he helped organize the Japanese Community Pioneer Center (JCPC) of Los Angeles to assist elderly Issei. Kochi coedited a hsitory of the Okinawan community, first published in Japanese and later in English translation as *History of the Okinawans in North America* (1988).

Kochiyama, Yuri (b. 1921, San Pedro, Calif.): Human rights and political activist. The daughter of a fish market operator, Kochiyama was sent to Jerome relocation center in southeastern Arkansas during World War II. Upon her release, she and her husband, William Masayoshi Kochiyama (1921-1993), who had served with the all-Nisei 442ND REGIMENTAL COMBAT TEAM, went to New York.

There, in the 1950's, the Kochiyamas became active in the Civil Rights movement. In 1960 the Kochiyamas and their six children moved to mostly black Harlem, where Yuri launched a crusade to improve conditions for the residents of that community. She met African American leader Malcom X in 1963 and was strongly influenced by his outlook, becoming a member of his Organization for Afro American Unity when it was formed in 1964. She worked closely with Malcolm until his assassination on February 21, 1965.

Since that time Kochiyama has continued to oppose injustice wherever she perceives it. After the seizure of the U.S. embassy in Tehran in 1979 prompted calls for the deportation of Iranian students, she helped to organize Concerned Japanese Americans, a group that protested the proposed action, seeing in the plight of the Iranian students a parallel to the internment that she and thousands of other Japanese Americans suffered during World War II.

Koda, Keisaburo (1882, Fukushima, Japan—1964, Japan): Rice farmer. Koda won the largest monetary settlement awarded by the U.S. government to former internment camp evacuees. Born to a former samurai,

Rice farmer Keisaburo Koda won the largest monetary settlement awarded by the U.S. government to former internment camp evacuees. (Japanese American National Museum)

Koda arrived in the United States in 1906. Moving up and down the Pacific Coast, he took on a string of odd jobs before starting a wholesale fish distribution company in Southern California in partnership with other Japanese, becoming especially successful during World War I. He later sold his share of the business and then went to Sacramento to become a rice farmer. Again he prospered until, by 1932, he was planting rice on ten thousand acres. Koda was also the first to devise a method of using airplanes to scatter rice seeds across large tracts of land. By the late 1930's he had a personal net worth of several million dollars.

Following Japan's surprise bombing of Pearl Harbor, Koda was sent to the GRANADA relocation center in southeastern Colorado. He returned to California upon his release, only to find that most of his property had been sold without his permission. In hope of getting it back, he appealed to the U.S. government and the courts for relief. Meanwhile, he persevered and, aided by his sons, was able to resurrect his rice-production business. His Kokuho brand rice soon brought him new prosperity.

When Koda died in 1964 during a visit to Japan, his claim still had not been settled. Finally, in 1965, the government, under authorization of the Japanese American Evacuation Claims Act of 1948, awarded the Kodas more than $360,000 to compensate them for losses traceable to the internment. This was the largest settlement awarded under the act, but even this sum was swallowed up by what Koda had spent litigating the two-decades-old claim.

Koden: Japanese American funeral custom in which mourners give money to the family of the deceased to help pay expenses. The practice of *koden* (incense money) began in Japan as a Buddhist or Shinto tradition.

Kodomo no tame ni: Japanese saying, literally meaning "for the sake of the children," that characterizes the inspiration and motivation of early Japanese American immigrants to make sacrifices in order to ensure a better future for their children.

Kogawa, Joy (Joy Nozomi Goichi: b. June 6, 1935, Vancouver, British Columbia, Canada): Writer and activist. An accomplished and distinguished writer, Kogawa garnered much acclaim for her award-winning *Obasan* (1981), a novel that portrays the travails of a Japanese Canadian family of Vancouver that was forcibly "removed" from the Canadian west coast

during World War II. It depicts the wrongheaded and hysterical racism of the Canadian authorities who perpetrated this unjust action, and it records in a brilliantly poetic narrative the fortitude and resilience of the Japanese Canadians who suffered in various ways as a result. A children's version of this novel was published as *Naomi's Road* (1986). Kogawa's second novel, *Itsuka* (1992), a sequel to *Obasan*, deals with the struggle of Japanese Canadians to obtain redress for the injustice of the wartime evacuation and internment.

Kogawa grew up in Vancouver, where her father was a minister and her mother a kindergarten teacher. Her family was evacuated during World War II, and she also spent some of her childhood years in Alberta. She attended the University of Alberta, the Anglican Women's Training College, the Conservatory of Music, and the University of Saskatchewan. Kogawa has also been active in civil rights causes, having been director of the Canadian Civil Liberties Association. She married David Kogawa in 1957; they were divorced in 1968.

Kogawa's first books were volumes of poetry: *The Splintered Moon* (1967), *A Choice of Dreams* (1974), and *Jericho Road* (1977), followed by *Woman in the Woods* (1985). Her poetry is characterized by crisp, brilliant images drawn from her experience of life and nature in Canada and from her travels in Japan.

When *Obasan* was published, it received many awards, among them the First Novel Award from Books in Canada, the Book of the Year Award from the Canadian Authors Association, the Before Columbus Foundation American Book Award, and a Notable Book citation from the American Library Association. In recognition of her writing Kogawa was also made a Member of the Order of Canada (1986) and was awarded honorary doctorates by the University of Lethbridge (1991) and the University of Guelph (1992).

Kojong (Yi Myong-bok; 1852, Korea—Jan. 22, 1919, Korea): King of Korea. At eleven years of age, he became the penultimate king of the Yi Dynasty (1392-1910). With nationalist pride, he supported U.S. missionary Horace N. ALLEN's project to increase Korean immigration to Hawaii, since the Chinese were excluded. In 1907, Japanese officials forced him to abdicate his rule to his son.

Kokuryukai (Black Dragon Society; also, Amur River Society): Japanese ultranationalist organization.

Founded in 1901 to promote Japanese expansion on the Asian mainland, it was one of Japan's most influential right-wing organizations throughout the years leading to World War II (1939-1945). Never large, it exerted its influence through propaganda and close ties to Japan's business, political, and military leaders.

The society was founded by Uchida Ryohei, an anti-Russian zealot heavily influenced by the powerful nationalist Toyama Mitsuru. Its initial aim was to secure a more aggressive Japanese approach in northeast Asia in response to increased Russian activities there. It chose its name to highlight its belief that Japan's national territory should extend to the Amur River, which formed Manchuria's northern boundary. its stated goals also called for nationalization of public education, an increased martial spirit, and greater efficiency in Japan's political system.

The society propagated its positions through a journal called *Kokuryu*, various pamphlets, and a training school for activists. Graduates of the school were dispatched to China and northeastern Asia to gather intelligence and stir up anti-Russian activities.

In the early years, the society's leaders took credit for helping to convince prime minister Ito Hirobumi to support military action against Russia; after the Russo-Japanese War (1904-1905), they called for annexation of Russian territory as far west as Lake Baikal and led demonstrations against what they saw as a weak peace agreement.

The society exerted an impact on Asians abroad by supporting such revolutionary nationalists as China's Sun Yat-sen and the Philippines' Emilio Aguinaldo. Though favoring the independence of these nations, the society's leaders primarily hoped to extend Japanese influence throughout Asia.

From the 1920's, it turned its focus to the domestic scene, joining other organizations in fanning flames of nationalism. Its members urged greater governmental control by the emperor, a stronger international posture, and the end of the corrupt party system of government. In the early 1930's, they joined the vocal opposition to the London Naval Treaty of 1930, in which Japan agreed to continue cooperative policies with the United States and Great Britain. The society was disbanded by American occupation authorities at the end of World War II in 1945.

Komagata Maru incident (1914): Significant event in the history of Asian Indians in North America, named after a Japanese ship chartered by an Indian Sikh labor contractor from Singapore. The incident highlighted the Canadian government's discriminatory immigration policy.

Sailing from Hong Kong on April 14, 1914, the *Komagata Maru* arrived in Vancouver, Canada, on May 23, carrying 376 Asian Indian laborers picked up en route from Shanghai, China, and Kobe and Yokohama, Japan. The purpose of their journey was to challenge a 1908 Canadian law that required immigrants to travel directly to Canada from their countries of origin. The aim of this law was to bar immigration from India, which had been increasing since 1900. When the law was passed, there were no ships sailing regularly from India directly to the Pacific Coast of North America. Following the law's passage, Indian immigration to Canada was almost entirely cut off; between 1909 and 1920, only 118 South Asians entered Canada as immigrants.

The *Komagata Maru* incident took place when the ship reached Vancouver harbor. The Canadian government remained firm in its resolve not to allow the passengers to disembark, and, as a result, they remained on the ship for more than two months. Meanwhile, the Indian community in Vancouver made representations, in vain, on behalf of the passengers to the Dominion government in Ottawa and the British India office in London to negotiate an arrangement for disembarkation. Thereafter, the Indians resorted to court action to challenge the legality of the exclusionary regulations, but the court decision was against them.

When the Canadian authorities ordered the captain of the ship to remove the ship from the harbor, the passengers, most of whom had military training, took over the ship to prevent its departure. A police unit that was sent in by tugboat to enforce the orders had to retreat as the passengers began to bombard the tug with coal and whatever else was available to them on the ship. The event was hailed as a victory by the Asian Indian community, as a concession was made by the Canadian authorities to allow the Indians to represent their case before a cabinet official. Through the ensuing negotiations, the passengers agreed to leave and arrangements were made for their return directly to India, though without the right to disembark at any other port.

The *Komagata Maru* left Vancouver on July 23, 1914. When the ship reached harbor near Calcutta, India, all the passengers were arrested by the British police and sent to their home state of Punjab in special trains. Realizing the fate that awaited them after reaching Punjab, they resisted, and in the violent confrontation that took place there were twenty-six casualties, including twenty passengers.

The *Komagata Maru* incident, which received global press coverage, increased the political consciousness of the Asian Indian community in North America. Indians in North America began to establish a link between the racial, economic, and legal discrimination they faced and the colonial oppression of British rule in their homeland. (See GHADR MOVEMENT.)

Kondo Masaharu (1877, Kyoto, Japan—1948, Tokyo, Japan): Commercial fishing pioneer. Kondo studied fisheries and oceanography in his native Japan, then began a teaching job at the Imperial Fisheries Institute, for which he traveled the world studying global fishery technologies. He reached Los Angeles in 1908 and, recognizing the opportunity to expand the Southern California fisheries market, made plans to start a San Diego-based fishing company. As head of the MK Fishing Company, established in 1912, Kondo won exclusive rights from the Mexican government to ply the waters of Turtle Bay, off Baja, California. He then imported contract fishermen from Japan—the first ever to arrive in Mexico—and introduced technologies that became the basis for fisheries in that region.

In 1915 Kondo helped rescue the crew of a Japanese ship that ran aground at Turtle Bay. As a result, a year later he was the first Japanese American to win a national honor from the government of Japan—the Sixth Order of Merit of the Order of the Sacred Treasure. In 1920 he began to fish for tuna and so hired more fishermen from Japan.

Kondo and his fishermen are credited with many innovations, including the use of flexible and sturdy bamboo fishing poles, more effective lures and use of bait, refrigerated boats, and ways of locating schools of fish using radio-tracking.

Kong Chow Company (also, Kong Chow Benevolent Association; Gangzhou Huiguan): District organization, or *huiguan*, for people whose ancestry was from Xinhui and Heshan counties in Guangdong Province, China. Its beginnings may be traced back to the See Yup (Sze Yup) company founded in 1851 by immigrants from Xinhui, Xinning, Kaiping, and Enping with headquarters at Sacramento and Stockton streets in San Francisco. The association also enrolled people from Heshan and Sihui, but this group left after the 1880's to join the Sam Yup Company.

In 1853 Xinning people, except for the Yu (Yee) clan, withdrew from the organization to form the Ning Yung Company. The same year the See Yup Company sold its property to the Presbyterian Mission and built a new building and the See Yup Asylum (Kong Chow Temple) on Pine Street near Kearny on land donated by Yee Ahtye. In 1862 the Yu clan from Xinning withdrew from the See Yup Company together with Kaiping and Enping clans. Xinhui people inherited the See Yup Company property and incorporated it as the Kong Chow Beneficial Society in 1867. In 1882 the company's president, Chun Num Chueng (Chen Wenquan), became the first president of the newly founded Chinese Consolidated Benevolent Association.

Under the Kong Chow Association are the Fook Hang Association (Fuqingtang), which takes care of charitable activities for Xinhui people, and the Teh Hou Association (Dehoutang), which does the same for Heshan people. From 1926 to 1936 the association also ran Kong Chow Chinese School, a school of about thirty students. During the days of the *tong* wars Bow On Tong (Baoantang) was established for self-defense under the leadership of the association. Branches were founded in Los Angeles, Fresno, Stockton, Seattle, and Portland. Over the years Kong Chow Associations were also founded in Los Angeles, Philadelphia, Seattle, and Honolulu. New York, however, has a Sun Wei Association, while Hok San societies are found in Philadelphia and New York.

The Kong Chow Association held a national convention in 1954, during which it became the first *huiguan* to abandon the practice of rotating the officers by clans and geographical origin. A second convention in 1964 made a decision to sell the headquarters building. Although Yee Ahtye's descendants contested the action, the land was sold in 1969. A new headquarters building was dedicated during the third convention in 1977. Three more conventions were convened in 1982, 1987, and 1990 in San Francisco, New York, and Los Angeles, respectively.

Kongnip Hyop-hoe (Mutual Assistance Association): First Korean American political organization, established on September 22, 1905, in San Francisco, California, by Ahn Chang-ho and other members of the Chinmok-hoe (Friendship Society), also founded by Ahn. Its main objective was to work for the restoration of Korea's national independence, but some leaders acted as employment agents for new Korean immigrants. The organization also published *KONGNIP SINPO* (*News of the Kongnip*), the first Korean-language newsletter in the continental United States.

Kongnip Sinpo (*News of the Kongnip*): Korean American newsletter, published by the Kongnip Hyophoe (Mutual Assistance Association), the first Korean American political organization, beginning on November 22, 1905. It was the first Korean-language newsletter to be published in the continental United States.

Konko-kyo (Religion of Konko): One of the syncretistic Shinto movements that arose in the pre- and early Meiji period; founded in 1859 by Kawate Bunjiro (later known by the title "Konko Daijin"), a farmer in Bitchu Province (now part of Okyama Prefecture). Kawate experienced a series of family misfortunes and a serious illness, but then he said he had received revelations from the kami Konjin, traditionally considered a malevolent deity. Kawate believed that this kami had taken possession of him and appointed him to be mediator between the kami and humanity. People from the surrounding area came in great numbers to seek Kawate's mediation as he received and interpreted the words of Konjin for them. Eventually Konko-kyo was recognized by the government as one of the thirteen Sect Shinto groups.

Konko-kyo holds that Konjin is really Tenchi-kane-no-kami (the golden kami of heaven and earth), the one kami uniting all others, the parent deity of the universe. All humans are children of kami's family. Kami and humans are mutually interdependent, like parents and children; humans cannot exist apart from kami, and kami can only be complete through humans. This interrelationship is key to the central Konko-kyo practice of *toritsugi*, or "intermediation." *Toritsugi* is practiced daily in Konko-kyo churches; ministers listen to parishioners tell of their problems and spiritual state and they provide guidance and reconciliation with kami. Konko-kyo places much emphasis on a monotheistic belief in kami, sincerity and piety in life, and concern for social welfare and world peace.

Konko-kyo has grown and spread as a vigorous movement in the post-World War II period in Japan. Konko-kyo's headquarters are in Konko Cho, Okayama Prefecture, and there is a nationwide organizational network in Japan, with about a half-million adherents. In Konko-kyo's organizational structure the office of Leader (*Kyoshu*) is held by a descendant of the founder.

Konko-kyo was established in the United States in the 1920's in Seattle, Tacoma, Los Angeles, and Honolulu. In the United States the movement grew, although it was hurt by the internment of most of its leadership during World War II. The present leadership in Japan supports work outside Japan and encourages the production of English-language materials. (See SHIN SHUKYO.)

Kono, Tamio "Tommy" (b. June 27, 1930, Sacramento, Calif.): Weightlifter. Born to Issei parents who were employed as cannery workers in Sacramento, Kono suffered from severe asthma as a child. During World War II, he and his family were sent to the Tule Lake internment camp. While living at the camp, Kono's health improved and he took up the sport of weightlifting.

When his family returned to Sacramento at the end of the war, Kono enrolled in Sacramento Junior College. A highly successful lifter, Kono was drafted in 1952 to serve in the army during the Korean War, but was given duty as a cook in Hawaii in order to continue competing. Kono trained with a Korean American physician named Richard W. You, who helped him win his first national title as a lightweight in 1952. Kono competed on the U.S. Olympic team as a weightlifter at the summer games in 1952 held in Helsinki, Finland, and in 1956 held in Melbourne, Australia, winning back-to-back gold medals. At the 1960 Olympic Games in Rome, Italy, Kono won a silver medal.

Tommy Kono won Olympic medals in weight lifting. (Asian Week)

All three of his Olympic medals were won in different weight classes, a feat unmatched in Olympic history.

Kono had settled permanently in Hawaii in 1955, married Florence Rodrigues, and established a family. His aggressive weight training regimen for weightlifting allowed him to compete in world-class body-building events as well. During his career, Kono won six world weightlifting championships, established twenty-six world records, and won titles as Mr. World and Mr. Universe. After his retirement as a competitor in 1965, he served as a coach and adviser for various Olympic weight lifting teams in 1968, 1972, and 1976. In 1988, the International Weightlifting Federation ranked Kono first among the thirty greatest weightlifters of all time, and he was inducted into the U.S. Olympic Hall of Fame in 1990.

Koo, [Vi Kyun] Wellington (Ku Wei-Chun; 1887, Shanghai, China—Nov. 14, 1985, New York, N.Y.): Diplomat. Koo's career was a distinguished, active one that spanned forty of the most critical years in modern Chinese history. His life mirrored the changing fortunes of his country in the international arena.

Born of well-to-do parents, Koo studied in mission schools in Shanghai before coming to the United States for college. He studied at Cornell and Columbia, distinguishing himself in public speaking and in Chinese student politics.

After receiving a Ph.D. degree in political science from Columbia in 1912, Koo returned to China to enter government service. From 1915 through 1918 he was China's minister to the United States. As a member of China's delegation to the Paris Peace Conference, he pleaded eloquently for China's position on the "Shandong Question." Appointed to the commission for drafting the constitution for the League of Nations, Koo argued successfully for the principle of regional representation for membership in the League Council.

Diplomat Wellington Koo. (AP/Wide World Photos)

His efforts resulted in China being elected to the council as a nonpermanent member.

Subsequently Koo participated in the Washington Disarmament Conference (1921-1922), which settled the Shandong Question and finalized the Nine-Power Treaty (1922) guaranteeing the administrative and territorial integrity of China. In the mid-1920's he served twice as foreign minister and once as acting premier of the Beijing government. Sidelined by the establishment of the Nationalist Government in 1928, he returned to international diplomacy after the Japanese seizure of Manchuria in 1931.

With the approach of World War II and rising international tension, China needed a man of Koo's caliber to defend her interests at the League of Nations. To bolster his position in the protocol-conscious society of Geneva, he was concurrently appointed as China's ambassador to France. After the fall of France, he became ambassador to Great Britain. He participated in the Dumbarton Oaks Conference and signed the United Nations charter on behalf of China. His last diplomatic posting was at Washington, D.C., where he served as China's ambassador. During the Chinese civil war (1946-1949) he sought to steer U.S. aid to his government; after the relocation of the Nationalist government to Taiwan, he assisted in the negotiations that resulted in the Sino-American Defense Treaty of 1954. From 1957 through 1967 he served on the International Court of Justice at The Hague. After 1946 he made his home permanently in the United States.

Koopmanschap, Cornelius (Feb. 13, 1828, Weesperkarspel, near Amsterdam, The Netherlands—1882, Rio de Janeiro, Brazil): Labor contractor. After arriving in California in the early 1850's, he set up shop in San Francisco and began importing goods from China. He began living in Hong Kong in the 1860's having traveled there frequently on business trips. Using his connections with Chinese firms, he became a contractor and importer of Chinese labor to all parts of the world, including the United States. Responsible for having imported thirty thousand Chinese laborers into California, he addressed the Southern Planter's Convention in Memphis, Tennessee, in 1869, and offered to make Chinese laborers available to Southern plantation owners. The latter had been experiencing a Reconstruction era labor shortage.

Korea: Mountainous peninsula situated prominently along the continental fringe of northeast Asia. Its strongly seasonal climate and diverse resources have

offered an attractive human habitat for the long evolution of Korean civilization. Settled early, the subsequent success and durability of Korean peninsular life has culminated in a robust Korean ethnic identity.

Korea's site and situation as a sovereign state is that of a geopolitical linchpin centered within the circumference of its three often aggressive neighbors—China, Japan, and Russia. Twentieth century Korean modernization began under Japanese colonialism (1910-1945), followed by a tragic civil war (1950-1953). Hostilities ended with the estrangement of the Korean nation into two parts: the Republic of Korea (South Korea, capital in Seoul), and the Democratic People's Republic of Korea (North Korea, capital in Pyongyang). They are separated by the military demarcation line (MDL), a temporary administrative boundary surrounded by a demilitarized zone (the DMZ).

South Korea has rapidly evolved from postwar penury to become a newly industrialized democracy with a booming export economy. North Korea, over the same four decades, traded off its economic growth rates relative to South Korea in order to maintain ideological purity under the monocratic patriarchy of KIM IL SUNG: Kim's ideology of *juche* (communal self-reliance) long extolled central planning, national isola-

Independence Hall near Chonan, South Korea, commemorates the long struggle for Korea's independence. (Korea National Tourism Corporation)

tion, and militarism. By 1990 the per capita gross national product (GNP) in South Korea had already become about four times greater than that of North Korea, and experimentation with minor economic reforms in the north indicated some growing concern there with this widening disparity of wealth and power. Territorial division of the Korean nation-state persisted, this despite increasing internal and external pressures for peaceful reunification.

Land. The Korean peninsula and archipelago comprise a mountainous environment of about 85,700 square miles, approximate in size and comparable in latitude to Utah. It extends southward and away from Chinese Manchuria over a distance of six hundred miles through nearly ten degrees of latitude to within twenty-one miles of Japanese territory. Nature has reinforced the physical and psychological separation of its inhabitants from outsiders. There are isolating seas to the east (East Sea, or Sea of Japan), south (East China Sea), and west (Yellow Sea). In the north a rugged riverine boundary is formed by the diverging flows of the Amnok (Yalu) and Tumen rivers from their sources near Paektu Mountain.

Popular lore describes the irregular elongation of Korean territory in profile as "rabbit-shaped." The waist of this rabbit narrows to 120 miles in the vicinity of the DMZ, which cuts a 2.4-mile-wide swath across the 38th parallel for 151 miles between coasts. North Korea shares a long land border with the People's Republic of China (PRC) for 640.7 miles, which extends into a border with Russia at the tip of the rabbit's ears for an additional 10.4 miles. This border spans Korea's greatest width, through six degrees of longitude. South Korea shares its only land border with North Korea, along the DMZ. North Korea is slightly larger than South Korea, comprising about 55 percent of the peninsula, but it has less level land than does South Korea. Cheju Island is the southernmost landmark of Korea.

Climate. Though often described as a "temperate" climate, seasonal change throughout Korea is more dramatic and invigorating than that term suggests. Long summers (hot and humid) and winters (cold and dry) are separated by shorter springs and autumns that are invariably clear and pleasant. Annual wind and temperature shifts are monsoonal, bringing summertime rains that are regular and predictable. Regional variations in temperature and moisture on the penin-

Korean performers dress in traditional garb. (Korea National Tourism Corporation)

sula relate to differences in latitude, altitude, and proximity to the sea. North Korea has a greater range of temperature throughout the year than does South Korea, but South Korea is more exposed than the north to damaging summer typhoons. Floods, droughts, winds, and temperature extremes are some of the less predictable weather hazards of peninsular life.

Resources and Environment. Korean soils, carefully enhanced during past centuries of subsistence agriculture, remain productive but require careful management. Industrial and energy resources are widely scattered throughout the peninsula yet overall are inadequate to support a self-sufficient, mature industrial economy. Coal is available, but petroleum is lacking. Mountainous terrain suits hydroelectric power development, and much untapped potential remains. Generally speaking, North Korea has more resources for industrial development than does South Korea.

Little of Korea's once-magnificent but poorly managed timber resource has survived to the 1990's. Degradation of the forest environment has occurred concomitant with declines and extinctions among Korea's diverse wild floral and faunal resources. Ironically, the DMZ has unintentionally created the largest contiguous "protected" area for many wild species of plants and animals in Korea. Air quality has declined with excessive auto emissions in the southern cities and increasing pesticide drifts in the countryside. Korea's important freshwater and ocean resources are also increasingly jeopardized by overexploitation, toxic runoff, and siltation.

Korea remains rich in human resources, as Koreans continue to value family ties and education. South Korea's population was approximately 44.6 million in 1993. Although the North Korean population was half that size, the rate of population increase in North Korea was about twice that of South Korea.

Civilization. The character of the Korean people is inseparable from their peninsular origins and heritage. Korean history is highlighted by some remarkable achievements during the rise of its stable and productive premodern Korean agricultural civilization. Most of the peninsula was first unified under one government during the Silla period, which began in 668. The name "Korea," however, derives from the kingdom of Koryo, ruled by a dynastic line that reigned over the peninsula from 935 to 1392 during its "golden age" of Buddhism. The peninsula was called "Choson" under the subsequent Yi Dynasty (1392-1910). The Yi Dynasty was notable for its longevity and high cultural achievements, administered largely by scholar-

Seoul, Korea, circa 1900. (The Korea Society/Los Angeles)

bureaucrats guided by neo-Confucian ideas adapted from Chinese models. The fundamental symbolism of neo-Confucian cosmology is called "Taeguk" (the great ultimate) and appears on the South Korean flag.

The outcome of Korea's geopolitical situation has tempted pundits to focus mainly on the nonattributes—rather than the attributes—of Korea's size and location. History, however, ultimately belies the oft-quoted metaphor that "Korea is a shrimp between whales": Whereas shrimp are devoured and cease to exist, modern Korean civilization still flowers upon its ancient roots in the peninsula, never destroyed or dislodged despite numerous destructive foreign invasions. Thus have Koreans demonstrated to the world their remarkable resiliency amid adversity.—*David J. Nemeth*

SUGGESTED READINGS: • Henthorn, William E. *A History of Korea*. New York: Free Press, 1971. • Lautensach, Hermann. *Korea: A Geography Based on the Author's Travels and Literature*. Translated and edited by Katherine and Eckart Dege. Berlin: Springer-Verlag, 1988. • Lee, Chang-Sik, ed. *Korea Briefing, 1990*. Boulder, Colo.: Westview Press, 1991. • McCune, Shannon. Korea's Heritage: A Regional and Social Geography. Rutland, Vt.: Charles E. Tuttle, 1956. • Macdonald, Donald Stone. *The Koreans: Contemporary Politics and Society*. 2d ed. Boulder, Colo.: Westview Press, 1990. • Nahm, Andrew C. *Korea, Tradition and Transformation: A History of the Korean People*. Elizabeth, N.J.: Hollym, 1988.

Korea, Christianity in: Korean Christians celebrated the bicentennial of Catholicism and the centennial of Protestantism in 1984. Christianity has been a powerful influence in the modernization of Korea, and it has become a highly visible, dynamic religion in contemporary Korea. With more than nine million believers, South Korea is the most Christianized nation in Asia after the Philippines. The Korean church since 1945 has been regarded as perhaps the most rapidly growing church in the world. Christianity has been and will probably continue to be a major social and political force in South Korea.

Historical Background. Korea's initial contact with Christianity took place in the late sixteenth century during the Japanese invasion of Korea. Korea's first known Christian church, however, began in 1784, when a small group of Silhak (school of practical learning) scholars gathered to found a lay congregation of Catholics. The group included Sung-hun Yi, a son of a Korean tribute envoy to China, who had been christened "Peter" in Beijing. The church began to grow, but the pope's condemnation of ancestor worship rendered Christianity heretical to the Confucian ideals of Yi Dynasty (1392-1910) Korea. The government arrested Christians and persecuted both Korean Christians and foreign missionaries until Korea signed a treaty of friendship and commerce with the United States in 1882.

Protestant missions to Korea began in 1884 with the arrival of Horace N. ALLEN from the Presbyterian Mission in China. The following year two ordained missionaries, a Presbyterian and a Methodist, started missionary work by building churches, schools, and hospitals. Under the precarious sociopolitical circumstances of the late Yi Dynasty, the church not only met the religious needs of the common people but also represented a major source of Western culture and modernization. Mission clinics, for example, provided modern medical service, and the Ewha Haktang (school), which had been established by a Methodist missionary in 1886, offered the first opportunity for girls to receive formal education.

After Japan won the Russo-Japanese War (1904-1905) and made Korea its protectorate, a mass conversion of the Korean people of the commoner class to the Christian faith reached a peak during what has been called the "Great Revival at Pyongyang" in 1907. Japan subsequently colonized Korea from 1910 to 1945. When, on March 1, 1919, Koreans staged nonviolent street demonstrations across the country to demand national independence from Japan (see MARCH FIRST

MOVEMENT), Christians along with Chondogyo (the religion of the heavenly way) believers played leading roles in organizing the demonstration. As a consequence Christian churches suffered persecution from the Japanese colonial government.

Since Korea's liberation from Japan in 1945, Christian churches have experienced explosive growth in democratic South Korea, while religion is forbidden in communist North Korea. More than nine million South Koreans, or about 21 percent of the total population of 44.6 million, are Christians. The imported alien religion of Christianity has now become Korea's leading religion, with Christians slightly outnumbering Buddhists.

Korean Christianity. Because of the particular history of foreign missionary work around the start of the twentieth century, Presbyterians and Methodists have become the most prominent Protestant denominations in terms of membership and influence among Chris-

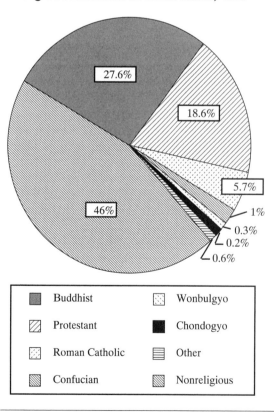

Religious Affiliation in South Korea, 1991

27.6%
18.6%
5.7%
46%
1%
0.3%
0.2%
0.6%

Buddhist   Wonbulgyo
Protestant   Chondogyo
Roman Catholic   Other
Confucian   Nonreligious

Source: Illsoo Kim, *New Urban Immigrants: The Korean Community in New York.* Princeton, N.J.: Princeton University Press, 1981.

tian churches in Korea. Emphasizing earthly blessings, many churches have rapidly grown, attracting the urban middle class in large numbers since the 1960's. This remarkable expansion of the Christian population is attributable in part to the strength of the Pentecostal movement, the emergence of new sectarian groups, and the development of new religious syncretism (as exemplified by the Unification Church movement established by Sun Myung Moon).

In general, conservatism and evangelism characterize mainstream Korean Christian churches of various denominations and sects. Korean churches are Bible-based churches that stress orthodoxy and are organized in a male-dominated hierarchical structure. Although women constitute about two-thirds of Korean Christians and have been active in church growth and evangelical outreach, they make up less than 3 percent of ordained ministers in the patriarchal structure of the Korean church. Many Christian leaders share in the belief that Korea is a chosen nation of God and that their mission is to Christianize first the nation and then the rest of the world. Korean churches have sent evangelical missionaries to numerous countries, including the People's Republic of China and the former Soviet Union.

Sociocultural Impact. In order to understand the powerful sociocultural impact of Christianity on Korean society, one must consider the particular historical circumstances of Korea at the beginning of the twentieth century under the Yi Dynasty, when Christian missionary work formally began. The Yi Dynasty was a highly stratified patriarchal society based on Confucian principles. The roles of women were strictly confined within the domestic sphere. Education in the Chinese classics was available mainly as a means for male members of the *yangban* (upper) class to obtain government office.

Thus when the missionaries established schools for girls as well as boys, they offered an unprecedented opportunity for the common people, especially women, to receive formal education and to move into positions of leadership. For example the majority of early women legislators, medical doctors, and teachers attended mission schools, where they not only received Western-style education but also became politically awakened to the injustice of colonial oppression. In the independence movement of 1919, some women teachers and students from Christian mission schools played important leadership roles. Their patriotism, fostered by strong Christian faith in justice, helped them endure various hardships, including police torture and lengthy imprisonment.

Christianity was thus inextricably enmeshed in the social and political life of colonial Korea and has continued to be a major force in the developmental process of the nation, influencing not only the religious but also the social, cultural, and political fabric of life in modern Korea. The church service offered a social space where men and women could interact outside the home. The use of *hangul*, the Korean alphabet, in the translation of the Bible contributed to the revitalization of the Korean writing system and to the promotion of literacy and nationalism under Japanese rule. Many leading South Korean politicians, businesspeople, and professionals of both sexes have been Christians. Some Christian leaders were prominent in their struggle against social injustice and political repression during the 1970's and 1980's. Espousing the *minjung* (people's) theology and the urban industrial mission, they advocated human rights for the oppressed. Christianity will continue to be a dynamic force in the development of Korean society in the twenty-first century.—*Chunghee Sarah Soh*

SUGGESTED READINGS: • Clark, Donald N. *Christianity in Modern Korea*. Lanham, Md.: University Press of America, 1986. • Kim, Chan-Hie. "Christianity and the Modernization of Korea." In *Religions in Korea: Beliefs and Cultural Values*, edited by E. H. Phillips and E. Y. Yu. Los Angeles: Center for Korean-American and Korean Studies, California State University, Los Angeles, 1982. • Moffett, Samuel Hugh. *The Christians of Korea*. New York: Friendship Press, 1962. • Palmer, Spencer J. *Korea and Christianity*. Seoul, Korea: Hollym, 1967. • Ro, Bong-Rin, and Marlin L. Nelson, eds. *Korean Church Growth Explosion*. Seoul, Korea: Word of Life Press, 1985. • Shearer, Roy E. *Wildfire: Church Growth in Korea*. Grand Rapids, Mich.: William B. Eerdmans, 1966.

Korea, Democratic People's Republic of (North Korea): The Democratic People's Republic of Korea was formed in 1948 in the wake of political conflict between the Soviet Union, whose troops occupied the northern part of the Korean peninsula after World War II, and the United States, whose troops occupied the southern portion. Kim Il Sung, a Korean who had served in the Soviet Army, was installed by the Soviets as the new nation's ruler; his secretive Communist regime, centered in Pyongyang, soon embarked on a consistent policy of hostility toward South Korea and its Western allies that in ensuing decades would result

Small village north of the capital of Pyongyang, North Korea. (AP/Wide World Photos)

in sporadic violence and one large-scale international conflict. (See KOREAN WAR.)

North Korea encompasses an area of roughly 46,800 miles, or slightly more than half of the Korean peninsula, between the Yellow Sea to the west and the Sea of Japan to the east. The country is bordered on the north primarily by the People's Republic of China and on the south by a demilitarized zone that separates it from South Korea (it also shares a small northern border with the former Soviet Union). The landscape consists primarily of alternating mountains and valleys. Outstanding physical features include the Nangnim Mountains, which run north-south through the center of the country and form a natural division between east and west, and the Yalu River, which flows for more than five hundred miles along the country's northern frontier. Climatic conditions are generally harsh, with a wide annual temperature range and an average annual rainfall of about forty inches. Deforestation has removed trees from most lowland areas, which are largely given over to the cultivation of rice, corn, wheat, and other grains; many mountainous regions, however, are still covered by expanses of fir, pine, and other coniferous trees.

Under KIM IL SUNG's doctrine of *juche* thought (communal self-reliance), social life in North Korea was extremely regimented. Images of Kim, who was generally known as "the Great Leader," were ubiquitous, from billboard-sized portraits on public buildings to lapel buttons.

North Korea's state-run economy is industrially based. Large mineral and ore deposits support extensive iron and steel production; machinery and textile manufacturing are also important. In the 1980's, the country became a prime exporter of missiles and other weaponry to Middle Eastern countries. The military accounts for more than a fifth of the country's gross national product, with approximately one million of the country's estimated 1993 population of 22.6 million serving in the armed forces. In the early 1990's, North Korea's nuclear industry became a focus of international concern, as widespread suspicions about the country's production of atomic weapons sparked worldwide controversy.

Korea, Republic of (South Korea): The Republic of ·. Korea was created by a United Nations resolution in 1948 following the partition of the Korean peninsula

Namhae Bridge is a tourist attraction at Noryang on the southern coast of South Korea. (Korea National Tourism Corporation)

along the 38th parallel in the wake of World War II. The division of the peninsula between Communist forces in the north and a Western-backed regime in the south made the area a Cold War hot spot, and tensions erupted into full-scale international conflict between 1950 and 1953. (See KOREAN WAR.) Since the war, North and South Korea have endured an uneasy coexistence punctuated by occasional acts of violence and more frequent hostile rhetoric.

South Korea occupies an area of slightly more than 38,000 square miles, or roughly 45 percent of the Korean peninsula, which lies between the Yellow Sea to the west and the Sea of Japan to the east. The largely mountainous terrain is broken by small valleys and coastal plains; the outstanding physical feature is the Taebaek mountain range, which runs north-south down the eastern side of the peninsula and gives rise to the region's major rivers. The western and southern portions of the country contain many harbors and small islands. Annual temperatures range from about 20 degrees Fahrenheit to about 80 degrees Fahrenheit, and annual rainfall averages about fifty inches in most areas.

Although slightly smaller in size than North Korea,

South Korea has twice as many people, with a 1993 population of 44.6 million. For most of its short history, South Korea has been under authoritarian rule, with some degree of democracy but with significant limits on freedoms. Following the Korean War, the South Korean government, headed by Syngman RHEE since its founding, used the real threat of renewed aggression from the North as a pretext to stifle dissent.

In 1960, shortly after Rhee was elected, unopposed, to a fourth term as president, mass protests broke out against the corruption of Rhee's regime and his party's routine rigging of election results. (See APRIL REVOLUTION.) The eighty-five-year-old Rhee resigned, but his successor was overthrown by a military junta led by PARK CHUNG HEE, a major general who had been active in a campaign to reform the army.

Between 1961, when he took power, and 1979, when he was killed by one of his hand-picked lieutenants, the head of the Korean Central Intelligence Agency, Park presided over an unprecedented surge in development and economic growth. A decade after his death, when South Korea's capital, Seoul, hosted the 1988 Olympics, Park's positive legacy was showcased to the world. Yet Park also grew increasingly dictatorial in his policies, maintaining only a semblance of democracy and creating a deeply entrenched system of political repression. Not until the election of ROH TAE WOO as president in 1987 did South Korea begin to move—very slowly—toward genuine democratic reforms, a process continued under Kim Young Sam, who became president in December, 1992.

As South Korea's first civilian president since 1961, Kim has had to contend with a slowdown in economic growth as well as with the challenges of establishing democratic institutions. South Korea's major industries include clothing, footwear, steel (in which it is a world leader), electronics, and automobile manufacturing. Between 1987 and 1991, sales of South Korean-made cars, household electronics, and computer chips more than doubled the per-capita gross national product, with a commensurate rise in living standards. Still, production dropped in 1990 and 1991, largely as a result of labor disputes.

In 1994, tensions with North Korea were higher than they had been for many years, in part as a result of the ongoing controversy over the North's nuclear facilities. Nevertheless, Kim continued to press for reforms, calling for measures to cut campaign spending, and scheduling for 1995 South Korea's first election of mayors and provincial governors since 1960.

Korea, reunification of: Reunification of the two halves of the divided Korean Peninsula has been a common aspiration of the Korean people since the end of World War II. Various proposals for affecting political reunification have been submitted by both North and South Korea since the creation of separate and competing regimes in 1948. While there has been some progress in reducing regional tensions and increasing contact between the two regimes, all attempts to achieve actual reunification have failed.

Causes of Division. A unified state since 668 C.E., Korea's strategic location in East Asia made it the target of great power rivalry for many centuries. Following victories in the Sino-Japanese War (1894-1895) and the Russo-Japanese War (1904-1905), Japan annexed Korea as a colony. With Japan's surrender to the Allies in August, 1945, the United States and the Soviet Union jointly occupied Korea. Soviet forces

This view of Seoul, South Korea, shows traditional and modern influences. (Korea National Tourism Corporation)

occupied areas north of the 38th parallel, and U.S. forces occupied the area south of that demarcation line. In Moscow in December, 1945, the Soviets and Americans agreed to a joint trusteeship plan that would lead to a unified and independent Korea within five years.

Announcement of the Moscow declaration provoked widespread opposition throughout the Korean population. A general resentment of foreign intervention was exploited and exacerbated by political factions vying for internal power. Korean domestic opposition coupled with the onset of the Cold War stalemated attempts to form a coalition Korean government acceptable to both domestic and foreign interests. Korea became a pawn in the emerging Cold War struggle.

When United Nations-sponsored elections failed to establish a unified Korean government in 1948, two separate and competing regimes were proclaimed: the Republic of Korea (ROK) under a pro-American leadership in the southern zone, and the Democratic People's Republic of Korea (DPRK) under pro-Soviet leadership in the northern zone. In this way enduring ideological and territorial divisions coincided with and reinforced one another.

On June 25, 1950, North Korean forces invaded

Former President Ronald Reagan chats with Army guard post commander while viewing North Korean positions from the South Korean side of the DMZ in 1983. (AP/Wide World Photos)

South Korea in an attempt to unify the peninsula by force. This civil war became an international war when various foreign powers intervened in support of one or the other side. An armistice ending the fighting was negotiated in 1953; however, the war is not technically over as no formal peace treaty has been signed. The suffering and bitterness of the KOREAN WAR solidified an apparently permanent national division between two mutually hostile regimes claiming the legitimacy to rule the entire peninsula.

Unification Efforts Since 1945. Efforts to reunify Korea have been viewed by historian Donald Macdonald as having occurred in seven phases. The first phase, 1945-1947, was the period of joint international trusteeship between the United States and the Soviet Union. This attempt failed because of strong opposition from the Korean people, who believed that it smacked of foreign intervention in their domestic affairs.

The second phase, 1947-1948, was that of United Nations (UN) involvement. A UN commission was authorized to negotiate a political compromise and hold elections to establish a coalition government. This attempt failed when the north refused to allow UN officials to organize balloting in its zone. As a consequence separate states had been established by the end of 1948.

The third phase, 1950-1953, was the attempt to reunify by military force. The initial attempt by DPRK forces was frustrated by U.S. and UN intervention on the side of the south. After UN forces crossed the 38th parallel in pursuit of defeated DPRK forces, Chinese troops intervened on behalf of the latter, and a military stalemate ensued.

The fourth phase was the attempt to return the problem to the UN for negotiated resolution. In 1954 representatives of the combatants met in Geneva to propose alternative solutions, but the conference broke up without reaching a consensus. While the UN continued to debate the Korean question annually until 1975, neither North nor South Korea were granted full membership in that body until 1992.

The fifth phase, 1954-1960, was characterized by North Korean attempts at armed subversion in the south while, at the same time, organizing public appeals for negotiations and a nonaggression pact with the Seoul government. The South Korean attitude was one of uncompromising intransigence and refusal to open a dialogue with the north.

The sixth phase, 1960-1971, was characterized by the North Korean proposal for the formation of a Con-

President Kim Young-sam of South Korea, 1993. (AP/Wide World Photos)

federal Republic of Koryo. This system would preserve the equal status of the separate political and economic systems of the two states, as well as their separate foreign alliance arrangements. A Supreme National Committee would preside over certain common issues of mutual concern. This initiative also failed to enlist the support of South Korea.

The seventh phase represents the opening of genuine dialogue between the two regimes. It began in 1971 when the north accepted Seoul's proposal for joint talks and exchanges on the sensitive issue of divided families involving their respective Red Cross agencies. In July, 1972, the two sides issued a Joint Declaration in which they pledged themselves to the principles of independence from foreign interference, unification through peaceful means, and the search for national unity. A South-North Coordinating Committee was established as well as a "hot line" linking Seoul and Pyongyang. Progress stalled, however, and

Late North Korean head of state Kim Il Sung (left) and his son Jong Il. (AP/Wide World Photos)

the north stopped answering the hot line in 1976. Until the mid-1980's, a "dialogue of the deaf" resumed.

Continuing Separation. In 1984 a thaw in relations began when the south accepted relief supplies from the north in response to a devastating flood. In the same year representatives of their respective legislatures met to discuss issues in the areas of sports, economics, the Red Cross, and parliamentary affairs. In 1985 members of fifty divided families were allowed to cross the demilitarized zone (DMZ) in search of relatives living on the other side. In 1989 South Korean business tycoon Chung Ju-Young visited Pyongyang to discuss the possibility of joint business ventures. In September of that year ROK President Roh Tae Woo proposed the creation of a Korean Commonwealth with two heads of state, a joint ministerial body of twenty members (ten from each side), and a joint legislature of one hundred (fifty from each side). This incremental approach was rejected by the DPRK, and national division continues.—*Michael A. Launius*

SUGGESTED READINGS: • Clark, Donald, ed. *Korea Briefing, 1992*. Boulder, Colo.: Westview Press, 1992. • Haas, Michael, ed. *Korean Reunification: Alternative Pathways*. New York: Praeger, 1989. • Kwak, Tae-Hwan, Chonghan Kim, and Hong Nack Kim, eds. *Korean Reunification: New Perspectives and Approaches*. Seoul, Korea: Kyungnam University Press, 1984. • Macdonald, Donald S. *The Koreans: Contemporary Politics and Society*. Boulder, Colo.: Westview Press, 1990. • Mazarr, Michael, et al., eds. *Korea 1991: The Road to Peace*. Boulder, Colo.: Westview Press, 1991.

Korea Herald: One of two major English-language daily newspapers circulating in South Korea. It was founded in 1953 originally as the *Korean Republic*, assuming its present name in 1965. The only other English-language daily is the *Korea Times*. Both newspapers are morning editions.

Korea Journal: Semimonthly, scholarly English-language journal published by the Korean National Commission in Seoul, South Korea, since 1961. The publication, with topics ranging from history to politics to culture, is produced for the United Nations Educational, Scientific, and Cultural Organization (UNESCO).

Korea Review: Monthly magazine issued from 1919 to 1922 by the Bureau of Korean Information in Philadelphia, Pennsylvania. The journal was devoted to the cause of political and religious freedom for Korea, at that time under Japanese colonization. The reports included accounts of atrocities inflicted by Japanese forces and other suppressions of the Korean independence movement.

Korea Society: Private, nonprofit New York City-centered organization dedicated to promoting mutual understanding between the United States and Korea, and among Koreans, Korean Americans, and other Americans. Formed in 1993 by the merger of an earlier Korea Society, also headquartered in New York City, and the Washington, D.C.-based U.S. Korea Foundation, the society fosters knowledge and awareness of Korean and Korean American culture. Its Festival of Korea, a year-long celebration of Korean art and music beginning in the fall of 1993, included musical performances and a traveling exhibition, "Korean Arts of the 18th Century: Splendor and Simplicity."

Korea Times: Korean-language general newspaper, the North American branch of which was founded in New York City in 1967. This newspaper has the largest circulation of any non-English daily newspaper printed in the United States a total circulation of 150,000 copies daily (except on Sunday, when the paper is not published). The *Korea Times* is also the only Korean-language newspaper in the United States that prints an English edition, which comes out weekly in an eight-page format. In addition, the *Korea Times* published the *Korea Times Magazine*, a quarterly English-language popular magazine.

The parent office of the *Korea Times* is in Seoul, South Korea. The newspaper's first North American branch was established by Peter H. Ohm, a Korean emigrant and an American university graduate. By the 1990's, the newspaper was being published in nine major North American cities: Los Angeles, New York, Chicago, Houston, Honolulu, Seattle, San Francisco, Toronto, and Vancouver. The Los Angeles office, established in 1969 and head of all U.S. branch offices, has the largest North American circulation, at 50,000 copies daily. All North American offices remain affiliated with the parent office.

The scope of the *Korea Times* is impressive. Its length, averaging eighty to ninety pages daily, rivals that of the *New York Times* or the *Los Angeles Times*. A broad range of topics is also covered, as the paper is the primary source of printed news for many of its readers.

Korea-U.S. Treaty of Amity and Commerce (1882): First treaty concluded between CHOSON Korea and the Western countries. It was a historic turning point for Korea because it opened doors for other Western countries to enter similar treaty relations with Korea, effectively introducing the hermit kingdom to the world community.

The United States did little to open Choson Korea even after signing a treaty with Japan in 1854. Until then, Choson Korea was generally known to the West as a Chinese dependency, a misrepresentation that Qing China was most anxious to preserve. A major turning point came when in 1866 an American merchant ship was attacked and burned on the Daedong

River near Pyongyang after it defied the local authorities' order to withdraw. After the attack, Washington tried to no avail to get the Choson court's explanation of the matter. The United States dispatched its naval squadron briefly landing at Ganghwa Island in 1871. Still, the Choson court did not respond to American gunboat diplomacy.

After Korea signed a forced treaty with Japan in 1876, the United States renewed its efforts to open Korea. In 1880, it dispatched Admiral Robert W. Shufeldt to Korea to negotiate a treaty, mainly to secure the Choson court's cooperation in relation to American shipwrecks in Korean waters. Encountering Choson's indifference and Japan's lukewarm cooperation, Shufeldt sought the help of Viceroy Li Hung-chang, the Qing court's strongman. Li urged the Choson court to open its doors to the United States to counter growing Japanese influence in Seoul. In 1882, the Choson court signed the agreement with minor revisions, thus first formally opening its door to a Western power. The Korea-U.S. treaty was similar to the one signed with Japan. The pact designated open ports, extraterritoriality for diplomats of both countries, and other commercial provisions. President Chester A. Arthur's administration sent its first ambassador to Korea in 1883.

King Kojong of Choson was anxious to bring in a Western power to curb the increasingly abusive Japanese influence in Seoul. The Qing Dynasty, however, pursued its own extensive ambitions. Throughout the negotiation process, Qing officials pressured Americans to acknowledge Qing overlordship over the Choson court. Americans persistently refused to agree to this, believing that the treaty would be useful only when Choson was a free, independent state rather than a tributary state of China. In the end, the treaty became the second international document that clearly and unambiguously declared Choson's independent, equal status in the world community.

Koreagate (1977): Scandal that resulted from allegations of bribery and influence-peddling activities involving members of the U.S. Congress and agents of the South Korean government in the 1970's. The term "Koreagate" was an allusion to the Watergate scandal, which had rocked American politics only a few years before. The incident damaged the image of South Korea in the United States and strained diplomatic relations between the two governments.

In October, 1976, the American media reported questionable political and financial relationships between American politicians and agents of the South Korean government, some of whom were officials of the KOREAN CENTRAL INTELLIGENCE AGENCY (KCIA) while others were Korean Americans or Korean permanent residents in the United States. Mots of the politicians were congressmen connected to the lucrative rice trade between the United States and South Korea. Others were in positions of influence over South Korea's national security affairs.

The scandal had launched five separate U.S. government investigations by the spring of 1977. The investigations centered on whether and to what degree the South Korean government had utilized financial rewards to influence the voting behavior of members of Congress toward policies affecting South Korea.

A central figure in the scandal was Park Tong Sun, a Korean resident in the Washington, D.C. area. It was alleged that Park bribed American politicians at the behest of the South Korean government. Another central figure was Suzi Park Thompson, a Korean American staffer in the office of then house speaker Carl Albert. She was accused of seeking to influence Albert's political positions as well as supplying confidential information to the KCIA. Neither Park nor Thompson was successfully prosecuted for their actions.

In the end only one American Congressman, Richard Hanna of California, was convicted and sentenced to prison for bribery. The scandal tarnished the reputation of Congress, and, in exposing attempts by the Korean government to buy influence in the United States, it damaged Korean American political relationships. Given the historic mutual security and economic interests that bind South Korea and the United States together, however, such damage proved to be temporary.

Korean Air Lines incident (1983): Aviation disaster in which an unarmed South Korean commercial airliner was shot down by a Soviet jet fighter, killing all 269 persons aboard. The airliner had been traveling from New York to Seoul and had apparently strayed into Soviet airspace.

At about 4:00 P.M. Greenwich mean time on September 1, Korean Air Lines (KAL) flight KE007 came to the attention of Soviet radar as it began drifting into Soviet airspace. The aircraft had strayed more than three hundred miles off course twice, first over the Kamchatka Peninsula and again over Sakhalin Island, a strategic military area north of the Japanese island of Hokkaido. The Soviets tracked the commercial airliner for some two-and-a-half hours. At 6:12 P.M. a Soviet pilot reported visual contact with the Korean aircraft. At 6:26 P.M. the pilot reported that he fired a missile and that the target was destroyed. At 6:38 P.M. the aircraft disappeared from the radar screen.

The Soviet Union said that the fighter pilot had been ordered to stop the flight of the Korean airliner as it flew over Sakhalin Island after the aircraft failed to obey the fighter pilot's instructions. Soviet leaders contended that the United States was ultimately responsible for the loss of the aircraft, which was said to have taken a "preplanned spying mission" for the United States over the restricted Soviet territory.

There was speculation that the Soviet pilot could have confused the Korean commercial jetliner with a military reconnaissance plane used by American forces off the Pacific coast of the Soviet Far East. In response, however, it was strongly argued that no circumstances could have justified the unprecedented attack on an unarmed civilian aircraft. Members of the United Nations (UN) denounced the Soviet Union for the "massacre" as the UN Security Council began reviewing the evidence. The international pilots' union called for a sixty-day suspension of flights to Moscow

in retaliation for the downing of the Korean jetliner.

A Soviet delegate attending a conference in Scotland told the British Broadcasting Corporation (BBC) on September 21 that the Soviet pilot had mistakenly identified the Korean aircraft as a spy plane and had, therefore, wrongly destroyed it. The occasion marked the first time that the Soviet government confessed to acting in error when it downed the other aircraft.

Korean American-African American relations: Although post-1965 Korean immigrants have high levels of education, because of language barriers and other disadvantages many of them have not found occupations to match their education and ability. As an alternative to menial blue-collar work, many Korean immigrants have turned to self-employment in labor-intensive small businesses. A significant proportion of Korean-owned businesses are located in low-income African American neighborhoods where big corporations and white independent store owners are reluctant to invest because of high crime, vandalism, and the low spending capacity of the residents. In fact, the majority of stores in many low-income black neighborhoods in Los Angeles, New York, and other cities

Demonstrators gather outside the boycotted Korean-owned Red Apple grocery store in 1991. (AP/Wide World Photos)

are owned by Korean immigrants.

Community Hostility. One consequence of Korean immigrants' involvement in African American neighborhoods is the interracial conflict between the Korean American and African American communities. Korean merchants in black neighborhoods in Los Angeles, New York, and other cities have been subject to black hostility and rejection in different forms: verbal and physical attacks, murder, boycotts, arson, and looting. Black hostility toward Korean merchants has not been limited to black residents and customers. Black community leaders, black nationalist organizations, and

Korean American owner of boycotted Red Apple grocery store displays letter of support and $100 that was delivered by an unidentified African American man. (AP/Wide World Photos)

Jesse Jackson meets with leaders of the Korean American coalition after the 1992 Los Angeles riots. (Steve Yang)

black mass media have joined forces in attacking Korean merchants and the Korean community as a whole.

One form that African American hostility toward Korean merchants has taken is the long-term boycott. The New York and Los Angeles Korean American communities have experienced several major long-term boycotts of Korean stores. The longest and most publicized boycott occurred in 1990 in Brooklyn, New York. It started in January after a scuffle between a Haitian black woman, who paid only two dollars for a three-dollar item, and the manager of a Korean produce retail store, who allegedly beat up the customer. The boycott of this Korean store and another one nearby lasted one and a half years. The New York Korean community responded to the boycott by raising a large amount of money to help the owners of the two stores. Unhappy about Mayor David Dinkins' lukewarm effort to terminate the boycott, Koreans in New York held a rally in front of city hall in which some seven thousand Koreans participated. The boycott came to an end in May, 1991, when the owner of Red Apple, the main target of the boycott, sold his store to another Korean.

The most severe instance of Korean American merchants' conflict with the African American community took place in Los Angeles in 1992. On April 29 of that year, after the verdicts were announced in the first Rodney King trial, with acquittal for three of the police officers charged with using excessive force against King and a mistrial declared for the fourth defendant, racial tensions exploded in Los Angeles. (See LOS ANGELES RIOTS OF 1992.) Between 2,000 and 2,500 Korean stores were targets of destruction during three days of rioting.

In part the high Korean losses reflected the fact that a disproportionately large number of Korean stores were located in African American and Latino neighborhoods in South Central Los Angeles, where the destruction was most severe. An investigation by the Federal Bureau of Investigation (FBI), however, indicated that black gangs, who played an active role in the riots, specifically targeted Korean-owned stores for arson and looting. Many Latinos as well as many African Americans were participants in the violence, but

Korean American schoolgirls pass a National Guardsman on duty in South Central Los Angeles in the aftermath of the 1992 Los Angeles riots. (AP/Wide World Photos)

there is evidence that African Americans and Latinos participated in rioting for different reasons. South Central Los Angeles has a higher percentage of African Americans than Koreatown and other areas where violence occurred. An assessment of riot damage shows that a higher percentage of Korean stores in South Central Los Angeles were damaged by arson and that alternatively a higher percentage of Korean stores in other areas were simply looted. This suggests that more residents of the predominantly African American community of South Central participated in the destruction of Korean stores out of their hatred of and revenge against Korean merchants, whereas the residents of other areas simply stole stock from Korean stores.

Roots of the Conflict. Middleman minority theory offers an insight into the nature of Korean American-African American conflicts. Historically, middleman merchants engaged in distributing products made by the ruling group to minority customers have been subject to hostility. Korean merchants, like middlemen in other societies, have become targets of black hostility partly because they play a middleman role in American society. Although the larger system is mainly responsible for black economic problems, Korean merchants as middlemen between black residents and big corporations bear the brunt of black economic frustrations.

Although middleman minority theory is useful in understanding the basic nature of the conflict, it fails to assess the multiple sources of the problem. From this theoretical perspective, the middleman position of Korean immigrants is mainly responsible for the conflict, and nothing else is an important contributor to the problem. This approach fails to take account of two other important factors which help to explain the conflict.

Every major conflict between Koreans and African Americans started with an altercation between a Korean merchant/employee and an African American customer on the premises of a Korean-owned store. One frequently heard African American complaint, whenever a major racial conflict occurs, is that Korean merchants do not treat black customers respectfully. This suggests that cultural differences, including Koreans' language barrier, and mutual prejudice between Korean merchants and black customers, have partly contributed to these kinds of altercations.

Altercations between Korean merchants and African American customers are sometimes violent. In 1991, after a dispute over payment for a container of juice, Latasha Harlins, a fifteen-year-old African American, struck Soon Ja Due, a Korean merchant in South Central Los Angeles. As Harlins was walking away, Soon shot and killed her. When Soon received an extremely light sentence and was released on probation—the judge declared that she was not a threat to the community—African Americans were outraged. Some observers have suggested that the destruction of Korean businesses in the 1992 riots was in part in retribution for this incident.

On the other side, Korean merchants feel extremely vulnerable to assault. In 1993, there were more than fifty gun-related crimes against Korean merchants in Los Angeles, a number of them resulting in deaths. According to a report on anti-Asian violence issued by the National Asian Pacific American Legal Coalition in April, 1994, eighteen of these cases may have involved racial motivation.

Although cultural differences and mutual prejudice have contributed to merchant-customer altercations, these social-psychological factors are not sufficient to account for the long-term boycotts of Korean stores. A more important factor that has led African American residents and leaders to boycott Korean stores is the black nationalist ideology that views outsiders' commercial activities in black neighborhoods as economic exploitation. Black nationalist leaders have typically organized boycotts of Korean stores. This has been particularly true in New York City, where in the tradition of Marcus Garvey and Malcolm X black nationalism has had a great influence on black community politics. Sonny Carson, who has played an influential role in black nationalist movements in New York City, also played a significant role in organizing or at least intervening in all five major black boycotts of Korean stores. Influenced by black nationalist leaders and the black media, many African Americans have accepted the perception that Korean merchants are out to exploit them.

Despite this history of conflict, many individuals within both the Korean American and African American communities are working to improve relations between the groups. Moreover, there is a consensus among scholars who represent widely differing ideological positions that Korean American-African American conflict, especially as manifested in Los Angeles in 1992, has drawn attention to the dynamics of a multiethnic society, exposing the inadequacy of traditional models of race relations in the United States.—*Pyong Gap Min*

Suggested Readings: • *Amerasia Journal* 19, no. 2 (1993). Special issue: "Los Angeles—Struggles Toward Multiethnic Community." Edward Chang, guest editor. • Chang, Edward. "New Urban Crisis: Korean-Black Conflicts in Los Angeles." Ph.D. diss. Ethnic Studies Department, University of California, Berkeley, 1990. • Cheng, Lucie, and Yen Le Espiritu. "Korean Business in Black and Hispanic Neighborhoods: A Study of Intergroup Relations." *Sociological Perspectives* 32 (1989): 521-534. • Lee, Heon Cheol. "Black-Korean Conflict in New York City: A Sociological Analysis." Ph.D. diss. Department of Sociology, Columbia University, 1993. • Light, Ivan, Hadas Har-Chvi, and Kenneth Kan. "Black-Korean Conflict in Los Angeles." In *Managing Divided Cities*, edited by Seamus Dunn. Newbury Park, Calif. Sage Publications, 1994. • Min, Pyong Gap. "Ethnic Business, Intergroup Conflicts, and Ethnic Solidarity: Korean Immigrants in New York and Los Angeles." Unpublished manuscript, Department of Sociology, Queens College of CUNY, 1993.

Korean American businesses: Korean Americans participate in self-employed small businesses at high rates. According to the 1980 U.S. census, about 12 percent of Korean Americans who were economically active in 1979 were self-employed workers, whereas less than 7 percent of the U.S. general work force were self-employed. The concentration of Korean Americans in small businesses is most conspicuous in such large cities as New York, Los Angeles, and Chicago, where between 30 and 60 percent of Korean adult workers are self-employed business owners. When taking into account both unpaid family workers and Korean employees working for Korean businesses, more than half of Korean American workers partici-

pate in the Korean ethnic economy as either employers or employees.

Causes of High Rates of Self-Employment. For many Korean Americans, self-employment in business is a situational adaptation to limited opportunities for white-collar wage employment in the U.S. labor market. Although the majority of post-1965 Korean immigrants received a college education and came from white-collar occupational backgrounds in South Korea, the jobs initially available to them in the United States are low-skilled and low-paying manual, service, and sales jobs. The English-language barrier and the difficulty of transferring their Korean education and occupational skills to the American labor market are largely responsible for the immigrants' difficulty in obtaining white-collar employment. Under such circumstances, Korean immigrants turn to small businesses to earn more income and gain more independence by working for themselves rather than working for others.

In addition to Korean Americans' aspirations for upward economic mobility, the economic development of South Korea has been crucial for the growth of Korean American businesses. In 1962 South Korea started an export-oriented economic development that was highly dependent on foreign markets, especially those of the United States. In the early period, cheap consumer goods such as wigs, footwear, apparel, and accessories were South Korea's major export items. Large numbers of Korean immigrants had emerged in the late 1960's and early 1970's as agents of the export-import trade between South Korea and the United States, importing and distributing Korean-made products to Korean retailers in the United States. This international trade linkage provided Korean immigrants with initial business opportunities in minority neighborhoods of central cities, where inexpensive Korean-made products were in big demand among low-income customers.

The race-related demographic changes which affected both residential and business areas in U.S. central cities during the 1960's also aided the entry of Korean American businesses into minority neighborhoods. As African Americans moved into previously white-dominated neighborhoods, the white population moved out. The out-migration of whites from central cities was frequently followed by white shop-owners leaving, increasing the number of vacated businesses in those racially transitional areas. Such changes enabled Korean Americans to establish their businesses in minority neighborhoods without great resistance from local businesses.

Top 8 Types of Korean-Owned Small Businesses, New York City, 1992	
Total businesses	15,000
Delis and groceries	2,500
Vegetable markets	1,500
Cleaners	1,500
Variety stores	700
Fish markets	600
Nail salons	400
Garment factories	250
Korean restaurants	90

Source: Ann Hagen Griffiths, *The Korean Americans*. The New Americans series. New York: Facts on File, 1992.

Korea House Restaurant, San Francisco, California. (Robert Fried)

Characteristics of Korean American Businesses. Korean American businesses are generally small in size with respect to annual gross sales and the number of paid employees. According to the U.S. Bureau of the Census' Survey of Minority-Owned Business Enterprises, by 1987 Korean Americans owned 69,304 businesses nationwide, with total gross receipts of $47,683 million. The average gross receipts per business were $110,859, which were less than 60 percent of the average receipts ($189,000) of businesses owned by white proprietors. Of the 69,304 businesses, only 30 percent had paid employees, and the average number of paid employees (excluding businesses without paid employees) was 3.25. Ninety-four percent of Korean American businesses were owned by individual proprietors, and the owners and their family members were the major operators of those individually owned businesses.

Handicapped by limited capital, the English-language barrier, and the lack of prior business experience, Korean Americans tend to concentrate in labor-intensive retail and personal service trades, such as produce, grocery and liquor, apparel and accessory, general merchandise retail, dry cleaning and laundry, and res-

taurant businesses. To lower the entry-level costs further, many Koreans established their businesses in low-income minority neighborhoods of large central cities. Korean businesses in those neighborhoods fill a marginal market that is neglected by large retail stores because of the low profit margin and high crime rates.

Resource Mobilization. Korean Americans finance their businesses mainly through informal financial resources, such as personal savings, loans from relatives and friends, and Korean rotating credit associations called *kye*. The use of loans from banks and the federal Small Business Administration (SBA) is limited at least at the early stage of business formation.

The *kye* is an informal financial club where a group of people, often ten to twenty, contribute the same amount of money to a fund, which is loaned to one of them in a rotating order. It consists primarily of friends, family members or relatives, or church members among whom the personal trust is guaranteed through longtime relationships. By utilizing such informal resources, Korean Americans overcome the difficulty of getting loans from financial institutions.

The Prospects. Although Korean American businesses have been heavily concentrated in small-scale

Korean American small businesses thrive in this mini-mall in Garden Grove, California. (The Korea Society/Los Angeles)

Korean American Businesses in the U.S. by Type and Receipts, 1987

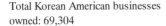

Total Korean American businesses
owned: 69,304

Total receipts: $7,683,000,000

Rank order among Asian Americans: 2nd
in businesses owned, 2nd in receipts

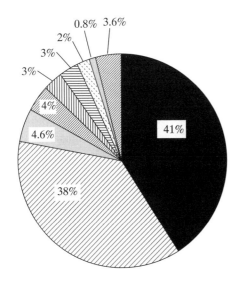

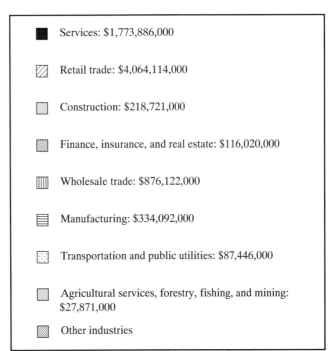

- Services: $1,773,886,000
- Retail trade: $4,064,114,000
- Construction: $218,721,000
- Finance, insurance, and real estate: $116,020,000
- Wholesale trade: $876,122,000
- Manufacturing: $334,092,000
- Transportation and public utilities: $87,446,000
- Agricultural services, forestry, fishing, and mining: $27,871,000
- Other industries

Source: Susan B. Gall and Timothy L. Gall, eds., *Statistical Record of Asian Americans.* Detroit: Gale Research, Inc., 1993.
Note: Receipt totals withheld for mining and "other" categories.

retail and service trades, there has been a noticeable transition toward more capital- and technology-intensive businesses. From 1982 to 1987, 6,494 new businesses were established in construction, manufacturing, wholesale trade, finance, insurance, and real estate, recording a 197 percent increase. In contrast, retail trade gained only a 104 percent increase, from 12,831 to 26,161 businesses. As a result of this upgrade in business types, the average receipts per business increased from $9,480 (in 1987 dollars) to $110,859.

While Korean immigrants will continue to engage in self-employed businesses at high rates, U.S.-born second- and third-generation Korean Americans will not follow the paths of their parents. Instead, they will seek professional and white-collar wage employment in the mainstream American economy. Accordingly, as increasing numbers of second- and third-generation Korean Americans enter the U.S. labor market, self-employment rates among Korean Americans are expected to decline.—*In-Jin Yoon*

SUGGESTED READINGS: • Kim, Illsoo. *New Urban Immigrants: The Korean Community in New York.* Princeton, N.J.: Princeton University Press, 1981. • Kim, Kwang Chung, and Won Moo Hurh. "Ethnic Resource Utilization of Korean Immigrant Entrepreneurs in the Chicago Minority Area." *International Migration Review* 19 (Spring, 1985): 82-111. • Light, Ivan, and Edna Bonacich. *Immigrant Entrepreneurs: Koreans in Los Angeles, 1965-1982.* Berkeley: University of California Press, 1988. • Min, Pyong Gap. *Ethnic Business Enterprise: Korean Small Business in Atlanta.* New York: Center for Migration Studies, 1988. • Yoon, In-Jin. "The Changing Significance of Ethnic and Class Resources in Immigrant Businesses: The Case of Korean Immigrant Businesses in Chicago." *International Migration Review* 25 (Summer, 1991): 303-331. • Young, Philip K. Y. "Family Labor, Sacrifice, and Competition: Korean Greengrocers in New York City." *Amerasia Journal* 10 (Fall/Winter, 1983): 53-71.

Korean American Coalition members register a new citizen to vote in Los Angeles. (Robert Park)

Korean American Coalition (KAC): Founded in 1983, a nonprofit, nonpartisan membership organization in Los Angeles that serves as an advocacy group for Korean Americans. The organization began as community leaders and activists recognized the need for an effective bilingual advocacy group. The KAC joins first-, second-, and third-generation Korean Americans to promote and advance the civic, legislative, and political interests of the Korean American community. The coalition, moreover, serves to establish a channel of communication between Korean American and other ethnic communities in Los Angeles.

The KAC is a voluntary organization consisting of a board of directors, officers elected by the general membership, and eight standing committees. The eight committees are as follows: Leadership Development, Public Affairs, Public Relations, Membership, Resource Development, Voter Registration, Historian, and Newsletter. These committees function to educate, organize, and empower the Korean American community through cultural, educational and political activities. The Leadership Development committee, for example, coordinates such programs as college internships in business, law, media, and politics with a goal

of encouraging personal and professional development among Korean American students.

The KAC also plays a pivotal political role within the Korean American community. One of the coalition's major objectives is to represent the community and its interest in the larger political arena. The group maintains communication and relationships with government agencies and elected officials to monitor services and representation for the community. The KAC, for example, took an active interest in the reapportionment process in redrawing the political boundaries of the state of California. The Public Affairs committee, moreover, monitors civil rights and community empowerment issues, coordinating such activities as media monitoring, legislative watch, and electoral politics. The group also occupies a prominent role in conducting voter education programs and in actually mobilizing Korean Americans to vote. In addition the KAC plays an important role for the Korean American community by communicating and coordinating issues with other minority communities. The group has worked actively to improve interracial relations between the Korean American and African American communities by serving as a forum in which the issues confronting the two communities can be effectively discussed.

Korean American Garment Industry Association:
Nonprofit, membership-supported community organization for Korean sewing contractors, established in 1978. It was formed to educate its members about U.S. labor codes and their rights and responsibilities as sewing contractors, as well as to find employment for those in need.

Korean American literature: Like the literature of other Asian ethnic groups in the United States, much of Korean American literature explores the experience of immigration and describes the economic hardships and racial discrimination confronting the immigrants upon arrival. A recurring theme is their effort to forge a Korean cultural and political identity in the midst of these transitions. One of the significant aspects of Korean American writings is the concern that many authors express for their Korean homeland. In *Asian American Literature: An Annotated Bibliography* (1988),

King-Kok CHEUNG and Stan Yogi list more than fifty works of poetry, prose, and epic drama by Korean Americans. Most of these works are out of print or are distributed by small presses, thus making them difficult to acquire. This entry highlights some of the more well-known works of Korean American literature.

Early Examples. The earliest works of Korean American literature were written by elite, Western-educated Koreans such as Younghill KANG, who were in the United States as students or political exiles. Kang's first book, *The Grass Roof*, published in 1931, was an autobiographical fiction based on his experiences in Korea. This book was widely read both in the United States and in Europe. In 1937, Kang wrote *East Goes West: The Making of an Oriental Yankee*. According to Elaine H. Kim in *Asian American Literature: An Introduction to the Writings and Their Social Context* (1982), Kang's American and European audiences were not as receptive to this second effort because the book emphasized life in the United States rather than describing the exotic customs of a foreign country. It pointed out the difficult and ambivalent

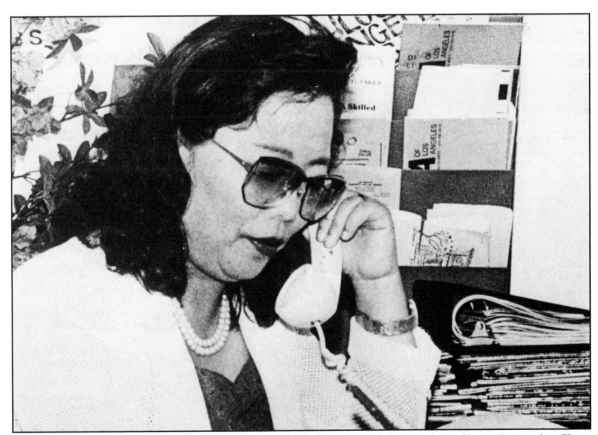

Mary Paik Lee wrote the autobiographical narrative entitled Quiet Odyssey: A Pioneer Korean Woman in America. (Korea Times)

Kim Ronyoung (Gloria Hahn), author of Clay Walls. (Richard Hahn)

experience of being a Korean immigrant.

Another early Korean American writer is Richard E. KIM, who published three books in the 1960's. *The Martyred* (1964) is a novel that explores the deaths of Christian missionaries during the Korean War (1950-1953); a second novel, about a military coup, is titled *The Innocent* (1969). In 1970, Kim published a collection of autobiographical pieces, *Lost Names: Scenes from a Korean Boyhood.*

Because of the severe restrictions on Asian immigration to the United States in the first half of the twentieth century, the Korean American community was relatively small, and therefore both Kang and Kim's audience would most likely have been composed of non-Koreans. With the liberalization of immigration laws in 1965, Koreans began to immigrate to the United States in large numbers. Several significant works have been produced since then by both first- and second-generation Korean Americans.

Post-1965 Works. In 1982, Theresa Hak Kyung CHA's *Dictee* was published. This book explores cultural identity and history as embedded in many other persons, histories, and languages, and demonstrates the influence of such seemingly diverse sources as Korean history, French film theory, Catholicism, and Greek mythology. One focus of the book, which addresses the Korean American experience, is the Japanese colonization of Korea, the Korean War, and the subsequent division of the country into North and South. The author and her family immigrated to the United States in 1963 to escape the political repression that followed these events. To conceive of different ways of writing about and representing these stories that would prevent them from being forgotten, the book utilizes diverse forms of representation such as narration, journal entries, photographs, old letters, maps, and language exercises.

Under the pen name Kim Ronyoung, second-generation Korean American Gloria HAHN published *Clay Walls* (1986). This novel tells the story of a Korean immigrant family in Los Angeles in the 1940's and 1950's. Separated into three sections that are narrated in turn by the father, the mother, and the daughter, *Clay Walls* relates the complex family dynamics of gender conflicts, intergenerational gaps, and class differences that are played out against the challenges of immigrant life in the United States. While the book is significant in its focus on the lives and thoughts of two generations of Korean American women, it is also remarkable for its attempt to draw sympathetic and complex portrayals of all three family members. Finally, *Clay Walls* is also insightful in terms of Korean American history and in describing the mother's involvement in the Korean independence movement.

Mary Paik Lee's *Quiet Odyssey: A Pioneer Korean Woman in America* (1990), edited by Sucheng CHAN, is an autobiographical narrative. Born in 1900 near Pyongyang, Korea, she was five years old when her family immigrated to Hawaii, and soon thereafter to California. Lee's memoir recounts her family's struggle against economic hardships and tells about her marriage, her three American-born children, and her interactions with other Korean immigrants. *Quiet Odyssey* is valuable not only for its first-person chronicle of early Korean American history but also for Sucheng Chan's substantial historical introduction and bibliographic essay. The experience of the first wave of Korean immigrants to the United States is also conveyed in Margaret K. Pai's *The Dreams of Two Yi-Min* (1989) and Peter Lee's *Mansei!*. All three volumes show the intense concern these Korean emigrants felt for the political situation in their homeland and describe their efforts to gain Korea's independence from Japan.

Poetry. In addition to these works of prose, significant contributions have been made to a growing body of Korean American poetry. In this genre, Cathy SONG, a Chinese Korean native of Hawaii, is perhaps the best known. Her first book, *Picture Bride*, was published in 1983 in the prestigious Yale Younger Poets series. The volume combines reflections upon her Korean heritage, the Hawaiian landscape, and the poet's relation to her various artistic endeavors. In 1988, Song published a second collection, *Frameless Windows, Squares of Light.* In *Under Flag* (1991), Myung Mi Kim, like Theresa Hak Kyung Cha, explores language in innovative ways and addresses questions of identity and citizenship in the context of immigration. Other Korean American poets include Willyce KIM (*Curtains of Light* [1971], *Eating Artichokes* [1972], *Under the Rolling Sky* [1976]), Sung-Won Ko (*The Turn of Zero* [1974], *With Birds of Paradise* [1984]), and Chungmi Kim (*Chungmi: Selected Poems* [1982]).—*L. Hyun-Li Kang*

SUGGESTED READINGS: • Cha, Theresa Hak Kyung. *Dictee.* New York: Tanam Press, 1982. • Kang, Younghill. *East Goes West: The Making of an Oriental Yankee.* New York: Charles Scribner's Sons, 1937. • Kim, Elaine H. *Asian American Literature: An Introduction to the Writings and Their Social Context.* Philadelphia: Temple University Press, 1982. • Kim, Ronyoung. *Clay Walls.* New York: Permanent Press,

1986. • Lee, Mary Paik. *Quiet Odyssey: A Pioneer Korean Woman in America*. Seattle: University of Washington Press, 1990. • Song, Cathy. *Picture Bride*. New Haven, Conn.: Yale University Press, 1983.

Korean American Political Association (KAPA): Political participation group founded in December, 1970, in San Francisco. How the KAPA came about has much to do with the turbulent 1960's, the time of the Civil Rights movement, during which many American minority groups developed a new political consciousness. It was during the 1960's that a group of Koreans believed that the time had come for Korean Americans to leave the fringes of American society and actively participate in the mainstream of the American political process.

Preparations began in late 1969 to draft a proposal for establishing an organization capable of providing leadership to this end. A year later, in December, 1970, a proposal was finally put before a plenary conference held in San Francisco, where more than three hundred participants, including delegates from sixteen regions in the United States, were represented. The approval of the organization's charter by delegates at this two-day conference gave birth to the KAPA, a nonpartisan organization dedicated to the development and participation of Korean Americans in American politics.

The KAPA operates with sixteen regional chapters headed by their respective chapter presidents, with the national chairperson overseeing regional chapters. The KAPA's most notable accomplishment in the 1970's was its participation in the Jerry Brown gubernatorial campaign in California. The KAPA's support for Brown's candidacy reportedly brought about Judge George Paik's judicial appointment to the Superior court of Monterey County, California.

The San Francisco KAPA chapter actively participated in the San Francisco Mayoral elections of George Moscone and Dianne Feinstein and in supervisorial elections. The Korean community's support for mayoral candidate Moscone was rewarded with Samuel Chung's appointment to the San Francisco Human Rights Commission in 1978. In the 1980 presidential election, the KAPA rallied behind President Ronald Reagan's candidacy. Subsequently, the Reagan Administration appointed Harry Bang, the former national executive director of the KAPA, to serve in the Civil Rights Division of the U.S. Department of Education.

The KAPA's Los Angeles chapter was headed for many years by Jay Kim, who was elected to the U.S. Congress from California's Forty-second Congressional District in 1992. Kim's successful bid to Congress is a credit to the vision the KAPA's founders had some twenty years before. Competing political organizations mushroomed in the 1980's among Koreans in the United States. The KAPA, the oldest such organization, is determined to work closely with these organizations.

Korean American women: The history of Korean American women's experience in the United States begins at the dawn of the twentieth century. The first wave of Koreans immigrated to the United States during the years 1903-1910. Forced from their native homes by poverty, heavy taxation, and the growing Japanese military presence, many Koreans saw emigration as an opportunity to improve both their economic and their educational situations.

Early years. The first Korean emigrants settled mostly in Hawaii. They were recruited by Hawaii plantation owners to act as strikebreakers against Japanese laborers, who at that time constituted the major portion of the plantation work force. Korean women came with their husbands to Hawaii and eventually worked on the sugar plantations with them. The lives of these women were often arduous and marked by physical hardship. While most worked alongside their husbands, some supplemented the meager household income by working as cooks for a number of bachelor Korean men living and working in Hawaii. Besides working outside the home, they were also responsible for such routine domestic chores as cooking, cleaning, and sewing. Within this first wave of immigrants, the family remained the primary focus of Korean women's lives. The predominance of family concerns, which limited their public activities, did not differ substantially from the ideology of separate gender spheres dominant in early American culture.

Picture brides constituted the next wave of Korean women who immigrated to the United States. They came during the years 1910-1924 to be the wives of single Korean men who had already established themselves in the United States. Although mostly poor, picture brides were generally younger, more educated, and more politically active then the previous group. Many of them had been teachers and had social contacts outside the home before they came to the United States. They transported their public experience by actively participating in church activities and uniting around organizations to further the social and political causes of their homeland.

Educational Attainment, Labor Status, and Occupation of Korean American Women, 1990

Education of Women 25 Years or Older	
	Percent
High school graduate	29%
Some college or associate degree	19%
College graduate	20%
Advanced or professional degree	6%
Total high school graduate or more	74%

Women 16 Years or Older	
	Percent
In labor force	56%
(Unemployed	6%)
Not in labor force	44%

Employed Civilian Women 16 Years or Older

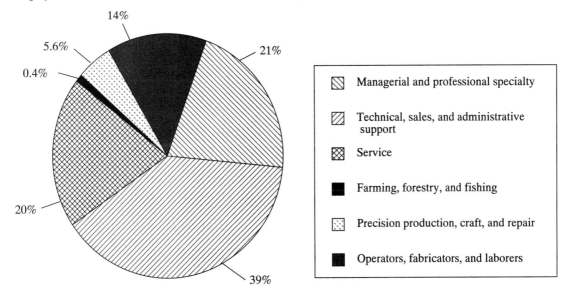

- ⬚ Managerial and professional specialty
- ⬚ Technical, sales, and administrative support
- ⬚ Service
- ■ Farming, forestry, and fishing
- ⬚ Precision production, craft, and repair
- ■ Operators, fabricators, and laborers

Source: U.S. Bureau of the Census, *1990 Census of Population: Asians and Pacific Islanders in the United States,* 1993.

Nationalist sentiment reached a peak among Koreans with the Japanese annexation of Korea in 1910. When the MARCH FIRST MOVEMENT of 1919, the largest mobilization of demonstrators to march against the Japanese occupation, broke out in Korea, Korean women residing in the United States became increasingly political. The march prompted Korean women, largely made up of picture brides by this time, to organize regional clubs in Hawaii and in such mainland cities as Los Angeles, San Francisco, and Sacramento. The mobilization led them to become more active in the political arena and contributed to the growth of their social expression. Such organizations as the Korean Women's Patriotic Society, established in 1919, called for greater power for women in the Korean independence movement and greater education for them as well.

Besides their political contributions, the inflow of picture brides into the immigrant community was pivotal in transforming Korean immigrants from temporary to permanent settlers. Korean women also gained greater equality within the highly patriarchal and traditional familial structure. Although patriarchy never disappeared, their political and civic participation, contri-

Korean Immigrant Householders' Weekly Work Hours by Wife's Work Status				
	Families with Wife Not Working		**Families with Wife Working**	
Roles	Husband	Wife	Husband	Wife
Paid work	56.9	0	56.8	50.7
Household chores	5.2	46.3	6.7	24.8
Total	62.1	46.3	63.5	75.5

Source: Pyong Gap Min, "Korean Immigrant Wives' Overwork." *Korea Journal of Population and Development* 21 (1992): 32.

butions, and accomplishments allowed the American Korean family to adopt a more egalitarian tenor.

Subsequent Immigration. The next two waves of Korean women to emigrate to the United States occurred after the Korean War (1950-1953). Following the war the wives of U.S. servicemen came to the United States to join their husbands. The next wave came shortly after 1960, when many professional women emigrated in search of better economic and social conditions. Both groups experienced social marginality and employment hardship.

Korean War brides were mainly poorer, less-educated women. Married to American soldiers and scattered across various parts of the country, their experience differed from that experienced by most other Korean immigrant women. Instead of residing in Korean communities, they were isolated form other Koreans because of their geographical diffusion, and they experienced great difficulties in adjusting as a result. Unable to receive much support from either the Korean American community or the mainstream American society, they have been one of the most marginalized groups among Koreans living in the United States.

Women who emigrated in the 1960's were the product of the rising educational and professional opportunities that had emerged in Korea. Political and economic instability at home, as well as U.S. preferential immigration status for certain professional occupations, especially nurses, permitted the immigration of a generation of relatively highly educated women professionals. Yet because of a lack of fluency in English, many suffered a decline in their status. Unable to qualify for or pass the nursing examinations, those who stayed in health care were relegated to lower-level occupations. Others became sewing women, maintenance or laundry workers, and grocery and hamburgerstand attendants. This demotion bred both frustration and determination to achieve success through their children via education.

Greater Diversity. Immigrants who have come to the United States since 1974 constitute the majority of the Korean American population. Changes in U.S. immigration law altered the composition of the immigration population in the 1970's by allowing immigrants of more diversified population, in contrast to the wave of predominately professional immigrants who came in the 1960's. Many single and married urban Korean women belong to this latest group. Theirs is also a story of hardship and perseverance. They have worked mainly in labor-intensive jobs that require little skill. Many work in garment factories as seamstresses, often doing piece work. Others have found employment in small family businesses. Nevertheless in such cities as Los Angeles a large concentration of Koreans has allowed Korean women to become increasingly active and public through forming and participating in various community organizations. Although many Korean American women still face sexism within the predominantly patriarchal familial and social structures, a growing number of them, especially those among the younger generation who have received their college education in the United States, have become active in civic, religious, and educational organizations. Korean American women still face many concrete challenges, but their growing public and civic activism reflect the accelerated movement into public roles in the United States.—*Haein Park*

SUGGESTED READINGS: • Houchins, Lee, and Chang-su Houchins. "The Korean Experience in America, 1903-1924." *Pacific Historical Review* 43 (November, 1974): 584-75. • Kim, Bok-Lim. "Asian Wives of U.S. Servicemen: Women in Shadows." *Amerasia Journal* 4 (November 1, 1977): 91-111. • Sunoo, Sonia S. "Korean Women Pioneers of the Pacific Northwest." *Oregon Historical Quarterly* 79 (Spring, 1978): 51-63. • Yu, Eui-Young, and Earl H. Phillips, eds. *Korean Women in Transition: At Home and Abroad.* Los Angeles: Center for Korean-American and Korean Studies, California State University, Los Angeles, 1987.

Korean Americans: Koreans first began immigrating to the United States at the beginning of the twentieth century. Not until the post-World War II period, however, and especially after the Immigration and Nationalty Act of 1965, did a substantial Korean American community begin to develop. (For a full account of the early period, see KOREAN IMMIGRATION TO THE UNITED STATES.) The Korean American population grew from less than 100,000 in 1970 to approximately 800,000 in 1990.

The 1990 census indicates that 82 percent of Koreans in the United States were foreign-born, with only 2.4 percent having immigrated before 1965. These statistics suggest that post-1965 immigrants make up an overwhelming majority of the current Korean American community.

Korean Immigrants' Concentration in Small Businesses. Probably the most distinctive aspect of the post-1965 Korean immigrants is their concentration in small businesses. This has significantly affected their family lives, intergroup relations, and overall community structure.

Korean merchants are found in almost any neighborhood in the Korean communities of Los Angeles, New York, and other major U.S. cities. Based on casual observations, the American public seems to believe that Korean immigrants are business-oriented people. Surveys conducted in major Korean communities tend to support the validity of these casual observations. A study conducted in 1986 showed that 45 percent of the Korean workforce in Los Angeles was self-employed. A study based on interviews with Korean married

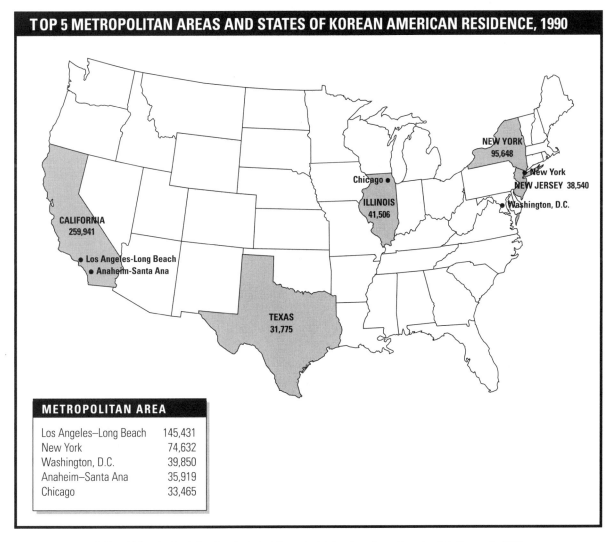

TOP 5 METROPOLITAN AREAS AND STATES OF KOREAN AMERICAN RESIDENCE, 1990

METROPOLITAN AREA	
Los Angeles–Long Beach	145,431
New York	74,632
Washington, D.C.	39,850
Anaheim–Santa Ana	35,919
Chicago	33,465

Source: Susan B. Gall and Timothy L. Gall, eds., *Statistical Record of Asian Americans.* Detroit: Gale Research, 1993.

Korean American family. (Robert W. Ginn)

Korean American-owned market, Brooklyn, New York. (Frances M. Roberts)

women in New York City revealed that 49 percent of Korean married women and 62 percent of their husbands were found to be self-employed; thus, the overall rate of self-employed married Koreans reached 56 percent. Another 30 percent of the New York respondents were employed in Korean-owned businesses; only 14 percent were employed in non-Korean firms. This means that Korean immigrants are highly segregated in their economic activities.

When minority/immigrant groups are overrepresented in small businesses, they are concentrated in a few or several business lines. Korean immigrants are heavily concentrated in grocery/green grocery retail, the retail of manufactured goods imported from South Korea and other Asian countries, dry cleaning, and a few other business lines. Grocery retail is the most common type of Korean-owned business in the United States. According to the Korean-American Grocers Association of Southern California, there were some 2,800 Korean-owned grocery/liquor stores in Southern California as of 1990, which accounted for 25 percent of the total independent grocery/liquor stores in that area. The Korean communities in Atlanta, Philadelphia, Seattle, and Washington, D.C., are also heavily

concentrated in grocery retail. In the New York Korean community, there are also a large number of fruit and vegetable stores, in addition to many grocery stores.

Another type of business common to major Korean communities is the retail of manufactured goods imported from South Korea and other Asian countries. These items include wigs, handbags, clothing, jewelry, hats, and shoes. This type of business has been made possible mainly because of the radical increase in Korean exports to the United States since the early 1970's. Many Korean immigrants took advantage of their native language and connections with South Korea and established import and wholesale businesses dealing in Korean-imported fashion items in the 1970's. They distribute Korean-imported merchandise mainly to Korean retailers.

Another popular Korean business line is dry cleaning. This business is attractive to Korean immigrants partly because it is very suitable for a family business involving husband-wife coordination and partly because it involves shorter hours of work and a lower level of physical strength than other types of retail businesses.

Few Korean immigrants who came to the United

New York City Married Koreans' Self-Employment and Economic Segregation Rates by Sex						
Job Type	Husbands		Wives		Total	
	Number	Percent	Number	Percent	Number	Percent
Self-employed	172	61.4	102	48.8	274	56.0
Employed in Korean firms	69	24.6	76	36.4	145	29.7
Employed in non-Korean firms	39	14.0	31	14.8	70	14.3
Total	280	100	209	100.0	489	100.0

Source: Pyong Gap Min, "Korean Immigrant Wives' Overwork." *Korea Journal of Population and Development* 21 (1992).

States in the late 1960's and the early 1970's planned to start their own businesses there. They expected to make successful adjustments in the white-collar and professional occupations for which they were originally trained. Most of the Korean immigrants at that time, however, had to switch to low-level, blue-collar occupations because of their inability to speak English and their unfamiliarity with U.S. customs. They reluctantly turned to small businesses as alternatives to undesirable blue-collar occupations. They were not prepared for self-employment in small business, nor were they familiar with it. Accordingly, it took them a long period of time to accumulate the capital and other elements necessary to start a business.

Recent Korean immigrants are better prepared to start their own businesses than the earlier post-1965 immigrants, since the former are told before leaving Korea that self-employment in small businesses is the only alternative for most Korean immigrants. Most recent Korean immigrants expect to run small businesses in the United States. In one predeparture survey conducted in Seoul in 1986, more than 70 percent of the male respondents and 60 percent of the total respondents reported that they would go into business when they came to the United States. In the early 1970's, many Korean immigrants attended language and vocational schools in Korea to increase their qualifications for employment in the U.S. labor market. By contrast, at present most prospective Korean immigrants try to bring enough money to establish their own businesses as soon as possible. Once they arrive here, Korean immigrants acquire business information and training easily from Korean-owned businesses. Consequently, recent Korean immigrants can start their own businesses much faster than the earlier immigrants.

Koreans' Middleman Role and Business-Related Intergroup Conflicts. An alien group specializing in minority-oriented businesses is referred to as a "middleman minority." A middleman minority, as is the case with Chinese in Southeast Asia and Asian Indians in South Africa, plays an intermediate role between the ruling class and the masses by distributing the products made by the former to the latter. Korean merchants in the United States play a middleman minority role in that they distribute products made by large corporations to low-income minority customers. According to the 1990 census, only 9.5 percent of New York City Koreans live in Brooklyn, yet more than 25 percent of New York City Korean businesses are located in this borough, which is heavily populated by African Americans. Approximately 10,000 Koreans in Southern California engage in indoor and outdoor swap meet businesses as of 1992, and 80 percent of Korean-owned swap meets are located in areas with largely African or Latino American residents. In addition, a large number of Korean-owned grocery/liquor stores, gas stations, and dry cleaning shops in Los Angeles are located in African and Hispanic American neighborhoods.

Historically, the ruling group has encouraged the use of the middleman minority since there has been no intermediate group to bridge the status gap existent in society. There is no evidence that either the U.S. government or U.S. corporations encouraged Korean immigrants to start small businesses. Some structural factors, however, encouraged Korean immigrants to operate businesses in minority neighborhoods. One type of Korean business heavily concentrated in black neighborhoods is the grocery/liquor business. Predominantly white neighborhoods have enough major grocery chain stores and therefore do not need Korean-owned small grocery stores. There are, however, few grocery chains in low-income black neighborhoods. Because of the low spending capacity of the residents, the high crime rates, and vandalism, big grocery chains are unwilling to invest in these areas. Accordingly, Korean independent grocers in low-income black neighborhoods do not encounter competition as

School friends, St. Paul, Minnesota. Race relations are often simpler on a one-to-one basis where it is easier to discover things we have in common. (Cleo Freelance Photography)

Owner of boycotted market in Brooklyn, New York, 1991. (Frances M. Roberts)

strong as that in predominantly white areas.

The other major type of Korean business in minority neighborhoods is the fashion business that deals in Korean- and Asian-imported items such as wigs, handbags, hats, clothing, shoes, and so forth. Korean retailers in minority neighborhoods have an advantage in operating the fashion business that has much to do with the structural change in the U.S. economy. In the contemporary post industrial economy, fashion cycles have become very short. Korean independent store owners can respond to fashion changes more effectively than department stores. Whereas big department stores, going through several channels for merchandise orders, have difficulty getting new fashion items quickly, Korean independent store owners can get popular items the next day from Korean suppliers. This suggests that the restructuring of the U.S. economy in the late 1970's and the early 1980's created the opportunity for Korean business owners to compete successfully against large department-store owners in low-income minority areas.

Middleman minorities specializing in businesses in minority neighborhoods have received hostility and rejection from minority customers in different forms. Korean merchants in black neighborhoods, like middleman merchants in other societies, have been subject to all forms of hostility, rejection, and violent reactions by blacks. Korean merchants in the ghettos of Los Angeles, New York, Philadelphia, Baltimore, and other cities have received black hostility and rejection in several different forms: verbal and physical assaults, attacks in local newspapers, murder, arson, boycott, and looting.

Black hostility toward Korean merchants has been most severe in New York and Los Angeles, the two largest Korean communities in the United States. Five major black boycott movements against Korean stores have occurred in New York since 1981. The boycott of two Korean produce stores in Brooklyn, New York, in January, 1990, drew national media headlines. In the 1980's, Koreans in Los Angeles maintained better relations with blacks than those in New York. Korean-African American tensions were, however, heightened in the spring of 1991, when a fifteen-year-old black girl was shot to death by the Korean owner of a grocery store, who had fought with the girl about trying to steal a bottle of orange juice. Blacks became more angry about the court decision than the incident when the store owner was sentenced only to probation in November, 1991. Five months later, the grand jury acquittal of four white police officers accused of beat-

ing black motorist Rodney King, sparked a major race riot in Los Angeles. Approximately 2,300 Korean stores in South Central Los Angeles and Koreatown became targets of destruction and looting during the rioting, which resulted in property damages of more than $350 million. Korean immigrants absorbed 45 percent of the total property damages.

Effects of Business-Related Intergroup Conflicts on Ethnic Solidarity. Members of a group tend to achieve internal solidarity when they encounter threats from the outside world. Korean merchants have encountered threats from different outside interest groups: black customers, white suppliers, white landlords, government agencies, and labor unions. These business-related intergroup conflicts have, in turn, contributed to the solidarity of the Korean community.

Of all forms of business-related intergroup conflicts, black hostility in the forms of robbery at gunpoint, physical violence, murder, arson, boycott, and looting has undoubtedly been the most serious type of threat that Korean merchants have encountered. Therefore, Korean-African American conflicts have had the most pronounced effects on Korean internal solidarity.

By establishing local business associations, Korean merchants in black neighborhoods have tried to solve problems with black customers and residents collectively. Yet black boycotts of Korean stores in New York and other cities and the destruction of Korean stores in the Los Angeles race riots have threatened the Korean immigrants' economic survival. These issues have led not only Korean merchants but also all other Koreans to be concerned about their common fate and marginal status in the United States.

While a number of major incidents of business-related conflicts with blacks have enhanced Koreans' solidarity, the destruction of so many Korean stores in the Los Angeles riots has most significantly affected the Korean community in terms of its ethnic solidarity and political consciousness. Koreans in Los Angeles were angry about the widespread destruction that the Korean community suffered during the riots. They were more outraged, however, by what they believed to be the white conspiracy behind the destruction. In their view, the American media intentionally focused on Korean-African American conflicts during the riots in order to vent blacks' frustrations on Korean merchants. Angry about the biased media coverage, a number of Koreans sent letters of protest to the various U.S. and Korean news organs. On May 2, 1992 Koreans in Los Angeles held a solidarity and peace rally at Admore Park in Koreatown, only a day after the riots

Jay C. Kim takes the oath of office in 1992 to become the first Korean American member of Congress. (Korea Times)

came to an end. Some 30,000 Koreans from all over the Los Angeles area participated in the rally, the largest Korean meeting ever held in the United States. Koreans also showed solidarity in their efforts to help the victims of the riots. In order to help the Korean victims of the riots in Los Angeles, Korean Americans all over the country participated in fund-raising campaigns, which raised approximately $4.8 million.

Many Koreans in Los Angeles and other cities felt that Koreans became innocent victims of black-white racial conflict in the 1992 riots mainly because of their lack of political power. Thus, the Los Angeles race riots have heightened Koreans' political consciousness. Keenly aware of their need for greater political power, more and more Korean immigrants have applied for naturalization since the riots, and more of them have registered to vote. In the 1992 elections, Jay KIM, representing the 41st District in California, was elected to the U.S. House of Representatives, becoming the first Korean member of Congress in American history. The same year, three other Koreans were elected to the state legislature of Washington, Oregon, and Hawaii. They were elected largely because they received the support of conservative, white voters. It

is, however, true that Koreans' support not only as voters but also as helpers in election campaigns also contributed to these successful campaigns.

The Los Angeles riots also heightened second-generation Koreans' sense of ethnic identity and solidarity. It was the first major event in Korean American history that provided the 1.5- and second-generation Koreans with an opportunity to think about their common fate as Korean Americans. Many young Koreans suspected that the police did not care about protecting Koreatown mainly because Korean Americans are a powerless minority group. Immediately after the riots, many young Koreans showed their response by writing articles in major English dailies in California in which they attacked the media bias and the police inactivity in protecting Koreatown.

Korean retail store owners generally depend on white wholesalers and manufacturers to supply their merchandise. The former have been subject to some discrimination from white suppliers in terms of quality of merchandise, price, the speed of delivery, and even parking allocations. Korean retailers have not, however, passively accepted unfair treatment by white suppliers. The retailers have established trade associations

Korean American (left) and Japanese American Guardian Angel volunteers patrol the grounds of Crotona Park, Flushing Meadows, New York. (Odette Lupis)

Korean American Statistical Profile, 1990

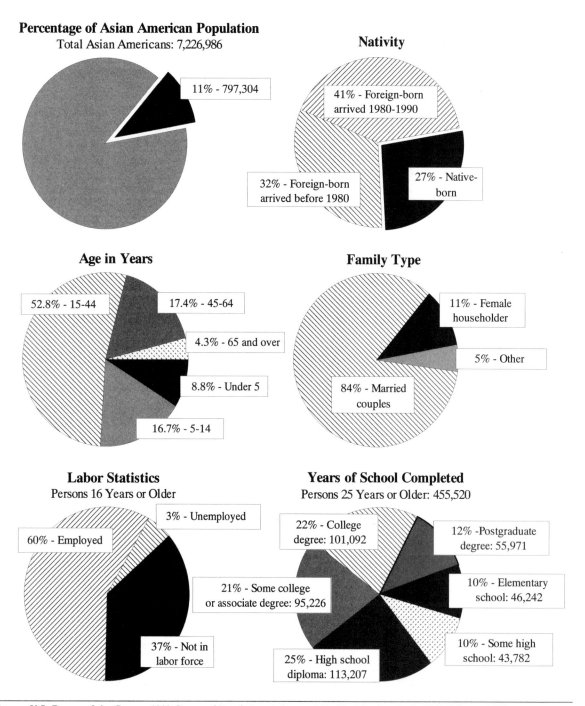

Percentage of Asian American Population
Total Asian Americans: 7,226,986

11% - 797,304

Nativity

41% - Foreign-born arrived 1980-1990

32% - Foreign-born arrived before 1980

27% - Native-born

Age in Years

52.8% - 15-44

17.4% - 45-64

4.3% - 65 and over

8.8% - Under 5

16.7% - 5-14

Family Type

11% - Female householder

5% - Other

84% - Married couples

Labor Statistics
Persons 16 Years or Older

60% - Employed

3% - Unemployed

37% - Not in labor force

Years of School Completed
Persons 25 Years or Older: 455,520

22% - College degree: 101,092

12% -Postgraduate degree: 55,971

10% - Elementary school: 46,242

21% - Some college or associate degree: 95,226

10% - Some high school: 43,782

25% - High school diploma: 113,207

Source: U.S. Bureau of the Census, *1990 Census of Population: Asians and Pacific Islanders in the United States,* 1993.

and used collective strategies to protect their interests. Collective actions taken by Korean merchants include boycotts, demonstrations, price bargaining, and group purchases. Korean merchants in New York boycotted white suppliers five times and demonstrated against them several times.

A very small proportion of Korean merchants (only about 10 percent) own the buildings that house their businesses; other merchants depend on white landlords. This relationship makes the merchant tenants vulnerable to exploitation. Typically, when Korean-owned businesses became successful, their landlords raised rents two or three times within a short period of time. Many Korean store owners have to keep their stores open for long hours partly to cover escalating

Occupation	
Employed Persons 16 Years or Older	Percentage
Managerial and professional specialty	25%
Technical, sales, and administrative support	37%
Service	15%
Farming, forestry, and fishing	1%
Precision production, craft, and repair	9%
Operators, fabricators, and laborers	13%

Income, 1989	
Median household income	$30,184
Per capita	$11,178
Percent of families in poverty	15%

Household Size	
Number of People	Percentage
1	14%
2	21%
3	21%
4	26%
5	12%
6	4%
7 or more	2%

Source: U.S. Bureau of the Census, *1990 Census of Population: Asians and Pacific Islanders in the United States,* 1993.

rents. Korean merchants' conflict over economic interests with white landlords has, however, also created solidarity. For example, in the 1980's Korean business leaders actively lobbied the New York City mayor and council members for a new law that would regulate commercial rents. Banding together, the merchants took a leading role in organizing three major multiethnic demonstrations in New York City to push regulation. Korean merchants also used collective bargaining techniques to lower or freeze rents.

Korean merchants have also responded collectively to conflicts with government agencies. City governments typically have many laws and administrative regulations concerning business licensing, commercial parking, commercial leases, disposal of commercial wastes, sidewalk obstruction, sanitary conditions of stores, and other aspects of business operation. While these restrictions are an inconvenience to all small-business owners, Korean merchants in particular have made collective efforts to moderate them since a majority of Koreans engage in small businesses. Korean trade associations have actively lobbied lawmakers and government agencies to make these regulations less strict. Such lobbying efforts have been generally successful.

The Radical Increase in Women's Economic Role. Confucianism, which has greatly influenced Korean culture historically, emphasizes a clear role differentiation between husband and wife, a distinction that has helped to establish an extreme form of patriarchy in Korea. In traditional Korean society, the husband was considered the primary breadwinner and decision-maker in the family and exercised complete authority over his wife and children. The wife was expected to obey her husband, devotedly serve him and his family members (including in-laws), and perpetuate her husband's lineage by producing children.

Much of the traditional gender role differentiation has been preserved in South Korea, for the last several decades the source of most Korean immigration. In spite of a high level of urbanization, industrialization, and economic development, only a small proportion of nonagricultural married women (less than 25 percent) participate in the labor force in South Korea. Traditional gender role orientation on the one hand, and employment/wage discrimination against women on the other hand, discourage married women from participating in the labor market in South Korea.

The immigration of Koreans to the United States has led to many changes in the traditional Korean family system, but the most noteworthy change is

Studies indicate that Korean American working women bear the main responsibility for domestic tasks, as is the case for most working women in America. (Ben Klaffke)

probably the radical increase in the number of Korean women joining the labor force. In 1988 70 percent of Korean married women in New York City held jobs. That compares to 57 percent for U.S. married women in general in 1988. More significant is the fact that Korean immigrant women work exceptionally long hours—an average of fifty-one hours per week, with 80 percent working full-time.

The high labor force participation rate of Korean immigrant women and their long hours of work can be explained largely by the concentration of Korean immigrant families in small businesses. To operate labor-intensive small businesses effectively, Korean male immigrants need the help of their wives. In fact, the coordination between the husband and the wife, along with their long hours of work, is the central factor that makes Korean small businesses successful. A New York City survey indicates that 38 percent of Korean married women who worked were engaged in the family business with their husbands.

Has the increase in the Korean immigrant wife's economic role led to the decrease in her domestic role? Several studies focusing on this issue indicate that Korean immigrant wives, whether they work outside or not, bear the main responsibility for traditional domestic tasks, and that their husbands' help is almost negligible. Few Korean immigrant dual-worker families have a housemaid working part-time or full-time, although most career women in Seoul and other large cities in Korea depend on housemaids for cooking and other housework. Only when Korean immigrant working women have elderly mothers or mothers-in-law living with them can they significantly reduce their housework. Since most Korean working women do not have that luxury, they suffer from double burdens. In 1988 Korean immigrant working wives spent 75.5 hours weekly on their job and housework, spending 12 hours more than their husbands.

Among Korean immigrants, both men and women tend toward overwork compared to the U.S. adult population in general. Overwork seems, however, to be more stressful to Korean immigrant women than to their husbands, since Korean women suffer from role strain, which their husbands usually do not experience. While U.S. working women also suffer from stress, role strain, and other forms of depression, overwork seems to be much more stressful for Korean immigrant wives, particularly because they also experience stress relating to language barriers and other adjustment problems.

A High Level of Ethnic Attachment and a Low Level of Assimilation. The extent to which members of an ethnic/immigrant group maintain their native cultural traditions and participate in ethnic social networks is referred to as "ethnic attachment." Korean immigrants in the United States maintain a high level of ethnic attachment, probably higher than any Asian ethnic group. The vast majority of Korean immigrants speak the Korean language, eat mainly Korean food, and practice Korean customs most of the time. Most Korean immigrants are affiliated with at least one ethnic organization and are involved in active informal ethnic networks. Comparative studies of Asian ethnic groups indicate that a much larger proportion of Korean Americans than other Asian groups have joined one or more ethnic associations.

There are three major factors that help Korean immigrants maintain a high level of ethnic attachment. First, Korean immigrants are a culturally homogeneous group, which provides the cultural basis for Koreans' ethnic attachment. South Korea is a small and culturally homogeneous country where there is only one racial group speaking one language. The cultural homogeneity of Korean immigrants becomes obvious when the group is compared with other Asian groups. Filipino immigrants consist of a number of subgroups differing in language and place of origin. The absence of a common native language and regional differences in customs contribute partly to the factionalism characterizing Filipino American community organizations. Asian Indian immigrants are also composed of many linguistic, regional, and religious subgroups. Therefore, close social interaction among Indian immigrants usually involves people from the same region or language group.

Second, Korean immigrants maintain strong ethnic attachment partly because most of them are affiliated with Korean ethnic churches. Some 55 percent of Korean adult immigrants attended Christian churches in South Korea prior to immigration, although Christians constitute only a little more than 20 percent of the population there. Many Korean immigrants who were not Christians in Korea attend the Korean ethnic church probably for practical reasons. Thus, more than 75 percent of Korean immigrants are affiliated with Korean immigrant churches, the vast majority of which are Protestant. There are 800 Korean churches in Southern California and 350 in the New York metropolitan area as of 1993.

Korean immigrant churches help to maintain social interactions among Korean immigrants by serving as places for meeting fellow Koreans. They also help to

Korean American Population by Census Year, 1910-1990

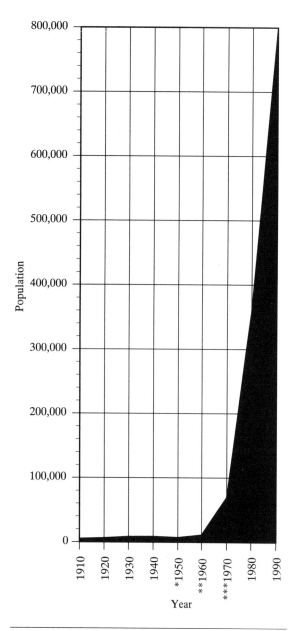

Sources: Susan B. Gall and Timothy L. Gall, eds., *Statistical Record of Asian Americans.* Detroit: Gale Research, Inc., 1993. Ong Bill Hing, *Making and Remaking Asian America Through Immigration Policy, 1850-1990.* Stanford, Calif.: Stanford University Press, 1993.
* Data for Hawaii only.
** Foreign-born Koreans only.
*** Does not include Alaska.

maintain the Korean cultural tradition through Korean language and other cultural programs. Ethnic/immigrant churches have contributed to maintaining ethnicity for other ethnic/immigrant groups as well, such as Jewish and Italian Americans and current Asian Indian immigrants. Nevertheless, they seem to be far more effective in sustaining the ethnicity of Korean immigrants than for other groups, since Koreans have a much higher level of affiliation with their ethnic churches than do other groups.

Third, Korean immigrants' concentration in small businesses also strengthens Korean ethnic attachment. As noted above, the vast majority of Korean immigrants are segregated in the ethnic economy either as small business owners or as employees of multiethnic stores. This enhances ethnic attachment and unity by tying Koreans together socially and culturally. Most Korean immigrants work for Korean businesses and therefore maintain social interactions with fellow Koreans at the workplace, speaking the Korean language and practicing Korean customs during most of the work hours. Korean immigrants in the Korean ethnic economy maintain more frequent social interactions with fellow Koreans even during off-duty hours and speak the Korean language more frequently at home than do those in the general economy.

Thus far, it has been noted that Korean immigrants maintain a high level of ethnic attachment, compared to other Asian immigrant groups. Their cultural homogeneity, high affiliation with Korean immigrant churches, and concentration in small businesses contribute to their strong ethnic attachment. What about Korean immigrants' level of assimilation compared to other immigrant groups?

Assimilation and ethnic attachment are not mutually exclusive. Nevertheless, it is also true that some components of ethnic attachment have negative effects on assimilation. For example, Koreans who speak Korean and eat Korean food more frequently depend on English and American food less frequently. Thus, while Korean immigrants maintain strong ethnic attachment, they are slower than other immigrant groups in achieving assimilation. Although Koreans achieve assimilation in proportion to their length of residence in the United States, only a small proportion of older Koreans speak English at home and depend on English newspapers and magazines for news and information.

Cultural homogeneity and economic segregation help Korean immigrants to maintain strong ethnic attachment. Yet the same factors also hinder Koreans' assimilation into American society. Since Korean im-

Young members of the Korean/American Heritage Association enjoy a lunch of pizza, rice, and fish soup at the Korean Presbyterian Church in Saginaw, Michigan. (Raymond J. Malace)

migrants were not exposed to significant subcultural differences in their home country, most of them have a low level of tolerance for the cultural differences that are found in the United States and are unwilling to learn English and American customs. Since new Korean immigrants usually find employment in Korean firms, they have little motivation to learn English. Moreover, the confinement of the vast majority of Korean immigrants to the ethnic market provides them with little opportunity to learn English and American customs at the workplace. Korean immigrants are self-employed in small businesses mainly because of the language barrier and lack of assimilation, but their concentration in small businesses further reduces their chances for assimilation.—*Pyong Gap Min*

SUGGESTED READINGS:

• Hurh, Won Moo, and Kwang Chung Kim. *Korean Immigrants in America: A Structural Analysis of Ethnic Confinement and Adhesive Adaptation.* Madison, N.J.: Fairleigh Dickinson University Press, 1984. This book, based on interviews with a sample of Korean immigrants in Los Angeles, provides information on several different aspects of Korean immigrants' adjust-

ment. The analyses of Korean immigrants' assimilation and ethnic attachment are particularly comprehensive and interesting.

• Hurh, Won Moo, and Kwang Chung Kim. "Religious Participation of Korean Immigrants in the United States." *Journal of the Scientific Study of Religion* 29 (1990): 19-34. Based on data collected through personal interviews with 622 Korean immigrants in Chicago, this article systematically analyzes the religious participation patterns of Korean immigrants in light of various theories of the immigrant church.

• Kim, Illsoo. *New Urban Immigrants: The Korean Community in New York.* Princeton, N.J.: Princeton University Press, 1981. This book provides Kim's observations of the dynamics of the New York Korean immigrant community in its early stage of development. His discussion of structural and cultural sources of New York Korean immigrants' commercial activities is insightful. His treatment of Korean ethnic churches and ethnic media as mechanisms of ethnic networks in a nonterritorial community deserves special attention.

• Light, Ivan, and Edna Bonacich. *Immigrant Entrepreneurs: Koreans in Los Angeles, 1965-1982.* Berkeley: University of California Press, 1988. This book offers a very comprehensive coverage of Korean immigrant entrepreneurship in Los Angeles between 1965 and 1982. Whereas Bonacich examines the external causes of Korean entrepreneurship, Light focuses on its internal causes. It is of great use in understanding both the Los Angeles Korean community and Korean immigrant entrepreneurship in general.

• Min, Pyong Gap. "The Cultural and Economic Boundaries of Korean Ethnicity: A Comparative Analysis." *Ethnic and Racial Studies* 14 (1991): 225-241. This article examines Korean immigrants' cultural homogeneity, affiliation with ethnic churches, and economic segregation as three major factors that contribute to Korean immigrants' ethnic attachment.

• Min, Pyong Gap. *Ethnic Business Enterprise: Korean Small Business in Atlanta.* Staten Island: Center for Migration Studies, 1988. Based on in-depth interviews with 159 Korean merchants in Atlanta, this book systematically analyzes the phenomenon of Korean immigrants' tendency to turn to small business. Specifically, he tries to answer three questions: What are the motivational factors for Korean immigrants decision to start small businesses?; what are the facilitating factors for Koreans' establishment of small business?; and what are the major factors that make Korean immigrants successful in small business?

• Min, Pyong Gap. "The Structure and Social Functions of Korean Immigrant Churches in the United States." *International Migration Review* 26 (1992): 1370-1394. Based on telephone interviews with 131 Korean head pastors in New York, this article analyzes four major social functions of Korean immigrant churches: providing fellowship, maintaining the Korean cultural tradition, providing social services, and providing social status and position.

• Yu, Eui-Young, Earl Phillips, and Eun Sik Yang, eds. *Koreans in Los Angeles: Prospects and Promises.* Los Angeles: Center for Korean-American and Korean Studies, California State University, Los Angeles, 1982. This is a collection of eleven articles on different aspects of the Los Angeles Korean community. It aims to portray "the characteristics, activities, problems, and feelings of the Koreans in Los Angeles in their initial stages of settlement as accurately as possible."

Korean Buddhism: This version of Buddhism is practiced, to varying degrees, by more than forty-five million Koreans, mostly in South Korea, Japan, the United States, and other places abroad. Nominally the twenty-five million Communist North Koreans are nonreligious, but some traditions still survive in spite of official governmental sanctions. There are more than seven thousand Buddhist temples, and some twenty-three thousand priests, in South Korea.

The Korean version of Buddhism coexists with quite a number of other belief systems, including Confucianism, Taoism, and several newly introduced Christian sects. The distinction between what is Buddhist, and what is not, is often unclear (thus, estimating the number of followers is difficult). Chondogyo (religion of the heavenly way, a monotheistic blending of Buddhism and several Eastern and Western philosophies, founded in the nineteenth century) is popular in both South Korea and North Korea (where the Communist government often uses it for moral teachings). Several hundred other of these so-called new religions—both large and small—have incorporated Buddhist elements in their teachings. Also, combinations of shaman and Buddhist practices are very common, especially among women in the rural areas.

Early History. Buddhism is said to have been introduced into the Korean peninsula when the Chinese monk Shun-dao (or "Sundo" in Korean) brought Buddhist scriptures to the Koguryo state in 372 C.E. This period in Korean history is usually referred to as the Three Kingdoms. At this time, Korea was not yet a unified nation, but three independent political units: Koguryo in the north, Paekche in the southwest, and Silla in the southeast. These warrior states had eliminated the previous Chinese colonizers in the area, but the cultural and religious influences remained.

Buddhism was attractive for at least three reasons. First, it offered an alternative to Confucianism and Chinese bureaucracy and political institutions. Second, Buddhist iconography and artwork was no doubt impressive and probably even carried mystical or magical connotations. Third, Buddhism offered a philosophical sophistication that the indigenous local religions often lacked. Buddhism presented more than simply ritual; it gave explanations for life, death, and the meaning of existence. Buddhism was avidly accepted by the Koguryo and Paekche courts, and Paekche sailors spread Buddhist scholarship and materials to Japan in the 550's. By the time Silla unified the Three Kingdoms into one kingdom in 668 C.E., Buddhism was in effect a state religion.

The early Buddhism brought to Korea was pragmatic and practical. It blended well with previously existing elements. Local animist beliefs became incor-

Pulguksa Temple is one of Korea's best-known temples. (Korea National Tourism Corporation)

porated into Korean Buddhist doctrine, and vice versa. For example, local dragon cults identified the dragon of Buddhist mythology as the protector of the state and the canon. The Silla king Munmu even vowed to be reborn as a dragon to return and defend the country. Buddhist monks could dance and sing and often performed many of the same rituals that shamans did. The most influential figure of this time was the monk Wonhyo, who sought to unify all the various sects under a common banner. More important, he spread Buddhism to the masses through legends, stories, and books.

Zen Buddhism and Korea. Many Westerners equate Zen with Buddhism in general, a mistake comparable to claiming that, for example, Presbyterians represent all Christians. There are dozens of different sects of Buddhism—even considering only the major denominations—and Zen is only one relatively small group. Still, Zen has been very influential among Buddhist theologians in both the East and the West. It has also been most important in the history of Buddhism in Korea.

Son ("Zen" in Japanese or "Chan" in Chinese) grew out of various Buddhist revival movements that tried to discard the formalized rituals and overintellectualization, which had accumulated after a millennium of doctrinal debate. Son, instead, tried to center on the essential and original teachings, applied to the here-and-now. Emphasis is placed on self-realization, enlightenment, and meditation.

By the 1200's, personal contacts and writings had spread Son Buddhism all over east Asia and Vietnam, though Son had been introduced into Korea from China in the eighth century. A military coup in 1170 in Korea lead to the suppression of Buddhism, and many practitioners retreated to the mountains or inaccessible areas. Around this time, the Korean Son master Chinul founded the influential Chogye-chong school. He introduced into Korea the practice of meditation upon special verbal paradoxes called *hwadu* (one famous example being, "What is the sound of one hand clapping?"). Solving these verbal puzzles was believed to shock the intellect into new thought patterns or perceptions. This Chogye-chong school of Korean Son became the dominant form of Buddhism in Korea and remains so even today. One reason for this is that later disciples continued the practice of trying to incorporate Son with other religions and Buddhist sects. For example, T'aego Pou, as a public teacher and advisor to kings, stressed the unity of Confucian ethics and the different Buddhist philosophies, integrating them together with various Son schools.

Buddhism and Household Practices. There is great diversity in contemporary Korean religious practices.

Korean Buddhist monk, New York City. (Richard B. Levine)

Even within a single family there may be adherents of different sets or religions. Also, individual Koreans may be quite iconoclastic, going to a Son Buddhist temple to pray for good fortune, while afterwards stopping off to visit a *mudang* (female priest) to have a fortune told or acquire some talisman.

Shamanism is especially popular in rural areas (even in North Korea) and is a particularly female domain. The *kut* is the shaman's most elaborate ritual and is used to cure illnesses, placate ancestors, and venerate the local and household deities. At divination sessions (*mugori*), clients may ask the shaman about marriage proposals, financial prospects, in-law problems, or career changes. To find answers, she may toss coins, rattle brass bells, or consult patterns of rice on a tray.

Buddhism and "New Religions." In the last hundred years, many "new religions" have evolved in Korea. Most have grown out of the Tonghak (Eastern learning) movement of the 1860's, which was a reaction against orthodox Catholicism (Western learning). Ch'oe Che-u, founder of the sect, claimed to have received a message from the Heavenly Emperor (Chonju) telling him to create a religion that would make Korea as strong as the West. After Ch'oe Che-u's arrest and execution by the authorities, his disciples changed the name to Chondogyo after eliminating its political aspects.

Today Chondogyo incorporates aspects from Taoism, Confucianism, Catholicism, and shamanism. This religion is, however, most strongly influenced by Buddhism, and Buddhist elements predominate. For example, followers recite a twenty-one-word phrase called a *chumum* (similar to a Buddhist mantra) as a means to gain enlightenment. As in Buddhism, there is no belief in an afterlife per se, as paradise and peace are to be found in this world. As in Son, individual self-discipline and self-improvement lead to enlightenment. Most other new religions are variants on the pattern of beliefs established by Chondogyo, though individual leaders or saviors may vary.

Some new religions have grown out of Buddhist movements in other countries. For example, the Chiangga Hakhoe (value creation learning society), introduced from Japan in 1963, is popular in urban areas among the working classes. This a version of lay Buddhism that began in Japan as the Soka-gakkai, a group of Nichiren Buddhist educational reformers.— *James Stanlaw*

SUGGESTED READINGS: • Buswell, Robert. "Buddhism in Korea." In *Buddhism and Asian History*, edited by Joseph Kitagawa and Mark Cummings. New York: Macmillan, 1989. • Janelli, Roger, and Dawnhee Yim Janelli. *Ancestor Worship and Korean Society*. Stanford, Calif.: Stanford University Press, 1982. • Kendall, Laurel. *Shamans, Housewives, and Other Restless Spirits*. Honolulu: University of Hawaii Press, 1985. • Lee, Peter, et al., eds. *Sourcebook of Korean Civilization*. Vol. 1. New York: Columbia University Press, 1993. • Pou Kuksa. *A Buddha from Korea: The Zen Teachings of T'aego*. Translated by J. C. Cleary. Boston: Shambhala, 1988.

Korean Central Intelligence Agency (KCIA): Established in 1961 as the South Korean government's primary source of national security information and intelligence gathering. The KCIA combined the functions of standard foreign intelligence gathering with those of an internal security police force. Throughout the PARK CHUNG HEE era (1961-1979), the KCIA functioned to suppress internal opposition to the government as well as to protect the country from foreign threats.

With a mandate to direct and supervise, the KCIA came to exercise practically unlimited powers of inquiry, arrest, detention, and interrogation over the whole of South Korean society. U.S. congressional hearings at the time of the KOREAGATE scandal (1977) associated the agency with intimidating and harassing Koreans living in the United States and other countries and uncovered covert efforts by the agency to influence U.S. foreign policy at the highest levels.

Until the end of the 1970's the KCIA was responsible only to the nation's president. The agency was organized into several functional bureaus charged with carrying out tasks related but not limited to counterintelligence, internal security, psychological warfare, foreign covert operations, and North Korean surveillance. The exact number of employees of the agency is unknown. By the late 1970's it had emerged as a major pillar of the Park regime.

In a dispute over domestic policy President Park was assassinated in 1979 by the then-director of the KCIA, Kim Jae Kyu. Kim was arrested, tried, and executed for the crime. In the aftermath of Park's assassination the agency was reformed because of public concerns over corruption, intervention in social and political affairs, and the agency's reputation for brutality toward dissidents. In 1980 the institution's name was changed to the Agency for National Security Planning (ANSP) and its ability to interfere in domestic affairs was reduced. It remains, however, an influential actor in national politics.

Traditionally the agency's leadership has come from the ranks of the military. In 1993, however, the first democratically elected civilian president, Kim Young Sam, appointed a university professor to the agency's directorship.

Korean children, adoption of: In the mid-1980's South Korea became the largest foreign source of adopted children, providing approximately 60 percent of all foreign infant adoptees and 10 percent of all children adopted into unrelated adoptive families in the United States.

In 1986, for example, Americans adopted 6,254 Korean children. That number, however, declined by about 75 percent and was in danger of dropping even further in the early 1990's, largely because of American television reports during the 1988 Seoul Olympics that accused South Korea of exporting its babies as a commodity.

When Americans began adopting South Korean children in 1955, most of the adoptees were Amerasians, children of American servicemen. By 1970, however, nearly all adoptees from South Korea were entirely of Korean ancestry. Most Korean adoptees were given up immediately after birth by unwed mothers to one of four government-regulated adoption agencies, which in turn provided child care until the infant could be placed with adoptive parents. Older Korean children were placed through orphanages, usually after being abandoned by their parents.

Traditionally, Korean families have been reluctant to adopt: Only about three thousand children were adopted within Korea in 1986. Yet with some two million American families waiting to adopt and only about twenty thousand healthy American children available for adoption each year, the Korean solution provided obvious benefits.

By the early 1990's the cost of Korean adoption averaged $8,000 to $10,000 per child, with much of the money going to the South Korean government, to defray child placement and care costs. Critics have charged that the businesslike efficiency with which the adoption agencies operated was demeaning, that the Korean government should have tried harder to improve people's attitudes about adoption and unwed mothers, and that the children could face discrimination in the United States.

In the mid-1980's South Korea became the largest foreign source of adopted children, a source of happiness for those facing the shortage of adoptees in the U.S. (Jim Whitmer)

Korean church in the United States: From its inception in 1903 the Korean Christian church has served as a most vital institution of the Korean immigrant community in the United States. It has experienced remarkable growth since the 1970's because of the rapidly increasing number of Korean immigrants into the country. Most Korean churches tend to be small and conservative. Aside from meeting spiritual needs, the Korean church has assumed important sociological functions. By offering various social services and programs, it has contributed to the maintenance of Korean culture and ethnic identity as well as to the adaptation of Koreans to American society.

Historical Background. The Korean church in the United States began after the first group of Korean immigrants settled in the Hawaiian Islands in 1903. Members of these early churches were actively engaged in political activities to support the national independence of their homeland, which was under Japanese colonial rule from 1910 to 1945. From the mid-1920's, when the Immigration Act of 1924 was adopted, to 1950 there was no systematic immigration from Korea to the United States. Korean immigration began to increase after the 1965 Immigration and Na-

Korean Methodist Church, Los Angeles, California, 1950. (University of Southern California East Asian Library)

tionality Act abolished the long-standing inequitable quota system discriminating against immigrants from Asia.

About thirty thousand Koreans have immigrated to the United States each year since 1976, and the number and size of the Korean churches have increased accordingly. For example the San Francisco Korean United Methodist Church, which was established in 1904 and is the oldest Korean church in the continental United States, decided in 1992 to sell the old building and to move to a bigger one in order to accommodate its growing membership, despite the opposition by those advocating the preservation of the old church as a historic monument of early Korean immigration. As of 1992 there were about seven hundred Korean churches in Southern California alone, ranging from the fundamentalist to the liberal denominations and millenarian sects. Since Koreans in Southern California constitute approximately one-third of all Koreans

in the United States, the total number of Korean churches in the United States may be well in excess of two thousand.

Organizational Characteristics. A survey of Korean churches in Los Angeles conducted by Marion Dearman found that two-thirds of them were established by immigrant ministers. The majority of Korean churches in the United States rent or share the buildings of American churches while those with large congregations tend to have their own buildings. The Korean church generally tends to be small, with the average size of the congregation below one hundred members. A few churches in big cities, however, have huge congregations. Young Nak (Presbyterian) Church in Los Angeles, for example, has a twelve-hundred-seat main sanctuary; its operating budget for 1992 was four and a half million dollars.

Presbyterians are the most numerous among Korean Christians in the United States, as they are in South

Korean American Churches, Selected Characteristics, 1992

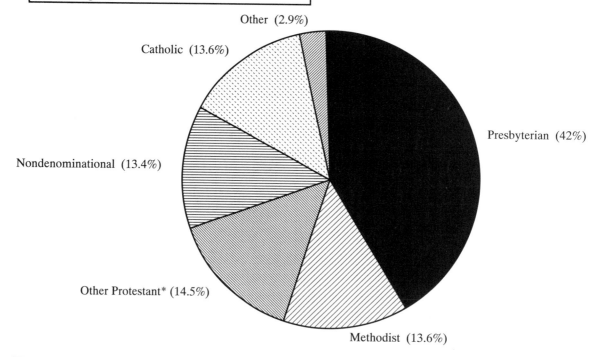

Total Korean churches in the U.S.: more than 2,000

Southern California: 600

New York City: 450

Chicago: 140

Washington, D.C./Baltimore: 120

Other (2.9%)

Catholic (13.6%)

Nondenominational (13.4%)

Presbyterian (42%)

Other Protestant* (14.5%)

Methodist (13.6%)

Sources: Ann Hagen Griffiths, *The Korean Americans*. The New Americans series. New York: Facts on File, 1992. Moo Won Hurh and Kwang Chung Kim, *Korean Immigrants in America: A Structural Analysis of Ethnic Confinement and Adhesive Adaptation*. Rutherford, N.J.: Fairleigh Dickinson University Press, 1990.
* Holiness, Baptist, Evangelical, and Seventh-day Adventist.

Korea. There are, however, more nondenominational churches among the Korean churches in the United States than in Korea. The Korean church usually offers separate services for adults and children, the former in Korean and the latter often in both Korean and English. The majority of churches hold worship services not only on Sundays but also during the weekdays. Some even offer dawn prayer services, following the tradition of the Christian church in Korea. Almost 99 percent of the ministers are men even though the majority of church members are women. The 1989 survey of New York Korean churches by Pyong Gap Min found that the proportion of women ministers in Korean churches in New York (1.3 percent) was lower than that in South Korea (2.4 percent). The figures reflect the conservatism of Korean Christianity generally and of the Korean immigrant church in the United States particularly. Most Korean churches in the United States are aggressively evangelistic like their counterparts in South Korea.

Nonreligious Functions. Aside from satisfying the religious needs of its congregation, the Korean church meets various sociological needs of the Korean immigrant community by offering many vital services. Studies indicate that between 70 and 80 percent of Korean immigrants attend church services regularly. This proportion of Christians in the Korean immigrant community is much higher than that in South Korea (about 20 percent), which may be attributable in part to the various important nonreligious functions that the church assumes for the membership.

Church attendance among Korean immigrants tends to be a regular outing for the whole family. Nearly all churches offer socializing hours with beverages and snacks on the premise immediately following Sunday services. Some churches even provide lunch for the whole congregation. New immigrants, especially those without relatives or friends, find this ritual of Christian fellowship and social interaction invaluable. Many Korean immigrants play active roles in various activities organized by their churches. Scholars have pointed out that official roles and formal titles at church assume important social psychological functions for Korean immigrants, because many of them—especially those with professional and/or managerial positions prior to immigration—often experience some loss of occupational status after immigration to the United States.

The church also provides various social services that include family counseling over marital conflict, children's education, and/or adolescent problems; translation or interpretation help with the English language; seminars and lectures on various aspects of American laws and social institutions; and Bible classes and Korean-language instruction for the children of the congregation. Thus the Korean church in the United States has led the way in preserving the Korean language and values, fostering social bonds, and maintaining a sense of ethnic identity. It has offered the organizational basis for the psychological security and the social adaptation of Korean immigrants.

After the Los Angeles Riots of 1992, however, which victimized many Korean immigrant shopkeepers, Korean church and community leaders have begun to look beyond the Korean immigrant community to combat racism and ethnic isolation. Service to the multiethnic local community and integration into the mainstream American society loom as new challenges to the Korean church as it approaches its second century of Christian ministry in the United States.— *Chunghee Sarah Soh*

SUGGESTED READINGS: • Dearman, Marion. "Structure and Function of Religion in the Los Angeles Ko-

Korean United Presbyterian Church, Los Angeles, California. (The Korea Society/Los Angeles)

rean Community: Some Aspects." In *Koreans in Los Angeles: Prospects and Promises*, edited by E. Y. Yu, E. H. Phillips, and E. S. Yang. Los Angeles: Center for Korean-American and Korean Studies, California State University, Los Angeles, 1982. • Lee, Kwang Kyu. "Hanin kyohoe" (Korean church). In *Chaemi Hangukin* (Koreans in America). Seoul: Ilchogak, 1989. • Min Pyong Gap. "Hanin kyohoe ui kujo mit kinung" (the structure and function of the Korean church). In *Miguk sok ui han'gukin* (Koreans in America), edited by P. G. Min. Seoul: Yurim, 1991. • Pai, Margaret K. "The Tragic Split." In *The Dreams of Two Yi-min*. Honolulu: University of Hawaii Press, 1989. • Patterson, Wayne. "Characteristics of the Immigrants and Why They Came." In *The Korean Frontier in America*. Honolulu: University of Hawaii Press, 1988. • Shim, Steve. *Korean Immigrant Churches Today in Southern California*. San Francisco: R and E Research Associates, 1977.

Korean Community Center of the East Bay: Nonprofit social service organization founded in 1977 in Oakland, California, dedicated to serving low-income limited-English-proficient immigrants. The group provides translation and medical assistance services; conducts citizenship classes and workshops on health, income tax, and small-business management; coordinates a youth drug prevention/educational program; hosts a monthly roundtable discussion on race relations; and houses a senior citizens center.

Korean Compound: Korean American school. It was originally called the Korean Language School, a residential school for boys, and was established by the Korean Methodist Church of Honolulu in 1906. In 1918, it merged with the Girls' Residential School, also known as the Girl's Seminary, and became the Korean Christian Institute, headed by the Korean political figure Syngman Rhee.

Korean dance. *See* **Korean music and dance**

Korean Evangelical Society: Korean American organization. It was founded by Korean Americans in Honolulu in 1903 and in San Francisco in 1905. It provided church services, housing and meals for Korean bachelors, and hosted social and political meetings.

Korean Family Counseling and Legal Advice Center: Private nonprofit service agency for Korean im-

migrants, founded in 1983 to meet the needs of the fast-growing immigrant population. Its purposes are to provide professional and bilingual counseling to abused women and those with marital and financial problems; prevent the proliferation of domestic violence; and lead educational workshops and training sessions on immigration law, parenting skill, and intercultural and intergenerational differences.

Korean Girls' Seminary (also, Girls' Residential School): Established by Syngman Rhee on June 29, 1914, with funds from the Korean National Association (KNA) in Hawaii. It merged in 1918 with the Korean Compound and became the Korean Christian Institute, headed by Rhee.

Korean Immigrant Workers Advocates: Nonprofit community service organization, founded in March, 1992. It provides bilingual job-related legal assistance and other services to the Korean immigrant community. Its mission is to empower Korean immigrants and to promote political and social awareness in the Los Angeles Korean community.

Korean immigration to the United States: Korean immigration to the United States is divided into three periods: the early immigration from 1903 to 1944, the post-World War II immigration from 1945 to 1964, and the recent immigration after 1965. Each wave of Korean immigrants was caused by different factors in Korea and the United States, and motivations and characteristics of Korean immigrants in each period were substantially different. The purpose of this article is to explain from historical and sociological perspectives the causes of Korean immigration to the United States, and the number and characteristics of Korean immigrants of each period.

The Early Korean Immigration, 1903-1944. Three sets of factors played important roles in initiating and sustaining the early Korean immigration to the United States: push factors that drove Koreans out of their homeland, pull factors that attracted Koreans to Hawaii and the West Coast of the United States, and agents who linked the push factors in Korea with the pull factors in the United States. The push factors in Korea were a series of political and economic upheavals and disasters at the end of the declining Choson (or Yi) Dynasty (1392-1910). After a five-centuries-long reign in Korea, the Choson Dynasty showed signs of decay and disintegration. The government lost its control of the ownership of land and taxation as the

Korean Immigration to the U.S. by Decade, 1901-1990

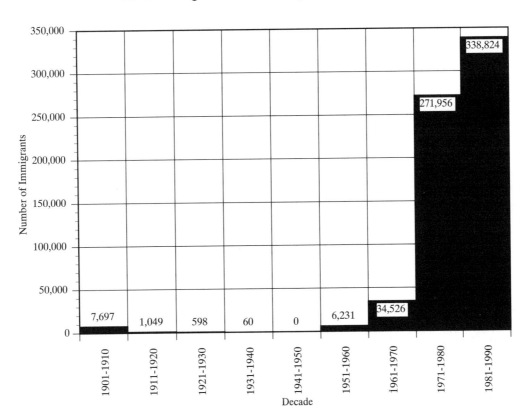

Source: Susan B. Gall and Timothy L. Gall, eds., *Statistical Record of Asian Americans.* Detroit: Gale Research, Inc., 1993.
Note: The first wave of immigrants settled mainly in Hawaii. Sources differ on early Korean immigration since the group was not counted separately by the Immigration and Naturalization Service until 1948.

yangban ruling class encroached on more land from which to extract taxes and rent directly from the farmers. Consequently, the financial basis of the government became increasingly precarious and the farmers found themselves squeezed more and more by the oppressive taxation by *yangban* landlords and corrupt officials. Pressed by poverty and food shortages during frequent famines, by the 1880's many farmers began to accept cash advances for sale of their crops after harvest from Japanese merchants, who began to penetrate the Korean economy under the Kanghwa Treaty between Korea and Japan in 1876. This resulted in a cycle of debt and dependency on Japanese merchants, eroding further the self-sufficiency of Korean agriculture. Furthermore, the entry into the Korean market of Japanese manufactured goods such as textile goods and metal products undermined Korea's primitive handicraft industries. As a result, many farmers and artisans became bankrupt. Food shortages, spiraling

debts, and oppressive taxation combined to produce intolerable conditions for many farmers. Such conditions led to a massive peasant uprising (the TONGHAK REBELLION) in 1894 in Cholla Province, the southwestern region of Korea, where agriculture was most highly developed and hence oppression of the farmers was most pervasive. The same conditions forced many farmers in Hamgyong Province, the northwestern region of Korea, to migrate northward to Siberia and establish farms on land under Russian control. Impoverished farmers also flocked in search of employment to such port cities as Inchon and Wonsan, the cities newly established by the 1876 Kanghwa Treaty to export Korean foodstuffs to Japan and import Japanese manufactured goods to Korea. This new urban population provided the source of much of the emigration to Hawaii from 1903 to 1905.

The internal disintegration of the Choson Dynasty's feudal order paved the way for the penetration into

Korean farmer plows a field, circa 1900. (The Korea Society/Los Angeles)

Korea of such imperialist powers as Japan, the United States, and Russia. After the Meiji Restoration of 1868, Japan emerged as a new industrial country and began to have an interest in Korea as a source of foodstuffs and other raw materials and as a market for manufactured goods. Japan succeeded in forcing the CHOSON rulers to sign the unequal Kanghwa Treaty, which opened Inchon, Wonsan, and Pusan to the Japanese for trade and residence and allowed the Japanese to exercise extraterritorial rights. Within two decades Japan achieved an unequivocal control over Korea, after defeating China in the Sino-Japanese War (1894-1895) and Russia in the Russo-Japanese War (1904-1905). With these wars and the Tonghak rebellion, Korea experienced three major armed conflicts between 1894 and 1905. Farmlands were ruined, houses were destroyed, and many people fled their villages to escape imminent danger and destruction. To make

matters worse, in 1901 a nationwide famine took place, caused by an unusual drought followed by floods. The farmers uprooted from their villages by famines and wars fled unemployed and dispossessed into cities such as Seoul and Inchon, where they engaged in miscellaneous low-skilled, urban work. These rootless refugees in their own country were cut off from traditional social norms and obligations, and consequently they became receptive to new ideas such as Christianity and new opportunities far away from their homeland.

Korean laborers who had drifted into urban cities of Korea were pulled into the United States by the demand for cheap labor in Hawaii's sugar plantation camps. Following Hawaii's development of large-scale, labor-intensive sugar plantations in the 1830's, immigrant laborers were recruited from various countries to work in the plantation fields. Chinese laborers began to arrive in sizable numbers in 1852, and around fifty thousand Chinese immigrated to Hawaii between 1852 and the end of the nineteenth century. Anti-Chinese agitation and legislation such as the CHINESE EXCLUSION ACT OF 1882, however, began to restrict the number of Chinese allowed to enter Hawaii, and consequently the import of Chinese laborers came to an end in 1886. Hawaii's sugar planters then recruited Japanese laborers as a new source of cheap labor. Japanese laborers began to arrive in Hawaii on a large scale in 1885, and they composed nearly 80 percent of the workforce on the plantations at the start of the twentieth century. As the Japanese gained a labor monopoly in Hawaii's sugar plantations, they launched numerous strikes in the 1890's against the sugar planters, demanding higher wages and better working conditions. Growing numbers of Japanese laborers also migrated to the U.S. mainland in search of higher-paying jobs in railroad construction camps and California's burgeoning agricultural economy. Under such circumstances, Koreans were recruited to meet the labor shortage on the one hand and to offset Japanese predominance on the other.

The roles played by Dr. Horace N. ALLEN, David W. DESHLER, and several American missionaries including the Reverend George H. Jones were crucial in linking the demand for cheap labor in Hawaii and the supply of such labor in Korea. Allen arrived in Korea in 1884 as a medical missionary for the Presbyterians and soon earned the trust of King Kojong (who ruled from 1864-1907) by saving one of the king's brothers-in-law, who was injured during a coup attempt in 1884. Shortly after he gained entry into Korean politics, Allen vigorously sought concessions and franchises for American businesses from the Koreans. He believed that the United States would involve itself in Korean politics as its economic interests in Korea increased. The U.S. involvement in Korea, Allen hoped, would in turn counter Japanese influence and regain Korean independence.

Allen became involved in Korean immigration to Hawaii after he met a representative of the HAWAIIAN SUGAR PLANTERS' ASSOCIATION (HSPA), who was eager to recruit Koreans as plantation laborers in Hawaii. Through his friendship with King Kojong, Allen persuaded the king to allow Koreans to emigrate to Hawaii. His arguments appealed to the kings, who thought that emigration would relieve the suffering of Korean famine victims, increase the U.S. economic interest in Korea, and consequently strengthen the re-

Chemulpo (now Inchon) harbor, 1900. (The Korea Society/Los Angeles)

lationship between Korea and the United States.

Following Allen's recommendations, a Department of Emigration was established in 1902, and Deshler, an American businessman, took charge of recruiting Korean laborers. Deshler's initial recruiting efforts, however, met with little success primarily because of reluctance and fear among Koreans of going abroad. Although Koreans had migrated to Siberia and Manchuria from the 1880's, overseas emigration was a totally new experience for them. The intervention of the Reverend Jones of the Methodist Episcopal church of Inchon was crucial in breaking the initial inertia. Jones was a personal friend of Allen and believed that emigration to Hawaii would be beneficial for Koreans and that mission work would be more successful away from Korea. He persuaded his congregations to emigrate to Hawaii, and half of them joined the first shipload of Koreans to Hawaii on December 22, 1902.

The first shipload, carrying 101 emigrants, sailed from Inchon and arrived in Honolulu on January 13, 1903. Fifteen additional shiploads in 1903 brought 1,133 more Korean immigrants. By 1905, when Korean immigration to Hawaii came to a halt because of Japanese opposition to Korean immigration, 7,226 Korean immigrants had arrived in Hawaii. That number included 6,048 male adults in their twenties, 637 women, and 541 children. Thus, the majority of the early Korean immigrants to Hawaii were young single males who came to Hawaii to make a quick fortune and return home rich and respected.

Because of their urban backgrounds in Korea prior to their emigration, Korean immigrants came from diverse geographic origins and occupational backgrounds. The majority were urban, manual laborers in port cities and towns. The remainder included former soldiers in the Korean army, household servants, policemen, woodcutters, miners, students, churchmen, and Buddhist monks. Farmers were, however, underrepresented in the early Korean immigration to Hawaii: Only one-seventh of the total were farmers. Despite a small proportion of farmers among the early arrivals, the majority of immigrants had in fact originally been farmers before drifting into port cities and towns and engaging in miscellaneous urban occupations there.

A distinctive characteristic of the early Korean immigrants was the prevalence of Christianity. It was estimated that nearly 40 percent of Korean immigrants to Hawaii were Christians in Korea, and gradually most of the Koreans in Hawaii became churchgoers. The overrepresentation of Christians among the early Korean immigrants to Hawaii resulted partly from the influence of American missionaries who encouraged their Korean congregations to emigrate to Hawaii. It

Korean church, Manteca, California, 1918. (University of Southern California East Asian Library)

Picture brides were sent for by Korean laborers in Hawaii and the U.S. mainland. (The Korea Society/Los Angeles)

also resulted from the fact that the majority of the early Korean immigrants were recruited in port cities and towns in the Seoul-Inchon area and northern Korea, where Christianity was more prevalent than elsewhere. Because of the settlers' strong Christian backgrounds and the absence of traditional associations based on kinship and region of origin, Christian churches became the center of social, cultural, and political activities of the Korean community in the United States.

Another important characteristic of the early Korean immigrants to Hawaii was an unbalanced sex ratio: There were ten men for every woman. The sojourning orientation among the early Korean immigrants was responsible for this skewed sex ratio. To redress that problem, Korean women were brought into Hawaii through an exchange of pictures between prospective brides and grooms. Between 1910 and 1924, when the picture marriage was banned, almost 1,000 brides arrived in Hawaii and another 115 in California.

Picture brides made significant contributions to the Korean immigrant community. First, Korean immigrants could establish families, and an increasing number of U.S.-born second-generation Koreans emerged.

Second, picture brides were generally more educated and enlightened than their husbands. They encouraged their husbands to change their occupations from plantation work to small businesses or other urban occupations in cities. As a result, Koreans left planation work faster than any other ethnic group in Hawaii. Between 1903 and 1915, a total of 1,087 Koreans moved to the U.S. mainland in search of higher wages in railroad construction camps and orchards. The picture marriage, however, had a tragic consequence on Korean families. Because of wide age discrepancy (an average of fourteen years) between husbands and wives, Koreans recorded the highest rate of divorce among all racial and ethnic groups in Hawaii.

During the decade after 1910, some 541 Korean students came to the United States to study at American schools and universities. Although their status at the time of entry was as students, they were essentially political refugees trying to escape Japanese rule over Korea (1910-1945). They soon became the intellectual and political leaders of the Korean immigrant community and organized and sponsored the Korean independence movement overseas. After 1924, when the Immigration Act effectively curtailed Asian immigration to a minimal level, until the end of World War II, there was virtually no more immigration from Korea. By 1945, when Korea was restored to independence from Japan, Koreans in the United States were a small and largely isolated minority, with about 6,500 in Hawaii and about 3,000 on the mainland.

The Post-World War II Korean Immigration, 1945-1964. Shortly after its independence from Japan, Korea was divided along the thirty-eighth parallel into a communist North Korea and a democratic South Korea. The United States governed South Korea between 1945 and 1948 through the military and became more deeply involved in South Korea during the KOREAN WAR (1950-1953). Since the Korean War, the United States had stationed more than forty-thousand troops in South Korea, until 1990, when a small reduction occurred. The presence of U.S. troops in South Korea produced a sizable number of intermarriages between Korean women and American soldiers stationed there. Between 1950 and 1964, six thousand Korean women entered the United States as spouses of American servicemen. During the same period, five thousand children, who were either war orphans or children of mixed parentage, were adopted by American families. These women and children accounted for two-thirds of the Korean immigrants admitted to the United States between 1950 and 1964. Unlike the early Korean immigrants who formed their own communities, these new immigrants were attached to American families and were scattered throughout the United States. For the most part, they are still cut off from the Korean immigrant community and lead isolated and marginal lives in the United States.

The post-World War II military, political, and cultural relations between the United States and South Korea were also responsible for the migration of Korean students to the United States. Between 1945 and 1965 about six thousand Korean students came to the United States to seek higher education at American colleges and universities. They entered the United States in expectation of high social prestige back in South Korea after obtaining American diplomas. Many of them, however, settled in the United States after they completed their study and laid a foundation for chain migration for succeeding generations of Koreans.

The Recent Korean Immigration After 1965. Korean immigration to the United States entered a new phase when the United States changed its immigration policy in 1965. Not only did the annual number of Korean immigrants allowed to enter the United States increase dramatically, but also the motivations and socioeconomic backgrounds of post-1965 Korean immigrants were substantially different from those of their predecessors. Since the second half of the 1970's, about 30,000 Koreans have emigrated to the United States annually. During the peak of Korean immigration between 1985 and 1987, more than 35,000 Koreans emigrated annually, making South Korea the third-largest immigration country after Mexico and the Philippines. Altogether, more than 660,000 Koreans have entered the United States as permanent residents between 1965 and 1990. As a result, the Korean population in the United States increased dramatically from 69,130 in 1970 to 350,000 in 1980 and 800,000 in 1990. The zeal of Koreans for U.S.-bound emigration, however, began to dwindle from 1988 onward, as the deepening economic recession in the United States made emigration to the United States less attractive. Since then, the annual number of Korean immigrants, particularly new arrivals, has been declining.

Korean War Memorial site dedication at Angels Gate Park, San Pedro, California. (The Korea Society/Los Angeles)

Korean Immigration to the U.S., 1966-1990

Number of Koreans Admitted to the U.S. as Permanent Residents

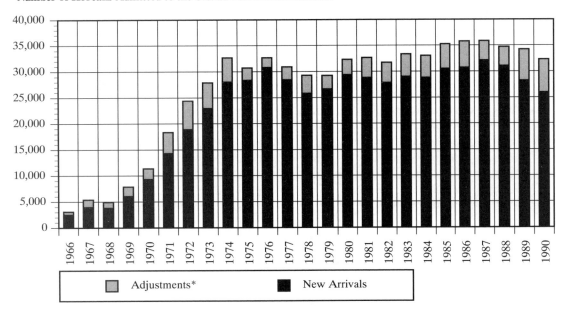

Trends in Class Backgrounds**

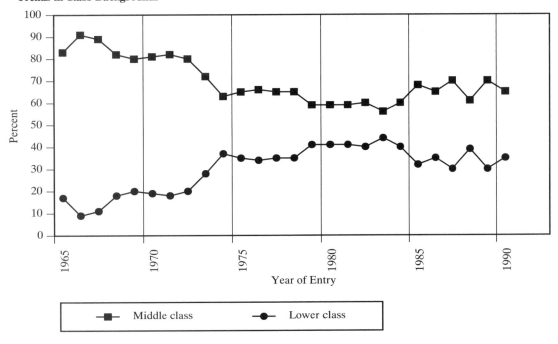

Sources: U.S. Immigration and Naturalization Service, *Annual Report,* 1966-1977. U.S. Immigration and Naturalization Service, *Statistical Yearbook,* 1978-1990.

* Adjustments apply to persons who previously entered the United States with a nonimmigrant status (such as student, visitor, or businessperson) and who changed their status to that of permanent resident.

** Data for 1980 and 1981 are unavailable.

The IMMIGRATION AND NATIONALITY ACT OF 1965 has also dramatically changed the demographic and socioeconomic profiles of Korean immigrants. The majority of post-1965 Korean immigrants came as nuclear families so that the family unit could be maintained intact. They also came from urban, college-educated, and white-collar occupational backgrounds in South Korea. More than half of post-1965 Korean immigrants came from Seoul, and the remainder came from Pusan, Taegu, and other large cities. Analyses of the 1980 U.S. census also show that about 30 percent of the Korean immigrants aged twenty-five and older who were admitted between 1970 and 1980 had received four years of college education. The corresponding figures were 22 percent for new immigrants of all nationalities during the same period and 16 percent for the U.S. native-born population. In addition, the majority of post-1965 Korean immigrants were professional, technical, managerial, or clerical workers before immigration. Laborers and farmers, in contrast, have been uniformly underrepresented in Korean immigration to the United States, although they made up more than half of the Korean labor force as recently

Many Korean professionals emigrated to the U.S. under the Immigration and Nationality Act of 1965. (Don Franklin)

as 1980. Thus, Korean immigration to the United States has been primarily a movement of middle-class Koreans.

The major motivation for emigration among middle-class Koreans was their sense of limited opportunity for social and economic mobility in South Korea, not only for themselves but also for their children. During the 1960's and 1970's, South Korea underwent a dramatic structural transformation from an agricultural society to a capitalist, industrial one. After 1961, when President PARK CHUNG HEE came to power through a military coup d'etat, his military government initiated an export-oriented economic development. That strategy has changed the industrial structure of South Korea in a short period of time. Agriculture declined rapidly during the 1960's and 1970's, but manufacturing and the service industries posted large gains. During this industrial restructuring, large numbers of rural out-migrants were drawn into the booming manufacturing industries or marginal service sectors in large cities. Massive out-migration from rural areas led to rapid urbanization and the concentration of population in several large cities, especially Seoul, from which the majority of post-1965 Korean immigrants to the United States came.

During the same period, Korean higher education expanded substantially because of foreign aid to education and the strong demand among Koreans for higher education. The latter desire resulted from the fact that education has been the single viable avenue of upward social and economic mobility in Korean society.

The industrialization, urbanization, and expansion of higher education during the 1960's and 1970's produced a new urban middle class, whose members were essentially urban, college-educated, white-collar workers. For example, the proportion of professional and white-collar workers, in the South Korean labor force grew from 14.6 percent in 1960 to 20 percent in 1970 and 27.2 percent in 1980. As members of the new urban middle class attained a college education and became professional and white-collar workers, their aspirations for upward social mobility were heightened. They could not realize their goal of upward mobility in South Korea, however, because of the limited opportunities available to them. One the most serious structural imbalances in South Korea has been that the supply of college graduates greatly exceeds the demand for such a highly educated labor force. The imbalance between the demand for and the supply of highly educated labor has resulted in the lack of employment opportunities congruent with higher education. Between 1965 and 1980, the average unemployment rate for male college graduates was 28 percent. The high unemployment rates among college graduates led some Koreans to migrate overseas. About 17,000 Koreans migrated to West Germany and the Middle East as contract mining workers, construction workers, and nurses between 1963 and 1974. Others sought emigration to the United States.

Korean American student proudly wears his letter sweater in a family picture, Kansas City, Kansas. (University of Southern California East Asian Library)

Another important motivation of middle-class Koreans to emigrate to the United States was aspirations for their children's education. The strong demand for higher education and the government's decision to restrict enrollment at the college and university level have resulted in fierce competition for a limited number of slots in colleges and universities. Every year more than 70 percent of college applicants fail the entrance examination and have to prepare for one or two more years to retake the examination. The annual number of repeat applicants is around 300,000, placing tremendous financial and psychological stress on stu-

dents, their families, and the society at large. Increasing numbers of middle-class Korean families have come to the United States to seek a second chance for their children or to bypass the stressful rite of passage.

Changing Class Backgrounds of Korean Immigrants. Between 1965 and 1976, middle-class Koreans had been overrepresented in the Korean immigration to the United States. In 1965, 84 percent of the Korean immigrants who reported their occupations in South Korea had been professional, managerial, sales, and clerical workers, who generally constitute the middle class in South Korea. That figure decreased to 81 percent by 1970 and 65 percent by 1975, but between 1965 and 1975 the majority of Korean immigrants had come from middle-class backgrounds.

The overrepresentation of middle-class Koreans among Korean immigrants before 1976 was attributable partly to U.S. immigration policy that favored highly educated and professional workers. Because of the shortage of professional workers in the American medical industry and engineering in the 1960's, Korean medical doctors, nurses, and engineers could enter the United States without difficulty. In addition, because of the small number of naturalized Koreans in the United States before 1965, Koreans could not use family preferences as an entry mechanism. Thus, between 1965 and 1974, occupational preferences were the most widely used entry mechanism among Korean immigrants, accounting for 30 percent of the Korean immigrants admitted to the United States each year.

Economic recessions during the 1970's led to political pressures on the U.S. Congress to amend the Immigration Act of 1965 to curtail the flow of immigrants admitted under occupational preferences. As a result, the proportion of occupational immigrants, including professional immigrants, was drastically reduced between the late 1970's and 1980's.

The increasing importance of social networks as an entry mechanism was also responsible for the changes in class backgrounds of Korean immigrants. As a growing number of Koreans became U.S. citizens after five years of permanent residence and thereby became eligible to sponsor the immigration of their parents and siblings, the proportion of family-preference immigrants increased. For example, in 1970, 68 percent of Korean immigrants obtained U.S. permanent residence through family preferences. That figure increased to 91 percent by 1977, and since then, more than 90 percent of Korean immigrants have arrived in the United States each year via family networks.

The growing importance of family networks as an

Korean immigrant, San Francisco. In 1970, 68 percent of Korean immigrants entered the United States on the basis of family ties. (James L. Shaffer)

entry mechanism resulted in a declining selectivity of Korean immigrants, because family-centered chain migration substantially reduced the uncertainty and requirements of international migration. As succeeding waves of new immigrants expected assistance from their family members in the United States in finding employment and housing, the former did not need to be as motivated and selective as their predecessors. Under such circumstances, since 1976 the proportion of Korean immigrants who had been manual laborers, farmers, and service workers, all of whom generally constitute the lower classes in South Korea, has been steadily increasing. Thus, after the early 1980's, lower-class Korean immigrants caught up with middle-class Korean immigrants.

The economic situation in South Korea and the United States is another contributing factor to the gradual increase of immigration of Koreans from lower-class backgrounds. Since the late 1970's, income inequality in South Korea has been increasing, especially disfavoring the lower classes. Absolute poverty in Korea has been significantly reduced, but relative poverty, measured by the percentage of the popu-

lation below one-third of the national median income, has increased—from 5 percent in 1970 to 14 percent in 1978. In addition, the desire for U.S.-bound emigration has been diminishing for the middle and upper middle classes because their economic conditions have improved, and they have become aware of the limitations of opportunities in the United States. The United States is no longer seen as the land of opportunity. Koreans realize that a large number of immigrants who were white-collar workers in Korea now engage in small-scale businesses in minority areas or in ethnic markets simply because they do not have other choices. Thus, middle-class Koreans have become increasingly reluctant to exchange their secure positions in South Korea for lower social and economic positions in the United States.

While economic conditions in Korea have been improving for the middle and upper middle classes during the 1970's and 1980's, a sense of relative deprivation has spread among the lower classes. According to a national opinion survey conducted in South Korea in 1987, lower-class Koreans are now more strongly motivated to emigrate than are the middle and upper classes: Emigration is favored by higher proportions of the working class (29 percent in favor) and the urban marginal class (45 percent) than by the upper middle class (22 percent) and the middle class (22 percent). It is expected that the number of immigrants from lower-class backgrounds will therefore continue to increase as long as the economic conditions of lower-class Koreans do not substantially improve in relation to those of middle and upper-middle classes.—*In-Jin Yoon*

The hope for economic mobility brought many Korean immigrants to the U.S. These cooks are employed by such an immigrant entrepreneur in Columbus, Ohio. (Chuck Doyle)

SUGGESTED READINGS:

- Choy, Bong Youn. *Koreans in America*. Chicago: Nelson-Hall, 1979. A pioneering study of Korean Americans. Choy provides detailed, rich, and lively description of Korea's political, economic, and cultural history, its relationship to the United States, and the history of the early and post-World War II Korean immigrants to Hawaii and the U.S. mainland. Also useful for understanding the Korean independence movement in the United States.

- Kim, Illsoo. *New Urban Immigrants: The Korean Community in New York*. Princeton, N.J.: Princeton University Press, 1981. Kim provides excellent analyses of the social, economic, and political conditions of the United States and South Korea in the 1960's that have affected the formation of U.S. immigration policy and South Korean emigration policy. Also useful for understanding patterns of occupational adaptation among Korean immigrants in the United States, including entrepreneurship.

- Koo, Hagen, and Eui-Young Yu. *Korean Immigration to the United States: Its Demographic Pattern and Social Implications for Both Societies*. Papers of the East-West Population Institute 74, Honolulu: East-West Center, 1981. Koo and Yu analyze structural causes and patterns of post-1965 Korean immigration to the United States, the effects of emigration of Korean society and economy, and the role of Korean immigrants in the American economy. They also critically evaluate the world economic system approach to international migration, including Korean immigration to the United States.

- Light, Ivan, and Edna Bonacich. *Immigrant Entrepreneurs: Koreans in Los Angeles, 1965-1982* Berkeley: University of California Press, 1988. Light and Bonacich explain Korean immigration to the United States as a response to economic and political dislocations in South Korea, which resulted from the penetration into the Korean economy by American and Japanese capitalists. The authors' explanation, however, does not adequately explain why middle-class Koreans have been overrepresented among Korean immigrants.

- Park, Insook Han, James T. Fawcett, Fred Arnold, and Robert W. Gardner. *Korean Immigrants and U.S. Immigration Policy: A Predeparture Perspective*. Papers of the East-West Population Institute 114. Honolulu: East-West Center, 1990. Park and her colleagues offer the most detailed and updated information available so far on the characteristics, motivations for emigrating, family networks, and postimmigration occu-

Korean American mother and daughter participate in Korea Day Parade in New York City. (Richard B. Levine)

pational choices among Korean immigrants based on scientifically selected samples of 2,383 adult Korean immigrants in 1986.

- Patterson, Wayne. *The Korean Frontier in America: Immigration to Hawaii, 1896-1910*. Honolulu: University of Hawaii Press, 1988. Patterson has extensively used archival materials in Korea, Japan, Hawaii, and Washington, D.C., to provide insightful and hitherto hidden information on the people involved in Korean immigration to Hawaii, their goals, and the tactics they employed to achieve their goals. A convincing explanation of how Korean immigration to Hawaii was sacrificed for the sake of Japanese American relations.

- Pomerantz, Linda. "The Background of Korean Emigration." In *Labor Immigration Under Capitalism: Asian Workers in the United States before World War II*, edited by Lucie Cheng and Edna Bonacich. Berkeley: University of California Press, 1984. Pomerantz explains in detail how the internal disintegration of Korea and penetration of such imperialist powers as Japan into Korea at the end of the nineteenth century produced conditions conducive for emigration to Hawaii. An excellent discussion of how the Japanese economic penetration into Korea impacted the breakdown of Korea's native industries and agriculture.

• Yoon, In-Jin. *The Social Origins of Korean Immigration to the United States from 1965 to the Present.* Papers of the East-West Population Institute 121, Honolulu: East-West Center, 1993. Yoon provides a comprehensive explanation of the social and economic changes in South Korea and the United States, as well as the post-World War II military, economic, and cultural relations between the two countries that have initiated and sustained post-1965 Korean immigration to the United States. Also useful for understanding the patterns and causes of changing class backgrounds of Korean immigrants to the United States from 1965 to 1990.

Korean immigration to the United States, sources of: South Korea has been a major source of post-1965 immigration to America. Between 1976 and 1989, more than thirty thousand Koreans arrived annually in the United States. South Korea was the third-largest source of immigration during this period, after Mexico and the Philippines. By 1990 the Korean American population had reached approximately 800,000, achieving an elevenfold rise in two decades.

Economic Considerations. The reasons for such accelerated migration from South Korea are several. The standard of living in the United States is higher than that in South Korea and is an important factor that has compelled many Koreans to leave their native country. Like Third World immigrants, many Koreans, especially those who came to America in the 1970's, were attracted by the prospect of a higher living standard. In the 1970's and early 1980's, many middle-class Koreans abandoned their white-collar occupations in Korea for the chance to enter lower-level positions in the United States. Even at a lesser position it was still possible, these immigrants realized, to maintain a higher living standard overseas than at home. In the 1970's many medical professionals discovered that working in the United States paid better than in South Korea.

South Korea has managed to upgrade considerably its domestic economic condition, particularly since the late 1980's. In 1975, Korean migrants to America earned eleven times more than they could earn in Korea (as of 1993, that figure was only about two and a half times more). Many middle-class families in Seoul and other large cities now have their own cars. South Korea's economic improvement, coupled with the dif-

As of 1993 Korean migrants to America earned two and a half times more than they were able to earn in Korea. (Robert Fried)

ficulties that many immigrants experience in adjusting to a foreign culture, has tended to moderate the influx of Korean immigration since about the late 1980's. The annual number of Koreans coming to the United States peaked in 1987 with nearly thirty-six thousand but then gradually diminished. The figure dropped below twenty-five thousand in 1991 for the first time since 1973. According to a 1990's survey conducted in South Korea, middle-class citizens have little incentive to migrate to the United States, although many working-class citizens do register a strong preference for overseas migration.

Occupational Considerations. Although middle-class Koreans are less motivated to move to the United States than they were fifteen years ago, immigration from Korea still includes a large proportion of the middle class. Many of the latter emigrated primarily because they could not find suitable or desirable jobs in Korea following their college graduation. Korean society's inability to absorb rapidly the growing surplus of college graduates has therefore become another source of immigration. Data show that the average unemployment rate of male college graduates in Korea, excluding those inducted into compulsory three-year military service, was thirty percent higher than in the previous quarter century. As a solution to their predicament, many of these jobless came to the United States as foreign students and subsequently became permanent residents. Many others chose to apply for naturalization.

U.S.-Korea Ties. The close political, military, and economic connections between the United States and South Korea have also produced a substantial crop of post-1965 immigrants. American military involvement in South Korea has directly influenced Korean migration, in that a large number of Korean women have come to the United States as the wives of American servicemen formerly stationed in Korea. Between 1975 and 1990, more than three thousand such women moved annually to the United States. Moreover, these interracial marriages have had a far greater effect on the Korean influx than the above figure indicates, since most of those Korean brides also arranged to have their family members and relatives brought overseas for permanent residence.

For many South Koreans, ties between the two countries have also meant greater exposure to the culture of the United States influencing these individuals' desire to emigrate to seek a better life for themselves and their families. South Koreans, particularly those of the middle class, have been exposed to the affluence of life in America through the presence of U.S. servicemen and the media since the KOREAN WAR. This has motivated many citizens to emigrate to the "land of opportunity."

The Primacy of Education. Finally, South Korea's inability to meet high aspirations for children's education is another important reason for the migration Westward. Strongly influenced by the Confucian cultural tradition, Koreans place great emphasis on education: According to a nationwide poll in South Korea, 90 percent of parents expected at least four years of college for their sons, while 72 percent expected the same for their daughters. Attending college in South Korea is, however, expensive. Moreover, the vast majority of college applicants fail to gain acceptance to

Michigan State University alumnus enjoys the lakeshore, Chicago, Illinois. (James L. Shaffer)

any school, since the Education Ministry tightly controls the freshman quota allotted each institution. In 1992 only 30 percent of all applicants were admitted to the country's colleges and universities. As a result, many aspiring students may spend several years preparing for the college entrance examination, imposing enormous financial and psychological burdens on both themselves and their parents. As one solution, many parents send their children to the United States to attend college. Others with younger offspring migrate overseas well before it is time to start worrying about college.—*Pyong Gap Min*

SUGGESTED READINGS: • Kim, Hyun Sook, and Pyong Gap Min. "The Post-1965 Korean Immigrants: Their Characteristics and Settlement Patterns." *Korea Journal of Population and Development* 21 (1992): 121-143. • Kim, Illsoo. "Korea and East Asia: Preimmigration Factors and U.S. Immigration Policy." In *Pacific Bridges: The New Immigration from Asia and the Pacific Islands*, edited by James Fawcett and Benjamin Carino. Staten Island: Center for Migration Studies, 1987. • Kim, Illsoo. *New Urban Immigrants: The Korean Community in New York*. Princeton, N.J.: Princeton University Press, 1981. • Park, Insook Han, James T. Fawcett, Fred Arnold, and Robert W. Gardner. *Korean Immigrants and U.S. Immigration Policy: A Predeparture Perspective*. Papers of the East-West Population Institute 114. Honolulu: East-West Center, 1990. • Patterson, Wayne. *The Korean Frontier in America: Immigration to Hawaii, 1896-1910*. Honolulu: University of Hawaii Press, 1988. • Yoon, In-Jin. *The Social Origins of Korean Immigration to the United States from 1965 to the Present*. Papers of the East-West Population Institute 121. Honolulu: East-West Center, 1993.

Korean Independence League (also Korean Independence Party): Korean nationalist group organized by PARK YONG-MAN after he lost control of the KOREAN NATIONAL ASSOCIATION (KNA) of Hawaii to Syngman RHEE in 1919. Its main objectives included supporting the Korean national independence movement, training soldiers in Hawaii and Manchuria, and raising funds for patriotic activities. The association also published a weekly Korean-language newspaper, *Pacific Times*, alternately called *Pacific News*.

Korean language: Spoken by more than seventy-two million people, most of them living on the Korean peninsula. There are approximately twenty-four million people in North Korea and forty-five million peo-

ple in South Korea. For the most part these countries are monolingual. According to these figures, Korean is one of the top fifteen most frequently spoken languages in the world, surpassing Italian, Cantonese, Tamil, Swahili, and many other important languages in terms of number of speakers. Also there are perhaps more than one million speakers of Korean in the People's Republic of China, a million and a half in Japan, and half a million in the republics of the former Soviet Union. In addition there are more than half a million speakers of Korean in the United States.

Historical Relationships. The linguistic affiliations of Korean are still subject to debate, and at one time many linguists thought it was a language isolate, such as Basque in Spain, showing no genetic relationships to any other language family. Current thinking in historical linguistics, however, generally places Korean in the Altaic family, along with Japanese, Turkish, Mongolian, and several languages spoken in Siberia, central Asia, and northern China. These proposed connections, however, are rather more distant than, for example, those found among the Romance or Germanic languages in Europe. It is clear that Korean is not related in any way to any of the Chinese languages, even though the Koreans borrowed the Chinese writing system (as well as many vocabulary items). The relationship to Japanese is somewhat more complicated. In terms of grammar Japanese and Korean are very similar, but phonology and word endings are rather different. Some linguists place Korean and Japanese in their own subfamily of the Altaic languages, along with languages of the Okinawan Islands and Ainu (the language/culture of the indigenous people of Japan).

The Korean Sound System. Linguists generally agree that there are about nineteen basic consonants, ten simple vowels, and two semivowels in most dialects of modern Korean. The phonology of Korean is, however, quite divergent from English. With the exception of the nasal sounds (*m*, *n*, and *ng*), most Korean consonants—and many vowels—are pronounced in a different manner. One of the main differences is not so much in the actual way that a particular sound is formed but more a matter of the underlying principles behind the sound system. In English, for example, there is a series of sounds that linguists call "bilabial stops," because air is prevented by the two lips from escaping immediately before these sounds are spoken; these sounds are *b* and *p*. The only difference between *b* and *p*, as they are normally spoken in English, is simply a matter of "voicing" (that is, whether or not

The Korea Times

제7524호　Thursday, October 20, 1994　〈제1판〉　**Los Angeles Edition**　141 N. VERMONT AVE., L.A. CA 90004　(213)487-5323　FAX (213)738-

오늘의 날씨
대체로 맑음. 최고 72～77도,
54～59도. 만조 하오 10시53분,
하오 4시38분.

「리커재건」5명 승소

의견과 함께 도시계획
회의 재건승인을 다시
복시키는 판결을 내렸
칠린 판사는 또 도시
위원회가 리커재건승
한 조건으로 부과한 경
외무고용 조항에 있어
「경비원고용조건을 정
시키는 증거제시가 없
했냐」고 지적, 시정부

This headline identifies the Korea Times. (Korea Times)

the vocal cords are used when pronouncing them). There is a whole series of pairs of sounds in English that differ only as a matter of voicing (for example, *t* and *d*, *k* and *g*, *f* and *v*). In the Korean series, voicing is not so important, but other qualities such as "aspiration" are. Aspiration refers to whether or not a puff of air occurs after a sound is uttered, as in the *p* sounds in "stop!" as opposed to "stop it." These two *p* sounds would be different kinds of sounds in Korean (and indeed have different "letters" in the Korean alphabet). Other differences include whether the speech organs are tense or lax when forming a consonant, or whether or not the lips are rounded or flat when saying a vowel.

Writing. Writing may have been brought to Korea as early as the first century B.C.E. by the Chinese who colonized much of the northern and western Korean peninsula. The original Koreans probably had no writing system before this. Until the thirteenth century C.E., Koreans wrote in the Chinese language or used Chinese characters to stand for either native Korean sounds or individual Korean words themselves. Along with the Chinese characters, many Chinese words were also brought into the language as well. Today more than half the total vocabulary items found in a Korean dictionary may have a Chinese origin (with about 10 percent of the basic vocabulary coming from China).

This system of using Chinese characters was not, however, especially elegant, as the two languages were (and are) completely different, in terms of both grammar and phonology. Chinese is monosyllabic (having words, or word-combinations, that consists of only one syllable) and non-inflecting (that is, Chinese verbs do not conjugate for tense or person, nor do nouns or adjectives decline for things such as case/part of speech, number, or gender). Korean, in contrast, is polysyllabic and highly agglutinative (having words consisting of stems with many added prefixes and suffixes). In 1446 C.E. King Sejong issued the procla-

mation of *Hunmin-jongum* (correct sounds for instructions to the people), giving Korea the HANGUL alphabet and making literacy possible for the masses (most of whom had no training in Chinese or Chinese characters).

Until the twentieth century, both Chinese characters and the *hangul* alphabet were used in a mixed fashion in Korea. After World War II, when North and South Korea became separate nations, different language policies were followed by the two governments. North Korea has officially abolished all Chinese characters, but while South Korea has highly curtailed their use, the government continues to teach students about eighteen hundred Chinese characters through high school.

Gramatical Structure. Korean, like Japanese, is an SOV language. That is, the basic word order of the sentence is subject-object-verb. This word order, however, is not especially strict as long as the verb always comes at the end of a sentence. Korean nouns are generally not marked for gender or plurality (distinguishing singular versus plural). Like many other Asian languages, Korean uses numeral classifiers when nouns are being counted. Certain kinds of counterwords must be included with the noun whenever it is used with a number. For example, one way to say "two letters" in Korean would be the phrase "phyyon-chi tu chang" (literally "letter two flat-object"). There are only a few such classifiers in English (for example, "six cups of coffee" or "a pair of glasses")

Verbs in Korean generally consist of a stem plus several optional and obligatory verbal endings. These include markers for honorifics, tense (past, present, future, remote past, past future), formality (plain or polite), aspect (things such as the so-called subjunctive in English), and mood or style (whether or not a sentence is declarative, interrogative, or imperative, and so forth).

Korean Sociolinguistics. The Korean Language, like Japanese, has very complex ways of showing respect within its grammatical structure. Even as speakers of English are required by their syntax to make a gender choice when using a third-person pronoun (that is, they must say "he" or "she" when referring to another person), Koreans must make decisions about politeness and speech levels. Respect language depends on several factors, including the sex, age, social status, and degree of intimacy between the speaker and the hearer. A competent speaker of Korean, then, needs to know not only the formal rules of syntax but also the cultural rules of behavior in order to communicate with others appropriately. For example, the two sentences "kamnita" and "ka yo" both mean "I go" (they could also mean "you," "he," "she," "we," "you all," or "they go," depending on the context). The first version could be said at almost any time among any two adults, but the second would be considered much more informal.—*James Stanlaw*

SUGGESTED READINGS: • Hoji, Jajime, ed. *Japanese/Korean Linguistics*, Stanford, Calif.: Center for the Study of Language and Information, 1990. • Kim, Man-Kil. "Korean." In *The World's Major Languages*, edited by Bernard Comrie. New York: Oxford University Press, 1987. • Korean National Commission for UNESCO, ed. *The Korean Language*. Seoul: Si-sa-yong-o-sa, 1983. • Martin, Samuel E. *Korean in a Hurry: A Quick Approach to Spoken Korean*. Rutland, Vt.: Charles E. Tuttle, 1954. • Martin, Samuel E., and Young-Sook C. Lee. *Beginning Korean*. 1969. Reprint. Rutland, Vt.: Charles E. Tuttle, 1986.

Korean Liberty Congress: Korean nationalist conference for Koreans in the United States, held in Philadelphia, Pennsylvania, from April 14 through April 16, 1919. Organized by prominent Korean-born activist Philip Jaisohn in order to publicize the plight of Korea in the wake of the harsh government crackdown on the MARCH FIRST MOVEMENT, the Korean Liberty Congress passed a ten-point resolution that called for official recognition of Korea as an independent nation by the League of Nations. Delegates to the congress also authorized Jaisohn to publicize the Korean situation by disseminating information through a centralized clearinghouse known as the Bureau of Korean Information.

Korean martial arts: Korean methods of self-defense are derived from ancient Asian fighting systems. Although there are various theories regarding the history and origins of Korean martial arts, most scholars agree that the major Korean systems developed from a combination of indigenous Korean arts and other Asian techniques. The major Korean martial arts are tae kwon do and hapkido. Other schools include tang soo do, hwarang-do, and the Sul Sa system.

Tae Kwon Do. In the seventh century C.E., during the Silla Dynasty, an independent Korean martial art, now called "tae kwon do," developed. "Tae" means "to kick or smash with the feet," "kwon" means "to punch or destroy with the hand or fist," and "do" means "method, art, or way." Often called the "Korean style" of karate, tae kwon do's basic five principles were formulated by Buddhist monk Won Kwang.

The three kingdoms of Koguryo, Silla, and Paekche fought bitterly for centuries. The Silla kingdom, the smallest of the three kingdoms on the Korean peninsula, developed an elite, well-educated fighting corps called the "hwarang-do," or "way of the flowering manhood." These warriors, often compared to the Japanese samurai, learned tae kwon do techniques from the Buddhist monks. In 668 C.E. the peninsula was unified under the Silla kingdom, and this martial art, called "tae kyon," became a popular sport.

In 935 C.E. the Koryo kingdom replaced the Silla Dynasty, and tae kyon developed further, as a compulsory art. During the fifteenth century, however, the Age of Enlightenment began. With the establishment of the Yi Dynasty, which favored scholarship over military arts, the practice of tae kyon was discouraged. Confucianism became the state religion.

In 1910 the Japanese annexed Korea. To discourage a Korean national identity, the Japanese forbade all martial arts activities.

The few Koreans who still knew tae kyon emigrated to Japan and China, where they were influenced by other systems of martial arts. At the end of World War II many of these martial artists returned to Korea. The Korean fighting system was now a blend of ancient Korean and other Asian styles of martial arts. In 1955 the Korean art was renamed tae kwon do, a name suggested by army general Choi Hong Hi. In 1961 the government established the Tae Soo Do Association. In 1965 the organization was renamed the Korean Taekwon Do Association, and all major *dojangs*, or schools, became members. In 1966 the first international federation was founded by Choi Hong Hi. Tae kwon do was part of the 1988 Olympics and has become one of the most widely practiced martial arts in the world.

The martial arts of Korea spread to the United States as a result of the Korean War, during which U.S. servicemen stationed in Seoul learned Korean fighting skills. The American soldiers brought this knowledge

Practitioners of tae kwon do exhibit the high kicks characteristic of their art. (Raymond J. Malace)

back to the United States, and the number of martial arts schools started to increase. American martial arts film star Chuck Norris started his training in tae kwon do and became an undefeated eight-time world champion.

Although hands as well as feet are used, tae kwon do emphasizes powerful kicks based on the "bound-spring" principle: A kick should be like a coiled spring that is suddenly released. As in other martial arts, balance, speed, and concentration are also important.

Hapkido. Hapkido is the popular Korean martial art that exists primarily for self-defense. It is the art of power coordination or harmony: "Hap" means "harmony" or "coordination," "ki" means "power" or "cosmic force," and "do" means the "way" or "art of."

During the 1950's hapkido was developed by Choi Yong Suhl, who had emigrated to Japan during the Japanese occupation of Korea. Already a master of the Korean tae kyun system, Choi learned the Japanese system of daito ryu, or dai jujitsu, the forerunner of judo and aikido. He combined the "hard" style kicks and punches of tae kyun with the "soft" styles of jujitsu.

After World War II Choi returned to Korea and established the first hapkido school in Taegu, Korea. Later, Choi and his disciple, Ji Han Jae, established a school in Seoul. When Choi retired, Ji Han Jae continued the tradition. He became president of the Korea Hapkido Association and the chief martial arts trainer for South Korean president PARK CHUNG HEE's corps of secret service bodyguards. After Park died, Ji went to San Francisco, where he founded a hapkido school. During the Vietnam War, American Green Berets were trained in hapkido.

The hapkido system combines the specialized kicking and punching techniques of tae kyon with the soft circular blocking of aikido. There are more than three hundred different techniques, but there are no *katas*, forms, or patterns, since hapkido is essentially an art of self-defense. The hapkido practitioner waits for the attack, deflects the blow, and then counterattacks with powerful kicks until the opponent is totally defeated. A knowledge of the pressure points of the body is a basic part of hapkido training.

Other Systems. Tang soo do, which had been devel-

Young tae kwon do enthusiasts await their turn to compete. (The Korea Society/Los Angeles)

oped by the first century C.E. in Korea, is also very popular in the United States. Originally known as soo bahk, tang soo do means "way of the tang hand" and resembles Japanese or Okinawan karate. After World War II Hwang Kee established the Moo Duk Kwan Academy in Korea, world headquarters for tang soo do.

In 1972 Joo Bang and Joo Sang Lee, two brothers from Seoul, established the first U.S. school for the ancient martial art of hwarang-do. Techniques include 365 kicks, one for each day of the year. Hwarang-do students also try to develop mind control and learn healing by finger pressure.

The late Michael Enchanis, an American who had studied with Joo Bang Lee, taught the ancient martial arts system of the Sul Sa, a secret sect within the hwarang-do. The Sul Sa were spies or assassins who apparently could cope with any situation. Enchanis introduced Sul Sa methods into American military training: acupressure for self-healing, psychological control of the enemy, and camouflage.—*Alice Chin Myers*

SUGGESTED READINGS: • Soet, John S. *Martial Arts Around the World*. Burbank: Unique Publications, 1991. • Spear, Robert K. *Hapkido: The Integrated Fighting Art*. Burbank: Unique Publications, 1988. • Williams, Boyn. *Martial Arts of the Orient*. New York: Hamlyn, 1975. • Yates, Keith D. *The Complete Book of Taekwon Do Forms*. Boulder, Colo.: Paladin Press, 1982. • Yates, Keith D. *Tae Kwon Do Basics*. New York: Sterling Publishing Company, 1987.